DUNS SCOTUS ON GOD

The Franciscan John Duns Scotus (c. 1266–1308) is the philosopher's theologian *par excellence*: more than any of his contemporaries, he is interested in arguments for their own sake.

Making use of the tools of modern philosophy, Richard Cross presents a thorough account of Duns Scotus's arguments on God and the Trinity. Providing extensive commentary on central passages from Scotus, many of which are presented in translation in this book, Cross offers clear expositions of Scotus's sometimes elliptical writing. Cross's account shows that, in addition to being a philosopher of note, Scotus is a creative and original theologian who offers new insights into many old problems.

D1598043

ASHGATE STUDIES IN THE HISTORY OF PHILOSOPHICAL THEOLOGY

Ashgate Studies in the History of Philosophical Theology provides students and researchers in the field with the means of consolidating and re-appraising philosophy of religion's recent appropriation of its past. This new Ashgate series offers a focused cluster of high-profile titles presenting critical, authoritative surveys of key thinkers' ideas as they bear upon topics central to the philosophy of religion. Summarizing contemporary and historical perspectives on the writings and philosophies of each thinker, the books concentrate on moving beyond mere surveys and engage with recent international scholarship and the author's own critical research on their chosen thinker. Each book provides an accessible, stimulating new contribution to thinkers from ancient, through medieval, to modern periods.

Series Editors

Professor Martin Stone, Katholieke Universiteit Leuven, Belgium
Professor Peter Byrne, King's College London, UK
Professor Edwin M. Curley, University of Michigan, USA
Professor Carlos Steel, Katholieke Universiteit Leuven, Belgium

Also in this series

Hegel's God
A Counterfeit Double?
William Desmond

Mill on God
The Pervasiveness and Elusiveness of Mill's Religious Thought
Alan P. F. Sell

Duns Scotus on God

RICHARD CROSS
University of Oxford, UK

ASHGATE

© Richard Cross, 2005

Published by

Ashgate Publishing Limited
Gower House
Croft Road
Aldershot
Hants GU11 3HR
England

Ashgate Publishing Company
Suite 420
101 Cherry Street
Burlington
VT 05401-4405
USA

Ashgate website: http://www.ashgate.com

British Library Cataloguing in Publication Data
Cross, Richard
    Duns Scotus on God. – (Ashgate studies in the history of philosophical theology)
    1.Duns Scotus, John, ca. 1266–1308 – Criticism and interpretation 2.God – History of doctrines – Middle Ages, 600–1500
    I. Title
    231

Library of Congress Cataloging-in-Publication Data
Cross, Richard.
    Duns Scotus on God / Richard Cross.
      p. cm. — (Ashgate studies in the history of philosophical theology)
    Includes bibliographical references and index.
    ISBN 0-7546-1402-6 (alk. paper) — ISBN 0-7546-1403-4 (pbk. : alk. paper)
    1. Duns Scotus, John, ca. 1266–1308. 2. God—History of doctrines—Middle Ages, 600–1500. 3. Trinity—History of doctrines—Middle Ages, 600–1500. I. Title. II. Series.

    B765.D74C753 2004
    231'.092—dc22

2003024004

ISBN 0 7546 1402 6 (Hardback)
        0 7546 1403 4 (Paperback)

Typeset by Owain Hammonds, Ceredigion.
Printed and bound in Great Britain by TJ International Ltd, Padstow, Cornwall

For Sue Beardmore

Contents

Acknowledgements

Thanks to Martin Stone and the editors of *Ashgate Studies in the History of Philosophical Theology*, for asking me to write the volume, and to other scholars who helped me by variously reading, discussing, and asking and answering questions: Stephen Dumont, Peter King, Brian Leftow, Chris Martin, and Calvin Normore. Errors, of course, are entirely my own. Sarah Lloyd at Ashgate was a very encouraging and enthusiastic editor, with seemingly endless reserves of patience. I should like to thank the copy-editor, Jenny Roberts, for her careful, efficient, and thoughtful work. As always, thanks as well to Essaka Joshua.

Abbreviations

Primary Sources

Anselm
  Monol.   *Monologion*
Aristotle
  An. post.   *Analytica posteriora*
  Cat.   *Categoriae*
  De an.   *De anima*
  Eth. Nic.   *Ethica Nicomachea*
  Int.   *De interpretatione*
  Ph.   *Physica*
  Metaph.   *Metaphysica*
Aquinas, Thomas
  ST   *Summa theologiae*
Augustine
  De Trin.   *De trinitate*
Avicenna
  Metaph.   *Metaphysica (Liber de philosophia prima sive scientia divina)*
Boethius
  Cons.   *De consolatione philosophiae*
  Eut.   *De persona et duabus naturis contra Eutychen et Nestorium*
Bonaventure
  In Sent.   *Commentaria in quatuor libros Sententiarum*
Duns Scotus, John
  DPP   *De primo principio*
  In Metaph.   *Quaestiones super libros Metaphysicorum*
  Lect.   *Lectura*
  Ord.   *Ordinatio*
  Qu. misc.   *Quaestiones miscellaneae*
  Quod.   *Quodlibetum*
  Rep.   *Reportatio Parisiensis*
  Super El.   *Quaestions in libros Elenchorum*
  Super praed.   *Quaestiones in librum Praedicamentorum*
Giles of Rome
  In Sent.   *In quatuor libros Sententiarum quaestiones*
Godfrey of Fontaines
  Quod.   *Quaestiones quodlibetales*
Gregory of Nazianzus
  Or.   *Orationes*

Henry of Ghent
  Quod.   *Quodlibeta*
  SQ   *Summa quaestionum ordinariarum*
Henry of Harclay
  In Sent.   *Quaestiones in libros Sententiarum*
Hilary of Poitiers
  De Trin.   *De trinitate*
John of Damascus
  Exp. fid.   *Expositio fidei* (*De fide orthodoxa*)
Lombard, Peter
  Sent.   *Sententiae in quatour libros distinctae*
Marston, Roger
  De em.   *De emanatione aeterna (Quaestiones disputatae)*
Olivi, Peter John
  In Sent.   *Quaestiones in libros Sententiarum*
Porphyry
  Isag.   *Isagoge*
Richard of Middleton
  In Sent.   *Super quatuor libros Sententiarum quaestiones*
Richard of St Victor
  De Trin.   *De trinitate*
  Sum. fr. Alex. *Summa fratris Alexandri*
Thomas of Sutton
  Quod.   *Quodlibeta*
  Qu. ord.   *Quaestiones ordinariae*

Versions, Translations, and Series

Alluntis and Wolter	Duns Scotus, *God and Creatures: The Quodlibetal Questions*, ed. and trans. Felix Alluntis and Allan B. Wolter
BGPTM	Beiträge zur Geschichte der Philosophie und Theologie des Mittelalters
Buytaert	John of Damascus, *De fide orthodoxa: The Versions of Burgundio and Cerbanus*, ed. Eligius M. Buytaert
CCSL	Corpus Christaniorum Series Latina
CSEL	Corpus Scriptorum Ecclesiasticorum Latinorum
DSDL	A. Vos and others, *Duns Scotus on Divine Love: Texts and Commentary on Goodness and Freedom, God and Humans*
Frank and Wolter	Duns Scotus, *Metaphysician*, ed. and trans. William A. Frank and Allan B. Wolter
Hoffmann	Tobias Hoffmann, *Creatura intellecta: Die Ideen und Possibilien bei Duns Scotus mit Ausblick auf Franz von Mayronis, Poncius und Mastrius*
Kotter	Bonifatius Kotter, *Die Schriften des Johannes von Damaskos*. Vol. 2: *Expositio fidei*
Macken	Henry of Ghent, *Opera Omnia*, ed. R. Macken and others

Moreschini	Boethius, *De consolatione philosophiae; opuscula sacra*, ed. C. Moreshini
Noone	Timothy B. Noone, 'Scotus on Divine Ideas: *Rep. Paris. I-A*, d. 36'
Paris	Henry of Ghent, *Quodlibeta* (Paris, 1518)
PhB	Les Philosophes Belges
PW	Duns Scotus, *Philosophical Writings: A Selection*, ed. and trans. Allan B. Wolter
St Bonaventure	Duns Scotus, *Opera Philosophica*, ed. Girard. J. Etzkorn and others
Söder	Joachim Roland Söder, *Kontingenz und Wissen: Die Lehre von den* futura contingentia *bei Johannes Duns Scotus*
Spade	Paul Vincent Spade (ed. and trans.), *Five Texts on the Mediaeval Problem of Universals: Porphyry, Boethius, Abelard, Duns Scotus, Ockham*
STGM	Studien und Texte zur Geistesgeschichte des Mittelalters
Vatican	Duns Scotus, *Opera Omnia*, ed. C. Balić and others
Vos	Duns Scotus, *Contingency and Freedom: Lectura I 39*, ed. A. Vos and others
Wadding	Duns Scotus, *Opera Omnia*, ed. Luke Wadding
WM	Allan B. Wolter, *Duns Scotus on the Will and Morality*, 1st edn
Wolter	Duns Scotus, *A Treatise on God as First Principle*, ed. Allan B. Wolter, 2nd edn
Wolter and Adams	'Duns Scotus' Parisian Proof for the Existence of God', ed. and trans. Allan B. Wolter and Marilyn McCord Adams

Manuscript sigla

| MS A | Assisi, Biblioteca Communale, MS 137 (Scotus, *Ord.*) |
| MS M | Merton College, Oxford, MS 53 (Scotus, *Rep.* 1A) |

Introduction

1 Duns Scotus: Life and Works

Beyond a few details, little is known of the life of John Duns Scotus (c. 1266–1308).[1] The generally accepted date and place of his birth are speculative. According to scholars, 1266 is most likely for the first of these, given a date that is secure, namely, that of Scotus's ordination to the priesthood in Northampton on 17 March 1291. Under canon law, 25 was the youngest age allowable for ordination. The Bishop of Lincoln (in whose huge diocese both Northampton and Oxford were then located) conducted an earlier ordination on 23 December 1290. Thus, assuming that Scotus was ordained at the first opportunity, this makes his birth sometime between late December 1265 and mid-March 1266. Scholars now hold that 'Duns' should be understood to refer to the town of that name just north of the border from England into Scotland, in Berwickshire, from which it may be presumed Scotus originated.

Ordination in Northampton implies that Scotus was in Oxford by 1291. Another concrete reference places Scotus in Oxford in 1300. Scotus's name appears in a letter, dated 26 July, as one of 22 friars presented to the Bishop of Lincoln for a licence to hear confessions. The list of names includes Philip Bridlington as the incoming Franciscan regent master (i.e. full professor) in theology. Bridlington was regent master for the year 1300–01. And we know that Scotus took part in a disputation under Bridlington during this year. These facts imply that Scotus remained in Oxford until at least June 1301. As part of their training for the professorship, theology bachelors were required to lecture on the *Sentences* of Peter Lombard (c. 1100–60), a kind of theological textbook consisting largely of discussion of conflicting sources from the early Church Fathers – predominantly Augustine – ranged under a series of theological topics.[2] We know that Scotus was busy revising the earliest portion of his lectures in 1300, because of a reference he makes explicitly to that year as the time of writing.[3] This suggests that he lectured on the *Sentences* between October 1298 and 1299. Two books of this early *Lectura* survive (along with a later third book), and the series formed the basis for Scotus's ongoing revision of his lectures for publication – the so-called *Ordinatio*.[4]

---

[1] For a useful summary of the current state of research, with full bibliographical information, see the editor's introduction in Thomas Williams (ed.), *The Cambridge Companion to Duns Scotus*, 1–15.

[2] For the university theological curriculum in Oxford, see most conveniently William J. Courtenay, *Schools and Scholars in Fourteenth Century England*, 41–8.

[3] Scotus, *Ord.* prol.2.un., n. 112 (Vatican, I, 77).

[4] For textual information on the *Ordinatio*, the best source remains the many editorial introductions to the various volumes of the Vatican edition of Scotus's theological *Opera* (ed. C. Balić and others).

We know from an early manuscript now in the library at Worcester Cathedral that Scotus was in Paris in the academic year 1302–03, lecturing for a second time on the *Sentences* in order to qualify for a chair in Paris. These lectures survive in the form of student notes corrected by the lecturer – a *reportatio examinata*. These lectures overlap in time with the margin additions to the *Ordinatio*. My impression is that what we have of the main text of the *Ordinatio* was complete before any of the examined version of the *Reportatio*, though it is hard to make any definitive claims in the absence of evidence external to the texts themselves. Scotus was forced to leave France, along with some 80 other pro-papal friars, in June 1303. The expelled students were allowed to return to Paris after April 1304. In 1305, Scotus became regent master in theology at Paris. From this period date Scotus's *Quodlibetal questions*: a series of disputed questions, originating in the lecture hall, on issues raised 'on anything by anyone' (*de quolibet a quolibet*) – a standard academic exercise held by a regent master during Advent and Lent in the university calendar. Scotus's single quodlibetal disputation was held probably in either Advent 1306 or Lent 1307. Scotus was moved to Cologne in the summer of 1307 to teach at the Franciscan house of studies there, where he died the next year, probably on 8 November.

Scotus was a member of the Franciscan order. Like the Dominicans, the Franciscans were founded in the early thirteenth century, and the presence of these two mendicant orders in the newly established universities was considerable. One of the explicit foundational aims of the Dominican order was education, and as a matter of practice the Franciscans quickly followed suit. Scotus was by profession a theologian. But – like many scholastic theologians – he has a substantial purely philosophical output: most notably, series of questions on various Aristotelian books: the *Categories*, *On interpretation*, *Sophistical refutations*, *On the soul*, *Metaphysics*, thought (with the exception of the last three books of the *Metaphysics* questions (7–9)), to be early works of Scotus's, dating from the 1290s. These are questions, not commentary, and Scotus uses Aristotle's text as a springboard for a range of questions of philosophical interest to himself. Scotus's early death prevented his completing the editorial work on his *oeuvre*. I use the best sources available for what is a complex and incomplete textual heritage.

Part of the reason for the poor state of the texts is the immediate desire of Scotus's many disciples to create as full a picture as possible of the general teachings of Scotus. In doing this they did not (and could not be expected to) pay the same kind of attention to critical accuracy as a modern editor would. It is a testament to Scotus's significance that he immediately attracted such close attention. His huge importance as a theologian and philosopher continued unabated until the seventeenth century,[5] and the undoubtedly great extent of his influence on later philosophical thinkers, particularly in the Rationalist tradition, has hardly yet begun to be explored.[6]

---

[5] See F. Bąk, 'Scoti schola numerosior est omnibus aliis simul sumptis', 144–56.

[6] A notable exception is Ludger Honnefelder, *Scientia transcendens: Die Formale Bestimmung der Seiendheit und Realität in der Metaphysik des Mittelalters und der Neuzeit (Duns Scotus, Suárez, Wolff, Kant, Pierce)*.

2 Intellectual Context

The theological tradition in the middle ages, particularly in the thirteenth and fourteenth centuries, was more intellectually vibrant than at perhaps any time before or since. So like all scholastics, Scotus found himself in constant debate and dialogue with other theologians, both his contemporaries and immediate predecessors. One reason for this is what we might call the 'professionalization' of theology. When the universities received their charters in the early thirteenth century, they acquired a structure organized around *faculties*: arts – the undergraduate faculty – and then the three graduate faculties of medicine, law, and (at least in Paris and Oxford, and, a little later, Cambridge) theology. Rather than being incorporated into general education as the central pedagogical focus, theology became a specialist discipline – an academic subject.[7] And in general it became a subject studied only by those who had completed a thorough grounding in the undergraduate arts degree.[8] The arts degree itself most resembles what we would call philosophy, with a clear focus on logic and related disciplines. This professionalization has both positive and negative results, of course, but perhaps the most important benefit was that theology became a highly rigorous and technical discipline.[9] In what follows, we shall see theology unashamedly at its most complex and specialized, in perhaps its most technically proficient philosophical practitioner.

Most important in this regard is Aristotle. By the second quarter of the thirteenth century, all the works of Aristotle that we now have were known in the West. The impact on theology was huge and sometimes bewildering. Aristotle, after all, provides a complete system, one that has no room for a Christian God – indeed, would find such a God philosophically unacceptable – and that, as I shall shortly discuss, often conflicts with the Christian faith. Throughout the thirteenth century, theologians existed in a sometimes uneasy relationship with Aristotle. On the one hand, all theologians, even professedly hostile ones such as Bonaventure (c. 1217–74) and Peter John Olivi (1248–98), relied heavily on Aristotelian logic, physics, and metaphysics. For example, the analysis of all sorts of change and composition in terms of potency and actuality, one of the most central features of Aristotelian philosophy, was universally accepted, and with it all sorts of further Aristotelian elaborations of this (matter and form, substance and accident, and so

---

[7] The most vivid account of this shift is still G. R. Evans, *Old Arts and New Theology: The Beginnings of Theology as an Academic Discipline*.

[8] In fact, members of religious orders were statutorily dispensed from following the arts course. But they were expected to provide some analogous philosophical education in their own *studia*, and it is evident that a theologian such as Scotus was trained in philosophy at least as well as any secular contemporary. On Franciscan education in this period, see Bert Roest, *A History of Franciscan Education (c. 1210–1517)*.

[9] The negative side, I suppose, is that theology tended to become detached from immediate social and political concerns, making it hard to associate other than in a very general and more or less meaningless way with contemporary cultural trends. Still, there are lots of ways of practising the Christian life, and the way of the scholastic theologians is surely one such way. On admittedly rare occasions, Scotus slips easily enough between scholastic and doxological voices: see most notably the fourth and concluding book of *DPP*. For Scotus then, doing theology is one way of living the Christian life. And it would be hard-hearted to object to this, at least from a theological point of view.

on: I discuss all of these notions at appropriate places below). Likewise Aristotelian syllogistic was (for obvious reasons) accepted without question. These were tools that all used without hesitation, and that help explain the vast advances made in both theology and philosophy during the period. On the other hand, certain key areas of difficulty developed during the thirteenth century, coming to a head in the 1260s and 1270s. Most notable are Aristotle's belief that the world lacks a beginning, his claim (at least in the interpretation of Averroes) that there is just one soul for all human beings, and his argument that the highest human good is the life of the philosopher.

These and other beliefs – apparently seriously entertained by professors in the Paris Arts Faculty – were condemned in 1277, when the Bishop of Paris, Stephen Tempier, issued a condemnation of some 219 propositions of largely Aristotelian provenance, including some taken from the recently dead Thomas Aquinas (1224/25–74).[10] From the point of view of Scotus, the most important of these condemnations was a series connected with contingency and God's power to do other than he has done. For example, proposition 53 asserted that God creates of necessity, and proposition 21 that 'everything comes about by necessity, and that all the things that will exist in the future will exist by necessity, and those that will not exist are impossible, and that nothing occurs contingently if all causes are considered'. Contingency was defended too through the condemnation of certain positions in natural philosophy, particularly the condemnation of proposition 34 ('That the first cause cannot make more than one world'), and proposition 49 ('That God could not move the heaven in a straight line, the reason being that he would then leave a vacuum'). Human freedom was likewise robustly maintained. Tempier condemned the views that the soul is not a self-mover (proposition 194), that it lacks the liberty of indifference (propositions 131, 134, and 135), and that the will is constrained by the intellect (propositions 159 and 163). Scotus clearly took the condemnations seriously, and it is evident that they pushed theologians in a new direction on questions such as freedom and possibility. A key player in the condemnations was the great Parisian theologian Henry of Ghent (c. 1217–93), a thinker who lay great stress on the freedom of the will and influenced Scotus on this matter directly.

Many of the condemned propositions owe their origins not to Aristotle – the Philosopher, as the medievals called him – but to the great Iberian Moslem exegete of Aristotle, Averroes (1126–98) – the Commentator, as the scholastics referred to him. Averroes produced no fewer than three commentaries on the works of Aristotle, and tended to push the interpretation of Aristotle in a way that theologians of both Islamic and Christian persuasions found unacceptable from a theological point of view. Thus, the belief that there is just one human soul for all human beings is one that is distinctive to Averroist interpretation of Aristotle, at least as understood by the medievals.[11] More important for Scotus was the earlier, more neoplatonically inspired Islamic philosopher Avicenna. From Avicenna, Scotus takes three

---

[10] For the condemned propositions, see *Cartularium Universitatis Parisiensis*, I, 543–55 (English translation in Lerner and Mahdi, *Medieval Political Philosophy*, 338–54). On the condemnations, see R. Hissette, *Enquête sur les 219 articles condamnés à Paris le 7 Mars 1277*.

[11] On this unicity thesis in Islamic thought, see H. A. Davidson, *Alfarabi, Avicenna, and Averroes on Intellect*.

argumentative structures that are very important in what follows. First, Avicenna famously rejects the primacy of Aristotle's 'physical' argument to the existence of a first *mover*, and replaces it with a 'metaphysical' argument from contingency to the existence of a necessary being. In the course of this argument, secondly, Avicenna rejects the Aristotelian association of modal concepts (necessary vs. contingent, and so on) with temporal ones (everlasting vs. temporary). And, thirdly, in his understanding of contingency, Avicenna develops the notion of an essence (paradigmatically, *horseness*, but any kind-nature will do) that is, in itself, neither one nor many. All of these Avicennian claims hold considerable importance for Scotus, as we shall see. (I deal with the proof for God's existence in Part I, chapter 2; with modal concepts in Part I, chapters 2 and 4; and with common natures in Part II, chapter 13 below, though in none of these cases do I explore more deeply the Avicennian background, since that is already covered well in the literature.[12]) But it is important to keep in mind that in many ways Scotus owes more to Aristotle than he does to any of these other philosophers. Certain important and characteristic neoplatonic structures that were important for Scotus's contemporaries and predecessors are almost entirely lacking in Scotus. I have in mind most particularly the use of the notion of *participation* as having some kind of explanatory or argumentative force. (It is not that Scotus is not happy with the language of participation; it is simply that he – like Aristotle – does not regard it as anything other than an ambiguous way of talking about relationships that can more perspicuously be talked about in other ways.)

Having said all of this, one remote predecessor seems to have had an influence on Scotus that approaches in importance that of Aristotle: namely, Augustine. Clearly a key theological influence, there are many parts of Augustine's philosophical system (if I may so label it) that were important for Scotus too. In what follows, Scotus makes full use of the inchoate philosophy of mind that Augustine begins to develop in *De Trinitate*. From Aristotle and later thought inspired by Aristotle Scotus takes an abstractive account of concept-formation. But from Augustine he develops a theory of occurrent acts of thought, and it is this that is central in the account of the Trinity that I discuss in Part II below. I deal with some of the relevant material in Part I, chapter 4 and Part II, chapter 10 below. I do not relate the discussion all that closely to Augustine himself, because a comparison of Scotus and Augustine on the issue of cognition would take me too far afield from my theological purposes here. Most of the issues that Scotus deals with have a complex background in thirteenth-century theology, and many of them have a history going back to the Patristic era. It would be a wonderful project to write about them, but here I have seen my main task as to focus on Scotus. I do not generally discuss passages where Scotus appeals to authority, though I occasionally note in passing Patristic and other texts that make a difference to the interpretation of Scotus. Assessing Scotus's reading of the relevant authorities, and placing these in the context of a theological tradition would be the task of another large book.

It is worth keeping in mind that Scotus engages in a serious way far more with his contemporaries and immediate predecessors than he does with the earlier

---

[12] On the first two, see Stephen Menn, 'Metaphysics: God and Being', 150–54; on the third Timothy B. Noone, 'Universals and Individuation', 102–5.

theological tradition. As will become clear, one thinker more than any other provides Scotus with material for discussion: the late thirteenth-century theologian Henry of Ghent, perhaps the most important scholastic thinker between Aquinas and Scotus, and someone from whom Scotus obviously learned a great deal. Other names from the second half of the thirteenth century crop up too, greater (Bonaventure, Aquinas, Godfrey of Fontaines, Richard of Middleton) and lesser (Roger Marston, Thomas of Sutton, Richard of Conington, among others).[13] I explain the various positions of these theologians, when relevant, in what follows.

3 Reason and Authority

The various pre-thirteenth-century philosophical and theological thinkers I have just discussed had something of the character of 'authorities', people whose views could in principle be thought of as trustworthy on the grounds that there was reason to suppose that they knew what they were talking about. Medieval attitudes to authorities were in some ways different from ours: an argument from authority is allowed to carry more explicit weight than we would perhaps allow today. But it is important not to overestimate this difference. We rely on authorities all the time, and often in a far less sophisticated way than the medieval theologians. Scotus, for example, devotes some space to a discussion of the nature and importance of *testimony* as evidence in favour of a particular view. The context is an attempt to provide motives for the credibility of the Christian faith, and a key feature of Scotus's account is an attempt to show the credibility of the witness of the Apostles, as found in the scripture. On the question of testimony, Scotus believes that, *ceteris paribus*, it is simply natural to believe the testimony of others, an assertion that Scotus makes in connection with the belief that the world existed 'before I did, and that there are parts of the world that I do not see'.[14] Equally, if there were not such a presumption in favour of belief in testimony, then there would result a situation that would 'destroy all political life':[15] the example Scotus gives here is refusing to believe that one's parents are such – something that for him, before the days of DNA testing, could obviously only be a matter of testimony. Scotus clearly believes that this presumption operates merely *ceteris paribus*. He insists, for example, on the importance of the moral worth of the person in question:

[1]
1 By faith acquired though hearing my parents and others, I believe that many eras have
2 passed, and that the world did not begin when I did. For I believe Rome to exist,
3 which I have not seen, from the belief related by the worthy.[16]

---

[13] For useful summaries of the life and works of these thinkers, see conveniently the relevant entries in Jorge J. E. Gracia and Timothy B. Noone, *A Companion to Philosophy in the Middle Ages*. On Conington, who does not receive an entry in this work, see Stephen D. Dumont, 'William of Ware, Richard of Conington and the *Collationes Oxonienses of John Duns Scotus*'.

[14] Scotus, *Ord.* 3.23.un., n. 5 (Wadding, VII, 461).

[15] Ibid. prol.2.un., n. 107 (Vatican, I, 68).

[16] Ibid. 3.23.un, n. 4 (Wadding, VII, 460).

And the Church is credible because 'it is a renowned and honest community'.[17] Scotus perhaps gives more place to mere fame than we would: thus, he likens believing something because the Church says so to believing 'other histories written or narrated by certain famous men'.[18] Despite this cultural difference between Scotus and us, the point, I take it, is that believing on the basis of the testimony of those whom we believe to have good reasons to know what they are talking about is a reasonable thing to do – much as many today have to rely on the testimony of scientists for all sorts of beliefs that we have about the origin and nature of the universe and the things within it. Equally, Scotus provides a large number of arguments in favour of the credibility of scripture that include considerations of the unlikelihood of the Apostles being either mistaken or deceivers.[19]

Having said this, Scotus is aware of the limitations of arguments from authority, and thus accords them less *rational* or *probative* force than arguments from reason. Scotus believes that, in relation to Christian belief, arguments from testimony result in *acquired faith*, and such faith does not have the certainty of divinely infused faith (or, presumably, of knowledge either, *a fortiori*):

[2]
1 Firm assent cannot come from acquired faith, because by acquired faith someone
2 believes only someone whom he knows to be able to be mistaken, and to be mistaken
3 even though he believes him not to wish to be mistaken: but no one can assent
4 perfectly to the sayings of someone whom he knows to be fallible, and to be mistaken,
5 in the things that he says. But every human being is like this.[20]

In the light of this, Scotus allows that the will has a role in the acceptance of something merely on the basis of testimony. Even given all the evidence in favour of acquired faith, someone could *by will* refuse to assent – and Scotus does not give us any indication as to how *reasonable* he thinks such a person would be.[21] Still, Scotus's acceptance of authority, be it of the Apostles, Fathers, or non-Christian philosophers, is philosophically principled in a way that is only rarely found in modern discussions.[22]

---

[17] Ibid. prol.2.un, n. 107 (Vatican, I, 69).

[18] Ibid. 3.23.un., n. 4 (Wadding, VII, 460).

[19] Ibid. prol.2.un., nn. 101–19 (Vatican, I, 61–85): I summarize the reasons in my *Duns Scotus*, 12.

[20] Scotus, *Ord.* 3.23.un., n. 15 (Wadding, VII, 469).

[21] Ibid.

[22] Scotus's respect for his authorities sometimes has a rather disconcerting result, namely the presence of flexible and frankly implausible interpretations of various texts with a view to 'saving' the authority (from an obvious or not so obvious error, for example). Scotus famously and very unpersuasively tries to show that his understanding of individuation – in terms of haecceity or thisness (see Part I, chapter 6 below) – can be found in Aristotle: see Scotus, *Ord.* 2.3.1.5–6, nn. 201–11 (Vatican, VII, 490–94; Spade, 110–13). And doubtless a serious discussion of Scotus's exegesis of Augustine, touched on in Part II below, would reveal similar problems.

4 Duns Scotus: A Philosopher's Theologian

Scotus, then, has the same respect for authorities as his contemporaries. But it must be said that the authorities he is most interested in are those whose habits of mind lead them to deal with questions that are fundamentally philosophical in nature, and to deal with them in a logical way. Rhetorical concerns are of no interest to him; neither is narrative as a way of practising theology. Perhaps more than any of his contemporaries, he is interested in arguments for their own sake. To this extent, he is *par excellence* the philosopher's theologian. Almost invariably, he provides multiple arguments for his positions, usually laid out in a way that makes their logical form very clear indeed. He delights in giving what he regards as unsound refutations to unsound arguments, for – it sometimes seems – the sole purpose of revealing the argumentative defect. He pauses over philosophical difficulties that are only tangentially relevant to his theological task. Indeed, Scotus came up with a huge range of philosophical insights, often discovering or inventing philosophical topics that are greatly relevant to modern debates in analytic philosophy: haecceity, contracausal freedom, logical possibility, to take just the most important ones. And his discussion of the problem of universals is probably without rival. It is perhaps not surprising that Scotus soon after his death became known by the sobriquet '*doctor subtilis*' – the subtle doctor.

What makes Scotus agreeable to the philosopher is likely to render him unappealing to the theologian. For it is hard to avoid the impression that he sometimes lets concerns about the philosophical coherence of a theological view outweigh other, perhaps more theological, considerations. He is of all theologians I have encountered (other than those in the fourteenth century who are, arguably, his methodological inheritors) the least likely to appeal to mystery, and most likely to try to solve a problem by intellectual gymnastics. Whether or not such an approach is legitimate, however, is best assessed by trying it; no one, not even the most apophatic theologian, should want to appeal to mystery in a case where the theological issue is philosophically unproblematic. (This is not to deny that doctrines are mysterious; it is to assert that sometimes the mystery lies in what we do not know, not in what we do know. I return to this question in the Appendix below.) And whether or not there are such philosophically unproblematic cases can be determined only by careful and rigorous intellectual discussion – the kind of which Scotus's discussions are examplars. Furthermore, the task Scotus sets for himself seems to me to have some very interesting theological consequences: sometimes, pushing as far as possible in the direction that Scotus leads can yield new theological insights that could be of interest to many systematic theologians. In what follows, it seems to me that Scotus has some very interesting things to say on the commonality of the divine essence shared by the three Trinitarian persons, and on the *filioque*. And, in line with his understanding of the commonality of the divine essence, he has a great deal to offer on the correct theological and philosophical understanding of the concept of *person*. He provides too an object lesson in the way that philosophical assumptions explicitly determine theological accounts of divine simplicity.

As we shall see, Scotus's discussions rarely engage even remotely with scripture. This might make it look as though Scotus is, from a theological point of view, somehow defective, even in comparison with some of his contemporaries.[23] Still, we should keep in mind that Scotus is working within a theological tradition the basic contours of which were well-established. This tradition, of course, was based on a close reading of scripture, and scriptural commentary was a compulsory part of the university curriculum. Scotus, in order to qualify as a master in theology at the University of Paris, must have lectured on the scriptures, and once a master he would have been required to lecture in detail on scriptural books. It is to be regretted that no copy of these lectures survives, though this fact itself is doubtless indicative of Scotus's own interests and abilities. But in so far as Scotus accepts the basic picture agreed upon by his contemporaries and predecessors, it is not clear that more explicit engagement with scripture would have made any difference to the content of his theology.

Furthermore, the theological world in which Scotus moved was more concerned with sorting out micro-problems with particular issues in what we would call systematic theology. These problems are not the sort of thing that can, on the whole, be decided by a close reading of scripture. Scotus and Aquinas, for example, differ vastly on many theological questions. But the sorts of thing that distinguish them – for example, whether there could be a proof of God's existence using intellectual material belonging merely to the realm of physics, or whether we should think of the divine essence as some sort of universal – are not the sorts of question upon which the scriptures could – or even should – cast any useful light. This does not, of course, mean that the theological questions that occupied Scotus are in any sense irrelevant, or even theologically decadent, despite the claims of the detractors of scholastic theology. One of the objections that the Arians made to the Council of Nicaea was that the Council introduced a non-scriptural term ('*homoousios*') to talk about the relation of Father and Son in the Trinity. On this anti-Arian view, the scriptures simply do not provide intellectual tools of sufficient rigour to deal with every question in systematic theology. Scotus is no worse off in this respect than any systematic theologian, and there is historical and authoritative precedent for this from Nicaea onwards. It seems to me that systematic theology is by its very nature an attempt to produce a coherent intellectual system, and such a system needs clear, and clearly defined, concepts, cogent arguments, and the like. And this is not the stuff of the Bible.

Scotus's project is remarkably ambitious, as we shall see, and – as is the way of ambitious projects – not all of it is successful. But there are good and bad reasons for supposing that a project of this nature is unsuccessful. It hardly does justice to a writer to reject an argument simply because it has an unexpected consequence. For example, Scotus thinks that a highly persuasive, though complex, argument can be formulated in favour of the doctrine of the Trinity. The argument may well fail at multiple points. But it would not be reasonable simply to reject the argument on the basis of some *a priori* assumption that there could not be an argument in favour of

---

[23] Aquinas, for example, cites the scriptures frequently: on this, see Wilhelmus G. B. M. Valkenberg, *Words of the Living God: The Place and Function of Holy Scripture in the Theology of St Thomas Aquinas.* In Scotus, by contrast, even in explicitly theological works, the Bible is cited but rarely. In the published volumes of the critical edition of Scotus's theological works, references to Aristotle outnumber those to the Bible by something approaching ten to one.

the Trinity; indeed, if Scotus's argument is successful, that assumption is shown to be false. That said, it is clearly the case that an argument with a counterintuitive conclusion needs to be particularly secure. As we shall see, Scotus's argument in favour of the Trinity makes some fairly sweeping assumptions about the philosophy of mind, assumptions that may well need more defence than Scotus gives them. But maintaining a healthy scepticism about an argument is quite different from dismissing it out of hand. More generally, there is a great deal of a philosophical and theological nature here with which one might wish to disagree. But I have found working slowly and carefully through Scotus's arguments has provided an unparalleled example of someone thinking painstakingly through a vast range of complex theological issues, and has thus been the opportunity to learn a great deal from a highly individual, creative, and thoughtful theologian. Scotus's beatification by Pope John Paul II in 1993 is testimony to the esteem in which Scotus's theological method is evidently still held.

5 Duns Scotus on God

As for all the scholastics, Scotus's God is the God of classical theism. I have tried to argue elsewhere that the key motivator for Scotus's account of God is the notion of God's being *wholly unconditioned*: being such that nothing can affect him.[24] On this view, God lacks any *passive capacities*. In what is now the most famous medieval account of God, that of Thomas Aquinas, the notion that God lacks passive capacities is associated with the view that God is identical with his own *esse* or existence.[25] Aquinas reasons that essence is actualized by *esse*; hence in God essence and *esse* cannot be distinct: essence cannot be actualized by *esse*. Scotus, as I note briefly below, does not accept this view, since he does not believe it is possible to make any sense of a distinction between essence and *esse*. But he certainly thinks that God lacks any passive capacities, and uses this belief to justify a moral theory based on divine command: if God's commands were somehow constrained by the natures of the things he has made, then God would fail to be wholly unconditioned: something external to God could have an effect in God, restricting God's absolutely sovereign freedom. The God of classical theism is one inherited from the Patristic era. But the medievals believed that it can be inferred from God's existence as first cause: the first cause must be such that nothing can cause an effect in it, for if something could cause an effect in it, then that thing would be prior to the first cause – which is impossible. Amongst modern theologians, I suppose this view is not particularly fashionable (though in theology today, what counts as fashionable entirely depends on the circles one is moving in), and it seems to me that there are good reasons for finding it objectionable, at least from a Christian perspective.[26] But almost all of what Scotus writes about God can stand quite independently of his claims about God's wholly unconditioned nature. To this extent, there will be material in Scotus that may be of interest or use to theologians who do not share his

---

[24] On this, see my *Duns Scotus*, 154–5, n. 6.

[25] See Aquinas, *ST* 1.3.4 c (I/1, 16ᵃ–17ᵇ).

[26] I discuss some of these reasons in my *The Metaphysics of the Incarnation*, 317–18.

fundamental belief in the God of classical theism – perhaps theologians who prefer to think of God as somehow *personal* (an adjective to which I return in a moment). Indeed, Scotus's theory of religious language, discussed in the Appendix below, certainly does not make metaphysical presuppositions about God's 'wholly otherness'. If anything, more apophatically minded theologians – the followers of Aquinas, perhaps – have criticized Scotus's theory for sanctioning a God who is insufficiently different from the creation.

The main text of what follows is divided into two parts. In the first, I deal with Scotus's proof for the existence and nature of God as first cause. In the second, larger part, I discuss how Scotus tries to show that this God must be a Trinity of persons. The two parts are likely to have slightly different appeals: the first to those interested in Scotus's natural theology, the second to those with a more theological interest in the technicalities of Scotus's Trinitarian theology. But both parts are about God as Scotus conceived him, and both parts are, according to Scotus, open to some kind of rational proof, as we shall see. In the first part, I consider initially Scotus's notion of causation (chapter 1), and then apply the concepts described there to Scotus's proof for the existence of a first cause (chapter 2). Fundamentally, Scotus believes that causal relations hold between substances. A cause is a substance with an active causal power; what it brings about is the actualization of some passive capacity in another substance (or, according to Scotus, sometimes and in certain circumstances in itself). Scotus believes that it is impossible for there to be an infinite regress of such causal relations, and that it is impossible for there to be self-contained circles of causes. Given this, he maintains that there must be a first cause. In Part I, chapter 3, I consider Scotus's relation to Anselm's so-called 'perfect-being' theology – the attempt to derive the divine attributes from a consideration of the 'pure perfections': attributes which, *ceteris paribus*, it is better to have than to lack. Scotus on the whole is agnostic (though inconsistently so) about this methodology, and in the remaining chapters of Part I, I show the alternative strategies Scotus develops for identifying his first cause as the God of classical theism. Since there is contingency (freedom) in the world, there must be freedom in God, and thus will; and this in turn means that there must be intellect in God too (chapter 4). And, as the first cause of all that there is and can be, God's knowledge must be infinite, and thus God must be infinite (chapter 5). An infinitely perfect being must be supremely simple, and I explore Scotus's account of this in chapter 6. Although Scotus firmly accepts divine simplicity, his general philosophical account of the relation between the various attributes of a thing leads him to suppose that even in God there are distinctions between various attributes that are not merely mind-imposed: a claim that places him at a considerable distance from more traditional classical theists. Scotus holds that divine infinity entails that there can be only one God (chapter 7), and that divine simplicity entails immutability (chapter 8).

In Part II, I explore Scotus's Trinitarian theology, starting with Scotus's account of the degree of proof available in favour of the doctrine (chapter 9). Chapters 10–12 contain the proof proper, more or less as Scotus presents it. Scotus believes that God, as an intellectual and voluntary agent, must have at least two internal productions: acts of knowledge and love (chapter 10). But according to Scotus there can be in God at most two internal productions, and must be exactly one unproduced producer (chapter 11). This producer and these products must be distinct from each other (since nothing produces itself). But there is just one God, so the relevant things must be *persons*: exemplifications of the numerically singular divine essence (chapter 12). The remaining chapters of Part II provide necessary clarifications to the account of the Trinity – again, claims Scotus believes to be known by natural reason, but extrinsic to the structure of his proposed proof of God's Trinitarian nature. The divine essence is an entity shared by the three persons, but in contrast with creaturely common natures it is not divided into numerically many particular natures or essences. As a numerically singular nature it is (weakly) subsistent – subsistent, but not in such a way as not to be shared by more than one person – and (weakly) prior to the persons, since it explains the fact that each person is God (chapter 13). Each divine person includes this divine essence, and in addition a further property that distinguishes the persons from each other – the so-called 'personal properties'. According to Scotus, these personal properties are causal relations and are distinguished from each other by their being different *kinds* of causal relation. This view allows Scotus to reject the standard Western argument in favour of the *filioque* (the belief that the Holy Spirit proceeds from the Father *and the Son*). Son and Spirit are distinguished from each other in virtue of the fact that each possesses a relation to the Father different in kind from the other's relation, irrespective of any causal relation between the Son and Spirit themselves (chapter 14). In chapter 15, I consider Scotus's treatment of the (standard scholastic) view that the divine essence is the causal power in virtue of which divine persons produce and are produced. This view gives Scotus an argument in favour of the *filioque*: if the Son possesses the divine essence 'prior' to the production of the Spirit, then the Son possesses a power sufficient to allow him, along with the Father, to produce the Spirit. In chapter 16 I discuss Scotus's view of the relation between the intellectual and volitional acts that produce the Son and the Spirit, on the one hand, with the intellectual and volitional acts that all three persons share. Related to this, I consider too the unity of the external activity of the three persons. Thinking that the persons all share intellect and will certainly means that the divine persons have a conscious life, even if that life cannot include the possibility of being affected by creatures in any way. Scotus holds too that the essence and the personal property of each person are fully real, and in chapter 17 I discuss his view of the reality and unity of these two 'components' of each divine person, in the light of considerations of divine simplicity. Again, Scotus's view moves him away from a rigorous kind of classical theism that would deny any extramental distinction between different divine properties. Since Scotus, like many of the Fathers and scholastics, is happy to think of the Father as *producing* the Son and Spirit, in the final chapter of Part II I show how Scotus addresses subordinationist worries that this causal account might suggest.

In the Appendix, I consider Scotus's view of religious language and divine ineffability, again showing that Scotus's view of God is not by any means as apophatic as that of many classical theists. Scotus holds that scholastic and Patristic theological method, using rigorously deductive arguments, requires that at least some of the concepts that we ascribe to God and creatures must be identically the same.

6 Theology and Metaphysics

As just noted, in what follows I deal first with Scotus's proof for the existence of one God, and secondly with his attempt to show that there must be three divine persons. It would not be possible to present the argument the other way round. This is not because Scotus thinks that God's Trinitarian nature is somehow secondary, or not reflective of what God truly is. It is merely a reflection of the *ordo inventionis* in the rational presentation of the Christian faith: in providing an argument for Trinitarian processions, it is first of all necessary to show that there is at least one divine person, and that this person has productive powers of a kind to produce a further such person or persons (the subject of Part II, chapters 10–12). And showing that there is at least one divine person first of all requires showing that there is at least one divine essence or substance (the subject of Part I).

In fact, the two parts just described reflect two different disciplines: metaphysics and theology, respectively. According to Scotus, metaphysics is the discipline whose subject is *being as being*, and whose object or aim is to show that an infinite being (God) exists.[27] Theology is the discipline whose subject is the God of revealed theology: specifically, God's unique Trinitarian essence.[28] Scotus believes that these two disciplines, while independent, complement each other. A belief that it is possible to provide good arguments in favour of the Trinitarian God of revealed theology was widespread amongst the scholastic theologians. I discuss it in Part II, chapter 9 below. Not all agreed; for example, the most famous of the scholastics, Thomas Aquinas, argues that we cannot demonstrate God's Trinitarian nature since demonstrations of God are *a posteriori*, and nothing about God's causal role relative to the universe seems to require that he is a Trinity of persons. Scotus believes that arguments in favour of the Trinity do not count as Aristotelian demonstrations. But he believes them to have some persuasive force, as I shall show.

Like Aquinas, and for that matter many of the thirteenth-century schoolmen, Scotus believes that both metaphysics and theology are *sciences*.[29] They understand science here in an Aristotelian sense that I discuss variously in Part I, chapter 2 §1, and Part II, chapter 9 §2. Basically, a science is a deductive system in which earlier parts *explain* later parts. A deductive argument is one such that, if the premises are true, the conclusion must be as well. In the *Posterior Analytics*, Aristotle distinguishes two sorts of such argument, which the Latin writers label '*propter quid*' and '*quia*', respectively. Aristotle's example of a *propter quid* argument is the following:

The planets are near;
Things that are near do not twinkle;
Therefore, the planets do not twinkle.[30]

Contrast Aristotle's example of a related argument *quia*:

---

[27] See my *Duns Scotus*, 147–8.
[28] See Ibid., 7–8.
[29] See Ibid., 8–10.
[30] Aristotle, *An. post.* 1.13 (78ᵇ1–3).

The planets do not twinkle;
Things that do not twinkle are near;
Therefore, the planets are near.[31]

Both of these are sound arguments (true premisses, valid logical form). The key difference is that in the first argument the premisses somehow *explain* the conclusion, giving the *reason why* the conclusion is true; in the second, an argument *quia*, they do not, merely showing *that* the conclusion is true. It is the nearness of the planets that explains their failure to twinkle, not *vice versa*.

Thus described, none of the material that I discuss below counts as strictly scientific. In Part I, the arguments for God's existence fail to be explanatory. For proofs for God's existence argue from effects to causes: if there is such-and-such an effect, there must be such and such a cause – a paradigm case of a demonstration *quia*. Although, as we shall see in Part I, chapter 2 §1, Scotus tries to build into his cosmological argument as many features of scientific argument as he possibly can, explanatoriness is bound to elude him: God explains the existence of creatures, and not *vice versa*. In Part II, the Trinitarian material is not scientific, in the sense that (again) the basic evidence comes from human experience – in this case, introspective experience of human mental life – from which Scotus generalizes to construct arguments about the Trinity. But human mental life is not explanatory of the Trinity. If anything, the explanatory order will go the other way. It is because God has a procession from intellect and a procession from will that our minds are constructed in the way that they are.[32]

What this shows is not that metaphysics and theology fail to be scientific. The scientific nature of theology and metaphysics, on medieval accounts such as Scotus's, is understood not in the context of an attempt to prove God's existence and Trinitarian nature. So in neither case does my exposition below follow the correct scientific order. This need not matter. When thirteenth-century theologians claim that theology is scientific, they do not mean that they intend to practise it scientifically. What they mean, rather, is that the material of theology *could* be arranged scientifically by someone so minded; by the time of Henry of Ghent, it was held that at least one mind actually did this: namely, the divine mind in its grasp of theological truth.[33]

---

[31] Ibid. (78ᵃ32–6).

[32] For example, Scotus holds that the distinction between different manners of production manifested in the Trinity is fundamental and basic, and that it is reflected in the operation of our minds, as we shall see in Part II chapter 11 below.

[33] On this, see my *Duns Scotus*, 7.

PART I

THE EXISTENCE OF
THE ONE GOD

Chapter 1

Theories of Causation

1 Efficient Causation

Medieval philosophical theories of causation are in many ways very different from modern ones. An understanding of some of these differences may help to make Scotus's account of God's existence intelligible, and perhaps even plausible. And it will help too with understanding Scotus's theology of the intra-Trinitarian relations of the divine persons. Medieval views of causation generally involve an analysis in terms of substances causing effects (in other substances). The causes here are substances with (active) *powers* to do things, and what they do is affect things with (passive) *potencies* or capacities to be affected in the relevant way: paradigmatically, x brings it about that y is φ, where x and y are two different substances, and where x has the relevant power (to make things φ), and y the relevant capacity (to be made φ). Modern views of causation tend to suppose that causal relations obtain between events. Talk of causation in this way has a great ontological advantage: it renders superfluous any talk of substances and their powers. This is an advantage of economy. But the advantage comes at a price (and so is, in a different way, uneconomical): namely, a loss of explanatory force. For in event–event analyses, causation is usually reduced to one or other of two sorts of relation: constant conjunction or counterfactual dependence. On constant-conjunction theories, all there is to causation is one event's regularly or constantly following another. Counterfactual-dependence theories specify the relation a little more closely: an event x counterfactually depends on an event y distinct from x, if both, x and y obtain, and if y did not obtain, x would not obtain. Neither of these accounts is very satisfactory. They both deny what seems to be central in our intuitive notion of causation, namely that there is some sort of *connection* between cause and effect. A definition of causation that is faithful to our intuitions on the matter would have to include the fact that a cause seems to make some genuine contribution to the effect: something that the cause is or does is responsible for the effect; the effect somehow derives from the cause.

Of course, the point of both of these theories is to try to do without causal powers: the strange, invisible, seemingly almost magical properties of a thing that enable it to reach out to other things and make a difference to them. With their robust acceptance of causal powers, medieval theories, I suspect, tend to conform to our intuitive understanding of causation more than modern ones do. Thus in everyday discourse we tend to operate with an account of causation modelled on our own abilities to do things, and to affect other things. And talk of active powers invites talk of passive capacities too: the liability of something to be affected. Medieval theories tend to root all of this in talk about *forms*. On Aristotelian theories, largely accepted by later medieval thinkers, material substances are composites of matter and substantial form – very loosely, stuff and essential structure – and these composites are the subjects of further forms – accidental ones, forms that the substance can gain or lose, and have or lack. Lying behind this sort of analysis is a rather crude account according to which causation fundamentally amounts to the transference or communication of a form from one substance or substrate to another. For example, in a much debated passage, Aquinas argues against the possibility of self-motion in a way which seems to imply that, in order to make something be in a certain way, the agent needs itself to be in that way – more technically, in order to give something a certain form, the agent must already possess the form:

> Everything that is in motion is moved by another. For something is in motion only if it is in potency to the thing to which it is moved. But something moves [another] only if it is actual, for to move is nothing other than to reduce something from potency to actuality. But something can be reduced from potency to actuality only by something actual, just as something actually hot, such as fire, makes a stick which is potentially hot, actually hot, and thereby moves and changes it. But it is not possible that the same thing be simultaneously actual and potential in the same respect, but only in different respects. For what is actually hot cannot be simultaneously hot potentially. Therefore it is impossible that something, by the same motion, is both mover and moved, or that it move itself. It is therefore necessary that everything in motion is moved by another.[1]

On the face of it, this seems to imply that possession of a form is a necessary condition for bestowing the form on something else. And one obvious way of understanding this claim is to suppose that forms – abstract objects such as heat – are somehow 'spread out' from agent to effect. I do not want to adjudicate on Aquinas's precise meaning here, or what might be grounding it.[2] But I do want to suggest that by the time of Scotus, the *prima facie* sense of Aquinas's text here was regarded as false. Scotus, for example, accepts the possibility of self-change, and to do this he has to allow that a power to make something φ does not require actually being φ.[3] Whatever it is, a causal power need not be an instance of, or be possessed by, the kind of thing effected in virtue of, or through, the power (though, presumably, it can be: hot things, but not only hot things, make other things hot). Understood in this way, there is nothing 'mystical' about the notion of a form (though there may remain something mysterious about it). In this context, talk of substantial forms is at root a way of talking about the essential properties, powers, and capacities of a thing; talk of accidental forms is at root a way of talking about contingent properties, powers, and capacities of a thing.

---

[1] Aquinas, *ST* 1.2.3 c (I/1, 12ᵃ).

[2] Suffice it to say that Aquinas certainly does accept the notion of so-called 'equivocal' causation – the production of an effect different in kind from the cause, and this entails that the possession of a form is not a necessary condition for bestowing the form on something else. In this light, of course, it is hard to see how the impossibility of self-motion could be sufficiently sustained on the grounds found in the quotation just given from Aquinas.

[3] For the definitive modern discussion of this, see Peter King, 'Duns Scotus on the Reality of Self-Change', 229–90.

Thus far, I have talked about material substances, and their powers and capacities to change other material substances, and to be changed by such substances. The medievals accept too a more specialized kind of causation. For x to bring it about that y is φ does not require the pre-existence of y, and one way for the relevant causal relation to obtain is for x to bring it about that y exists. Bringing about y's existence entails bringing it about that y has at least some properties, and one way for x to bring it about that y exists is for the causal relation between x and y to admit of a more basic explanation: perhaps what it is for x to bring it about that y is φ is for x to act on a substrate z, somehow contained or included in y, bringing it about that z is ψ (such that the inclusion relation between y and z entails that, if z is ψ, y is φ). In standard cases of generation, this could be exactly what happens: matter (for us, though not for the medievals, fundamental particles, or things made up of such particles), is basically rearranged, such that what previously was one kind of thing is made to be another kind of thing.[4] This account explains why Aristotle and his followers thought of matter as *potency*, and form as *actuality*. For something to have a form φ-ness is for it to be *actually* φ. Matter that is not φ (where φ-ness is a substantial form) but can be φ has a (passive) potency for being φ. Likewise, a substance that is not φ (where φ-ness is an accidental form) but can be φ has a potency for being φ; the accidental form φ-ness itself is actual relative to the substance, making the substance to be actually φ.[5]

Furthermore, however, for x to bring it about that y exists does not entail that there is any pre-existent thing out of which y is made: y does not need to be made from anything at all. And this is creation. Peter Geach many years ago suggested a way of understanding this, contrasting God's creative and non-creative causal activity in the following way:

> We may insert an existential quantifier to bind the 'x' in 'God brought it about that x is A' in two different ways:
>   (I) God brought it about that (Ex) (x is an A)
>   (II) (Ex) (God brought it about that x is an A)
> (II) implies that God makes into an A some entity pre-supposed to his action; but (I) does not; and we express the supposition of God's creating an A by conjoining (I) with the negation of (II), for some suitable interpretation of 'A'.[6]

Medieval accounts tend to think of this creation relation – in the case of material substances – in terms of an agent's causing both the form and matter of a material

---

[4] We do not need to suppose that there is a substrate here. x could make y out of w without anything of w surviving. Even in this case, x's making y requires something from which y is made. Dispensing with a substrate, however, makes the analysis in terms of passive capacities harder (though not impossible) to sustain. I do not want to go into any detail here. Suffice it to say that we do not need to talk of a substrate in order to ground a global explanation of causation in terms of causal powers and capacities, so the possible implausibility of appealing to a substrate for every case of change does not render impossible any talk of powers and capacities.

[5] I explain these notions in my *The Physics of Duns Scotus: The Scientific Context of a Theological Vision*, 17–20; see too 44–5, 106.

[6] Peter Geach, 'Causality and Creation', 75–85 (83). Taking into account Trinitarian productions – the subject of Part II below – would necessitate some clarification here. But I do not think we need pause over this now.

substance. It was a commonplace that material substances cannot themselves create.[7] So talk of creation was held to entail talk of immaterial substances. Since the medievals tend – like Aristotle and his ancient followers – to think of forms as explaining causal powers, it was natural for them to think of immaterial substances as forms without matter. Again, there is not supposed, I think, to be anything mystical about this. 'Form' here is an equivocal notion, and we could just as easily think of an immaterial substance as something like a Cartesian soul.

The basic model of causation, as I have been outlining it, is that of an agent's doing something to something else. Causing, then, is a kind of doing. But it is not the only kind of doing. Sometimes we just do things without obviously affecting anything. When I think, for example, I just do something. Scotus does not regard this doing as properly classifiable as an action: actions, for him, always involve patients – things affected by the action. Scotus makes a distinction between *producing* and *operating*. Producing is a causal relation of the kind I have been describing: making something to be φ (and perhaps, but not necessarily, doing so by making that thing to exist). Producing is acting in this technical sense. Operating, however, does not in itself involve a patient in this way. It is just *doing*. Scotus believes, nevertheless, that there is some sort of causal relation involved in this operating. A paradigm case of an operation is thinking:

[1]
1 'Action' in creatures is understood in one way for action in the genus [viz. category]
2 of action, and in another way for second act, which is an absolute quality. ...
3 Speaking only of the one sort of act [viz. categorial act: production], or only of the
4 other [viz. second act: operation], one power has only one act; but there can certainly
5 be two acts of one [power], of which one is an action and the other of the genus of
6 quality, just as our intellect, whose action in the genus of action is to generate a word,
7 has however another action in the genus of quality, namely the generated knowledge.[8]

Here we have distinguished two sorts of action: categorial[9] action **[1.1–2]**, and action considered as an absolute quality **[1.2]** – a non-productive *state*, second act properly speaking (though Scotus is not always rigorous in maintaining that only operation is second act properly speaking). Scotus elsewhere uses the word 'production' to pick out the first of these – act in the category of action – and the word 'operation' to pick out the qualitative state.[10] The basic difference is that an operation does not have some *further* result: to act is simply to be in a particular, active, state, whereas a production *causes* some further entity. According to Scotus,

---

[7] For a discussion of this, see my *The Physics of Duns Scotus*, 256–63.

[8] Scotus, *Ord.* 1.6.un., n. 14 (Vatican, IV, 92–4; see too *Ord.* 1.3.3.4, n. 601 (Vatican, III, 354); *Ord.* 1.2.2.1–4, nn. 311 and 326 (Vatican, II, 314, 321); *Quod.* 13, nn. 2, 27 (Wadding, XII, 301, 341; Alluntis and Wolter, 284, 307–8 (¶¶ 13.4, 13.81–13.82)). Translations throughout are my own. To give a flavour of Scotus's thought, which is syntactically convoluted in Latin, I have tried to keep as close as possible to his Latin prose within the bounds of sense and reasonable clarity. The translations, I hope, pressurize English syntax in a way analogous to that in which the originals strain the Latin.

[9] I use 'categorial' to refer to the well-known division of predicates found in Aristotle's *Cat.* 4 (1ᵇ25–7).

[10] For 'production' and 'operation', see the passages cited in footnote 8.

the act or operation of understanding is a state – properly, a quality **[1.7]** – and it is caused (produced or elicited) by the intellect (more properly, the memory: on this, see Part I, chapter 4 §3 and Part II, chapter 10 §2 below). In this case, operation – something which looks as though it involves no patient – is intricately and inseparably entwined with production – something which does involve a patient. I do not believe that Scotus holds that I have to do two things when I think: do the thinking, and produce the thoughts. By thinking, I produce thoughts. But there is nevertheless a logical distinction to be drawn between the operation and the production.[11]

2 The Impossibility of an Infinite Regress of Causes

The medieval philosophers noticed that some cause–effect relations exist as parts of ordered sequences of such relations. As Scotus understands it, there are two quite distinct sorts of sequences: those in which the relations between the causes and their effects are transitive, and those in which they are not. The basic point in transitively ordered series is that what the cause brings about is itself a further causal relationship: *a* makes *b* affect (or effect) *c*. The paradigm for such a relationship is *a*'s actualizing a form in *b* sufficient for *b*'s bringing about the relevant causal effect in *c* (paradigmatically, another form). One way for *a* to do this to *b* is for *a* to *affect* *b*; another is simply for *a* to *effect* *b*, bringing it about both that *b* exists and that *b* has a certain form sufficient for affecting (or effecting) *c*. Scotus distinguishes this sort of relationship from an ordered sequence in which the relationships are not transitive. Scotus describes the transitive series as 'essentially ordered', and the intransitive as 'accidentally ordered'. As he presents the distinction, there are three differences between the two cases:

[2]
1 Essentially and *per se* ordered [causal series] differ in three ways from accidentally
2 ordered ones. The first difference is that in *per se* [orders] the second, in so far as it
3 causes, depends on the first; in accidentally ordered ones [it does] not, though it may
4 depend [on the first] for its existence or in some other way. The second is that in *per*
5 *se* [orders] the causality is of another kind and order, because the higher cause is more
6 perfect; in accidentally [ordered ones it is] not. And this follows from the first
7 [difference], for no cause depends essentially in its causing on a cause of the same
8 kind, for in the causation of something one [cause] of any one kind is sufficient. A
9 third [difference] follows, that all *per se* ordered causes are simultaneously required
10 necessarily for causing, otherwise some *per se* causality would be lacking from the
11 effect; accidentally ordered causes are not required simultaneously.[12]

---

[11] Neither does Scotus believe that the operation of thinking is itself productive of some further product: on this, see his criticism of Aquinas's theory of the mental word at *Ord.* 1.27.1–3, nn. 55–6 (Vatican, VI, 86).

[12] Scotus, *DPP* 3, n. 2 (Wolter, 47 (¶ 3.11)). When citing *DPP*, I give full references to Wolter's serviceable and readily accessible edition. I give too the margin numbers from the widely available Wadding. Wolter includes a translation and useful commentary on the whole text. Note that the text in Wadding is in places defective, and that Wolter's text suffers from a few small misprints.

The key difference is the first: in essentially ordered causal series, an earlier member of the series actually causes the later member to cause [**2.2–3**]. It is this that ensures transitivity: if x causes y to cause z, then there is a clear sense in which x causes z. So it need not be *existence* that Scotus sees essentially ordered series as explaining [**2.3–4**], except – presumably – in the case that z is a substance.

The second difference is far more controversial, at least to the extent that Scotus believes it to be entailed by the first. The difference is that, in essentially ordered series, the kind of causal activity is different in each member of the series – and furthermore, it is more perfect in earlier members [**2.4–6**]. The reason why this is supposed to be entailed by the transitivity claim is that, in any kind of ordered causal relationship, 'one cause of any one kind is sufficient' [**2.8**]. What Scotus is thinking is that the relevant causal relation is ordered, and not (say) cooperative. He is not suggesting that different things of the same kind may not cooperate on an equal footing to produce the effect: four horses pulling a cart, or whatever. The horses here are not ordered in the required way – they do not pull each other along. Scotus's proposal is that one cause of any one kind is sufficient in cases where the relevant causal relations are transitive in the way described. The trouble is that there appear to be counterinstances. Consider a series of dominoes, each pushing another over. Dominoes are all of the same kind, and yet the series appears to be transitive in the required way. Scotus's point presumably is that, had the dominoes been slightly differently arranged, the first domino could have pushed over the last directly, without any intervention from other dominoes. But the arrangement of the causes here is crucial.[13] The perfection claim itself is perhaps less problematic. The point is simply that the relevant perfection consists in being able to activate something else's causal powers: earlier causes are directly or indirectly responsible for a greater amount and variety of such activation than later ones are.

The third difference – simultaneity – is posited by Scotus on the grounds that, if it is not satisfied, the effect would be lacking some causal explanation required for it [**2.10–11**]. This criterion seems to make more sense in the case that the relevant causes and effects do not involve physical – mechanical – processes. Perhaps some causal series are like this. Suppose I have a soul that can immediately move parts of my body, and suppose that a possible causal series consists of God immediately making my soul move part of my body. This certainly satisfies the simultaneity requirement. But many candidates for essentially ordered causal series are not like this. That is to say, there seem to be series that satisfy the first, or perhaps the first two criteria in [**2**], but not the third. (It is easy enough to think of something satisfying the first but not the third: many physical processes in a deterministic universe would do so.) Doubtless, the kind of example that Scotus has in mind is similar to the case that Aquinas cites when explaining the distinction: sun, element,

---

[13] There are disanalogies, though I am not sure whether they are sufficient to save Scotus's position. Dominoes, on medieval accounts of things, would not really count as anything more than instrumental causes, causes that in some way gain their power of operating, as well as the exercise of this power, from the principal agent (on this, see my *Duns Scotus*, 56, 136–7). So the series I am describing is not a case of an essentially ordered causal series. But for so long as the dominoes act, they have the relevant power. I am not sure how different the two cases will ultimately turn out to be for the purposes of assessing Scotus's second criterion for an essentially ordered causal series.

man, foetus,[14] an example that derives from Aristotle.[15] And it is hard not to be moved by Anthony Kenny's conclusion at the end of a detailed discussion of this kind of case: 'There is no reason, outside archaic astronomy, to believe that a man, in begetting, is a member of such a series'.[16] As I have just pointed out, there may be examples of such series involving immaterial substances and agents; but whether or not there are such substances and agents is precisely what is at issue in a proof for God's existence.[17]

The key claim – and certainly the one that does most of the philosophical work – is the first. Scotus holds that an infinite series of essentially ordered causes is impossible:

[3]
1 This is proved, both because the totality of essentially ordered causes is caused:
2 therefore by some cause that does not belong to the totality (for then it would be its
3 own cause), for the whole totality of dependent things depends, and on no member of
4 the totality; and because [otherwise] there would actually be infinite essentially
5 ordered causes simultaneously (from the third difference above), and no philosopher
6 posits this conclusion; thirdly, because the prior is closer to the first (from
7 *Metaphysics* 5): therefore where there is no first, nothing is essentially prior; fourthly,
8 because the higher is more perfect in causing (from the second difference): therefore
9 what is infinitely higher is infinitely more perfect, and thus of infinite perfection in
10 causing, and is therefore something that does not cause in virtue of anything else (for
11 every such causes imperfectly because it is dependent in causing).[18]

This is an important set of arguments in Scotus's attempt to prove that an infinite series of essentially ordered causes is impossible. Each of the four proposed proofs is of philosophical interest.[19]

The first [3.1–4] makes the important assumption that the first cause of any essentially ordered causal series is not itself a part of that series. Every member of

---

[14] Aquinas, *ST* 1.46.2 ad 7 (I/1, 238[b]).

[15] Aristotle, *Ph.* 2.2 (194[b]4).

[16] Anthony Kenny, *The Five Ways: St Thomas Aquinas' Proofs of God's Existence*, 45.

[17] As I have noted elsewhere, Scotus is ambivalent about attempts to prove the immateriality of the soul: see my 'Philosophy of Mind', 277–8, and esp. n. 76.

[18] Scotus, *DPP* 3, n. 3 (Wolter, 47–9 (¶ 3.13)).

[19] Scotus adds a fifth too: 'fifthly, because being a cause does not necessarily posit any imperfection: therefore it can be in some nature without imperfection; but if it is in none without dependence on a first, then it is in none without imperfection; therefore independent causality can be in some nature, and that [nature] is simply first. Therefore simply first causality is possible, and this is sufficient, for from this it will be concluded below that it is in reality': Scotus, *DPP* 3, n. 3 (Wolter, 49 (¶ 3.13)). This argument – elsewhere characterized by Scotus as merely 'persuasive' (see Scotus, *Rep.* 1A.2.1.1–2, n. 29 (Wolter and Adams, 269; Frank and Wolter, 51); on 'persuasive' arguments, see Part II, chapter 9 §1 below) – has been identified by some as almost a distinct argument for God's existence by itself (Timothy O'Connor, 'Scotus's Argument for a First Efficient Cause', 27–8). What it establishes is that if the property of being a cause can be instantiated without imperfection, the property of being a first cause can be instantiated. As we shall see in the next chapter, Scotus believes that a valid inference can be made from the possibility of there being a first cause to the real existence of a first cause. But the fifth argument here is different from the four in [3], in the sense that it does not by itself establish the impossibility of an infinite regress, merely the possibility of there not being one.

an infinite series is dependent; by removing the first member from the series in this way, Scotus can ensure that, since every member of the series is dependent, the whole series is. In the *Ordinatio*, Scotus makes the nature of his innovative argumentation rather clearer. Even if there were an infinite series of essentially ordered effects, then 'the whole series of effects is from some prior cause';[20] that is to say, some cause that is not part of the series. This allows Scotus to circumvent one obvious objection to the cosmological argument: namely that the dependence of effects on prior causes does not obviously entail their dependence on a first (compare Aquinas: 'in all ordered efficient causes, the first is the cause of the intermediate, and the intermediate the cause of the last. ... Therefore if there were no first efficient cause, there would be no last, and no intermediate':[21] clearly begging the question).

Still, Scotus's innovation here seems to lay him open to another charge. After all, someone who believed that an infinite essentially ordered series was possible would indeed agree that every member of the series is dependent, and would probably deny that we could infer from this that the whole series is. The point that Scotus is trying to capture has been expressed well in a clarification offered by James Ross and Todd Bates:

> An objection that such reasoning is a 'fallacy of composition' is mistaken. One is not attributing some feature to the series as a whole solely on the basis of features of the members, but contrasting something *always missing* in each and every member of the series with *something present* in the final effect: a sufficient condition for being. Another illustration: the predicate 'unexplained' applies in regression to every member of the series, whereas its *negation* is by supposition present in the granted effect. Where could 'explained' come from? It could not, at all. A logical analogue is that the modal operator of a whole conjunction, no matter how long, even infinite, is the weakest operator of any conjunct.[22]

The alternative to a first efficient cause in Scotus's sense – a cause outside the whole series of dependent effects – is that the final effect is unexplained. Of course, Scotus's argument is vulnerable precisely here. The final effect could be ultimately a brute fact – and this because the *whole series* could just be a brute fact. An opponent to Scotus's project could object that it is not at all clear that the series as a whole could not be a brute fact: we have no other examples of such series that are themselves unequivocally caused in the way required.

The second argument relies on the Aristotelian claim, widely accepted in the Middle Ages, that an actually infinite simultaneous multitude is impossible.[23] Given the simultaneity requirement of an essentially ordered causal series [**2.9–11**], an infinite such series will entail an actually infinite simultaneous multitude [**3.4–6**]. The third argument is disappointing: order requires relations of priority and

---

[20] Scotus, *Ord.* 1.2.1.1–2, n. 53 (Vatican, II, 157; *PW* 41–2).

[21] Aquinas, *ST* 1.2.3 c (I/1, 12b–13a); whether or not Aquinas elsewhere makes it clear that the first cause is not in fact included in the series (thus allowing him to formulate his argument in a way that is not susceptible to this objection) is a nice question on which I do not have a view.

[22] James F. Ross and Todd Bates, 'Duns Scotus on Natural Theology', 203–4.

[23] See e.g. Aristotle's extended discussion in *Ph.* 3.3–5.

posteriority; according to Aristotle, however, priority is defined in terms of a relation to a first [**3**.6–7].[24] The argument fails, however: it is simply wrong to suppose that priority can be defined only in relation to a first.

The rather obscure fourth argument appears to be an attempt to reduce to absurdity the claim Scotus wants to reject. If the relevant causal chain were infinitely long, then there would be something infinitely perfect in its causality [**3**.8–10]. But something infinitely perfect in causality would be such that it does not depend on anything else for its causal activity [**3**.10–11]. I take it that such a thing would thus be a first cause. The problem here has to do with the possibility of a really existent actual infinity. Scotus's opponent would doubtless resist the attempt to saddle him with some first thing – something infinitely perfect in its causality, on the grounds that an infinite series of causes does not require there to be an 'infinitieth' cause. Indeed, Aquinas made just this objection to those such as Bonaventure who accepted the impossibility of an infinitely old universe.[25] Now, it is certainly true that an infinite set of (say) natural numbers does not include an infinitieth number. This is because there is no infinitieth natural number. But this is not to say that the set cannot be assigned both a cardinal and an ordinal number; neither is it to say that it could be assigned a cardinal number without being assigned an ordinal number. Understood in this way, Scotus's objection has some force. How sympathetic we feel to it doubtless depends on our belief in the possibility of a really existent actual infinity.

Scotus holds too that there can be no accidentally ordered causal series without essentially ordered series:[26] thus, any cause–effect relationship in an accidentally ordered series is the end term of an essentially ordered series. His reason is that accidental series are not complete explanations: prior elements are necessary but not sufficient, and what we need is something sufficient for the effect.[27] And this entails, in turn, that *a fortiori* there can be no infinite causal regress unless there is an essentially ordered causal series.[28]

Outlining – in chapters 1 and 2 of *De primo principio* – the presuppositions of his proof for God's existence, Scotus makes various further points about the nature of causation relevant here. The second chapter contains a series of conclusions about essentially ordered series. The first is that no essentially ordered relationship is reflexive:[29] nothing, for example, causes its own existence; if it did, it would be both independent of itself (as cause), and dependent on itself (as effect).[30] The second conclusion follows directly from this: 'In any essential order, a circle is impossible',[31] for if it were not, then 'the same thing will be essentially prior and posterior to the same thing, and thus ... dependent and independent with respect to the same thing':[32] the relationship of essential ordering would be, contrary to the

---

[24] Scotus refers to Aristotle, *Metaph.* Δ.11(1018ᵇ9–11).

[25] See Aquinas, *ST* 1.46.2 ad 6 (I/1, 238ᵃ).

[26] Scotus, *DPP* 3, n. 3 (Wolter, 47 (¶ 3.12)).

[27] Ibid., n. 4 (Wolter, 49 (¶ 3.14)).

[28] Ibid. (¶ 3.15).

[29] Scotus, *DPP* 2, n. 1 (Wolter, 15 (¶ 2.2)).

[30] Ibid. (¶ 2.3).

[31] Ibid. (¶ 2.4).

[32] Ibid. (¶ 2.5).

first conclusion, reflexive. Given that any relationship of essential ordering is transitive, this second conclusion rules out symmetry. A further, third conclusion makes clear a presupposition of the whole account: any essentially ordered relationship is transitive.[33] As far as I can see, this last conclusion is just a definitional matter; it is certainly something that Scotus exploits in **[2]** above.

3 Varieties of Essential Orders

Scotus does not believe that efficiently causal relations are the only sort of essential order, and in chapter 1 of *De primo principio* he proposes an exhaustive list of essentially ordered series. As he sees it, there are two basic types of essential order: the 'order of eminence', or perfection, and the 'order of dependence', or causation.[34] The order of dependence is an ordering of necessary causal conditions: later members in the series require the existence of earlier members, but not *vice versa*.[35] According to Scotus, this dependence order can be divided into two sorts: a simple causal chain (*a* causes *b* causes *c*), or a case of the common ordered dependence of two effects on one cause (*a* causes *b*; *a* then causes *c*, such that *a*'s causing *b* is a necessary condition for *a*'s causing *c*).[36] Scotus thinks the ordering in the first of these cases is obvious enough.[37] In the second case, however, the situation is a bit more complicated. Scotus claims that, since the existence of *b* is necessary for the existence of *c*, even though there is no direct causal link between *b* and *c*, it is still true to claim that the whole sequence is essentially ordered such that *b* is prior to *c*.[38]

Scotus holds that simple causal chains can be of various sorts – specifically, any such causal chain must fit one of Aristotle's four causes:

[4]
1 *Cause* is famously subdivided into the four causes, sufficiently known: final, efficient,
2 material, and formal. And the posterior opposed to these [causes] is divided into four
3 things corresponding to these [causes], namely, into what is ordered to a goal (*finis*)
4 (which, to speak briefly, is called the *finitum*); into what is caused from matter
5 (which is called the *materiatum*); into the effect; and into what is caused through form (which
6 is called the *formatum*).[39]

I have already briefly discussed the last three of these. Scotus's proof for God's existence makes use of the notion of efficient causation, a notion that on the whole – as we have seen – requires some general claims about actuality (including form) and potency (including matter as substrate). Aristotle and his followers talk about material and formal *causes* because they believe that matter and form have some

[33] Ibid. (¶ 2.6).
[34] Scotus, *DPP* 1, n. 2 (Wolter, 5 (¶¶ 1.6–1.8)).
[35] Ibid. (¶ 1.8).
[36] Ibid. (¶ 1.9).
[37] Ibid. (Wolter, 7 (¶ 1.10)).
[38] Ibid., n. 3 (Wolter, 7 (¶¶ 1.11–1.12)).
[39] Ibid., n. 4 (Wolter, 9 (¶ 1.15)).

explanatory work to do: in addition to explaining the potency for substantial change, matter explains identity,[40] and a form φ-ness explains how it is that a substance is actually φ. The proof for God's existence also requires the notion of a final cause – the goal of something's existence – and the notion of the order of eminence. In Scotus's Aristotelian universe, existence and causation are both *teleological* – goal-directed. Things ideally function in particular sorts of ways, and these ideal ways enable them to become good instances of their kind. What this notion of teleology requires is that of degrees of perfection: it thus requires the order of eminence.

As we have just seen, Scotus begins chapter 2 of *De primo principio* by outlining the nature of the relations that obtain between the members of an essentially ordered series (irreflexive, asymmetrical, and transitive). The rest of chapter 2 describes the relations between the various sorts of essential order identified in chapter 1. As we shall see, Scotus makes use of the notions of efficient and final causation, and of eminence, in his proof for God's existence. So I shall focus on the relations that Scotus draws between these various orders, rather than giving a complete account of the material in chapter 2. Central is the connection between efficient and final causation. Thus Scotus argues that every effect is goal-directed (done for the sake of a goal; conclusion 4),[41] and that everything done for the sake of a goal is an effect (conclusion 5).[42] The considerations in favour of the fourth conclusion are entirely Aristotelian in inspiration. Efficient causation requires the notion of a goal or purpose, for every cause causes 'for the sake of a goal'.[43] Equally, a causal explanation is, for Aristotle, an explanation of 'why' something happens, and thus requires an explanation in terms of goal or purpose.[44] From this, Scotus believes he can infer too the fifth conclusion, on the grounds that what happens for the sake of a goal is so only if an efficient cause is moved by the goal to direct something to the goal.[45] If something is produced in this goal-directed way, it is the effect of an efficient cause.

Scotus believes too that it is possible to draw some conclusions about the interrelationships between the series of efficient and final causes, on the one hand, and the order of eminence, on the other. The key conclusion is the 16th: that everything that is done or made for the sake of a goal is such that there are things more eminent than it is.[46] The goal must be more perfect than the thing that is done or made for the sake of the goal, and the reason is that the goal can be neither worse than, or equal in perfection to, the thing that is done for its sake. Scotus spends some time on the second disjunct here. The goal cannot be equal in perfection to the effect brought about for its sake, for if it were the effect would be just as robust a motivation for the action of the cause as the goal is. And in this case the effect itself would be its own goal – it would be brought about for the sake of itself – and this

---

[40] On role of matter for identity in Scotus, see my 'Identity, Origin, and Persistence in Duns Scotus's Physics'.

[41] Scotus, *DPP* 2, n. 2 (Wolter, 17 (¶ 2.9)).

[42] Ibid. (Wolter, 19 (¶ 2.13)).

[43] Ibid. (Wolter, 17 (¶ 2.10)), citing Aristotle, *Ph.* 2.2 (198ᵃ28–30).

[44] Ibid. (Wolter, 17–19 (¶ 2.12)), citing Aristotle, *Metaph.* Δ.2 (1013ᵃ35).

[45] Ibid., n. 3 (Wolter, 19 (¶ 2.15)).

[46] Ibid., n. 10 (Wolter, 33–5 (¶ 2.47)).

would entail that there could be an essentially ordered series that includes a reflexive relation: contrary to the first conclusion of the chapter, a conclusion that asserts the impossibility of a reflexive relation in any essentially ordered series.[47] Although Scotus does not make the point in chapter 2, given the truth of the fourth conclusion – that every effect is goal-directed – the 16th conclusion entails that everything that is an effect is such that there are things more eminent than it. This claim assumes a degree of importance in Scotus's attempt to show that the first cause must too be the most eminent being.[48]

Clearly, there is a range of presuppositions here that we might not be happy with. As we shall see, not all stages of Scotus's argument make use of these various presuppositions. Still, it is clear too that the rich Aristotelian account of causation that Scotus accepts makes him less likely than we perhaps are to be moved by more empiricist objections to the whole theological project. For example, someone who believes that causation is really no more than the constant conjunction of events of a given kind or kinds may well believe that causal relations within the world cannot give any warrant for making inferences to causes beyond the realm of the empirically observable. But Scotus clearly believes that, even within the world, there are substances with causal powers, and that all material things appear to require such causes to explain them. And he could well argue that, given the impossibility of infinite causal regress, this gives us warrant for supposing against the Humeans that there is some cause of the material, contingent, universe that is itself beyond the general nexus of cause and effect within the universe.

---

[47] Ibid., n. 11 (Wolter, 35 (¶ 2.48)).
[48] Scotus, *DPP* 3, n. 9 (Wolter, 61 (¶ 3.36)).

Chapter 2

The Existence of a First Being

Scotus's proof for the existence of a first being builds on the distinction in types of essential order outlined in chapter 1 above. For he holds that it is possible to show that there is a first efficient cause, an ultimate goal of activity, and a maximally eminent being. And his view of the interrelations of these three kinds of primacy allows him to infer that anything that has one sort of primacy has the other two sorts too. The background to the argument is Henry of Ghent. Henry analysed all proofs for the existence of God into two basic types: arguments from causation, and arguments from eminence.[1] Scotus more or less follows this basic insight, though he subdivides the causal argument into efficient and final causation. But Scotus adds various further features of his own. Perhaps the most striking is that Scotus's argument is in effect a *modal* argument, based on premises that Scotus believes to be necessarily true. As is well known, Scotus was an important innovator in modal theory, effectively introducing the notion of *logical* modalities, definable in terms of consistency relations. But he does not make consistent use of his new theory in the context of his cosmological argument. As Calvin Normore has rightly noted,

> That Duns Scotus is a pivotal figure in the history of modal theory seems beyond doubt. Although apparently not the first to claim that the present is as contingent as the future, he argued for and employed the thesis with such verve that the doctrine became associated with him. ... A pivot can face in more than one direction, and so it is with Scotus. While his picture led easily to the divorce of time and modality, he himself never completely divorced the two.[2]

I shall have occasion to return to Scotus's modal theory in chapter 4 §§1 and 3 of this part, and in Part II, chapter 15 §3. In the first of those sections, we shall see Scotus making fuller use of his new modal notions. But here he does not, and I shall thus delay discussion of the innovative aspects of Scotus's theory until that section.

The key to understanding Scotus's modal cosmological argument is to keep in mind that possibility in this context requires reference to a causal power, such that (basically) a state of affairs s is possible only if there is something in the actual world that has it in its power to bring about s: more strictly, only if all causal conditions for the existence of s are satisfied. We thus go wrong if we attempt to understand Scotus's modal cosmological argument as trading on notions of *logical* possibility and necessity, at least in such as way as to make the existence of a first

---

[1] Henry, *SQ* 22.2 (I, fo. 132L); the fullest treatment of Henry's natural theology is still the three interrelated articles by A. C. Pegis: 'Toward a New Way to God: Henry of Ghent', 'Toward a New Way to God: Henry of Ghent II', 'Henry of Ghent and the New Way to God III'.

[2] Calvin Normore, 'Duns Scotus's Modal Theory', 155–6.

being a *logically* necessary fact, one whose opposite entails a contradiction. As James Ross and Todd Bates helpfully remark, Scotus in this context 'sees that consistency to a human is not sufficient for the formal possibility of some thing'.[3] This is not, of course, to claim that every case where Scotus talks about possibility and necessity is like this; as we shall see, there are other contexts where consistency does seem to be not only necessary but also sufficient for possibility.

1 The Existence of a First Efficient Cause

With this material presupposed, we can now look in more detail at the argument itself.[4] The first stage runs as follows:

[1]
1 First conclusion: *There is among beings a nature that can produce an effect.*
2 Which is shown thus: some [nature] can be produced, therefore some [nature] can
3 produce an effect. The consequence is clear by the nature of correlatives.
4 The antecedent is proved, first, since some [nature] is contingent, and thus it is possible for
5 it to be after not being – therefore [its being] is neither from itself, nor from nothing,
6 for in either way a being would come from non-being: therefore it is producible by
7 another [being]. Secondly, some nature is changeable or mutable, for it is possible for
8 it to lack some perfection possibly in it; therefore the end term of the motion can
9 begin, and thus be effected.[5]

As Scotus presents it, this stage concerns 'a being understood quidditatively', not about the 'existence of that quiddity':[6] universal, not existential claims are being made, and I gloss accordingly. Thus, the first conclusion **[1**.1] does not claim that there is an individual that can produce an effect; merely that the existence of such an individual is possible. And the sense of possibility here is *causal* – it is consistent with the causal constitution of the actual world that there be individuals that can cause. There is a universal, *being able to produce an effect*, that is in this sense possibly instantiated. (There is thus an 'existential' claim, but the quantification is over *properties*, not individual substances.) The claim as Scotus makes it thus involves considerable metaphysical baggage, specifically the claim that there is

    [3] Ross and Bates, 'Duns Scotus on Natural Theology', 198–9. These notions are explained fully and at length in Normore's 'Duns Scotus's Modal Theory', from which I have learned a great deal.

    [4] There is a plentiful literature on Scotus's argument for God's existence. I mention some below. In addition to this material, useful expository accounts include the following: Joseph Owens, 'The Special Characteristics of the Scotistic Proof that God Exists'; Allan Wolter, 'Duns Scotus on the Existence and Nature of God'; William Lane Craig, *The Cosmological Argument from Plato to Leibniz*, ch. 5; Rega Wood, 'Scotus's Argument for the Existence of God'. Robert P. Prentice, *The Basic Quidditative Metaphysics of Duns Scotus as Seen in his De Primo Principio*, Spicilegium Pontificii Athenaei Antoniani, 16 contains a treatment of the whole of *DPP*; still useful are the same author's 'Some Aspects of the Significance of the First Chapter of the *De primo principio* of John Duns Scotus' and 'The *De primo principio* of John Duns Scotus as a Thirteenth Century Proslogion'. For a creative reinterpretation, see Michael Loux, 'A Scotistic Argument for the Existence of a First Cause'.

    [5] Scotus, *DPP* 3, n. 1 (Wolter, 43 (¶¶ 3.4–3.5)).

    [6] Ibid. (¶ 3.6).

some sort of reality to common natures independent of their instantiations – an assumption that in the required sense Scotus standardly denies.[7] Let me use 'exist*' to pick out this non-existential reality. Scotus's first conclusion is thus as follows:

(C1) Some nature able to produce exists*.

There is on the face of it a further oddity about (C1), too, which is that the modality seems to appear twice over. For the claim that some nature φ exists* means that it is (causally) possible that some individual is a φ: φ-ness can be instantiated in the actual world. But the relevant nature here has a modal claim built into it, as it were: thus it is (causally) *possible* that some individual is *possibly* productive. To make sense of this, we need to keep in mind the medieval view outlined in chapter 1 above that things have causal powers. What (C1) asserts is that it is possible that something with causal powers exists. In this sense the modality does not appear twice over; the claim about being possibly productive is a claim about a real power; the claim that it is causally possible that some individual exists merely means that the existence of that individual is consistent with the causal constitution of the actual world.[8]

(C1) is a claim about the possibility of a relation (that of producing something), and, as Scotus notes [1.2–3], if (C1) is true, then its truth is entailed by the truth of the correlative premiss

(P1) Some producible nature exists*.

---

[7] I deal with the question of the reality of non-existent possible essences, and with Scotus's various claims about 'quidditative being' in chapter 4 §3 below. For a useful discussion of some of the issues raised here, as well as insight into the nature of Scotus's modal argument for the existence of a first being, see Stephen D. Dumont, 'The quaestio si est and the Metaphysical Proof for the Existence of God according to Henry of Ghent and John Duns Scotus'.

[8] While I think that this is the right reading, it faces an immediate problem, in the face of an alternative, apparently non-modal, conclusion that Scotus also accepts, namely, some producing nature exists* (see Scotus, *DPP* 3, n. 1 (Wolter, 43 (¶ 3.6)). This raises a difficulty for my interpretation of (C1). According to Scotus, the alternative conclusion is non-modal and contingent, a claim about actuality; and such claims are, according to Scotus 'contingent but sufficiently evident': Scotus, *DPP* 3, n. 1 (Wolter, 43 (¶ 3.6)). Furthermore, such a claim about actuality is, according to Scotus, about 'an existent being', not about 'being taken quidditatively', as for example (C1) is. I think the lesson that we learn from this is that Scotus's *DPP* formulation of the alternative conclusion is wrong; what he means to assert is the existential claim

(C1*) Some producer exists;

the appearance of the modalities twice over in (C1) has simply misled Scotus into a poor formulation of his non-modal argument. Interestingly enough, the version of the argument in *Ord.* states the conclusion as (C1*) ('*est aliquod efficiens*'): see Scotus, *Ord.* 1.2.2.1–2, n. 56 (Vatican, II, 161; *PW*, 44). The problem here is that the premiss from which Scotus infers (C1*) is 'some nature is produced' ('*aliqua natura ... est effecta*') – i.e. 'some produced nature exists*'. The inference is clearly invalid (indeed, the premiss is necessary, not contingent); when making his changes in *DPP*, Scotus should have left the *Ord.* conclusion alone, and argued instead from the existential premiss 'some effect exists'. In *Rep.* he states the contingent argument correctly: 'something is produced; therefore something is a producer' ('*aliquid est productum; ergo aliquid est producens*': *Rep.* 1A.2.1.1–2, n. 28 (Wolter and Adams, 267; Frank and Wolter, 50)). There are signs of editorial carelessness in *DPP* here, especially if it post-dates *Rep.*

Claiming that it is possible that something producible exists should be understood as presupposing the existence of passive liabilities or capacities: if something is produced, it has a capacity for being the end term of such a relation. Again, the importance of Scotus's non-logical understanding of the relevant modalities is highlighted: the truth of (P1) requires that any world in which such a nature is instantiated contains entities with passive capacities. (The capacity does not, of course, have to be temporally prior to the relation itself.) Why believe that (P1) is true? It is at this point that Scotus's distinctive understanding of the relevant modal operators in this context becomes important. For the premiss from which Scotus infers (P1) is: some nature is contingent **[1.4]** – equivalently, it is (causally) possible that something is contingent. Contingency here is not to be understood logically. For, as Scotus immediately notes, contingency here amounts to existing after not existing **[1.4–5]**.[9] Thus the premiss is equivalent to this: it is (causally) possible that something exists after not existing. But anything which exists after not existing is produced by something else, on the principle that nothing is a self-cause (noted in chapter 1 §1 above) and *ex nihilo nihil fit* **[1.5–7]**. (**[1.7–9]** is similar, and I do not discuss it here.)

Scotus's second conclusion is, he claims, entailed by (C1):

[2]
1 Second conclusion: *Something able to produce an effect is simply first, that is,*
2 *neither able to be produced, nor able to produce in virtue of anything else.* It is
3 proved from the first [conclusion]: something is able to produce an effect. Let it be A.
4 If [A] is the first, understood in this way [viz. in the second conclusion], the proposal
5 is shown. If not, then it is a producer later [than some other producer], for it can be
6 produced by another, or is able to produce in virtue of something else (for if a
7 negation is denied, the affirmation is posited). Let that other be given, and let it be B,
8 about which it is argued as it was argued of A. Either we will proceed to infinity in
9 producers (of which each will be second with respect to a prior), or we will reach
10 something not having anything prior. An infinity in an ascending [order] is
11 impossible. Therefore primacy is necessary, for whatever has nothing prior is not
12 posterior to anything posterior to itself, for the second conclusion of chapter 2
13 destroys a circle in causes.[10]

Scotus does not make existential claims about individuals until his fourth conclusion. So the first thing to be clear about here is that Scotus is still talking at the quidditative level, and his 'existential' claims are about natures, not individuals. So the conclusion **[2.1–2]** should be understood as follows:

---

[9] As noted above, Scotus is here operating with an account of modality that is distinct from any logical understanding. Here, indeed, Scotus adopts a definition of 'contingent' that conforms straightforwardly with what has been labelled the 'statistical' understanding of modality, following Aristotle in understanding modal operators as implicit temporal operators: on this, see the seminal study of Simo Knuuttila, *Modalities in Medieval Philosophy*. The 'causal' account of modality does not entail the statistical understanding, though it is perhaps entailed by a statistical understanding. Assuming that all causal relations involve real powers, the statistical account entails an understanding of the possible that makes it dependent on the existence of a real power, or at least dependent on the factual satisfaction of all the conditions necessary for its existence.

[10] Scotus, *DPP* 3, n. 2 (Wolter, 45 (¶¶ 3.7–3.8)).

(C2) Some simply first nature, able to produce, exists*.

This is an existential claim about the *nature*, and rules out there not being such a nature in the required sense. (C2) thus entails that it is possible that something is a first producer. But Scotus wants more than this entailment. For Scotus's claim is that, if there are causal chains, then it is not possible for there not to be a first producer. But the sense of 'possible' in this last claim is not *logical*, for Scotus believes that he needs a further argument to get from this sort of necessity to the real existence of a particular first producer or producers. This further argument, as we shall see, makes explicit use of Scotus's causal understanding of the relevant modalities.

(C2), then, amounts to something like the following: it is possible that something is a first producer, and it is not possible that there are any essentially ordered infinite causal regresses. The two conjuncts here are not equivalent: the negation of the second is not the contradictory of the first. What (C2) amounts to is that if there are essentially ordered causal series, then there is a first cause. But Scotus wants his argument to go through without making any existential claims about individuals, and so he does not exploit this argumentative strategy. In favour of (C2), Scotus reasons as follows. Supposing (C1) – [2.2–3] – either it is possible that anything which causes an effect is itself caused, or something exists which is uncaused. And suppose – as Scotus showed in *De primo principio*'s chapter 2 – a circle of causes is impossible [2.11–13]. Then if the first disjunct is true, it is possible that there is an infinite causal regress [2.3–10]. But

(P2) An infinite regress of productive causes is impossible [2.10]

(as seen in chapter 1 above). Scotus clearly believes that the conjunction of this impossibility with (C1) entails that it is possible that something is a first producer. And this claim is to be understood as asserting the possibility of something that both cannot be produced by anything else and is such that its causal activity is independent of anything else [2.2]. I take it that these are results of its being *first* in a causal sequence (though note that by calling it first 'in' a causal sequence, I do not mean to imply that it should be considered to be a member of this sequence: as noted in the discussion of [3] in chapter 1 §2 above).

'To be produced' is to be caused efficiently, and Scotus's next move in his argument is to show that any such nature – *being a first producer* – is such that no instantiation of it can be caused in any way at all:

[3]
1 Third conclusion: *Anything that is able to produce an effect, and that is simply*
2 *first, is uncausable, because it cannot be produced as an effect and is*
3 *independently able to produce an effect.* This is clear from the second
4 [conclusion], for if it were produced as an effect, or causative in virtue of anything
5 else, there would be a regress to infinity, or a circle [of causes], or else we would
6 reach something that cannot be produced and is independently productive. And I call
7 this the first, and it is clear that the other is not the first, from what you grant. It is
8 further concluded that if the first cannot be produced, it is uncausable, for it cannot be
9 the caused for the sake of a goal (*non finibile*) (from the fifth [conclusion] of the

10 second [chapter]), nor caused from matter (*non materiatum*) (from the sixth
11 [conclusion] of the same [chapter]), nor caused from form (*non formabile*) (from the
12 seventh [conclusion] there), nor of matter and form simultaneously (from the eighth
13 [conclusion] there).[11]

Again, Scotus is not making any existential claims about individuals, and is restricting himself to claims about natures. So the third conclusion should most perspicuously read:

(C3) Any simply first nature, able to produce, is uncausable.

(C3) basically makes explicit certain features of anything able to produce that is simply first. Most notably, anything simply first cannot be the result of any of Aristotle's four causes [**3**.7–13], as Scotus shows by the application of conclusions from *De primo principio*'s chapter 2 (discussed in chapter 1 §3 above). Importantly, Scotus shows that the existence of any first efficient cause cannot itself be the purpose of the causal activity of any other thing – so there cannot be any final goal more ultimate than the first efficient cause.

The fourth conclusion introduces an argument of a different type, attempting to reason from possibility to actuality:

[4]
1 Fourth conclusion: *Something simply first, able to produce an effect, is actually*
2 *existent, and some actually existing nature is thus able to produce an effect*. It is
3 proved: anything with whose nature is it incompatible to have the possibility of
4 existence from another (*cuius rationi repugnat posse esse ab alio*), has the possibility
5 of existence from itself, if it can be. But it is incompatible with the nature of anything
6 simply first, able to produce an effect, that it have the possibility of its existence from
7 another (from the third [conclusion]); and it can exist (from the second [conclusion]). ...
8 Therefore anything simply first, able to produce an effect, has the possibility of
9 existence from itself. But what does not exist of itself does not have the possibility of
10 existence from itself, for then non-being would produce something in being, which is
11 impossible; and furthermore the thing would then cause itself, and thus would not be
12 entirely uncausable.[12]

The conclusion amounts to an existential claim about an individual or individuals:

(C4) Something simply first, able to produce, exists.

This is by far the most complex and, indeed, contentious stage of Scotus's argument. The phrase that I have translated 'to have the possibility of existence from another' [**4**.3–4] requires that the modal claims here are tied to *real* powers: x has the possibility of existence from another if there is some real thing by which x can be caused. Much the same presupposition informs the claims made in [**4**.9–12]. For the formal possibility of x's existence is required the satisfaction of whatever real causal

[11]   Ibid., nn. 4–5 (Wolter, 51 (¶¶ 3.16–3.17)).
[12]   Ibid., n. 5 (Wolter, 51–3 (¶¶ 3.18–3.19)).

conditions are necessary for x's existence. In the case of something simply first, these causal conditions cannot be extrinsic to the thing [**4**.5–7]. So if there is something simply first, the relevant causal conditions must be intrinsic [**4**.3–5, 8–9]. But any such thing can exist [**4**.7]. So whatever causal conditions are required, they will be satisfied: anything simply first exists from itself [**4**.8–9].

Scotus clearly takes this as supporting his intended conclusion, namely, that some such thing exists [**4**.1–2]. On the face of it, inferring an existential claim from a universal in this way is unsound. But I think that sense can be made of Scotus's argument, provided that we keep in mind the basic modal presuppositions here. Possibility is tied to causal powers, and if something is possible, then whatever the relevant causal explanation, that explanation must be *real* (if it were not real, the *explanandum* would not be possible: its very possibility is tied to the existence of a real explanation). Any first efficient cause is really possible, and its explanation is intrinsic to itself. Some such efficient cause must, then, be real, else, as Scotus has it, 'non-being would produce something in being, which is impossible; and furthermore the thing would then cause itself, and thus would not be entirely uncausable' [**4**.10–12].

Scotus makes some of his modal intuitions even clearer in the fifth conclusion:

[**5**]
1 Fifth conclusion: *Anything uncausable is of itself necessarily existent.* It is proved:
2 excluding every cause with respect to its existence, other than itself (both intrinsic and
3 extrinsic), it is of itself impossible for it not to be. Proof: nothing can not-be, unless
4 something positively or privatively incompossible with it can be, for at least one of a
5 contradictory pair is always true. Nothing positively or privatively incompossible
6 with the uncausable can exist, for either [such a thing would exist] of itself, or from
7 another. Not the first [viz. exist of itself], because then it would exist of itself in the
8 same way [as the uncausable] – from the fourth conclusion – and thus incompossibles
9 would exist simultaneously (and for the same reason neither would be, because you
10 concede by that incompossible [assertion] that the uncausable would not exist, and the
11 same follows *vice versa*). Nor the second [viz. exist from another], for nothing caused
12 has existence from its cause more forcefully or powerfully than the uncausable has
13 from itself, for what is caused depends in existing, whereas the uncausable does not.[13]

The key claim is that it is non-existence, rather than existence, that requires explanation [**5**.3–4].[14] And the non-existence of a thing is explained by the existence of something incompatible with it [**5**.4–5]. This key claim relates precisely to the relevant account of modality: if something can be, at some time it is, and this is because its possibility is precisely the result of the causal constitution of the actual

---

[13] Ibid., n. 6 (Wolter, 53–5 (¶¶ 3.21–3.22)).

[14] This is a very puzzling claim, for which I have no explanation. Calvin Normore summarizes: 'What exists exists in every situation in which its causal requirements are met and nothing preventing it exists. Hence, if something does not exist but could, then there is a privative or positive cause of its nonexistence' ('Duns Scotus's Modal Theory', 140). This Scotist claim entails, but is not entailed by, the causal theory of modality. Holding that the satisfaction of certain causal conditions is necessary for formal possibility does not of itself involve the additional claim that the satisfaction of such causal conditions is sufficient for real existence.

world. Scotus, in line with this key claim, spends the rest of the proof attempting to show that there could not exist anything incompatible with the existence of something uncaused. Such a thing could not exist of itself, for then the same considerations about the factual existence of anything existing of itself would apply in the case of two entities *ex hypothesi* incompossible with each other, and thus – impossibly – two such entities would exist [**5**.7–11]. Neither could the thing exist from another, because its caused existence would always be 'trumped', as it were, by the (already existing) necessary existent with whose existence it is supposed to be incompossible [**5**.11–13]. The argument here explains too the odd-looking inference in [**4**.1–2, 7]. Anything that can exist of itself does so unless some real thing prevents it from so doing. Thus,

(C5) Anything uncausable is a necessary existent,

because a necessary existent is something that exists and cannot be caused to exist.

All this shows, I think, how far Scotus is in this proof from anything like Anselm's ontological argument. Elsewhere, indeed, Scotus considers Anselm's argument, and his modifications ('colourations', as Scotus puts it[15]) are informative:

[6]
1 [Anselm's] description is to be understood thus: God is that than which, when thought
2 without contradiction, a greater cannot be thought without contradiction. For anything
3 the thought of which involves a contradiction is not said to be thinkable. And so it is.
4 For there are in that case two opposed thinkable things, in no way making one
5 thinkable thing, for neither determines the other. It follows, firstly in the realm of
6 quidditative being, that the highest thinkable thing, mentioned above – through which
7 [viz. 'that than which, when thought without contradiction, a greater cannot be
8 thought without contradiction'] God is described – exists in reality, for in such a
9 highest thinkable thing the intellect is most highly satisfied. Therefore it includes the
10 notion of the first object of the intellect – that is, *being* – and to the highest degree. [It
11 follows] further, in the realm of existential being [that the highest thinkable thing
12 exists in reality]: the highest thinkable thing does not exist merely in the thinking
13 intellect, for then it could be (because thinkable) and could-not be (because existing
14 from something else is incompatible with its definition – from the third and fourth
15 [conclusions] of the third [chapter]).[16]

The crucial contrast here is between 'quidditative being' [**6**.6] and 'existential being' [**6**.11]. For something to exist in quidditative being is for there to be a coherent concept of it [**6**.2–3, 7–9]. For something to exist in existential being is for that concept to be satisfied [**6**.11–12]: for there to be an individual thing satisfying the relevant description. Again, the contrast is between universal and existential claims, and the conclusion of the first part of the argument [**6**.5–10] is that a certain nature – that of the highest thinkable thing – exists*. How does Scotus defend this first conclusion? The highest thinkable thing does not involve a contradiction – if it did, it would not be thinkable [**6**.2–5]. And if it can be coherently thought, then it must exist in quidditative being –

---
[15] Scotus, *DPP* 4, nn. 24, 25 (Wolter, 123 (¶ 4.65)).
[16] Ibid., n. 24 (Wolter, 123 (¶ 4.65)).

there must be a concept of it [**6**.5–10].[17] (This does not seem to establish very much at all, since assuming that all concepts can be categorized hierarchically, it seems to follow trivially that there is one or more concept of something than which nothing higher can be thought – that is to say, that there is a highest (coherent) concept.)

The second part of the argument is of a very different sort: an attempt to infer that this concept must be satisfied – that the highest nature must be instantiated. The assumption that Scotus seems to make is that the nature of the highest thinkable thing includes the property of *being uncaused* [**6**.13–15]. I take it that Scotus is simply assuming here that *being uncaused* is a great-making property. Given this assumption, Scotus attempts to reduce to absurdity the claim that there fails to be an instance of this nature. Suppose there is no instance of this nature. Then it follows both that it is possible that there be such an instance (since the concept is coherent), and that it is not possible that there be such an instance [**6**.12–13]. It is the second of these contradictory conjuncts that does the relevant work: if there is no instance of an uncaused being, this is because the causal constitution of the actual world is somehow incompatible with there being such an instance [**6**.13–15]. And, Scotus asserts, this is a contradiction.

Now, it seems to me that there is a problem here. For the allegedly contradictory conclusion seems to equivocate on the relevant senses of 'possible'. Claiming that the concept is coherent means that it is logically possible for the concept to be instantiated. But claiming that the concept has to be instantiated because of the causal constitution of the world means that it is causally (physically, nomologically, factually) necessary that the concept be instantiated. It is not *causally* possible for the concept not to be instantiated given the constitution of the actual world. But an opponent should claim that the causal constitution of the actual world is irrelevant to the logical possibility or necessity of the instantiation of some concept. Perhaps, the opponent could suggest, nothing in the actual world can bring a first cause into existence, and nothing about the concept of God *logically* requires that God exist.

That Scotus's colouration of Anselm's argument moves it away from an understanding of the relevant modalities as logical or broadly logical is not to say that Scotus could not have formulated anything like Anselm's argument. To have done so, however, he would have needed to make proper use of his non-statistical account of modality – an account which, as I shall show later, Scotus certainly develops and uses elsewhere.

Given Scotus's claim that his premises for his cosmological argument are necessary, what distinguishes the argument from an *a priori* argument of Anselmian or other kind? Scotus explicitly rejects the claim that our knowledge of God's existence could be *a priori*.[18] For Scotus, an *a priori* claim is one that can be known

---

[17] This is a very revealing claim. For here, existence* is a predicate of concepts, and does not *ipso facto* ascribe some kind of reality to possible but non-actual natures. But what does existence* assert about a nature? That the nature includes only elements that are compossible with each other. And this suggests that the relevant modalities are *logical*: that it is logically possible that the concept be satisfied. So Scotus has, with one hand, given us a much lighter metaphysical baggage, but with the other shifted his understanding of the modalities involved in his argument. As I shall show in a moment, this move vitiates the colouration of the *ratio Anselmi*.

[18] Scotus, *Ord.* 1.2.1.1–2, nn. 15–19, 28, 35–6 (Vatican, II, 131–4, 140, 145–6).

immediately by the mind, simply on the basis of the knowledge of the terms of the proposition. What Scotus is rejecting, then, in rejecting that knowledge of God's existence could be *a priori*, is any *non-inferential* knowledge of God's existence.[19] Still, this is a specialized sense of '*a priori*'. For we might think of an *a priori* argument as one that is inferential but not reliant on any empirical claims. Would this describe Scotus's cosmological argument? The premiss from which the whole argument starts is simply this: it is (causally) possible that something exists after not existing. This is certainly entailed by the empirical claim that something exists after not existing. Indeed, the claim seems to be *a posteriori* – how could I know that anything was causally possible, given the *actual* constitution of the universe, without inference from empirical experience of the actual constitution of the universe?

I do not think much can be done to salvage Scotus's argument, in this modal form, and the reason is that the understanding of modality here seems to entail that the argument is ultimately question-begging: we do not know that the possibility of such a first efficient cause is *real* unless we already hold that there is a first efficient cause. Equally – going all the way back to (P1) – we do not know that things have passive capacities for being causally affected or effected unless we already know that there are things with causal powers that can affect or effect them. (I have elsewhere attempted to salvage the argument on the assumption that the relevant modalities are logical or broadly logical, rather than real, and others have attempted similar tasks.[20]) Scotus does not rely on this modal form of the argument. Thus, he clearly accepts too a non-modal argument of the following form:

(P1*) There exists something produced;
(C1*) Some producer exists.
(P2) An infinite regress of productive causes is impossible;
(C2*) Some first producer or producers exists.[21]

(P1*) is just empirically obvious, and indeed non-inferentially so (on this, see Part II, chapter 9 below). (C1*) is immediately entailed by (P1*). I discussed Scotus's reasons for accepting (P2) in chapter 1 §1 above, and the conjunction of (C1*) and (P2) entails (C2*).

Given the availability of a non-modal alternative, and the problems associated with the modal version of the argument, why did Scotus feel the need to develop a modal form of the argument at all? Scotus's reason for wanting to propose a modal version of the cosmological argument is tied up with Aristotelian notions of demonstration. Basically, according to Scotus's reading of Aristotle, a strictly demonstrative argument is such that its premisses satisfy the following conditions: they must be (1) certain, (2) necessary, (3) self-evident, and (4) explanatory of their

---

[19] I discuss these important clarifications to the notions of proof and demonstration in Part II, chapter 9 §1 below.

[20] See e.g. my *Duns Scotus*, 19–23; O'Connor, 'Scotus's Argument'.

[21] Scotus, *Rep.* 1A.2.1.1–2, n. 28 (Wolter and Adams, 267; Frank and Wolter, 50); *DPP* 3, n. 1 (Wolter, 43 (¶ 3.6)); *Ord.* 1.2.2.1–2, n. 56 (Vatican, II, 161; *PW*, 44). I have phrased this argument in line with the version in *Rep.* 1A: see n. 8 above.

conclusion.[22] I deal briefly with the third and fourth of these conditions in Part II, chapter 9 §1 below, and with the third in Introduction §6 above. Certainty requires not being open to doubt, and is entailed by (though does not require) self-evidence.[23] Necessity is more complex. The relevant modality is not – or at least need not be – understood *logically*, or broadly logically, for Scotus believes that his modal cosmological argument has premises that are necessary in the required sense. But the premises make claims about the causal constitution of the actual world.[24] We could perhaps suggest, in line with this, that the claim is that it is not possible, given the causal constitution of the actual world, for there to fail to be causal relations between causes and effects.

In the case of a non-modal argument for God's existence, none of the last three conditions can be fully satisfied. An argument from the existence of contingent reality to the existence of God cannot be explanatory, since the existence of the world in no way causally accounts for the existence of God; quite the reverse, in fact. Neither can premises gleaned from empirical observation be self-evident in the sense of *a priori* – evident simply from knowledge of the terms of the premiss. (As we shall see in Part II, chapter 9 §1 below, there is a different sense in which empirically undeniable claims are self-evident.) But Scotus believes that an argument is stronger the more of these conditions it satisfies, and hence prefers to advance a modal argument whose premises are, so he believes, necessary, even if not self-evident (*a priori*) or explanatory.

In *De primo principio*, Scotus rounds off his proof for the existence of a first efficient cause with a proof of a sixth conclusion:

(C6) No more than one nature has necessary existence of itself,

which is to say that there can be no more than one kind of thing whose instantiations are uncaused. I return to this argument later.

2 The Existence of an Ultimate Goal of Activity

Thus far, then, I have given an account of Scotus's complex argument for the existence of a first cause. Scotus believes too that it is possible to demonstrate, along very similar lines, that there is an ultimate goal of activity, and a maximally excellent being. The arguments exactly parallel those for (C1) to (C4). Scotus does not spell out the arguments for all the stages of these proofs. But they can easily be

---

[22] See Scotus, *Ord.* prol. 4.1–2, n. 208 (Vatican, I, 141); *Ord.* 3.24.un., n. 13 (Wadding, VII, 482–3). The list derives from Henry of Ghent, *SQ* 6.1 arg. 1 and c (I, fo. 42A, B–D), and Scotus claims that it can be derived from Aristotle, *An. post.* 1.2 (71ᵇ9–12), on which it is loosely based.

[23] See e.g. Scotus, *Ord.* 3.24.un., n. 17 (Wadding, VII, 485), where Scotus makes clear that certainty can be caused directly by God, since 'every effect that God can bring about with the mediation of a secondary efficient cause he can bring about directly' – where the relevant effect is the sort of certainty that would in the normal run of things be had only in virtue of the self-evidence of the relevant object of cognition.

[24] Scotus, *DPP* 3, n. 1 (Wolter, 43 (¶ 3.6)).

reconstructed. The first of the conclusions about an ultimate goal of activity is the seventh conclusion of *De primo principio*'s third chapter:

[7]
1 Seventh conclusion: *Among beings, some nature is a goal of activity (finitiva).*
2 Proof: because something can be produced – from the proof of the first [conclusion] of
3 this [chapter] – therefore, also, [that thing] can be directed to a goal. The consequence
4 is clear from the fourth [conclusion] of the second [chapter].[25]

The claim that 'among beings' some nature is a goal of activity [7.1] is simply supposed to assert that it is causally possible that something that is a goal of activity exists; thus,

(C7) Some nature able to be a goal of activity exists*.

The fourth conclusion of the second chapter is that every effect is goal-directed – an Aristotelian claim that I discussed in chapter 1 §3 above. If there are effects, then, there are things directed to goals [7.2–4]. So (C7) is true. Furthermore, Scotus holds that goal-directedness is an instance of an essential order. Hence there cannot be an infinite regress of such explanations.[26] Thus, parallel to (C2),

(C8) Some nature able to be a simply first goal of activity exists*.[27]

The idea is that final causes are paradigmatically supposed to provide explanations, and according to Scotus no genuinely explanatory causal chain can be infinite.
    The interrelation of the various sorts of causal explanation allows Scotus to infer a conclusion exactly parallel to (C3) of the argument from efficient causation:

[8]
1 Ninth conclusion: *the first thing able to be a goal of activity is uncausable.* It is
2 proved: because it cannot be directed to a goal (otherwise it would not be the first),
3 and furthermore, because it cannot be produced (from the fourth [conclusion] of the
4 second [chapter]); furthermore, as above, in the proof of the third conclusion of this
5 third [chapter].[28]

The statement of the various arguments here is very compressed. Here is the conclusion:

(C9) Any nature, able to be a simply first goal of activity, is uncausable.

---

[25] Ibid., nn. 8–9 (Wolter, 59 (¶¶ 3.27–3.28)). I translate 'finitiva' as 'goal of activity' on the grounds that Scotus clearly supposes that goals are themselves goal-directors: goals move or direct things to themselves: on this, see the discussion of final causation in chapter 1 §3 above. Later, Scotus certainly assumes that (C8) should be understood simply as amounting to the claim that there is a first (ultimate) goal of activity: see *DPP* 3, n. 12 (Wolter, 67, ¶ 3.55)).

[26] Ibid., n. 9 (Wolter, 59 (¶ 3.30)).

[27] Ibid. (¶ 3.29).

[28] Ibid. (¶¶ 3.31–3.32).

To get to it, Scotus appeals again to the crucial fourth conclusion of the second chapter, namely that every effect is goal-directed [8.3]. The first goal of activity is something that by definition is not goal-directed [8.2]. So it is not an effect. And something that exists that is not an effect is uncausable, as in (C3).

Again, Scotus thinks that he can get from these claims about natures to the existence of an instantiation of the nature, as in (C4). Thus:

(C10) Something able to be a simply first goal of activity exists.[29]

As he puts it, this 'is as for the fourth [conclusion] of the third [chapter]'.[30] Presumably, the proof would trade on the insight that if it is possible that something is goal-directed, there must be a real goal in the world to ground this possibility. If, Scotus is thinking, there is no real goal, then how can there exist the possibility of goal-directedness? Again, the modal theory is very far from the theory of logical possibility that Scotus elsewhere espouses. What is at stake are the real powers and capacities of really teleological entities.

3 The Existence of a Maximally Perfect Being

Scotus sketches out a similar argument for the existence of a maximally perfect being too. The first conclusion states simply that there is an essential ordering amongst perfections:

(C11) Some nature more perfect than some other nature exists*.[31]

Scotus believes that (C11) is entailed by (C7), on the basis of the 16th conclusion of chapter 2 of *De primo principio*, namely, that everything that is goal-directed is such that there are things more eminent than it is – namely, the goal itself.[32] Scotus takes it that, given the impossibility of an infinite series of essentially ordered items,[33] (C11) entails

(C12) Some simply most perfect nature exists*.[34]

It seems that Scotus is being a little ambitious here. For (C12) seems to equivocate between two distinct claims:

(C12*) Some nature more perfect than any other existing* nature exists*

and

---

[29] Ibid. (Wolter, 61 (¶ 3.33)).

[30] Ibid. (¶ 3.34).

[31] Ibid. (¶ 3.35).

[32] Ibid. (¶ 3.36).

[33] Ibid. (¶ 3.38).

[34] Ibid. (¶ 3.37).

(C12**) Some maximally perfect nature exists*.

The distinction is that (C12**) is a claim about a nature that is logically unsurpassable, while (C12*) asserts no more than that some nature unsurpassed by anything causally possible in the actual world exists*. Scotus's modal system here entails that (C12*) is the required sense. But it is not obvious that (C12*) entails (C12**). Scotus would perhaps claim that there is no nature that could surpass the most perfect nature possible given the causal constraints of the actual world. Conceivability is not, on this system, sufficient for formal possibility.[35]

The interrelations of the various essentially ordered series means that (C12) entails

(C13) Any nature more perfect than any other nature is uncausable.[36]

The reason is that a nature more perfect than any other cannot be goal-directed. And if it cannot be goal-directed, then according to conclusion 4 of chapter 2, it cannot be caused.[37] (C13) – like (C9) – is important for Scotus in establishing the causal possibility of the existence of a most perfect individual (or, in other words, of establishing the existence* of a most perfect nature). There would be no possibility of such an individual's existing unless the relevant real causal conditions for its existence are satisfied. And Scotus's way of guaranteeing that those real causal conditions are entirely intrinsic to the relevant individual is by asserting that the individual, if it existed, would be such that it could not be caused. (C12) coupled with (C13) thus, according to Scotus, entails

(C14) Something more perfect than anything else exists,[38]

proved, as Scotus notes, as for (C4).[39]

4 The Existence of One Kind of First Being

Thus far, Scotus's argument, if successful, has shown the following existential conclusions: (C4), (C10) and (C14), respectively, about the existence of a first cause, final goal, and most perfect being. The interrelation of the various sorts of causal order entail that anything more perfect than anything else cannot be goal-directed, and thus cannot be caused. But these claims do not establish that there is just one kind of first cause, final goal, or most perfect being. Neither do they establish that anything that is uncaused is not goal-directed, or is more perfect than anything else.

---

[35] It is perhaps worth pointing out too that some considerations raised by Scotus on the nature of divine infinity appear to entail that God is *logically* unsurpassable: see the discussion of [6] in chapter 5 §1 below.

[36] Scotus, *DPP* 3, n. 9 (Wolter, 61 (¶ 3.39)).

[37] Ibid., n. 10 (Wolter, 61 (¶ 3.40)).

[38] Ibid. (Wolter, 63 (¶ 3.41)).

[39] Ibid. (¶ 3.42).

The rest of chapter 3 of *De primo principio* is aimed at the establishment of these various additional conclusions. Thus far, I have ignored the crucial sixth conclusion:

(C6) No more than one nature has necessary existence of itself.

(C6) is necessary for the derivation of various of the remaining conclusions of the chapter, and I discuss it here.

One feature of (C6) to note immediately is the relevant sense of 'necessary'. For Scotus seems to be presupposing a distinction between something's having necessary existence *of itself*, and something's having necessary existence *from another*. I take it that, in line with the understanding of the modalities elsewhere in the proof, necessary existence is existence required by the causal constitution of the universe (i.e. the totality of things including God), and it matters not to the proof of (C6) whether or not there be anything that has necessary existence from another. Something that has necessary existence from another is, on Scotus's modal theory in this part of *De primo principio*, such that all causal conditions sufficient for its existence are extrinsic, and all necessarily satisfied; something that has necessary existence of itself is such that all causal conditions are intrinsic, and all necessarily satisfied: since nothing causes itself, the satisfaction of such intrinsic causal conditions really amounts to there being no extrinsic condition necessary for its existence, and nothing extrinsic to it incompatible with the existence of such a being. In point of fact, Scotus holds, as we shall see, that all divine external activity is *contingent* – logically contingent – and this entails that nothing about the causal constitution of the universe *requires* the real (i.e. extramental) existence of anything other than God. So nothing has necessary existence from another. But Scotus wants his presuppositions to be as few as possible for the purposes of his proof, and does not trouble himself with contentious clarifications until a much later stage in the argument.

Scotus offers three lengthy proofs for (C6), of which I give the first:

[9]
1 Sixth conclusion: *One nature alone has necessary existence of itself.* It is proved
2 thus: if two natures could exist necessarily of themselves, then necessity of existence
3 is common [to them]. Therefore there is too some quidditative entity, according to
4 which [necessity of existence] is common to them – from which there is derived as it
5 were a genus of them [viz. the natures]. And beyond this, they would differ by their
6 ultimate actual formalities. From this two incompossible things follow.
7   First, that each will be primarily necessary through the common nature, which
8 is of lesser actuality, and not through the distinguishing nature, which is of greater
9 actuality. For if one is necessarily existent formally through that [distinguishing
10 nature], it will be necessarily existent twice over, for that [distinguishing nature] does
11 not formally include the common nature, just as a difference does not [include] a
12 genus. But it seems impossible that a lesser actuality is that by which something is
13 primarily necessary, while by the greater [actuality] something is neither primarily or
14 *per se* necessary.
15   The second impossible [consequence] is that neither [nature] is necessarily
16 existent through the common nature by which it is posited that each is necessarily
17 existent primarily. For neither [nature] exists sufficiently through that nature
18 [common to them]. For any nature is that which it is through the highest formal

19 feature [of it]. But it is through the thing through which it is necessarily existent –
20 excluding everything else – that something [necessary] exists in reality. If you say that
21 the common nature is sufficient for existence, without the distinct natures, then the
22 common [nature] is actual of itself, and not distinct, and consequently
23 undistinguishable, for a really existent necessary existent is not in potency to existence
24 simply speaking; the being of a genus in a species is, with respect to [the genus],
25 existence simply speaking.[40]

The claim in [**9**.1] is a universal one: Scotus is not making a claim about the number of necessary individuals there can be, but merely about the number of natures whose instantiation is necessary in his sense. There can be no more than one kind of thing having necessary existence of itself. Since anything that is a first cause has necessary existence of itself, this entails that there cannot be more than one kind of first cause. The basic argument is that, if two natures could have necessary existence as a feature (such that any instantiation of the nature is a necessary existent), it would follow that necessary existence is a common feature of the two natures – rather like a genus can be a common feature of two species (*animal*, for example, common to *dog* and *cat*) [**9**.2–5]. Furthermore, each of the two natures would include some further feature distinguishing them from each other – rather like a species includes, in addition to the genus, a *specific difference* distinguishing it from all other species in the same genus [**9**.5–6]. Scotus refers to these distinguishing features as 'ultimate actual formalities' [**9**.6]. What he means is most easily seen by considering Scotus's preferred analogue here, the features of a species – say, rationality (specific difference) and animality (genus) in the paradigm species case, humanity. Rationality and animality are distinct features of the species *human*. But they are not distinct as two concrete things are; they are in some sense merely abstract entities. Scotus's word for such entities is 'formality'. So each of two natures that shared the feature of necessary existence would have a formality, something like a specific difference, distinguishing it from the other. These features are 'ultimate', in the sense that – like specific differences – they prevent division into further species.[41] And they are 'actual' since, like specific differences, they are considered as 'actualizing' the genus's potential to be of such-and-such a kind (there are no animals unless there are specific sorts of animal – dogs, cats, or whatever).

The key metaphysical claim here is the last: that specific differences are actual relative to genera. For Scotus holds that the scenario he is describing involves two logical contradictions [**9**.6], and the first requires the assumption that specific differences are actual relative to genera. More precisely, if the common nature is something like a genus, and the distinguishing feature something like a specific difference, then the distinguishing feature will be of greater actuality than the common nature [**9**.8–9]. And, according to Scotus, this raises a problem. For, clearly enough, the common nature is sufficient to explain the necessary existence of its instantiations: that is just what Scotus's claim about the common nature in [**9**.2–4] is intended to secure. And if the common nature is sufficient, then the distinguishing differences cannot have any role in explaining necessary existence [**9**.9–10]. (In

---

[40] Ibid., n. 6 (Wolter, 55–7 (¶¶ 3.23–3.24)).

[41] What Scotus means is that, if there is a shared common nature – *being necessarily existent* – it would be possible ultimately to arrive at most basic 'species' of this nature.

[**9**.10–12] Scotus rules out the possibility of the distinguishing difference's somehow *including* the common nature, such that the difference could be alone necessary and sufficient, on the technical grounds that, according to Scotus's theory of the predicables, the intension of a specific difference does not include the intension of a genus.) So, given that the distinguishing difference cannot have a role in explaining necessity, and given that the common nature is of lesser actuality than the distinguishing difference, it follows that it is the feature of lesser actuality that explains necessity. And this, according to Scotus, 'seems impossible' [**9**.12–14].

There looks to be an equivocation here. For it is one thing to say that the common 'generic' nature could not be instantiated without its being instantiated in some species of it, and quite another to say that the specific difference is more actual than the genus. But the actuality claim here is just a commonplace, and I take it that Scotus has at least two different things in mind: specific differences distinguish between species, and the existence of something is not explained formally by any mere genus. I exist in virtue of my being human, not in virtue of merely being an animal.

The second argument – [**9**.15–25] – seems to give more substance to the kind of thing Scotus wants to urge in his first argument. While the argument is not entirely clear in all its stages, the basic thrust is an attempt to generate an explicit contradiction from the opponent's assumption that there could be two necessary existents. Suppose there are in reality two necessary existents. The contradiction is that the existence of each one is (formally speaking) both sufficiently explained and not sufficiently explained by their shared common nature. For, on the one hand, the existence of the necessary existents cannot be sufficiently explained by the common nature [**9**.15–18]. The reason is that, in order to exist, a thing must belong to a kind. But kind-membership cannot be sufficiently explained by a genus alone, or anything analogous to a genus (such as the common nature of *necessary existence*) [**9**.18–19]. This, then, gives us one horn of the dilemma. Scotus proves the second more straightforwardly: if a necessary existent exists, how could this existence be explained, formally, other than through the property of *being a necessary existent* [**9**.19–20]? So this property looks to be a sufficient formal explanation of existence. According to Scotus, then, the position of his opponent involves accepting the conjunction of two contradictory claims.

Scotus's opponent offers a counterargument: why not just accept the second disjunct, and assert that the common nature is a sufficient explanation of existence [**9**.20–21]? Scotus's reply is that, if so, *being a necessary existent* would be a species, or something analogous to a species. And on the kind of analysis that Scotus and all his contemporaries accept, the point about a species is that it cannot be the case both that there are instances of the species, and that the species can be a genus for some lower-order species too (this, I take it, is the point made rather cryptically in [**9**.24–25]; and on this reading it is certainly not a controversial point). If there are things that are blackbirds, then there cannot be other things that are *just* birds, and not birds of any given kind. Contrariwise, if there are things that are *just* blackbirds, then there cannot be other things that are more specific kinds of blackbird too.[42] If, then, the common nature *being a necessary existent* were

---

[42] Species and hybrid – in, say, plant-growing – are not counterinstances to this *taxonomic* point. The distinction in this case is simply to do with the *ancestry* of particular species.

something like a species, then there could not be more specific kinds of necessary existent. Scotus's opponent, in effect, has conceded the very thing Scotus wants to show, namely that there cannot be more than one kind of necessary existent [**9**.22–24]. Thus, the nature would be 'actual of itself, and not distinct, and consequently undistinguishable' – like a species, in other words. 'Not being in potency to existence simply speaking' is another way of stating the same claim: in order to be a (formal) explanation for an individual's existence, a nature needs to explain the kind of the individual (its 'existence-simply-speaking'). But a species is, paradigmatically, such an explanation, and is thus 'not in potency to existence-simply-speaking'. Equally, a really necessary existent is not such that there could be further kinds of it.

What Scotus is worrying about is the problem of a substance having the (shareable) property *being a necessary existent*. The possession of such a property is supposed to provide a formal explanation of the existence of the substance – it *by definition* guarantees its existence – and it is hard to avoid the conclusion that possession of such a property would render the substance's possession of any further necessary property superfluous. Now, this seems to prove too much, since, if sound, it would make necessary existence the only necessary property of any substance that possessed it. Scotus himself, as we shall see in chapter 6, §5 below, makes a distinction between 'genuine' attributes and modes of those attributes. Necessity is a mode (of every genuine divine attribute), and in some way is not supposed to perform precisely the explanatory role that genuine attributes do.

What this shows, then, is that, if there is a common nature, *being a necessary existent*, this nature will be species-like, not genus-like. But it seems to me that, whatever we make of this argument, there is a more general problem. Why should we suppose that there is a real common nature – loosely, an extramental universal – *being a necessary existent*? As I explain in the Appendix below, Scotus is generally a nominalist about non-categorial (transcendental) universals. Thus he is a nominalist about necessary properties that are neither natural kinds nor Aristotelian *propria*. Indeed, what he says elsewhere on this topic – as I shall show – makes it clear that he is a nominalist about the universal *being a necessary existent*. Realism is supposed among other things to provide an explanation of kind-membership, and nominalism lacks, among other things, this explanatory power of realism. But Scotus's argument in [**9**] certainly trades on the alleged explanatory power of *being a necessary existent*: the argument proceeds on the assumption that this property serves some real explanatory function, explaining something's necessary existence. I do not see why Scotus's opponent could not simply deny that there is a common nature *being a necessary existent*. Of course, being a nominalist about this nature does not mean merely that there can be no more than one such thing; what it means too is that, even if Scotus's arguments in [**9**] are valid, there could be more than one *kind* of necessary existent.

Assuming (C6), Scotus goes on to try to show that anything that has one of the three primacies – being a first cause, being an ultimate goal, being a most perfect thing – has the other two as well. These three properties are for Scotus necessarily coextensive. This does not amount to showing that there could be only one such being. Scotus's claim is merely that, however many there are, any which has one of the three properties has the other two as well. Scotus states the key claim in the argument for his 15th conclusion:

[10]

1 Fifteenth conclusion: *The above-mentioned threefold primacy in the three*
2 *essential orders – namely, of efficiency, of finality, and of eminence – is in some*
3 *one and the same actually existing nature.* This fifteenth [conclusion] is the fruit of
4 this chapter. It follows evidently from the things shown thus: if in just one nature is
5 necessary existence of itself (from the sixth [conclusion] of this [chapter]), and [if]
6 whatever has any primacy of the three mentioned has necessary existence of itself
7 (from the fifth, and third about one primacy [viz. of efficiency], from the fifth and
8 ninth about the other primacy [viz. of finality], and from the fifth and thirteenth about
9 the third primacy [viz. of eminence]), then any of the above-mentioned primacies is in
10 just one nature, in which nature the others also are, for each is actually in some nature
11 (from the fourth, tenth, and fourteenth [conclusions]), and not in different natures;
12 therefore in the same [nature]. The minor is proved, for then many natures would be
13 necessary existents (from the second argument just made). Again, the proposal is
14 proved from the uncausable, for that is just one first thing; any of the [natures]
15 mentioned is uncausable, therefore etc. The major is proved: how could a multitude
16 [of uncaused things] arise of itself?[43]

Scotus's argument for his 15th conclusion is both rather compressed and also curiously repetitive (perhaps evidence of a rather sloppy editorial assistant?). The conclusion:

(C15) The threefold primacy is in some one and the same actually existing nature

– **[10**.1–3**]** – is not quite that there can be only one *kind* of first entity, though this is entailed by the argument offered for (C15). It is rather that at least one nature exhibits the relevant threefold primacy. Scotus presents it as the 'fruit' of the proof thus far; it is the important conclusion that Scotus wishes to establish **[10**.3–4**]**. Scotus reserves his proof of divine unicity – that there can be only one God – until the very end of *De primo principio*, and I thus discuss divine unicity in chapter 7 below. The basic argument in **[10]** is very straightforward. Scotus has already established that anything that is a first producer is of itself a necessary existent; and likewise for anything which is a final goal, and a most perfect being. The argument is that anything that has any one of the three primacies is uncausable – (C3), (C9), and (C13) – and that anything uncausable is a necessary existent – (C5) **[10**.6–9**]**. Since there can be just one kind of necessary existent – (C6) **[10**.4–5**]** – it follows that there can be just one kind of thing having any one of the three primacies, and thus that anything that has any one of the three primacies has the others too **[10**.9–10**]**. Furthermore, we know that each of the three primacies is instantiated – (C4), (C10), and (C14) **[10**.10–11**]**. And this yields not only (C15) but the stronger conclusion that entails (C15), namely that there can be only one kind of first entity. **[10**.12–13**]** simply repeats, in a different form, the argument in **[10**.6–10**]**. (The argument is that if any of the primacies is instantiated, then it is so in just one kind of thing, and the relevant 'minor premiss' that Scotus talks about is that the primacy is instantiated in just one kind of thing.) **[10**.13–16**]**, however, contains a different argument in favour of (C15), arguing directly from the claim that anything that has

---

[43] Scotus, *DPP* 3, n. 10 (Wolter, 63 (¶¶ 3.43–3.44)).

any one of the three primacies is uncausable. Scotus reasons that there can be just one kind of uncausable thing. Hence (C15). The benefit of this argument is that it bypasses the rather weak (C6). But it requires Scotus to make plausible the claim that there can be just one kind of uncausable thing. Scotus's strategy is simply to wonder what explanation there could be for more than one kind of uncausable thing [**10**.15–16]. Scotus is making a metaphysical application of Ockham's razor: if there is some kind of multiplicity, then that multiplicity requires an explanation.[44] Now, the sort of thing that we are talking about here is something *uncausable*. Hence a multitude of uncaused things requires some explanation intrinsic to the domain of such things. But how could multiplicity be self-caused?

The result of the argument for (C15), then, is that there cannot be more than one kind of first being. Scotus in fact proceeds to attempt to infer this stronger conclusion from (C15) – a wholly superfluous project, since the stronger conclusion is warranted by the argument for (C15) in any case. The key conclusion (the 19th, that just one existent nature is first in the threefold order mentioned above, with respect to every other nature, such that each other is thus posterior in the threefold way to that one nature[45]) is defended by Scotus, as (C15) is, by an appeal to (C6). The result of the argument for the existence of a first being, then, is that at least one such being exists, and that there can be at most one kind of such being.

---

[44] Scotus is explicit in his acceptance of the principle of parsimony, a principle that he attributes to Aristotle (see e.g. Scotus, *Ord.* 4.11.3, n. 27 (Wadding, VIII, 630), referring to Aristotle, *Ph.* 1.6 (189ª15–16)).

[45] Scotus, *DPP* 3, n. 12 (Wolter, 69 (¶ 3.57)).

Chapter 3

Perfect-being Theology

As I have presented it thus far, Scotus's argument for the existence of a first being does not give much detail about the attributes of this first being. In the rest of this Part, I shall examine Scotus's attempt to derive the attributes of the first being, and in this chapter I shall outline a method that Scotus discusses in great detail – and tends to reject – to get clear on the strategies that Scotus believes are open to him.

Near the end of chapter 3 of *De primo principio*, Scotus proposes an 18th conclusion, containing three 'sub-conclusions', as it were: (i) the first producer is the most actual thing, because it virtually contains all possible actuality; (ii) the final goal is the best thing, because it virtually contains all possible goodness; (iii) the most eminent being is the most perfect, because it eminently contains all possible perfection.[1] Scotus notes that the three conclusions are inseparable, since 'if one [primacy] were in one nature, and another in another [nature], then it could not be granted that one of them is simply eminent'.[2] I take it that the point of these conclusions is to clarify some of the notions introduced in chapter 2 above, rather than to add substantively to the proof for the existence of a first being. Scotus does not provide any explanation of the technical notion of containment. Rather, he focuses on the ways in which the three primacies relate to the notion of the highest good, claiming that the three notions are entailed by that of the highest good, since the highest good is maximally communicative, maximally lovable, and maximally whole or integral – corresponding, respectively, to the primacy of efficiency, finality, and eminence. The claims are basically traditional, stemming from Aristotle and Avicenna, both of whom Scotus cites here.[3] I take it that the claim about efficiency here is that God has whatever actuality is required to produce (actual) things. A goal of activity is that which is the object of an inclination or desire; hence God, as the final goal, is sufficiently lovable to be such a goal. And something perfect is something fully 'whole' – the Latin term '*perfectus*' means 'completed'.

Scotus could in principle use this material to infer various further divine attributes, namely the so-called 'pure perfections'. This kind of strategy – now sometimes known as 'perfect-being theology' – was developed by Anselm, and Scotus is often happy to endorse it. For example, in the late *Quodlibet*, Scotus appeals to Anselm's strategy in support of the claim that pure perfections are in God:

---

[1] Scotus, *DPP* 3, n. 12 (Wolter, 67 (¶ 3.55)).

[2] Ibid. (¶ 3.56).

[3] Ibid. (Wolter, 67–9 (¶ 3.56)). For the identity of goodness and perfection, Scotus cites Aristotle, *Metaph.* Δ.16 (1021ᵇ18–20); for the identity of perfection and wholeness, Aristotle, *Ph.* 3.6 (207ᵃ13); for the identity of goodness and desirability, Aristotle, *Eth. Nic.* 1.1 (1094ᵃ3); and for the highest good's communicativity and liberality (acting without expectation of return: see Part II, chapter 10 §2 below), Avicenna, *Metaph.* 6.5 (II, 341–3).

[1]
1 [That something essential in God is a pure perfection] is clear from the mind of
2 Anselm, *Monologion* 15, where he posits this distinction: 'whatever is, other than a
3 relation, is either such that it is entirely better to be it than not it, or such that it is
4 better in something not to be it than to be it'. And having explained and clarified this
5 distinction, he concludes: 'Just as it is impious to think that the substance of the
6 highest nature is something which it is better not to be than to be, so it is necessary
7 that it is entirely whatever it is better to be than not to be.' And then he infers in
8 particular what it is not. 'Therefore', he says, 'it is not a body, nor anything of those
9 things that bodily senses apprehend.' And after he adds in particular what kind of
10 thing it is. 'Therefore', he says, ' it is necessary that it is living, wise, omnipotent,
11 true, just, eternal, and whatever absolutely it is better to be than not to be.' But it is
12 clear that many of these things are essential in God.[4]

According to Anselm, every non-relational attribute is either a pure perfection
('entirely better to be it than not to be it') or not such a perfection (such that at least
one thing is better without the attribute than with it) **[1.2–4]**. God's substance can
include only pure perfections **[1.5–7]**. And Scotus quotes – seemingly with approval
– Anselm's attempt to list such pure perfections **[1.8–11]**, and ascribes them to the
divine substance **[1.11–12]**.

In *De primo principio*, however, Scotus appears to suggest very considerable
reservations about the utility of the principle.[5] Perhaps, then, we should understand
the argument in **[1]** to be simply an appeal to authority in order to show that God
has pure perfections, rather than an endorsement of Anselm's principle itself. I begin
with Scotus's attempt to understand the relevant principle:

[2]
1 Every unqualified perfection, to the highest degree, is necessarily in the highest
2 nature. An unqualified perfection is said to be that which is *better in anything than*
3 *what is not it*. This description seems to be nothing, for if it is understood of an
4 affirmation and a negation, as they are in themselves, an affirmation is not better than
5 its negation, whether in itself or in anything, if it can be in it. If however, it is
6 understood not only in itself and in anything if it can be in it, but unqualifiedly in
7 anything, then it is false. For wisdom is not better [than non-wisdom] in a dog, for
8 nothing is good for that thing which it contradicts. Reply: this is a famous description,
9 and is expounded thus: *better than what is not it* – that is to say, than any positive
10 incompossible thing in which [what is] *not it* is included. It is thus better *in anything*,
11 not for anything, but *in anything*, in so far as it is of itself, for it is better than what is
12 incompossible with it, on account of which [incompossible thing the unqualified
13 perfection] could not be in [its subject]. It is said, briefly, therefore: an unqualified
14 perfection is that which is unqualifiedly and absolutely better than anything

---

[4] Scotus, *Quod.* 1, n. 8 (Wadding, XII, 10; Alluntis and Wolter, 12 (¶ 1.22)), quoting Anselm, *Monol.*
15 (*Opera Omnia*, I, 28–9). Scotus's main proof of omniscience is similar: see *DPP* 4, n. 14 (Wolter, 101
(¶ 4.42)).

[5] Scotus appears equivocal here, for his most critical discussion of the principle – **[4]** below (Scotus,
DPP 4, n. 8–9 (Wolter, 87–9 (¶ 4.22))) – follows immediately on a proof of God's intellectuality that Scotus
seems to accept: 'A living thing is better than any non-living one, and among living things, an intellective
one is better than any non-intelligent one' (Scotus, *DPP* 4, n. 7 (Wolter, 87 (¶ 4.21))), a classic application
of the perfect-being methodology. See also n. 4 above.

15 incompossible with it. And it is thus that *[better] in anything than what is not it* is
16 expounded, that is, [better than] whatever is not it.[6]

[**2**.1–2] states the conclusion that the first being has, to the highest degree, every
pure perfection. The proof for this holds no surprises:

[**3**]
1 I prove the ... conclusion thus understood [i.e. in accordance with [**2**]]: an unqualified
2 perfection has some order, according to nobility, to everything incompossible [with
3 it]. But not of what is exceeded – by definition – and therefore of being more eminent.
4 Therefore, either [this perfection is] incompossible with the supreme nature, and thus
5 exceeds it, or [it is] compossible, and thus can be in [the supreme nature], and also to
6 the highest degree, for it is thus compossible with that [nature] if it is compossible
7 with anything.[7]

'Everything incompossible with' an unqualified perfection [**3**.2–3] is anything with
which the perfection is incompatible, be it substance or accident. Wisdom, for
example, is incompatible not only with folly but also with being a dog. And Scotus
supposes that any perfection has some 'order according to nobility' to every such
thing [**3**.2–3]. What order? No divine perfection can be exceeded; so every divine
perfection must be better than anything with which it is incompatible [**3**.3]. Suppose
the relevant perfection were incompatible with the divine nature. It would, by [**3**.3],
then exceed the divine nature in nobility [**3**.4–5]. Although Scotus does not state it,
this argument is a *reductio*: for something to exceed the divine nature in nobility is
impossible. So any unqualified perfection is compatible with the divine nature
[**3**.5–6]. And, drawing on a conclusion that I outline below – [**6**] – Scotus infers that
the perfection is in the divine nature 'in the highest degree' [**3**.3–6].

This might make it look as though Scotus wants here to endorse a perfect-being
theology. But Scotus in fact places some restrictions on the kinds of inference
available to a perfect-being theologian, since, as Scotus sees it, it is not always
possible to know in advance of our knowledge of the perfections exhibited by the
first nature what counts as a pure perfection. So, as we shall see in the next chapter,
Scotus has to find other ways of determining what the list of pure perfections
includes. First, then, what of the complex set of clarifications offered in [**2**]? The
Anselmian definition is stated in [**2**.2–3]. A pure perfection is something that it is
better to have than not to have. Scotus immediately embarks on a complex objection
to the principle. [**2**.3–5] states an extreme view – no attribute is better than its
contradictory – and Scotus, while he clearly regards this claim as false, does not
even bother replying to it. In the *Quodlibet*, Scotus states as obvious the claim that
Anselm's principle should not be understood to assert that a pure perfection is
anything that is better than its 'contradictorily opposed negation', on the grounds
that 'anything positive is simply better than its contradictorily opposed negation'.[8]

The crucial claim is [**2**.5–8]: there is no such thing as a pure perfection, since a
pure perfection should be better *for everything*; wisdom, however, is not better for

---

[6] Scotus, *DPP* 4, n. 3 (Wolter, 79 (¶ 4.10)).

[7] Ibid., n. 4 (Wolter, 81 (¶ 4.11)).

[8] Scotus, *Quod.* 5, n. 13 (Wadding, XII, 128; Alluntis and Wolter, 119 (¶ 5.31)).

a dog than non-wisdom, since dogs cannot be wise. The reply takes its lead from this insight, one that turns out to be very important for Scotus's own agnosticism about pure perfections. A pure perfection is one that is better than whatever is incompatible with it [2.9–10, 13–16]. Wisdom is better both than folly and than being a dog. The point of [2.10–13] is purely expository: how to get this understanding out of Anselm's principle. A pure perfection is one which is such that it is better than anything incompatible with it; this does not entail that a pure perfection is a perfection *for everything*, because there are some imperfect things with which the pure perfection is incompatible.

It is easy to see, given this, why Scotus is agnostic about our capacity for identifying pure perfections in advance of the fact. Later he offers a defence of his agnostic understanding of the pure perfections:

[4]
1 If you take wisdom denominatively, it is better than any incompossible denominative,
2 and yet you still have not proved that the first being is wise. I say that you beg the
3 question. You can have only that something wise is better than something not wise,
4 excluding the first being. In this way the first angel is better than any being, taken
5 denominatively, incompossible with it, other than the first being. Rather, the essence
6 of the first angel, in the abstract, can be simply better than wisdom. You may say that
7 it is incompatible with many, and therefore it is not better denominatively for
8 everything than its opposite is. I reply that neither is wisdom better denominatively
9 for everything; it is incompatible with many. You may say, indeed, it would be
10 [better] for everything, if it could be in it, for it would be better for a dog if a dog were
11 wise. I reply, so it is for the first angel: if it could be a dog it would be better for it;
12 and if [a dog] could be the first angel, it would be better for the dog. You may say,
13 that would rather destroy the nature of the dog; therefore it is not good for the dog. I
14 reply: so too being wise destroys its nature.[9]

The crucial point is [4.1–4]; the rest of the passage simply gives examples of the kind of problem Scotus believes his opponent will encounter. In [4.1] Scotus outlines his opponent's claim, that wisdom taken denominatively is better than anything incompossible with it. 'Taken denominatively' simply means 'taken as a predicate' (of this or that individual) – here, Scotus is talking not about *wisdom* in the abstract, but about wise individuals, and ascribes to his opponent the view that individuals who are wise are better than individuals who possess a property incompatible with being wise. It is this claim that Scotus wants to take issue with. For he does not see that we can know that wise things are better than things possessing a property incompatible with being wise unless we already know that the first being is wise. For if it should turn out that the first being is not wise, then wisdom would not be a pure perfection. The opponent, then, begs the question, for the claim that wisdom is a pure perfection can be made only by inference from the fact that the first being is wise; but this last claim – that the first being is wise – is precisely what the opponent is trying to prove [4.2–4].

In the rest of the passage, Scotus reinforces his position by thinking of a similar example that his opponent is bound to concede. The first angel is supposed to be the

---

    [9] Scotus, *DPP* 4, n. 8 (Wolter, 87–9 (¶ 4.22)).

most perfect creature, and the claim is that, setting aside the first being, the first
angel is more perfect than anything possessing a property incompatible with being
the first angel [**4**.4–5]. The only reason that we know that *being the first angel* is not
a pure perfection is that we already know that this attribute is incompatible with the
nature of the first being. The point is that much the same could be claimed for
wisdom: unless we already know that the first being is wise, we do not know
whether wisdom is or is not a pure perfection. [**4**.6–14] shows that the parallel
between the two cases is exact.

This does not mean that all cases are problematic:

[5]
1 It is different in the case of the attributes of being (*de passionibus entis*) in general,
2 whether a common attribute or one of [two] disjuncts, for they follow every being.[10]

The attributes of being are the so-called 'transcendentals', here trans-categorial
attributes that can be predicated trivially of any substance or accident. I deal with
these sorts of attributes in more detail in chapter 6 §5 of this Part, and in the
Appendix below. Scotus here identifies two such groups of attributes: those
'common attributes' [**5**.2] said to be 'convertible with being' – the list includes *one,
good, true*[11] – and various disjuncts, generally though not invariably contradictories,
likewise predicable of everything – the list of metaphysically interesting ones
includes disjunctions such as *necessary-or-contingent, finite-or-infinite, prior-or-
posterior*, and so on. In [**5**], Scotus makes it clear that God – like everything else –
has all of these attributes. This is, of course, a trivial claim. But it can get us some
distance. For Scotus also maintains the following:

[6]
1 Whatever is intrinsic to the supreme nature is such in the highest degree. It is proved:
2 ... it is entirely the same as that nature on account of simplicity. Therefore, just as
3 that nature is a nature to the highest degree, so that [feature intrinsic to the nature] is
4 such to the highest degree, for it is the same [as the nature]. Otherwise, if it could be
5 understood to be exceeded according to its entity, then the nature too could be
6 understood to be exceeded according to its entity, which is the same as the entity of
7 that thing [viz. the nature].[12]

I shall deal with the simplicity claim [**6**.2, 4, 6–7] in chapter 6 §4 below. What
Scotus wants to assert is that, since the divine nature is supreme [**6**.3] – as he has
established above – and since any intrinsic feature of that nature is the same as it

---

[10] Ibid. (Wolter, 89 (¶ 4.22)).

[11] The presence of truth on this list strikes the modern reader as odd. For we tend to think of truth as
a property of signs or representations, the property of conforming to the reality represented. For the
medievals, truth can be a property not only of representations, but also of things: of creatures, that they
conform to their divinely understood pattern, and of God, that he is the supreme exemplar for all other
truths. We would probably want more helpfully to substitute a different notion: perhaps *accuracy* rather
than truth would be a less ambiguous way of thinking of the relevant creaturely property. Both, of course,
carry the implication of *conformity*.

[12] Scotus, *DPP* 4, nn. 2–3 (Wolter, 79 (¶¶ 4.7–4.8))

[6.4, 6–7], any intrinsic feature of that nature must be a supreme case of that kind of feature **[6**.3–4]. **[6**.4–7] make much the same point. **[6]** means that the common attributes are had by God in the highest degree: maximally one, good, and true. What about the disjunctive attributes alluded to in **[5**.2]? **[6]** might seem to give us warrant for ascribing to God the higher of each two. Indeed, Scotus accepts a '"law of disjunctive transcendentals", namely that it is impossible that there be a case of the inferior without there being a case of the superior'.[13] But, as Ross and Bates point out, 'The proof of that law seems ... to be cognitively a consequence of a proof of the existence of a divine being rather than a premise for it'.[14] Indeed, Scotus does not, in *De primo principio*, derive God's possession of these attributes by a perfect-being strategy. As we see in later chapters of this Part, Scotus infers God's possession of these attributes in other ways.

---

[13] Ross and Bates, 'Duns Scotus on Natural Theology', 196: see Scotus, *Lect.* 1.39.1–5, n. 39 (Vatican, XVII, 491; Vos, 96). I mention the disjunctive transcendentals at slightly greater length in chapter 6 §5 below.

[14] Ross and Bates, 'Duns Scotus on Natural Theology', 196–7.

Chapter 4

The Knowledge and Volition
of a First Being

1 The Will and Intellect of a First Being

On the face of it, one obvious way of showing that a first being has intellect and will is by arguing from the apparent status of intellect and will – and indeed wisdom and love – as pure perfections.[1] As we might expect, Scotus does not accept this inference. As we saw in chapter 3, Scotus holds that the correct understanding of a pure perfection is one that is better than anything incompatible with it. But he believes it to be hard to tell whether something is a pure perfection unless such a property is simply better for everything. So Scotus's own arguments for the first being's intellect and will use rather different insights. They turn on the fact that the first being's activity is directive and contingent. Scotus believes that these activities of the will require intellect: if the first being is to direct things to their ends, he must know their ends, and if his activity is contingent he must be able to choose between known options.[2] Scotus offers a few brief arguments for the directive role of the first cause, of which the most extensive is this:

[1]
1 The first efficient cause directs its effect to a goal. Therefore, [it does so] either
2 naturally or by loving it. But not in the first way, because something lacking
3 knowledge directs nothing other than in virtue of something that knows, for the first
4 ordering belongs to the wise. The first [efficient cause] does not direct in virtue of
5 anything [else], just as it does not cause [in virtue of anything else].[3]

Efficient causes aim at goals **[1.1]**: minimally, they are inclined or disposed to certain sorts of effect. There are, according to Scotus, two kinds of inclination: natural and voluntary **[1.1–2]**. Scotus's account of this distinction is of extreme complexity, spelled out at length in book 9 of his *Metaphysics* questions.[4] I examine

---

[1] Scotus, *DPP* 4, n. 8 (Wolter, 87 (¶ 4.22)). See chapter 3, n. 4 above.

[2] Ibid., nn. 4–6 (Wolter, 81–3 (¶¶ 4.12–4.15)). I sometimes talk about God in what follows, for convenience, and likewise refer to 'the' first being rather than 'a' first being; in strict propriety, I should refer to a first being, or first efficient cause. Many of the passages I cite below come from contexts other than the proof for God's existence, and thus use 'God' to refer to the first being. But none of the passages I use below presupposes revelation; it is thus possible and useful to treat them all as part of a detailed and sophisticated proof for divine existence – as I am attempting to do here. Equally, Scotus later presents proofs to the effect that there could be at most one first being – I examine some of them in chapter 7 below – so nothing turns on my terminological inexactitude here.

[3] Scotus, *DPP* 4, n. 5 (Wolter, 83 (¶ 4.14)).

[4] Scotus, *In Metaph.* 9.15, nn. 20–34 (St Bonaventure, IV, 680–4).

it when discussing passage **[2]** below. But all that he requires here is a distinction between conscious and unconscious inclinations. A voluntary inclination is one based on a conscious act of knowledge **[1.3]**. Nothing unconscious could be goal-directed unless something directs it – teleology requires conscious purposiveness **[1.2–4]**. If, then, a first efficient cause lacked consciousness, it would be directed to a goal by something else. But this contradicts its being a first cause **[1.4–5]**. So a first efficient cause must have both intellect and will.

Scotus devotes rather more space to the argument from contingency, providing, in addition to the argument in **[2]**, various objections and responses that I do not examine here:

[2]
1 Something is caused contingently; therefore the first cause causes contingently;
2 therefore it causes voluntarily. The first consequence is proved: any second cause
3 causes in so far as it is moved by the first cause. Therefore, if the first cause moves
4 necessarily, every [cause] is moved necessarily and everything is caused necessarily.
5 Proof of the second consequence: there is no principle of acting contingently other
6 than will, or something requiring the will, for everything else acts by the necessity of
7 nature, and thus not contingently.[5]

Scotus develops a complex account of contingency as – in effect – liberty of indifference. As he sees it, the basic feature of a contingent cause is that it is not 'determined of itself to acting'. The kind of determination Scotus is denying – the determination proper to a natural power – is in fact twofold: determination to one kind of effect, and determination to produce that effect whenever there is no impediment. This twofold determination is the feature of a natural (non-contingent) power. A free power is 'not determined of itself, but can cause this act or the opposite act, and act or not act'[6] – presumably in the self-same circumstances, since the feature of a natural power is that the circumstances determine whether or not it actually causes an effect. These features entail, for Scotus, that a free power can 'determine itself' in both ways (that is, both to act, and to act in one way rather than another),[7] and this on the basis of its 'unlimited actuality' (such that it is not, or need not be, in passive potency to any causal activity external to it).[8] In line with these sorts of consideration, the second part of **[2]** is devoted to showing that contingency entails will **[2.2]**. The reason is that Scotus believes that the only power in virtue of which something can act in a non-determined (non-natural) way is will **[2.5–7]**. He does not believe, for example, that things could arise just randomly. And he believes – plausibly enough – that all material processes are determined.

This understanding of freedom requires a notion of contingency rather different from that appealed to in chapter 3 of *De primo principio*, discussed in chapter 2 §1 above. And Scotus observes as much:

---

[5] Scotus, *DPP* 4, n. 5 (Wolter, 83 (¶ 4.15)).
[6] Scotus, *In Metaph.* 9.15, n. 22 (St Bonaventure, IV, 680–1).
[7] Ibid., n. 32 (St Bonaventure, IV, 683).
[8] Ibid., n. 31 (St Bonaventure, IV, 683).

[3]
1 I do not here call contingent everything that is neither necessary nor everlasting, but
2 that whose opposite could have happened when this did. For this reason I did not say
3 'something is contingent', but 'something is caused contingently'.⁹

Scotus clearly notes that the understanding of 'contingent' here is distinctive [3.1]. [3.2] gives the relevant definition, and the definition makes it plain that 'contingent' is to be understood as that whose non-existence does not entail a contradiction. The significance of the simultaneity claim is that contingency – and modality in general – is to be thought of not temporally or diachronically, but *synchronically*, in terms of conceivable states of affairs. The notion of contingency here 'is thus understood to involve a consideration of several alternative states of affairs with respect to the same time'.¹⁰ Such alternative states of affairs are in some sense possible, and elsewhere Scotus makes it clear that the relevant sense of 'possible' approximates to what we would think of as logical, or broadly logical, possibility: the possible is whatever does not entail a contradiction.¹¹ This notion is not quite our logical possibility, if logical possibility is defined in terms of conceivability, for, as we saw in chapter 2 §1 above, Scotus believes that positing the existence of something both contingent and uncaused would generate a formal contradiction. But Scotus does not believe that every logical possibility has to correspond to some real power in the world; thus, 'not all logical possibilities are real alternatives in the actual world', and so realization 'in the actual world is no longer the criterion of real possibility'.¹² Since on this understanding freedom entails contingency, and since contingency is to be understood synchronically, for Scotus a free power is one that has at one and the same time more than one outcome under its scope. This, of course, is fully consistent with Scotus's claims about the self-determining nature of a free power. Equally, this understanding of contingency entails Scotus's contracausal notion of freedom – as in [2.5–7]. The reason is tied in with Scotus's residual Aristotelianism on the question of modalities. Scotus believes that positing the existence of something both contingent and uncaused would generate a formal contradiction. So *real* contingency requires a real free power.

The key claim in **[2]** is the first: 'something is caused contingently' [2.1]. Scotus clearly regards this premiss as obvious, and I shall note in a moment how he defends it on the assumption that some creatures have free will. Scotus is envisaging here a series of causes, and his claim is that if later members of the series are such that they cause contingently, then the first cause must be such too [2.1–2]. Scotus's proof for this requires that within the domain of what is possible, whatever is not contingent is necessary: something that seems to be a matter of definition. Suppose the first cause caused necessarily, and was causally responsible for everything lower down in the causal chain. In this case, every cause–effect relation

---

⁹ Scotus, *DPP* 4, n. 6 (Wolter, 85 (¶ 4.18)).

¹⁰ Simo Knuuttila, 'Modal Logic', 353; see also his *Modalities in Medieval Philosophy*, 139–49.

¹¹ See e.g. Scotus, *Ord.* 1.2.2.1–4, n. 196 (Vatican, II, 249): 'The possible is that which does not include a contradiction'; see too *Ord.* 1.7.1, n. 27 (Vatican, IV, 118); *Lect.* 1.39.1–5, nn. 49–51 (Vatican, XVII. 496–7; Vos, 116–20).

¹² Knuuttila, 'Modal Logic', 354.

in the chain would be necessary [2.3–4]. The problem with this argument, of course, is that it seems to prove too much. If the first cause is causally responsible for everything lower down in the causal chain, then it seems that there can be no contingency in the chain other than the contingency of the first cause. Thus, [2.3–4] presupposes that the only independent agent is the first agent. But the evidence in favour of [2.1], as we shall see, requires that there is indeed observable contingency lower down in the causal chain. We might hold, for example, that any being with free will is, to that extent, an independent agent. But, as we have seen, Scotus believes himself to have shown that anything that causes completely independently must also be maximally perfect. Since no free creature is maximally perfect, no free creature is a completely independent agent. This looks odd, however. For the premiss of the argument is that contingency exists, and Scotus's evidence for this is presumably that we can observe contingency – that is, *freedom* – in secondary causes.[13] And the notion of genuinely contingent, indeterminate freedom is incompatible with the notion that the activity of a free agent could be brought about by anything other than itself.

In effect, Scotus requires the causal concurrence of two independently contingent agents, and the problem of how such causal concurrence could obtain is not one that Scotus managed to find a viable solution to. Scotus is aware of this difficulty, and troubled by it. For, on the one hand, he rejects the view, associated with Peter John Olivi, that the human will is the sole cause of free human activity[14] – and thus that God's causal activity does not have a role in free human activity – for two reasons: such a view is incompatible with God's knowledge of future contingents, and such a view is incompatible with divine omnipotence. As we shall see below, Scotus holds that God knows the future by understanding the contingent determinations of his will. If a creaturely will were the sole cause of that creature's actions, then God's knowledge of the future could not be in the way Scotus describes it.[15] Neither, according to Scotus, could God be omnipotent. Omnipotence for Scotus requires the power to bring about directly anything which is brought about through a secondary cause. If my will is wholly independent, God can directly causally affect its activity only by overriding it – something incompatible with the notion of freedom.[16]

On the other hand, Scotus does not know how to give an account of the joint causal responsibility of God and a free creature for that free creature's acts. Dealing with the problem of God's non-responsibility for sin, Scotus presents an account of

[13] In the parallel context in the *Sentence* commentaries, Scotus cites Aristotle to the effect that, if there were no contingency, there would be no need for counsel or deliberation (see Scotus, *Lect.* 1.39.1–5, n. 40 (Vatican, XVII, 491; Vos, 100); *Rep.* 1A.39–40.1–3, n. 30 (Söder, 247), citing Aristotle, *Int.* 9 (18ᵇ31–3), and in the latter text adding too a reference to Boethius, *Cons.* 5.3, nn. 31–2 (Moreschini, 144) to the effect that, unless there were contingency in the sense described, there could be no virtues, precepts, merit, reward, punishment, or honour, and 'in short all polity and human relations would be destroyed'). Elsewhere, Scotus offers a range of different proofs, the most significant of which is introspective (to the effect that we are aware that, when we do *a*, we could have done not-*a*, or refrained from acting altogether): see *In Metaph.* 9.15, n. 30 (St Bonaventure, 682–3); for other arguments, see my *Duns Scotus*, 86.

[14] Scotus, *Ord.* 2.34–7.1–5, n. 119 (Vatican, VIII, 418), rejecting Olivi, *In Sent.* 2.116 (III, 336–8).

[15] Scotus, *Ord.* 2.34–7.1–5, n. 120 (Vatican, VIII, 418–19).

[16] Ibid., nn. 121–2 (Vatican, VIII, 419).

human action according to which the action is the result of two necessary and jointly sufficient causes: God and the creature. The way Scotus sees it, God's action is not causally prior to the creature's; rather, the two causes are both immediately necessary for the effect. As Scotus puts it, 'In one instant of nature ... the two efficient causes cause a common effect, such that neither then causes without the other'.[17] In terms of the moral goodness or badness of an action, God always causes in a way necessary for the goodness of the action. But a creature does not always do so: and thus morally bad actions are the creature's responsibility.[18] Indeed, Scotus goes further: if God's causal activity were sufficient for a sinful action, then creatures would not be responsible for their own sin. Clearly they are; so God's activity cannot be sufficient.[19] This position, however, does not seem better able to allow for God's knowledge of free creaturely actions than does the view of Scotus's strongly libertarian opponents. In order for God to know the future in the manner Scotus describes, his choice must be not merely necessary for the outcome of a creaturely choice: it must be sufficient.[20]

In terms of the argument for the existence of God, the problem is that the sufficiency of God's activity undermines the claim that there is clear empirical evidence for contingency; and the mere necessity of God's causal activity for creaturely acts undermines the claim that contingency in divine activity is required for contingency in creaturely actions. God can perform his role as the necessary condition for a human action *necessarily*; contingency can enter in as a result of the creature's own free choice. I do not see what can be done to rectify this problem.

One final note. Scotus holds not only that the first cause causes contingently, but that *everything* that it causes it causes contingently.[21] He argues that **[2]** entails that everything that God immediately causes is caused contingently, which entails that everything further down the causal chains that result from that immediate causation is contingent too.[22] Scotus does not make clear why he supposes that **[2]** entails that everything that God immediately causes is caused contingently. Later, however, he gives a reason, namely that the only necessary goal of the causal activity of the first being is himself. This entails that all divine external activity is contingent. On this, see passage **[30]** below.

2 God's Knowledge of the Divine Essence

I have already mentioned in passing God's self-knowledge. Scotus discusses it mainly in the context of his Trinitarian theology, since he thinks that the presence of God's essence to the divine mind entails the production of an act of self-knowledge, which Scotus then – in standard Augustinian fashion – identifies as the Son. He

---

[17] Ibid., n. 145 (Vatican, VIII, 429–30).

[18] Ibid., nn. 143–4 (Vatican, VIII, 428–9).

[19] Ibid., n. 150 (Vatican, VIII, 431–2).

[20] This whole problem causes Scotus no little difficulty. I return to it briefly in the final section of this chapter below.

[21] Scotus, *DPP* 4, n. 9 (Wolter, 91 (¶ 4.23)).

[22] Ibid. (¶ 4.24).

reasons likewise for God's self-love and the Holy Spirit. So I discuss the issue fully in Part II, chapters 10 and 11. But I mention one aspect of his teaching here. Scotus persistently distinguishes intellectual knowledge into two kinds: abstractive and intuitive. Very roughly, abstractive knowledge is knowledge of (or by means of) universals and mental representations. Intuitive knowledge is immediate knowledge of real individuals.[23] I deal with the question of abstractive knowledge of God's essence in the Appendix. Creatures who enjoy the beatific vision enjoy intuitive knowledge of the divine essence, and God's self-knowledge is of this kind too: direct intellectual knowledge of the divine essence as an individual entity.[24] As we shall see below, there is some sense in which all divine knowledge is identical with the divine essence. Setting aside the Trinitarian context for the time being, this identity means that, while it is true to claim that God has an act of knowing his own essence, this act is not itself really distinct from the divine essence.

3 God's Knowledge of Creaturely Essences

God's omniscience entails, for the medieval theologians, that he has concepts of all the kinds of things that there can be. These concepts are the so-called divine ideas, and provide the patterns or types for things that God causes or can cause.[25] These ideas do not correspond merely to the kinds of thing that there actually are, however; they include all the kinds of thing that there could be. Clearly, these ideas can be combined in any number of possible ways, and these combinations will give God an understanding of any number of different individuals too. Scotus holds, however, that individuals are not just collections of shareable properties, but include too haecceities – *thisnesses*: wholly non-qualitative or non-quidditative individuating principles.[26] We cannot have knowledge of haecceities, since such things are irreducibly particular and hence undescribable.[27] God, however, has knowledge of actual haecceities.[28] Whether or not God has knowledge of possible haecceities I will discuss below.

According to the most well-known medieval account of the divine ideas – that of Aquinas – God's knowledge of his own essence somehow includes knowledge of all

---

[23] For the distinction, see Scotus, *Quod*. 6, nn. 7–8 (Wadding, XII, 172–3; Alluntis and Wolter, 135–7 (¶¶ 6.18–6.19)); *Ord*. 1.1.1.2, n. 35 (Vatican, II, 23–4); *Ord*. 2.3.2.2, n. 321 (Vatican, VII, 553).

[24] Scotus, *Ord*. 1.1.1.2, n. 43 (Vatican, II, 27–30); *Ord*. 2.3.2.2, n. 322 (Vatican, VII, 553); on God's intuitive knowledge of his own essence, see Part II, chapter 10 §1 below. There are various sorts of intuitive cognition in Scotus. Imperfect intuitive cognition provides, via representations of particulars, knowledge of individual things in the past and future; perfect intuitive cognition is (as I suggest in the text here) a form of *direct* realism – knowledge unmediated by any kind of sensible or intelligible 'species' or form. On the distinction, see Allan B. Wolter, 'Duns Scotus on Intuition, Memory, and Our Knowledge of Individuals'.

[25] Scotus, *Ord*. 1.35.un., n. 35, 38–40 (Vatican, VI, 259, 260–1); *Ord*. 1.45.un., n. 7 (Vatican, VI, 373). On omniscience, see chapter 3, n. 4.

[26] On this, see my 'Medieval Theories of Haecceity' and the bibliography cited there.

[27] For the irreducible particularity of haecceities, see e.g. Scotus, *Ord*. 2.3.1.5–6, n. 186 (Vatican, VII, 483; Spade, 106); on their unknowability by humans, see e.g. *In Metaph*. 7.13, n. 158 (St Bonaventure, IV, 271); *In Metaph*. 7.15, n. 20 (St Bonaventure, IV, 301).

[28] See e.g. Scotus, *Rep*. 1A.36.3–4, n. 47 (Noone, 441).

possible created essences: 'God sees himself in himself, for he sees himself through his essence. He sees things other than himself, however, not in themselves but in himself, in so far as his essence contains the likeness of things other than himself.'[29] This account is very appealing. It avoids making God's knowledge of possible essences the result of anything external to him, while avoiding too the problem of making possible essences dependent on God's knowledge or will – in the way perhaps that Descartes later proposed. But it is open to a powerful objection. How is it that God's knowledge of his essence gives him knowledge of anything other than himself? Aquinas attempts to solve this by appealing to God's knowledge of his *power* (something which is of course identical with his essence, according to Aquinas):

> It is evident that [God] perfectly understands himself, otherwise his existence would not be perfect, since his existence is his understanding. If something is perfectly known, however, it is necessary that its power is perfectly known. But the power of something cannot be perfectly known unless those things are known to which the power extends.[30]

But even this is little help. On the one hand, bare knowledge of the extent of a power, given that that power extends over every possible object, is not itself sufficient for knowledge of the possible objects that fall under that power. Knowing that a power extends over all possible objects does not reveal just what those objects may be. On the other hand, Aquinas clearly intends this as an argument to show that God's self-knowledge entails knowledge of creaturely essences. But the argument is non-explanatory: it shows that God must have knowledge of creaturely essences, but does not explain how such knowledge is possible, or how it can be derived from knowledge of the divine essence. To this extent, Aquinas's position amounts to no more than an argument to the effect that God has knowledge of creaturely essences; it does not explain how this knowledge is possible.

Aquinas's view – the 'power' view – makes knowledge of the divine essence sufficient for knowledge of all creaturely essences. There is, however, a further question that could be asked: is God's knowledge of his own essence *necessary* for his knowledge of creaturely essences? Some of Scotus's predecessors answered this question affirmatively, asserting that God's knowledge of creaturely essences required knowledge of his essence as *imitable* or capable of participation – the 'participation' view. Thinkers who held this view often made knowledge of the divine essence both necessary and sufficient for knowledge of creaturely essences. Scotus focuses on the account of this given by Henry of Ghent, though he also uses a version found in Aquinas.[31] *Being imitable* is a relation, and the position is that

---

[29] Aquinas, *ST* 1.14.5 c (I/1, 80ᵃ).

[30] Ibid. (I/1, 79ᵇ). The view can also be found in e.g. *Summa* that emanated from the circle of Alexander of Hales (*Sum. fr. Alex.* 1.1.5.1.un.2.2, n. 165 (I, 248ᵇ)) and in Bonaventure, *In Sent.* 1.35.un.1 (*Opera Omnia*, I, 601ᵃ).

[31] See e.g. Henry of Ghent, *Quod.* 9.2 (Macken, XIII, 32). On Henry's theories in general here, see Jean Paulus, *Henri de Gand: Essai sur les tendances de sa métaphysique*, 87-90. Aquinas develops a similar theory in *ST* 1.14.6 (I/1, 81a). God knows creatures in so far as his essence can be participated by them; Scotus summarizes at *Rep.* 1A.36.1–2, n. 21 (Noone, 402). For Aquinas's view, see in particular Vivian Boland, *Ideas in God according to Saint Thomas Aquinas*, 202–14.

God's knowledge of creatures is in effect knowledge of the complete set of relations of imitability that the divine essence has. In Henry of Ghent, this account is buttressed with a theory of the reality of non-existent essences: if there are genuine relations of imitability in the divine essence, this requires that there are objects to which the divine essence is related; it requires, in short, that the divine essence is really imitated. This requirement results in one of the most distinctive features of Henry's metaphysics, the claim that essences have in themselves some kind of non-existential being: *esse essentiae*, the being of an essence, distinguished from *esse existentiae*, the being of an (individual) existent.[32] It is important to understand that Henry does not believe that these essences are the *objects* of God's knowledge. The only object of his knowledge is his essence. The reason for positing real non-existent essences is precisely so that the relations in the divine essence can be in some sense real: nothing could be related without there being something for it to be related to. Still, in principle there are two distinct claims here: one that knowledge of God's essence is necessary for God's knowledge of creatures, and a second that the object of this knowledge requires the reality of non-existent essences. It is the first of these issues that is important here, and I consider the second only in passing.

Scotus is absolutely explicit that knowledge of the divine essence is not necessary for God's knowledge of created essences. As far as I can see, he denies too that knowledge of the divine essence is sufficient for knowledge of created essences, but his position on this second question is a bit harder to dissect. Scotus's denial that knowledge of the divine essence is necessary for his knowledge of created essences follows simply from his own replacement account of the issue. According to Scotus, God comes to know created essences through his *producing* them as thought-objects – items with what Scotus calls '*esse cognitum*': thought-existence:

[4]
1 The divine intellect is actual by its essence as the basis for understanding, and by this
2 fact it has first act sufficient to produce everything else in *esse cognitum*, and by
3 producing it in *esse cognitum* produces it as something that has dependence on [the
4 divine essence] as intelligence (and the intellection is of that [other] thing because that
5 other thing depends on this intellection as on an absolute), just as in other things it is
6 said that a cause considered as merely absolute is a first act, from which an effect
7 proceeds, and the effect produced has a relation to the cause.[33]

Following Augustine, Scotus makes a distinction between two cognitive faculties – memory and intelligence. Memory is the storehouse of our habitual intellectual

---

[32] For a helpful summary of Henry's position, see Mark G. Henninger, *Relations: Medieval Theories 1250–1325*, 44–6. The background to this is a passage in Avicenna (*Metaph.* 5.1–2 (II, 227–45; see esp. pp. 228–9)), a passage that both Aquinas and Scotus cite in different contexts (see Aquinas, *De ente* 3 (pp. 24–5); Scotus, *Ord.* 2.3.1.1, n. 31 (Vatican, VII, 402–3; Spade, 63)). While Aquinas and Scotus may disagree on the ascription of some sort of entity to these 'common natures' – Scotus tending more to the view that they have some kind of entity in themselves – neither believes that such natures are required as extramental foundations for divine knowledge of kinds. (On the relative positions of Aquinas and Scotus on the common nature, see my 'Medieval Theories of Haecceity'.)

[33] Scotus, *Ord.* 1.35.un., n. 47 (Vatican, VI, 264–5); see too nn. 55, 58 (Vatican, VI, 269, 270); *Ord.* 2.1.1, nn. 29, 31 (Vatican, VII, 16, 17–18).

knowledge, and is according to Scotus also the faculty responsible for producing occurrent acts of thought; intelligence is the faculty that actually has such thoughts.[34] In the context of the divine mind, Scotus holds that memory is responsible too for producing the objects of God's thoughts of creatures,[35] and that the divine intelligence understands these objects (recall the production/operation distinction from chapter 1 above: memory produces thought-objects; the intelligence has an operation directed to them – that of understanding them). In [4.1–2] Scotus talks about the productive capacity of the divine memory, able to produce thought-objects of 'every' possible creaturely essence. These thought-objects ground God's actual knowledge of such essences. This knowledge is an act of the divine intelligence [4.2–3]. What makes a divine thought i a thought of an essence e is that precisely essence e, as thought-object, is causally dependent on i itself [4.4–5].[36] As in all cause–effect relations in which the effect is not necessary for the existence of the cause, Scotus holds that there is no real relation between cause and effect – though there is, of course, such a relation between the effect and the cause [4.5–7].

Scotus goes into considerable detail on the precise steps involved in the production of these thought-objects:

[5]
1 God in the first instant understands his essence as merely absolute. In the second
2 instant he produces [for example] a stone in *esse intelligibile* and understands the
3 stone, such that there is a relation in the understood stone to the divine intellection, but
4 no [relation] in the divine intellection to the stone. Rather, the divine intellection is
5 the end term of the relation of the stone, as understood, to [the divine intellection]. In
6 the third instant, perhaps, the divine intellect can compare its intellection to any
7 intelligible to which we can relate [an intellection], and then, by comparing itself to
8 the understood stone, can cause in itself a relation of reason. And in the fourth instant

---

[34] For memory and intelligence, and their respective roles in the production of an occurrent thought, see in particular Scotus, *Quod.* 15, n. 20 (Wadding, XII, 430–1; Alluntis and Wolter, 362–3 (¶¶ 15.60–15.63)); *Ord.* 1.2.2.1–4, nn. 221, 291–2, 295 (Vatican, II, 259–60, 299–301, 301–2); Ibid. 1.3.3.4, n. 580 (Vatican, III, 343); see too Ibid. 1.27.1–3, nn. 20, 46–8 (Vatican, VI, 72, 83–4). What is stored are *intelligible species* – in creatures, universal objects of thought that are the result of abstraction from particulars of the same kind – and what Scotus has in mind is that the intelligible species is (partially) causally responsible for the production of the occurent act of thought – the mental word. Since the species inheres in the memory, the memory will be at least a cause *per accidens* of occurrent acts of thought (since some accidental feature of it is a component of the *per se* cause): *Quod.* 15, n. 20 (Wadding, XII, 431; Alluntis and Wolter, 362 (¶ 15.61)).

[35] See Scotus, *Ord.* 2.1.1, n. 26, *text. int.* (Vatican VII, 14–15); Ibid. 1.10.un., n. 41 (Vatican, IV, 368–9). Scotus holds that, in created intellects, the agent or active intellect is responsible for producing thought-objects (by abstraction from particular instances; see Ibid. 1.3.3.1, nn. 359–60 (Vatican, III, 216–18)). God, of course, has no active intellect since he does not know by abstraction from particulars. As we see here, he knows by producing such intelligible objects prior to the real existence of any particular.

[36] Note that in creatures the identity goes the other way: what makes a creaturely thought i_c a thought of an essence e is that e is a partial cause of i_c: see e.g. Scotus, *Ord.* 1.3.1.1–2, n. 35 (Vatican, III, 21–4; *PW*, 22–3; Frank and Wolter, 112–14). On memory and object as joint partial causes of an occurrent act of thought in a creature, see Scotus, *Ord.* 1.3.3.2, nn. 407–503 (Vatican, III, 247–98).

9 it can reflect on the relation caused in the third instant, and then that relation of reason
10 will be known.[37]

The 'instants' in **[5]** are simply steps in an ordered causal sequence (such that later
'instants' require the earlier 'instants' or steps in the sequence). Such a causal
sequence does not, for Scotus, entail a temporal sequence. The first step is God's
knowledge of his absolute (non-relational) essence: God's self-knowledge **[5.1]**.
The second step is the production of a thought-object – in this case, the concept of
a stone **[5.1–2]** (*'esse intelligibile'* is a synonym for *'esse cognitum'*). The
production of such a thought-object is equivalent, according to Scotus, to
understanding the concept – thus in the second step in the sequence Scotus places,
presumably without distinction, the production of (a) stone in *esse intelligibile* and
the divine understanding or intellection of this concept **[5.2–3]**. For the concept to
be understood there must be a relation between the concept and the divine act of
understanding **[5.3]**: so a relation is also a necessary feature of step two of the
sequence. Since the concept is causally dependent on God's act of understanding
(God's act of understanding causes the concept of the stone), but not *vice versa*, the
relation is non-mutual, existing merely in the concept: the concept is really related
to God's understanding, but God's act of understanding is not thus really related to
the concept of the stone **[5.3–5]**.

The rest of **[5]** is concerned to relate Scotus's account to those of Henry of Ghent
and others. According to these thinkers, God's ideas necessarily involve knowledge
of rational relations in God. For Henry of Ghent, the relations are relations of
imitability: God understands his essence to be imitable in certain ways. Scotus holds
that, in the case of God's knowledge of creatures, a real relation in the cognized
object is sufficient for cognition. Thus, his third step in **[5]** is the production of a
rational relation between the divine mind and the cognized object – God's
comparing the cognized object to his essence. Rational relations, in Scotus's
account, require a mind specifically to cognize the real relation between one object
and another – in the case at hand, the real relation between the thought-object and
the divine essence **[5.5–8]**. Since nothing about God's knowledge of a stone requires
that God think about the stone's relation of imitating God's essence, nothing about
God's knowledge of a stone requires a relation of reason between his mind and the
stone – hence Scotus adds 'perhaps' in his comments on the third step **[5.6]**. And
knowledge of this rational relation – such as Henry holds to be necessary for divine
knowledge – is a further step, since thinking of the real relation between the divine
essence and the thought-object does not involve thinking of the rational relation
itself. This final step, then, is to think of the rational relation **[5.8–10]**. Of course,
only steps one and two are required for knowledge of the stone. And this is why
Scotus denies that knowledge of the divine essence is necessary for God's
knowledge of created essences. Put baldly: knowledge of a possible essence seems
to be unrelated to knowledge of God's essence. We, after all, seem to be able to think
of possible essences without knowing anything about the divine essence – a point
that Scotus makes explicitly and at length elsewhere.[38]

---

[37] Scotus, *Ord.* 1.35.un., n. 32 (Vatican, VI, 258); see too Ibid., n. 49 (Vatican, VI, 266).
[38] See Scotus, *Ord.* 1.3.1.4, nn. 261–9 (Vatican, III, 160–5).

What about the claim that God's knowledge of his essence is *sufficient* for his knowledge of creaturely essences? The important steps three and four in **[5]** relate to God's knowledge of his essence considered as imitable. Could, in other words, step three exist without steps one and two? It seems to me that Scotus denies this:

[6]
1 The relations in the essence follow the comparative act of the intellect, by which the
2 essence is compared to other things. But the divine intellect does not compare [the
3 essence] to unknown things, for the comparison of things to each other presupposes
4 knowledge of both extremes. For just as nature compares only to a pre-existent thing,
5 so it seems that the intellect does not compare the essence to those other things
6 through relations of this kind unless it first of all knows the other things. Therefore
7 these relations are not necessary in order to know other things determinately, for the
8 [relations] presuppose cognition of those things.[39]

Knowledge of the divine essence alone simply cannot yield knowledge of creaturely essences. The divine essence is indeed imitable by creatures, but the ways in which it is imitated cannot be known until the imitations are known **[6.2–6]**. This is not an implausible thought. Suppose I know that Caesar can be represented in many different ways – perhaps by different artists, in different media, and so on. What these possible representations are I do not know until someone thinks of them.[40]

Scotus puts his complex account of God's knowledge of creaturely essences to use in explaining how it can be that his representations of creaturely essences can be *true*:

[7]
1 God's knowledge (*theologia divina*) is of all knowable things, for the first object of his
2 knowledge makes all other things actually known in his intellect, such that in the first
3 instant of nature his essence is primarily known by his intellect; and in the second
4 instant of nature the quiddities virtually containing proper truths; in the third instant
5 are known the truths virtually contained in those quiddities. There is no causal order
6 from the second to the third, as if those quiddities caused something in his intellect.
7 There is merely an order of effects ordered to one and the same cause: for example, for
8 his essence causes those known quiddities before, as it were, the truths about them are
9 known.[41]

---

[39] Scotus, *Rep.* 1A.36.1–2, n. 38 (Noone, 409); see too *Ord.* 1.35.un., n. 22 (Vatican, VI, 258–9).
[40] Scotus sometimes seems to claim the contrary: for example,

> If [the participation opinion] is understood thus, that if God perfectly understands his imitable essence, then he perfectly understands every mode in which it can be imitated, and the imitations, and the foundations for the imitations as entities which imitate (for an imitation is perfectly known only if the foundation for the of imitation is known), then it is true. (Scotus, *Rep.* 1A.36.1–2, n. 23 (Noone, 403))

I suspect that the correct gloss here is that to know his essence *as imitable*, God needs to know not only his essence but also the produced thought-objects that imitate it. Scotus is not suggesting here that bare knowledge of the divine essence is sufficient for knowledge of its imitations.
[41] Scotus, *Ord.* prol.3.1–3, n. 200 (Vatican, I, 135).

The knowledge of truths talked about here as taking place in the third 'instant of nature' [7.4–5] is the comparison between the secondary objects and the divine essence, outlined in [5.5–8]. For the secondary objects to be 'true' they must be accurate representations of the divine essence. It is here that Scotus appeals to his account of the divine essence as imitable: what makes the representations *true* is that they conform to the divine essence as imitable:

[8]
1 All things actually intelligible by the divine intellect have *esse intelligibile*, and all
2 truths about them shine out in them, such that the intellect understands them, and
3 understands in virtue of them all necessary truths about them, since it sees in them, as
4 in an object, those necessary truths. In so far as they are secondary objects of the
5 divine intellect, they are truths, because in conformity with their exemplar, namely the
6 divine intellect.[42]

Presumably the thought is that, once produced, God understands that the objects produced imitate his essence, and that it is in virtue of this that all creaturely essences are 'true'.

Scotus holds, then, that God's knowledge of creaturely concepts is a matter of his *producing* such concepts. As we shall see, the relevant kind of production does not involve God's *omnipotence*, since his omnipotence is concerned with the production of real creatures *ad extra*. Concepts are produced by the divine intellect. These produced thought-objects are necessary for God's knowledge of creaturely essences. Scotus holds that God would 'not be [wise] if he did not have knowledge of a creature – which creature "as understood by God" is the idea, and thus if God did not understand the ideas, he could not be entirely wise'.[43] These thought-objects are the exemplars or patterns according to which God creates whatever he creates. Thus, he proposes the following terms as synonyms with *esse cognitum*: being in an opinion (*esse in opinione*), being in an intellection (*esse in intellectione*), being as an exemplar (*esse exemplatum*), being as a representation (*esse repraesentatum*).[44] This list brings out the role of the ideas in God's knowledge and exemplarity. Perhaps the most suggestive term is the last – *esse repraesentatum*: a divine idea is a (mental) representation of a (possibly extramental) essence.

What is this *esse cognitum* or *esse intelligibile*? Scotus contrasts *esse intelligibile* with real, extramental, existence. Basically, what have *esse intelligibile* are the *contents* of a concept. Like Aquinas, Scotus holds that this intelligible existence is just a mode or manner in which common natures exist. Following a lead found in Avicenna, medieval thinkers sometimes hold that common natures have two sorts of existence: real, as particular things, and mental, as thoughts, or as objects of

---

[42] Ibid., 1.3.1.4, n. 262 (Vatican, III, 160).

[43] Ibid., 1.35.un., n. 43 (Vatican, VI, 263). Scotus is not entirely happy with the word 'idea', which he describes as 'Greek and Platonic ... predicated of [God] by philosophers', to which, in contrast, the truths of Catholic theology need to be added (see *DPP* 4, n. 37 (Wolter, 147 (¶¶ 4.85–4.86)).

[44] Scotus, *Ord.* 1.36.un., n. 34 (Vatican, VI, 284). The obvious translation of '*esse exemplatum*' is something like 'exampled being', and of '*esse repraesentatum*' 'represented being'. But the context requires that active senses, not passive ones, are intended: hence, 'being as an exemplar', and 'being as a representation'.

thought.[45] In terms of the theory of mental existence, however, Aquinas and Scotus diverge in a crucial way. For Aquinas, the mentally existent universal is identified as the intelligible species: the habitual (non-episodic) understanding that an intellect has of the kinds of thing that there are – of, in other words, common natures. Intelligible species are the result of abstraction. As Aquinas is usually understood, these species are not in any sense the *objects* of thought. They are simply the intentionally – mentally – existent natures of things. This yields the famous Thomist thesis – derived from Aristotle – that knower and known are in some sense identical.[46] For Aquinas, the intelligible species is in some way the form or nature of the external object, existent or inhering in the mind. Forms in the usual run of things in the extramental world make their subjects to be of the kind determined by the form. The form of horseness in some sense makes something a horse. But on Aquinas's theory, although such a form is really in the mind in some way, it is not in the mind in such a way as to make the mind a real instance of the form. In knowing the form of horseness, the mind does not become a horse (with e.g. four legs and a predilection for oats). The form is in the mind not really but, we might say, intentionally.

On Aquinas's view, these species are not in any way objects of thought. What is known – *directly* – are the extramental objects, the things with real existence.[47] Scotus finds this Thomist notion of intentionality defective. In the case of creaturely knowledge, Scotus maintains that there cannot be any mental contents without some real accident for these contents to inhere in.[48] The reason why the mind itself cannot be the subject is that the presence of intelligible species in the mind is episodic (even if, in the technical sense of the word, 'habitual'), and Scotus is presumably thinking that any mental act or habit is more than *just* contents; it is an act or habit as well, and this act/habit must be a real accident. If this were not the case, then the notion of a change in mental content, or of any episodic mental event, would be wholly mysterious. As Scotus might put it, it is not possible for something with merely objective existence (existence 'as thought') to inhere directly in the mind. Inherence is something that real accidents do: acts, states, and the like.[49] Scotus holds that the contents of an act or object of thought somehow 'shine out' in the real accident that bears these contents. The real accident, subjectively inhering in the mind (having the mind as its subject of inherence), is simply the 'vessel' in which the extramental object is represented. The intelligible species, then, is for Scotus a real form that contains a mental representation of an external object. This mental representation is

---

[45] For the references to Avicenna, Aquinas, and Scotus, see n. 32 above. As I noted there, Scotus tends more to claim a third sort of reality for the nature too: the common nature itself has some kind of being as the subject of these different sorts of existence (real vs. mental). This distinction between Aquinas and Scotus is irrelevant to the question about mental existence that I am about to discuss.

[46] See e.g. Aquinas, *ST* 1.84.2 c (I/1, 408b–9a).

[47] See e.g. Ibid., 1.85.2 c (I/1, 418b–19a).

[48] See e.g. Scotus, *Ord.* 1.3.3.1, nn. 375, 382, 386 (Vatican, III, 228, 232–3, 235); Ibid. 1.27.1–3, n. 54 (Vatican, VI, 86). On the questions of intentional existence in Scotus, see most usefully Peter King, 'Scotus on Mental Content'; for a brief summary of the relevant issues and passages, see Robert Pasnau, 'Cognition', 287–90. My debt to Peter King on this topic is obvious.

[49] See e.g. Scotus, *In Metaph.* 7.18, n. 37 (St Bonaventure, IV, 346–7).

the immediate object of thought, caused jointly by the agent intellect and the external object itself.[50] What distinguishes different (kinds of) species – the forms – is presumably the (efficiently) *causal* relations that they have to different (kinds of) external objects. (Contrast Aquinas: the species is something like a *formal* cause of knowledge; it is (merely) the form of the object existing intentionally.) The contents, of course, are distinguished by their being different *representations* – representations of different kinds of objects: presumably again to be given a causal explanation. The contents of the representation are identified as the mentally existing nature, and the common nature exists mentally or intentionally in so far as it is an (internal) *object* of thought. Scotus, then, tends to the view that an intelligible species is a representation, and the immediate (though not ultimate) object of cognition because he believes that the sophisticated Thomist account is simply too mysterious to do any explanatory work.

In the case of God, the picture is a little different, for, as we have seen, God knows not by abstraction but by straightforwardly causing representations of creaturely essences in himself prior to the real existence of any instantiations of these essences. Unlike creatures, these representations do not have any real subject other than God himself – they do not require real accidental forms, inherent in the divine mind, as their bearers. But Scotus still believes that they are the immediate objects of God's thought, something that I return to below.

A further clarification is in order too, for thus far I have been speaking as though there are *causal* relations between God's essence/memory and the concepts of creatures produced by this essence/memory. But the unreal status of these mental representations means that it is hard to envisage these relations as properly causal: nothing unreal, after all, is caused. In **[9]**, Scotus makes the point both about the produced concepts, and about the mental acts that have these concepts as their objects:

[9]
1 God's intellection, although it is not absolutely caused, is nevertheless quasi-
2 principiated as it is of this secondary object, and is so by the essence as (so to speak
3 (*quasi*)) by the formal objective equivocal principiator (*ratione*) – and thus is more
4 principiated than [is the intellection] of the primary object, for this is principiated (so
5 to speak) [by the essence as] by the formal objective univocal basis (*ratione*) [of
6 understanding]. For an intellection of this thing [viz. a secondary object] to be
7 equivocally quasi-principiated is for this thing [viz. a secondary object] to be
8 principiated in diminished existence (*esse diminutum*). ... Neither does it seem
9 inappropriate for a divine act to be quasi-principiated (not in itself, but as it is of this
10 object), for this has to be posited of a volition ... since a volition is contingently of
11 this object, and nothing contingent is entirely uncaused.[51]

'Principiation' is in Scotus's jargon a general term for all sorts of causal relation. It thus includes those relations that result not in the production of real objects, but in the production of merely intentional or mental objects or acts of the kind just

[50] See e.g. Scotus, *Ord.* 1.3.1.1–2, n. 35 (Vatican, III, 21–4; *PW*, 22–3; Frank and Wolter, 112–14) – a passage about concepts in general, not merely intelligible species.

[51] Scotus, *Ord.* 1.36.un., n. 39 (Vatican, VI, 286–7).

described. I take it that 'quasi-principiation' is a technical term for the production of unreal (i.e. intentional or mental) items. I translate '*ratione*' as 'by the principiator' in [**9**.3] because as Scotus sees it the divine essence is the basis for God's understanding essences other than his own by principiating secondary objects of divine cognition [**9**.1–2].

What Scotus is attempting to claim in [**9**] is that God's understanding is the result of a 'causal' process. This is true both for his self-understanding and for his understanding of secondary objects. His self-understanding is quasi-principiated by his essence as its object [**9**.4–6]. A univocal cause is one whose effects are the same in kind as the cause. Here, the 'causal' relation is between the divine essence as object, and the produced act of self-knowledge. (I deal with the nature of this productive activity in Part II, chapter 10 §2 below, since Scotus identifies this thought-act as the second person of the Trinity.) There is a further 'causal' relationship between the divine essence and the secondary objects of his understanding, and this relationship is 'equivocal' [**9**.2–3], in the (relevant technical) sense that the 'effects' – the secondary objects, the creaturely concepts – are *different in kind* from the divine essence. Still, the parallels with God's self-knowledge are not all that close, in the sense that God's knowledge of creaturely essences is caused precisely because the objects of that knowledge are caused. Since the divine essence is in every way uncaused, God's self-knowledge cannot be caused in just the way that his knowledge of creaturely concepts is caused.

It is important to see, too, that in neither case does the object precede the act. For there to be an act of understanding is exactly for there to be an object understood [**9**.6–8].[52] In the case of God's knowledge of creatures, but not in the case of God's self-knowledge, this object is caused. But Scotus does not want to posit too strong a distinction between God's self-knowledge and his knowledge of creaturely essences, and is inclined to think of all of this knowledge as just one act: he speaks of God's act of self-knowledge being 'extended' (*protendi*) to creaturely concepts, and claims that the further causal component added by the secondary objects is simply the identification of the act (since intellectual acts are identified by their objects).[53] In [**9**.9–10] Scotus makes much the same point: quasi-principiation here is a relation that is fundamentally responsible not for the existence of an act, but for its identity.

Whatever the nature of Scotus's worry here, it is clear that he is not concerned about items internal to God being caused (quasi-principiated) by himself. For he believes that free divine acts are internal to God and caused, at least to the extent that the *identity* of the act is contingent [**9**.8–11]. In fact, it seems that Scotus ought to claim that the *existence* of every contingent act is contingent too, since he holds that God could in principle fail to will anything other than himself at all.

4 God's Knowledge and Modality

As I noted above, Aquinas's view – that God 'sees' creaturely truths in his own essence – is open to the objection that it is unclear just how the divine essence can

---

[52] See Ibid. (Vatican, VI, 286).
[53] Ibid., nn. 42–3 (Vatican, VI, 287–8).

contain such truths. It may be thought that Scotus's view is open to an analogous objection: there seems to be no explanation as to how it is that the divine essence produces just the concepts that it does. Scotus, after all, insists that the production of creaturely concepts is *necessary*.[54] On one level, Scotus will have a straightforward answer to this. God produces all possible concepts, and he does so because he is omniscient. The context of **[10]** is a worry about why it is that an angel, in knowing its own essence, does not thereby know the essences of all angels less perfect than itself:

[10]
1 A higher angel has more perfect entity than a lower one, but does not however include
2 the whole entity of the lower one, such that the lower one differs from it merely by a
3 negation: for species are universally distinguished not by negations but by their proper
4 definitions. The divine essence, however, which is infinite, eminently includes all
5 perfections. For this reason no higher thing other than the divine essence is a
6 sufficient basis for knowing a lower thing.[55]

Less perfect species of angels are not distinguished from higher ones merely by lacking some features of higher ones **[10**.1–4**]**. So in knowing itself, a higher angel does not thereby know all the features of the lower angel. God's essence, however, 'eminently includes' all creaturely perfection **[10**.4–5**]**. For this reason, perfect knowledge of the divine essence is sufficient for knowledge of all lesser things **[10**.5–6**]**. Presumably, Scotus does not mean that the divine essence somehow 'contains' concepts in the sort of way envisaged by Aquinas. Including a perfection 'eminently' is here to be contrasted with the view of perfection-inclusion associated with Aquinas – the notion that Scotus labels 'formal containment'.[56] What he means is that God's intellect – the cause of secondary objects – has the capacity for producing (concepts of) all possible perfections.

Claiming that God has a sufficient capacity for producing concepts of all possible perfections does not in itself provide an explanation of why it is that God causes just the concepts that he does – that is to say, concepts of all possible objects. For it could be held that the modal notions such as *possible* are themselves the result of God's productive thought, or it could (at least) be held that the identity of certain perfections as possible and others as impossible is simply the result of God's productive thought. In either case, the fact that God produces the concepts that he does still requires further explanation – and, indeed, further explanation from within God and his mind. One way, of course, of dealing with this is to claim that the fact that God thinks some things (and thus makes them possible) and does not think other things (and thus does not make them possible) is just the result of the kind of thing that God is. Scotus, however, is unhappy with this sort of solution, I suspect because it seems to suggest that there are some things that God could think of and has not. Scotus holds instead that what is possible and what is impossible is in some sense independent of God's intellectual activity. Thus the fact that God thinks just

---

[54] See e.g. Ibid., n. 40 (Vatican, VI, 287); Ibid. 1.3.1.4, n. 268 (Vatican, III, 163–4).

[55] Ibid. 2.3.2.3, n. 395 (Vatican, VII, 594).

[56] See e.g. Ibid. 1.36.un., n. 39 (Vatican, VI, 286).

those things that he does ultimately springs from the fact that he thinks all possible things. On the face of it this sort of solution leaves the ontological status of modal notions unclear, and there has indeed been a great deal of controversy on the whole issue.

Let me start with the simplest part of the problem: what it is to think up a concept. For, as we shall see, Scotus holds that any mind can think up concepts, and that the same constraints about possibility exist for any mind, divine or created. I have suggested thus far that, according to Scotus, God is responsible for thinking up concepts. But Scotus holds too that we can think up concepts in much the same way that God can. The only difference is that, if our concepts are coherent, God has got there first, as it were. Arguing against Henry's claim that objects thought by God must have at least *esse essentiae*, Scotus draws an explicit and relevant parallel between God's thinking and our thinking:

[11]
1 If something does not exist, it can be understood by us (and this whether its essence or
2 its existence), and it does not follow from our intellection that the thing has real *esse*
3 *essentiae* or *esse existentiae*; neither is there any difference between the divine
4 intellect and ours in this respect, other than that the divine intellect produces these
5 intelligibles in *esse intelligibile*, whereas ours does not produce [them] firstly. ...
6 Likewise, our active intellect produces a thing in *esse intelligibile*, though it is
7 produced earlier [by the divine intellect], and it does not follow from this production
8 of our active intellect that a thing thus produced has existence simply speaking (*esse*
9 *simpliciter*).[57]

Talk of the agent or active intellect here is a way of signalling that we cause concepts (things in *esse intelligibile*) by abstraction **[11.6–9]**.[58] In doing so, we mimic God's thinking up concepts in the first place **[11.3–5]**. But I see no block on our just thinking of them – perhaps we could just speculatively 'stumble across' possible concepts, and Scotus certainly suggests that, in the counterpossible absence of God, our minds would indeed be able to think up some of the concepts that God has now thought up.[59] If we think up things that God has not thought up, this is simply because these things are impossible:

[12]
1 A figment ... or a thing including a contradiction is not any one conceivable thing,
2 other than by an errant intellect, and what is conceivable only by an errant intellect as
3 errant is nothing.[60]

Here, Scotus suggests that things including contradictions – that is to say, logically impossible things – are unintelligible **[12.1]**, and in fact Scotus in this sort of context

---

[57] Ibid., nn. 28–9 (Vatican, VI, 281–2).

[58] This is what Scotus means when he claims elsewhere that our intellects are 'measured by' things – whereas God just thinks of them – such that his thought is the 'measure' of concepts: see e.g. Scotus, *Ord.* 1.35.un., n. 27 (Vatican, VI, 256).

[59] See e.g. Scotus, *Ord.* 1.7.1, n. 27 (Vatican, IV, 118–19).

[60] Scotus, *Rep.* 1A.43.1 (Hoffmann, 319).

claims generally that any intelligible concept is possible.[61] Now, as we have seen, God is responsible for first of all thinking up such concepts. So there is a sense in which God is responsible for logical possibilities: God thinks up the concepts that are the bearers of such possibility:

[13]
1 A stone is formally possible in itself (*ex se*); therefore – reducing (so to speak) [this
2 possibility] to the first extrinsic principle – the divine intellect will be that from which
3 the first reason for possibility in a stone exists.[62]

[13.1] makes it clear that the contents of the concept of a stone are such that the concept is coherent – logically possible: it is 'formally possible *ex se*'.[63] But the existence of this logical possibility requires the existence of a concept to be the bearer of the possibility, and this existence – the existence of a concept – requires an in some sense 'causal' explanation: in this case, the divine mind. So the divine mind explains the existence of the possibility **[13.2–3]**. It is an originative principle extrinsic to – independent of – both the concept and the possibility **[13.1–2]**. **[13]** makes it clear that there is a sequence here, and Scotus elsewhere describes the sequence more carefully:

[14]
1 A thing produced in ... *esse intelligibile* by the divine intellect in the first instant of
2 nature has in itself (*ex se*) possible existence in the second instant of nature, because
3 existence is not formally incompatible with it.[64]

Stage one is the production of a thing in *esse intelligibile* **[14.1–2]**; stage two is the existence of the logical possibility inherent in the intelligible thing **[14.2–3]**. Scotus is not suggesting here any further productive or originative activity on God's part over and above the activity of the first stage. The production in *esse intelligibile* is 'causally' and logically sufficient for the existence of the logical possibility. Thus the intelligible object, once produced, has possible existence *ex se*, and the reason is that its content is not incompatible with real existence – it can be instantiated **[14.3]**.

Why should Scotus want to claim that there are two distinct instants of nature here? The reason, I think, is that Scotus believes that any sort of modal property – such as possibility – presupposes some subject. So the existence of the subject is in some sense prior to the existence of the possibility. It is in this sense that

---

[61] See Scotus, *Ord.* 1.35.un., n. 40 (Vatican, VI, 261); Ibid. 1.36.un., n. 48 (Vatican, VI, 290); *In Metaph.* 6.2, nn. 36–7 (St Bonaventure, IV, 50–1).

[62] Scotus, *Ord.* 1.43.un., n. 6 (Vatican, VI, 354).

[63] I am reasonably sure that Scotus would hold that the contents of such a concept would entail certain further properties too: *propria*, for example. (On this, see n. 82 below.) But Scotus is clear that these entailments are distinctly thought of by the divine intellect (see *Ord.* prol. 4.1–2, *text. int.* (Vatican, I, 143, l. 20–p. 144, l. 14)). Scotus does not mean that God could have failed to think of these entailments, or that he could have invented different ones instead. It is simply that – as a matter of fact – the entailment would not obtain if God were to fail to think of it. (I take it the same would hold *mutatis mutandis* in the absence of God: the entailment requires some sort of bearer for its reality.)

[64] Scotus, *Ord.* 1.43.un., n. 15 (Vatican, VI, 358).

possibilities come from God: God produces the subjects – in this case, simply concepts – that are the bearers of these modal properties. But he does not produce the modal properties in the sense of determining which concepts are subject to which modal property. The properties follow automatically from the contents of the concepts. Equally, while he holds that possibilities are (in this limited sense) from God, Scotus is most emphatically not saying that something is possible because God *causes* it, in the sense that it depends in any way on his power to produce things external to himself (it is for this reason that I glossed 'causal' as 'originative' above, and talked (equivalently) about production). Indeed, Scotus takes great pains to avoid this misunderstanding:

[15]
1 The active power which omnipotence is does not give anything existence other than by
2 producing it, for it [omnipotence] is a power productive of a thing external [to God].
3 But before any production of anything external, a thing has possible existence, because
4 ... for a thing to be produced in *esse intelligibile* is not for the thing to be produced in
5 existence simply speaking (*esse simpliciter*), and if it were [produced in *esse*
6 *intelligibile*] it would not be so by that power by which God is called omnipotent. It is
7 not, therefore, by the power that is omnipotence that a thing other than God is firstly
8 possible.[65]

Possibilities are from God in the sense that God thinks of every possible concept, such that, given God's existence, if he were not to think of these concepts, then they would not be possible. Of course, given God's existence, it is a necessary fact that he thinks of all and only those concepts that are possible: the blocks on impossible concepts are – as we shall see in a moment – intrinsic, not simply the *result* of God's failing to think of them. But since in actual fact God's thinking of concepts is sufficient for the existence of these concepts, logical possibility is in this sense traceable to God's intellect.

In order to understand this, we need to keep in mind that the sorts of concepts that can be possible are both simple and complex. Impossibility, however, is a feature only of complexes, and springs from the incompatibility of the various component concepts.[66] What God thinks of are all simple concepts (which are possible by definition, as it were, not possibly containing incompatible features), and all possible combinations of such concepts. Scotus employs the same formula for both logical possibility and logical impossibility: possibles are possible, and impossibles are impossible, 'formally *ex se* and principiatively from God'.[67] Nevertheless, Scotus sometimes wants to claim that there is a sense – I do not believe it to be a very important sense – in which possibles are from God and impossibles are from themselves.[68] As just noted, the sorts of concepts that can be possible are both simple and complex, whereas impossibility is a feature only of complexes. There thus seems to be an additional (originative or explanatory) stage in impossibility: a block, preventing possibility. It is presumably for this reason that Scotus wants to claim that

---

[65] Ibid., n. 9 (Vatican, VI, 355).
[66] Ibid., nn. 16–18 (Vatican, VI, 359–61).
[67] See e.g. Ibid., nn. 16, 17 (Vatican, 359, 360).
[68] Ibid., n. 15 (Vatican, VI, 359).

impossibility is not 'primarily from the side of God',[69] whereas possibility is (see **[13]** above). But we should not be misled by this into thinking that Scotus proposes a radically different account for the explanation of impossibility. The basic structure is the same: God originates the bearers of these modal properties, but the modal properties are borne by these things automatically. In **[14]**, Scotus makes it clear that possibility has no further *formal* explanation than itself, and this is compatible with **[13]** provided that we understand **[13]** as proposing that possibility is *originatively* explained by God (producing the bearers of the modality). And in this case, possibility is explained in just the way that impossibility is.

What does it mean for something to be formally possible, or formally impossible, *ex se*? The explanation is just that the concepts are the concepts they are. This is, of course, just what Scotus means when he claims that possibility and impossibility are formal features of the concepts. The contents of the concepts explain their modal properties. Scotus considers the contrasting cases of man and chimera, and notes that it is true of both concepts that they fail to be instantiated *eternally*, though for different reasons:

[16]

1 *Not being something* inheres in *man*-in-eternity, and *not being something* inheres in
2 chimera. But the affirmation which is being something is not incompatible with man;
3 rather, the negation inheres only on account of the negation of a cause not positing
4 [man's being something]. It is, however, incompatible with chimera, for no cause
5 could cause *being something* in it. And why it is not incompatible with man, and it is
6 incompatible with chimera is because this is this and that that. ... For whatever is
7 incompatible with something formally in itself (*ex se*), is incompatible with it, and
8 whatever is not incompatible with something formally in itself, is not incompatible
9 with it.[70]

The statement 'a man exists' is not always true **[16.1]**. The reason for this is not that it is logically impossible for there to be human beings **[16.2]**. Rather, the reason is simply that, for a considerable time in the existence of the universe, nothing factually caused any human beings **[16.3–4]**. The statement 'a chimera exists', however, is false **[16.1–2]**, and necessarily so, because it is logically impossible for there to be chimeras **[16.4–5]**. And the explanation for the difference in the two cases is reducible simply to the contents of the relevant concepts **[16.5–6]**: no further explanation can be given, and none should be sought **[16.6–9]**. Thus, the modal status of these concepts – the fact that they have the modal status that they have – is not originated by God, even though the concepts are.

Not surprisingly, this complex view has been the subject of considerable controversy.[71] As I see it, the problem lies in the distinction between originative and

---

[69] Ibid.

[70] Ibid. 1.36.un., n. 60 (Vatican, VI, 296).

[71] For an excellent account of the controversy, see Tobias Hoffmann, *Creatura Intellecta: Die Ideen und Possibilien bei Duns Scotus mit Ausblick auf Franz von Mayronis, Poncius und Mastrius*, 201–5, on which I rely here – though my conclusion is rather different from Hoffmann's (for which, see *Creatura Intellecta*, 205–14). Hoffmann includes a useful discussion of the debate between two seventeenth-century Scotists – Poncius and Mastrius – that closely parallels the modern debate that I am about to outline.

formal explanation. The problem has been sharpened in the literature by considering cases in which God fails to produce the concepts that are the bearers of modal properties. One such case would be that in which God fails to exist at all. Scotus considers this case, and it seems to me that his answers point in a very clear direction.[72] Simo Knuuttila, for example, holds that on Scotus's view it makes sense to think of modalities as 'non-existent preconditions of thoughts and beings and logical possibilities',[73] such that 'it is not the intrinsic possibility that depends on God, but the existence, whether mental or real, of something in which it is instantiated'.[74] For Knuuttila, this means that logical modalities – the structure of reality – 'would be similarly actualized by any omniscient intellect, because the absolute totality of intelligibility can be actual only in one way'.[75] Calvin Normore, contrariwise, holds that Scotus generally maintained that God's existence is necessary for the existence of modalities:

> If, per impossibile, there were no God, then there would not be the simple *notae* which ground repugnance or non-repugnance and there would be no possibilities. Thus I claim that, for Scotus, God gives to the constituents of natures the ontological status required of possibilities but does not make these constituents to be or not be repugnant.[76]

My view is that both of these overstate their respective cases. Suppose absolutely nothing were to exist. It would not then be the case – contrary perhaps to the suggestion made by Knuuttila – that there are non-existent modalities awaiting actualization or instantiation. This is far too realist an account of modalities, making them akin to universals that are instantiated by particulars. Nothing about Scotus's account suggests any more than a nominalist account of modalities. To this extent, Normore's reading is more plausible. But nothing about Scotus's account requires that God be the origin of modalities. Scotus explicitly affirms, for example, that any mind could cause modalities, simply by causing concepts, and to this extent Knuuttila's reading is on the right lines:

[17]
1 And why it is not incompatible with man, and it is incompatible with chimera is
2 because this is this and that that, and *this is the case whatever intellect conceives* [*of*
3 *them*].[77]

This passage begins at **[16**.5**]**, and continues through the ellipsis. I believe that **[17**.2–3**]** makes it sufficiently clear that the activity of any mind would be sufficient for the existence of the modalities, given that – as we have seen – Scotus holds that

[72] See e.g. Scotus, *Ord.* 1.7.1, n. 27 (Vatican, IV, 118).

[73] Simo Knuuttila, 'Duns Scotus and the Foundations of Logical Modalities', 138.

[74] Ibid., 139, both quoted in Hoffmann, *Creatura Intellecta*, 202.

[75] Ibid., 137, quoted in Hoffmann, *Creatura Intellecta*, 203.

[76] Calvin Normore, 'Scotus, Modality, Instants of Nature and the Contingency of the Present', 162, quoted in Hoffmann, 205. Note that Normore, while remarking Scotus's tendency to gloss logical modalities in terms of real powers, has somewhat retreated from the uncompromisingly universal claim here: see Normore, 'Duns Scotus's Modal Theory', 159, n. 26

[77] Scotus, *Ord.* 1.36.un., n. 60 (Vatican, VI, 296).

any mind has the power to think up concepts (even though only the divine mind, from its unlimited perfection, has the power to think up every possible concept). In fact, Scotus does not even seem to believe that the existence of thought-objects is necessary for the existence of modalities. Real objects, too, seem to be the bearers of modalities:

[18]
1 The entirely first reason, not reducible to another, why being is not incompatible with
2 man, is that man is formally man, and this *whether in reality or intelligibly in the*
3 *intellect.*[78]

Scotus uses 'logical possibility' ('*possibilitas logica*') to talk about the possibility inherent in concepts and propositions (complexes of concepts).[79] In [18.2–3], Scotus talks about this possibility when talking about man existing 'intelligibly in the intellect'. But he also talks about a possibility related to this, but inherent in states of affairs (e.g. in this case, there being a man) – what we call 'broadly logical' or 'metaphysical possibility'. And the point in [18.2] ('whether in reality ...') is that the existence of any real object is sufficient for the existence of broadly logical modalities.[80] Scotus's account of the origin of modality does not require that there not be at least one logically possible world with neither God nor logical modalities. Now, every world with logical modalities in includes God; despite appearances, however, this should not be understood as entailing that there is a *logical* link between God and logical modalities. The link is, rather, *originative* or principiative: God is principiatively sufficient for modalities in any world in which he exists. But the existence of anything in that world is likewise principiatively sufficient for at least some modalities; God simply gets there first.

How can we make this interpretation of Scotus consistent with the material in [16.1–2], according to which possibility presupposes intelligibility, and apparently presupposes intelligible existence, existence precisely as a thought-object? For if possibility presupposes existence as a thought-object, then the existence of real objects in the absence of any mind will not be sufficient for the existence of possibility.[81] There is a simple answer here. What possibility requires is intelligibility. Now, intelligibility can come from any mind thinking intelligible

---

[78] Ibid., n. 62 (Vatican, VI, 296–7).

[79] See Ibid., n. 61 (Vatican, VI, 296); Ibid. 1.7.1, n. 27 (Vatican, IV, 118).

[80] In fact, towards the end of his life, Scotus seems to have contemplated the possibility that modalities require absolutely no subject at all – rather like the position that Knuuttila ascribes to him globally. The suggestion is made in book 9 of *In Metaph.* – a portion of this work usually assumed to be late in Scotus's *oeuvre*. Scotus reiterates the view that logical possibility abstracts from every real active power (*In Metaph.* 9.1–2, n. 18 (St Bonaventure, IV, 514)) – a view that I believe can be found in some form in the various *Sentence* commentaries too, as I have been arguing. But he goes on to suggest that possibility obtains in the absence not only of any active *power*, but of any *subject* as well (Ibid., n. 35 (St Bonaventure, IV, 522–3)), and claims that this view 'seems to be probable, especially if it is posited that essence and existence differ only by reason' (Ibid., n. 36 (St Bonaventure, IV, 523)).

[81] Hoffmann has made considerations of this kind central in his interpretation of Scotus, according to which the existence of the divine mind is necessary for intelligibility and possibility: see *Creatura Intellecta*, 205 and esp. 211–12.

things. But intelligibility does not require any mind at all. A finite universe, without God, and inhabited merely by non-rational beings, is still intelligible – even though, in the strictest sense, there is nothing that has *esse intelligibile*: nothing that is a *mere* thought-object. (Such a universe is still intelligible: nothing intrinsic to it prevents its being understood. The blocks are all extrinsic, as it were: the lack of a mind to do the understanding.) And if it be doubted that anything is intelligible in the lack of any mind able to understand it, I can argue that, since Scotus accepts that such a universe as I describe would include modalities [**18**.2], and since modalities logically entail intelligibility, Scotus should accept that such a universe is intelligible.

The upshot of all this is that modalities are the same come what may. Scotus does not believe that there is a mechanism (such as instantiation) that explains this fact. The explanatory bedrock of the fact that modalities are the same come what may is simply the contents of the (non-modal) concepts that are the subjects of the modal properties. And this is what Scotus means by claiming that modalities are *formally* 'from themselves'. The modalities require something to bear them, and this is what Scotus means when he claims that, principiatively, it is not the case that the modalities are from themselves. In fact, they are principiatively from God. But if there were no God, then they could be principiatively from anything real: a finite mind, or even just the real objects themselves in the absence of any mind thinking the relevant thoughts.

If I have presented this picture correctly, then at least one question remains. If the mere existence of anything is sufficient to generate modalities, then why would Scotus hold that modalities do not supervene automatically on God's nature, without God's needing to principiate them by the cognitive mechanism that Scotus supposes? Why, in other words, accept that the modalities *in fact* supervene precisely on things with *esse intelligibile*, existence merely as thought objects? Perhaps Scotus holds that modalities can be principiated in various ways. Thinking of a stone generates them; God's thinking of himself generates them; but perhaps Scotus supposes that God's very existence sufficiently principiates them irrespective of God's thinking of himself or anything else. The problem, of course, is that Scotus's claims about principiation relate not to the supervenience of modalities on objects, but merely to the origination of thought objects in the divine mind.

5 God's Knowledge of Possible Individuals

As I noted above, God has knowledge of all possible essences and forms, essential and accidental. Scotus also holds that God has knowledge of genera and inseparable accidents, on the grounds that, as creator, his understanding of things must extend to what we might think of as the metaphysically micro-level: *all* of the formal components of a thing must be known by the agent responsible for creating it – responsible for bringing it into existence without *any* presupposed components.[82] Since God knows all possible combinations of such properties, it follows that God knows the complete range of combinations that can be realized by individuals. But

---

[82] On this, see Scotus, *Rep.* 1A.36.3–4, nn. 25–8 (Noone, 433–5).

this is not, for Scotus, the same thing as knowing the individuals themselves. As I have shown elsewhere, Scotus holds that individuals are distinct from their life-stories,[83] and he holds too that two individuals could be qualitatively indiscernible,[84] and even occupy the same place.[85] For Scotus, knowledge of an individual – the noumenon, as it were, not just the phenomenal spatio-temporal continuant – requires knowledge of a haecceity. As I have noted above, Scotus accepts that God can know actual haecceities. But he also holds that God knows all possible haecceities – presumably by positing them in intelligible existence, just as he does for quiddities.

That God knows individuals is not, amongst medieval theologians, a controversial position – Aquinas, for example, holds it (though Scotus mistakenly supposes that he does not).[86] Still, positing haecceities makes a big difference to the way in which the doctrine is spelled out. For a haecceity is both knowable and *irreducibly* particular: indeed, irreducibly *this* particular. There is nothing in Aquinas's account that fits this description: what is ultimately *this* particular, for Aquinas, is (other than in the case of God) simply the relevant combination of common components. (Matter is not irreducibly *this* particular, for whatever it is it is common to successive particulars. Neither is it knowable, which – I would suppose – would make it strange to think of it as *this* particular at all. As such – in abstraction from any and every form – it has no identity whatever.[87]) Still, Scotus wants to hold too that God knows all possible individuals – and presumably what God needs to do to achieve this is to know the haecceity (along, presumably, with the common nature to which the haecceity is united).[88]

Scotus's opponent on God's knowledge of individuals (possible and actual) is Henry of Ghent. Henry holds that knowledge of species is sufficient for knowledge of individuals. His reason for this has to do with his account of individuation. What

---

[83] See my 'Identity, Origin, and Persistence'.

[84] On this, see e.g. *In Metaph.* 7.13, n. 158 (St Bonaventure, IV, 271).

[85] On this, see my *The Physics of Duns Scotus*, 200–1.

[86] Scotus, *Rep.* 1A.36.3–4, nn. 29–32 (Noone, 435–6). For Aquinas's acceptance of divine ideas of individuals, see *ST* 1.15.3 ad 4 (I/1, 92ᵇ). For Scotus's misunderstanding of this point, see Timothy B. Noone, 'Scotus on Divine Ideas: *Rep. Paris. I-A*, d. 36', 378–9. Certain thinkers between Aquinas and Scotus rejected God's knowledge of individuals: most notably Godfrey of Fontaines: see John F. Wippel, *The Metaphysical Thought of Godfrey of Fontaines*, 124–30.

[87] It is for this reason that Aquinas – understandably – believes that even God lacks an idea of matter: *ST* 1.15.3 ad 3 (I/1, 92ᵇ). Scotus, of course, believes that matter has its own quidditative content, and hence has no trouble accounting for God's knowledge of it: see *Rep.* 1A.36.3–4, n. 30 (Noone, 435–6); for the quiddity of matter, see my *The Physics of Duns Scotus*, 17–23.

[88] It is hard to think that it could be a contingent matter that such-and-such a haecceity is united to such-and-such a nature – such that (e.g.) Socrates' haecceity could have been the haecceity of the greenness of a blade of grass, and thus that Socrates could have been the greenness of a blade of grass. Scotus is a committed essentialist, and thus must suppose that, for any haecceity, it is a necessary matter that the haecceity is united to the nature that it is. On this, see Scotus, *Rep.* 1A.36.3–4, nn. 41–2 (Noone, 439–40), where Scotus makes it clear that, although the extension of a species is not part of its definition, it is nevertheless the case that all possible instances of the species are essentially instances of the species. The distinction of an individual from its life-story cannot extend so far that it is no longer possible to talk of kinds at all. It is worth noting that, since Scotus holds that there are ideas of all possible individuals, he must believe too that the *possible* extension of a species is a necessary matter.

accounts for individuation is not, according to Henry, anything real added to a nature. It is simply a twofold negation: indivisibility (into further instantiations), and non-identity with every other thing.[89] As Scotus presents the denial of divine ideas of individuals, this denial entails Henry's theory of individuation. Since he believes that there is good reason to suppose that the theory of individuation is false, it follows by *modus tollens* that God must have ideas of individuals. Against the theory of individuation, Scotus reasons that the twofold negation is precisely what needs explaining; Henry has simply restated the problem without providing any kind of explanatory solution to it.[90] In accordance with this, **[19]** clearly entails that Scotus understands God to have ideas of haecceities, not just possible combinations of properties:

[19]
1 If the individual were perfectly known through the idea of a species, then whatever
2 positive that an individual implies is contained in the specific nature. And thus
3 nothing is added over and above a species other than a privation or negation, and thus
4 the individual in itself would be a non-being. And consequently either species and
5 individual would differ in nothing positive; or, if they differed in some way and the
6 individual adds something positive to the quiddity of the species, then according to
7 that thing [the individual] would not be perfectly known through the idea of the
8 species, but [would be perfectly known] through an idea proper [to it].[91]

This rather tortuous argument is an attempt to show that, if the individual is perfectly known through the idea of a species, then the individual adds nothing positive to the species **[19**.1–2**]**. This is Henry's view. Scotus's view is that the individual adds something positive to the species; and this yields the contrapositive of Henry's argument, and thus that the individual is not perfectly known through the idea of a species **[19**.5–8**]**. Rather, individuals must be known 'according to their proper notions', that is, 'through proper and distinct ideas of them'.[92]

Since Scotus holds that ideas are fundamentally thought-objects produced by the divine mind, in themselves independent of, and prior too, all divine external activity, this entails that God has ideas of all possible individuals. But he later makes the point more explicitly, and he does so for both his own notion of an idea as a thought-object, and for his opponents' notion of an idea as a relation of imitability. First, Scotus's own view:

[20]
1 There is a distinct ... idea ... of every positive thing other than God, whether it can
2 be made in itself, or in another, whether relational or non-relational. ... If an idea is

---

[89] See Henry, *Quod.* 5.8 (Paris, II, 166M); for a discussion of Henry's position, see Stephen F. Brown, 'Henry of Ghent (b. ca. 1217; d. 1293)', 195–219. Presumably Henry would claim that possible individuals are simply more or less loosely specified combinations of different common natures, essential and accidental. Henry makes more or less this point in the passage cited in n. 96 below.

[90] Scotus, *Ord.* 2.3.1.2, n. 51 (Vatican, VII, 414–15; Spade, 70).

[91] Scotus, *Rep.* 1A.36.3–4, n. 40 (Noone, 439).

[92] Ibid., n. 39 (Noone, 439).

3 posited to be a thought-object (*obiectum cognitum*) – which I believe to be
4 Augustine's intention – it is clear that any positive thing (in whatever way it has
5 existence) has in itself a proper and distinct idea in God. For from the fact that it is a
6 known object, whatever is an object distinctly knowable by God has a distinct idea.
7 But any of the things mentioned – whether it can be made in itself, or in another,
8 whether non-relational or relational – is an object distinctly knowable by the divine
9 intellect, for it is a perfection in our intellect that it can know all of these as distinct
10 knowable things. Therefore all or each of them has a proper and distinct idea.[93]

Ideas are (divine) internal thought objects [**20**.2–3]. God has ideas of all positive things – substance (a thing 'made in itself'), accidents (things made 'in another'), and relations [**20**.1–2, 7–8]. Crucially, real existence makes no difference to the extent to which something can be known: God knows any possible object '*in whatever way it has existence*', and thus whether real or not [**20**.4–5]. Equally, Scotus's concern here is not merely with actual objects – things that are made – but with possible objects – things that 'can be made' [**20**.7]. This requires God to have ideas of all possible individuals.

Scotus argues on behalf of his opponents that their view about the divine ideas – as relations of imitability – also entails that God has ideas of (possible) individuals: presumably on the assumption that Henry's double-negation theory of individuation is false:

[**21**]
1 To whatever objects, howsoever many, a created intellect can compare the divine
2 essence as imitable by them (since this is a perfection in it), to as many the divine
3 intellect can compare itself. But our intellect can compare the divine essence to every
4 positive thing, whether it be a whole or a part, absolute or relational, as more or less
5 imitable by them. Therefore the divine intellect can do the same. ... And if it can ...
6 compare itself, as imitable in various ways, to all things thus distinctly knowable, it
7 does distinctly compare itself.[94]

Suppose an idea is not a thought-object but a relation of imitability.[95] In this case God's intellect can compare his essence, as imitable, to any positive entity [**21**.5–7]. But Scotus clearly understands all positive entity to include all possible individuals, whether or not actual.

6 God's Knowledge of Real (Extramental) Objects

How does God know contingent things? How does he know which of all possible objects actually exists, and (since no creature is identical with its life-story) what the life-stories of existent things are? The problem is a general one, but it is nicely exemplified by that of God's knowledge of future contingents. One theory Scotus suggests – associated with Bonaventure and Henry – is that God knows such facts

---

[93] Ibid., nn. 46–7 (Noone, 441).

[94] Ibid., n. 49 (Noone, 441–2).

[95] Ibid., n. 48 (Noone, 441).

since they are simply built in to the divine ideas.[96] Another – clearly intended to be Aquinas's view – is that God knows these things by 'seeing' them as present to his eternity.[97] Scotus rejects both of these views. The view of Bonaventure and Henry does not, Scotus believes, allow for contingency. After all, as Scotus presents it, the production of divine ideas is necessary.[98] Against Aquinas, Scotus holds that, if God's seeing contingent creatures is a sufficient explanation of God's knowledge of them, it follows that God's knowledge is caused by creatures, and thus that God fails to be wholly unconditioned:

[22]
1 According to this position, things actually existing and coexisting with the 'now' of
2 eternity would cause determinate certitude, so that, with the things themselves present,
3 both the view (*aspectus*) is certain, and the intellect is made certain by this, and for
4 this reason is demeaned.[99]

Temporal things are somehow all present to divine eternity [**22**.1–2]. God sees things 'as they are' ('the view is certain'), and for this reason has certain knowledge of things as they are [**22**.3]. The fact that the external things are the cause of God's knowledge [**22**.2] 'demeans' God's intellect [**22**.4]. Nothing in God can be caused by anything external to him.

Scotus's own belief is that contingent things are the result of the free determination of God's will, and thus God's knowledge of contingent things is the result of his knowledge of the free determinations of his will:

[23]
1 Every act of the intellect, which in God precedes that act of will, is merely natural and
2 not formally free, and consequently, whatever he understands prior to any act of the
3 will is merely natural. Therefore the divine intellect, merely naturally apprehending
4 the terms of some future contingent complex (*complexionis*) is indifferent, or in itself
5 neutral, for it does not conceive the truth of some complex other than one whose truth
6 is included in the definitions of the terms, or which follows necessarily from the truth
7 of some complex knowledge (*notitiae complexae*). But [the divine intellect], as
8 neutral about it, offers the terms of a future contingent complex to the will; the terms
9 of the future contingent do not include knowledge of the contingent complex, for the
10 terms are not the cause of this truth, for then it would be an immediate truth. And for
11 this reason the divine intellect has only neutral understanding of such terms prior to an
12 act of the will, just as my intellect is neutral on this complex: whether the stars are
13 even or odd [in number]. When, however, the intellect offers these complexes to the
14 will, the will can freely elect or not elect the union of these terms, or the conjunction

---

[96] Ibid. 1A.38.1–2, n. 30 (Söder, 232); see Bonaventure, *In Sent.* 1.35.1 (I, 601[ab]); Henry, *Quod.* 9.2 (Macken, XIII, 28–33).

[97] Scotus, *Rep.* 1A.38.1–2, nn. 14–15 (Söder, 227–8); see Aquinas, *ST* 1.14.13 c (I/1, 87[a]). It may be that Aquinas's 'vision' language here is merely a way of drawing attention to the fact that the things known are external to God, and not a way of providing him with an additional cognitive mechanism in such a case. It is the putative additional mechanism that Scotus subjects to criticism.

[98] Scotus, *Rep.* 1A.38.1–2, n. 31 (Söder, 232).

[99] Ibid., n. 24 (Söder, 230). Scotus has other worries about Aquinas's position too, which I deal with in the next section of this chapter.

15 of these terms and the division of those, such as Socrates or Peter to be beatified,
16 Judas however to be reprobated and not joined but rather divided from beatitude. And in
17 the same instant (and not before) in which the divine will wills Peter to be joined to
18 beatitude, this is primarily true, 'Peter will be beatified.' And thus every such
19 contingent [complex] is true, because its truth is primarily caused through an act of the
20 divine will, and it is not that the will wills it to be true because [it is] true, but rather
21 *vice versa*. And for this reason, when the truth caused in complexes of such terms is
22 determined by an act of will, the divine intellect then first knows one part of a
23 contradiction of contingents to be true.[100]

The 'complexes' Scotus is talking about are combinations of divine thought-objects, and it is tempting to translate the term as 'proposition' (indeed, I would have done so had I been able to think of a way of doing so while remaining syntactically close to Scotus's Latin). The idea is that the intellect necessarily ('naturally') combines terms in any way possible [**23**.1–5]. Analytic truths and necessary consequences of such truths the intellect knows automatically [**23**.5–7]. But for all other propositions, the intellect offers contradictory pairs of such propositions (*p*; not-*p*: the subject and predicate respectively 'joined' and 'divided') to the will. The will then freely selects one of the pair for actualization [**23**.13–16]. It is this free actualization that makes the contingent propositions true [**23**.18–20]. Prior to this free act of the divine will, the intellect does not know which ones are true, and which ones are false, since the relevant truth-making condition is absent [**23**.10–13]. The 'instants' which Scotus refers to are not, of course, distinct temporal instants, but stages in a logical sequence. The claim in [**23**.16–18, 21–23] is that the intellect's knowledge of the truth of the relevant propositions is an immediate consequence of the will's free decision to make some of them true, and some false.

Thus far, it looks as though Scotus is committed to God's knowing not external objects but merely intelligible or willed objects within his own mind. But Scotus's position is a little more complex than this. For Scotus, to know an object external to the mind is for a representation of the object to exist in the mind. By (causing) representations of contingent realities, God knows these things. God knows facts; and to do this, he needs thoughts. But this does not entail that it is his own thoughts that he knows; what he knows are the facts: real, extramental objects. Scotus does not always make this clear, but I think it can be inferred from some things that he says about God's knowledge of tensed facts. (I will return in a moment to the whole question of God's knowledge of temporal facts as such.) Basically, Scotus wants God to be able to distinguish between past, present, and future events. The way that Scotus envisages this happening is by different real relations between thought-objects (in the divine mind) and the divine mind itself. Suppose, to use Scotus's example, God creates the soul of the Antichrist at t. God knows that, at t_{-n} he is going to create this soul, and that, at t, he actually creates it. Scotus distinguishes these in terms of two distinct real relations in the soul of the Antichrist, one of 'going to be created', possessed at t_{-n} (at which time the soul is merely a possible being with so-called 'objective' potency, as the *object* of some power); and one of 'being created', possessed at t_n. This latter is a relation possessed by the Antichrist's soul 'as actually

---

[100] Ibid., n. 37 (Söder, 233–4).

existing',[101] and Scotus elsewhere clearly implies that actually existing things have the real relation of being known by God.[102] This makes Scotus an indirect realist on the question of God's knowledge: he knows external objects simply by knowing directly his own internal thought-objects.[103]

7 God's Knowledge of Temporal Facts

It is important to grasp that divine knowledge of (future) contingents, as usually understood, does not entail knowledge of tensed facts. The reason is that some theologians believe God to be timeless. These theologians usually claim that the whole of time is directly accessible to a timeless God, and that God thus knows temporal facts by, as it were, seeing them. On this view, since God directly knows things as they actually are, the whole of time is extramentally actual. This entails that God cannot know *tensed* facts, or any facts that require the one who knows them to have a temporal location – though it does not, of course, prevent God knowing the temporal *order* of events: that some things happen before others, and that some things are simultaneous.

As I noted above, Scotus objects to Aquinas's account of God's knowledge of future contingents on the grounds that, if this account provides a sufficient explanation, then God's knowledge is caused by things external to himself. But Scotus has other objections too, and these relate to the theory of God's relation to time implied in Aquinas's account. Scotus rightly understands that Aquinas's account entails that all of time is equally actual, and his main objection is simply that God cannot be present to things that do not exist (such as past and future):

[24]
1 I do not hold this, and I argue similarly against them about eternity as about
2 immensity: God through his immensity is not present to a place other than that which
3 actually exists. Therefore, similarly, God does not coexist, through the 'now' of
4 eternity, with any part of time other than the 'now' of the present time.[104]

If only the present is actual, then there is (now) no other part of time with which God timelessly coexists. Conversely, if the soul of the Antichrist (to use Scotus's example) is present to God, then the soul of the Antichrist must (now) exist: and this, of course, is false.[105] Overall, the objection is that, if Aquinas's view is right, there will not be facts about the future at all, because nothing will be really future.[106]

---

[101] Scotus, *Ord.* 1.30.1–2, n. 41 (Vatican, VI, 187–8).

[102] Scotus, *Rep.* 1A.38.1–2, n. 24 (Söder, 230); compare *Ord.* 1.39.1–5, *text. int.* (Vatican, VI, 410, l. 15–p. 411, l. 1).

[103] As I made clear above, Scotus's account of cognition tends distinctly towards some sort of indirect realism, since he does not find the available direct realist theories satisfactory. But in contrast to creaturely knowledge, God's knowledge is wholly and directly caused by God himself. A creature's knowledge is at least in part caused by the external object.

[104] Scotus, *Rep.* 1A.38.1–2, n. 20 (Söder, 229).

[105] Ibid., n. 22 (Söder, 229).

[106] Ibid., n. 23 (Söder, 229–30).

Scotus's point is not that the future states of affairs need to be future for God – as we shall see, Scotus holds that God is timeless. What he is arguing is that if the states are really present to God, and as present to God as the present instant is, then all facts are really and tenselessly actual. And this Scotus believes to be false. The problem with Scotus's view is that the view that God coexists with different times successively – entailed by the claims in **[24**.3–4**]** – seems inconsistent with his timelessness, since it entails at the very least that God undergoes the 'merely Cambridge' change of existing first with one set of things, and later with another. As a result of this, it may be that Scotus's overall view ultimately turns out to be inconsistent.

Nevertheless, what Scotus in effect replaces all of this with is a claim that all of time is tenselessly actual, but not *really* or extramentally so; it is actual *merely* as a thought-object or collection of thought-objects in the divine mind. (The present, of course, is actual in some other way too; but that is another issue.) These thought-objects are in fact eternal, just as God is, but they include in their content representations of temporal relations. God knows the temporal relations between different events, since he can ascribe time-indices to the different items of knowledge, and know thus that some are before others (e.g. knowledge that the soul of the Antichrist is created at t, and not-yet created at t_{-n}). God's knowledge may be a perfect representation of all that there is, but it is not temporally fleeting in the way that extramental created objects are.

In effect, Scotus has severed relations of accessibility between God and time: God does not 'see' things at all, and the way that he knows temporal things, external to himself, is by inspecting his own cognitive and volitional states. Scotus thus exploits his indirect realism here to allow both for God to be timeless and for past, present, and future to be, *in different ways*, real (that is to say, not in such a way that the whole of time is equally actual). This does not mean that God does not coexist with his creatures, according to Scotus: God coexists with every time, successively.[107] But what this means, presumably, is not that God has successive relations to them, simply that they have successive relations to him.

Scotus's view makes God timeless and denies that creation is directly cognitively accessible to him. The advantage of Scotus's denial of accessibility, as he sees it, is that it allows him to accept both divine timelessness and the reality of past, present, and future, since his view – unlike that of Aquinas – does not commit him to the equivalent real actuality of all time.[108] Past, present, and future are all actual as

---

[107] See Scotus, *Ord.* 1.9.un., n. 17 (Vatican, IV, 336).

[108] Scotus is clearly supposing that Aquinas's account entails that all of time is equally actual, and thus that (distinctions between) past, present, and future are unreal. One modern commentator who agrees is William Lane Craig: see his *The Problem of Divine Foreknowledge of Future Contingents from Aristotle to Suarez*, 116–18. It seems to me that there is plenty of evidence to show that Scotus wants to be committed to the reality of tensed time; it is less clear to me that he has a successful account of it, however: on this see my *The Physics of Duns Scotus*, ch. 13; though see now, for a convincing case to the contrary, Neil Lewis, 'Space and Time', 83–7. Note that I no longer accept the reading offered in my 'Duns Scotus on Eternity and Timelessness': not that Scotus's God is not timeless, but that he does not coexist in such a way as to give him direct cognitive access to the universe. In the article, I supposed that, according to Scotus, God's knowledge of time required him to have some kind of access to the created universe. According to Scotus, however, God knows this universe, but not by direct inspection of it.

thought-objects; only the present is really actual, but this actuality has no bearing on God's knowledge of temporal facts.[109]

8 Divine Simplicity and God's Cognitive and Appetitive Activity

I deal at length with the question of divine simplicity in chapter 6 below. I shall discuss there, for example, the relationship between God and his intellect and will. But here I would like to mention one issue that seems to create problems for Scotus's account of the contingency of free divine decisions. Scotus holds that all divine acts of knowledge and will are identical with God. I take it that he means not only the items with *esse intentionale* but the real bearers of such contents. (In a creature, it would be odd to claim that the intentional items were real things over and above the intellect that includes them, but not at all odd to claim that the real accidental bearers of such items were real things over and above the substance that includes them. I dealt with this distinction above.) The seventh conclusion of *De primo principio*'s chapter 4, for example, runs as follows:

[25]
1 No knowledge can be an accident of the first nature. It is proved: for that first nature
2 is shown to be in itself the first producer; therefore it has of itself, excluding
3 everything else, the ability to cause any causable thing, at least as first cause of that
4 causable thing. But if we exclude its knowledge, it does not have the ability to cause
5 that thing. Therefore the knowledge of anything is not other than its nature.[110]

The assumption is that the first cause can only cause consciously, and Scotus goes on to spend some time reminding us of his proof for this from the coincidence of efficient and final causation in God.[111] The argument in **[25]** does not make a strong identity claim. All Scotus is suggesting is that all of God's knowledge is necessary to him. For the argument is that the first producer has in itself the power to cause **[25**.2–4]. Suppose this agent's knowledge were somehow not included in the description of what this agent is. Since the first agent cannot cause other than knowingly, this would entail – absurdly – that the first agent could not cause **[25**.4–5].

Scotus tries in various ways to show that what is true of one sort of knowledge must be true of all the sorts of knowledge that the first agent has. Thus:

---

[109] See Scotus, *Ord.* 1.30.1–2, n. 42 (Vatican, VI, 188). Here, an objector wants God to have knowledge of something he does now. Scotus deflects this by saying that God knows what he does at *t*. I am not sure whether Scotus is claiming that there is a group of facts (tensed ones) that God simply cannot know, or whether he believes that God's knowledge of what happens at given times is sufficient to allow God knowledge of tensed facts. If the latter, he is clearly mistaken. Supposing the former, there is one clear disadvantage of Scotus's account against Aquinas's. Aquinas has simply to deny that there are tensed facts. Scotus does not have to deny this (an advantage!), but the disadvantage is that there is a set of facts – tensed facts – that God does not know.

[110] Scotus, *DPP* 4, nn. 11–12 (Wolter, 97 (¶¶ 4.33–4.34)).

[111] Ibid., n. 12 (Wolter, 97 (¶ 4.34)).

[26]
1 All the intellections of the same intellect have a similar relation to the intellect,
2 whether according to essential or accidental identity. This is clear of any created
3 intellect, which is shown: for they [viz. the intellections] all seem to be perfections of
4 the same kind; therefore if some are received [into a subject] they all are, and if some [one]
5 is an accident, then every one is an accident. But some cannot be an accident in the
6 first [nature]; therefore none [can].[112]

Scotus's point is that occurrent acts of thought are all the same sort of thing
[26.3–4], and therefore have the same sort of relation to their intellect **[26.1–2]**.
Being an accident and *being received into a subject* are different ways of naming
the same relation, and the argument is that if, for one agent, one act of thought is an
accident, then all that agent's acts of thought are accidents; conversely, if one fails
to be an accident, then they all do **[26.4–6]**. Since according to **[25]** some of the first
nature's occurrent acts of thought fail to be accidents **[26.5–6]**, none is an accident.

Scotus argues likewise for acts of will. The most interesting is an unashamed
piece of perfect-being theology:

[27]
1 Since the highest perfection of any being in first act consists in the second act by
2 which it is conjoined to what is best – especially if it is operative, and not merely
3 productive. But every intellectual being is operative, and the first nature is intellectual
4 (from the first [conclusion of chapter 4]), so it follows that its highest perfection is in
5 second act. Therefore if that is not its substance, its substance is not the best, for
6 something else is best for it.[113]

The assumptions here are Aristotelian and teleological: things are such that they act
in certain specified ways, and acting in these ways is what perfects things' natures.
To be in first act is simply to have a particular kind of nature; second act is *activity*.
Thus, second act is perfective of a nature **[27.1–2]**. Teleological goals are
understood in terms of the inclinations of a substance (for a certain sort of goal)
[27.2], and in intellectual substances such inclinations are free and voluntary –
associated, in other words, with will. The properly cognitive and appetitive acts of
an intellectual substance do not result in the production of anything: they are simply
and irreducibly operations – internal acts. Having this kind of perfective second act
is, it seems, better than having productivity as a perfective second act **[27.2–3]**.
Thus, the perfection of an intellectual substance is whatever act it is that joins it to
its goal **[27.3–5]**. This second act cannot be distinct from the first nature, for then
the nature would not be the best conceivable: its perfection would be something
distinct from it, over and above the nature itself **[27.5–6]**. So the beatific operation
of the first nature must be essential to it: the first nature must always have an
occurrent act of self-love.

Still, all of this raises a problem. I showed above that Scotus believes some divine
willing to be contingent, and thus too some divine knowledge to be contingent. How
can this be if all divine acts are somehow essential? Scotus himself raises this

112 Ibid. (¶ 4.35).
113 Ibid., n. 11 (Wolter, 95 (¶ 4.30)).

problem in the context of his discussion of God's contingent causation: if God's knowledge of what is produced is 'in' him, then it must be necessary, not contingent. His reply is revealing:

[28]
1 I say that something can be in God in two ways: either formally, or objectively. What
2 is in God in the first way is, in real entity, necessarily God. What is in God in the
3 second way is not necessarily in him, for such is a secondary object in him. Whence
4 the act [of knowledge] neither requires nor presupposes such an object, and for this
5 reason a divine act, whether understanding or willing, is necessary with respect to the
6 first object, but not necessary with respect to, or by reason of, a secondary
7 object.[114]

The first contrast here is between something real (here 'formal') and something merely 'objective' – merely an object of thought. Amongst 'real' things here we can doubtless include real mental acts, but not the (merely mental) *contents* of those acts. The contents of mental acts are things that have merely *objective* existence as thought-objects [28.1–3]. A second contrast is between the first object of God's cognitive acts – the divine essence – and secondary objects of God's cognitive acts – creaturely essences [28.5–7]. God's essence is a real thing, and thus God's self-knowledge has a real object, really identical with God himself [28.4–6]. But secondary objects known by God have merely objective existence, and nothing real in God is affected by the identity of such objects [28.2–3]. Thus the identity of divine cognitive and volitional acts is not (it seems) affected by their contents [28.4]. Neither are any such acts necessitated merely by their objects [28.6–7]. So God can have contingent mental contents without the identity of the mental acts, whose objects such contents are, being in any way affected.[115]

9 Morality and the Divine Will

As we saw above, Scotus holds that everything that God causes is caused contingently. Part of his reason for this has to do with his seeing God as the only ultimate goal of activity:

[29]
1 Something is willed necessarily only if it is that without which that which is willed
2 about the goal cannot remain. God loves himself as goal, and whatever he loves
3 concerning himself as goal can remain if nothing other than himself exists, for what is
4 necessary of itself depends on nothing. Therefore from his volition [viz. of himself]
5 he does not will anything else necessarily; therefore neither does he cause
6 necessarily.[116]

---

[114] Scotus, *Rep.* 1A.39–40.1–3, n. 70 (Söder, 260).
[115] On this, see too the discussion in Scotus, *Ord.* 1.10.un., *text. int.* (Vatican, IV, 356, l. 13–p. 357, l. 21).
[116] Scotus, *DPP* 4, n. 9 (Wolter, 91 (¶ 4.25)); see too e.g. Scotus, *Ord.* 3.37.un., n. 4 (Wadding, VII, 879; *WM*, 275).

God, as necessary of himself, is wholly independent **[29**.4**]**. His act of love for himself thus depends on nothing other than himself, having nothing other than himself as a necessary condition **[29**.2–4**]**. So God does not require anything else, and his willing of everything else is thus contingent **[29**.1–2, 4–5**]**. So every external causal activity of God's is contingent **[29**.5–6**]**.

Scotus understands this in the strongest way possible. He supposes not only that the fact of divine external activity is contingent; he supposes that there are no constraints other than logical on what God can do. This has consequences for God's goodness. I do not want to dwell long on this, since it relates more to Scotus's views about morality than to his account of the divine nature as such. Basically, Scotus believes that whatever God wills for creatures, with the exception of commands and prohibitions that have God as their object, is just or right in virtue of being willed by God. God is a sufficient source of moral goodness by commanding and prohibiting,[117] and with the exception of commands and prohibitions related to creatures' dealings with God, God's choices are unrestricted.

[30]
1 Whatever God knows prior to the act of his will, he knows necessarily and naturally,
2 such that there is no contingency to opposites. In God there is no practical knowledge,
3 since if before the act of his will his intellect were to understand something as 'to be
4 done' or 'to be produced', the will would either will this necessarily, or not
5 necessarily. If necessarily, then it would be necessitated to producing the act; if not
6 necessarily, then it would will against the dictate of the intellect, and thus be bad
7 (since that dictate cannot but be right).[118]

If, prior to any act of his will, there were any obligations placed on God (if God had 'practical knowledge') with regard to the actions he directs towards creatures, then either God would be bound to will them, or he would not be so bound **[30**.2–5**]**. In the first case God would fail to be free with regard to his creature-directed actions **[30**.5**]**. And this would make his actions dependent on the natures of creatures; which in turn would mean that God failed to be wholly unconditioned – such that he could not be affected by anything external to him. But, given that God has no passive potencies,[119] this contradicts **[29]**, according to which every divine creature-directed action is contingent. In the second case, God could will against some of his obligations – and this really would make him bad **[30**.5–7**]**. But, just as (for the medievals) it is impossible for God to be affected by anything external to himself, so it is impossible for him to act badly. So there cannot be any obligations placed on God – with regard to the actions he directs towards creatures – prior to any act of his will. I take it that the way Scotus sets up the disjunction – lack of freedom versus (moral) badness – entails that there really are no restrictions on how God can behave to his creatures in relation to these creature-directed actions, and thus that he can command creatures as he will, at least with regard to their behaviour towards each

---

[117] Though, as I have argued elsewhere, not a necessary one, even in relation to the moral obligations binding creatures in their relations to other creatures: see my *Duns Scotus*, 90–1.

[118] Scotus, *Lect.* 1.39.1–5, n. 43 (Vatican, XVII, 492; Vos, 104–6).

[119] On this, see chapters 2 and 6 in this Part.

other. If God were to do so, he would still be just, of course; the whole point of **[30]** is to preserve divine justice.

With regard to Godward aspects of creatures' moral duties, however, the case is rather different: God's nature is an automatic source of moral obligation:

[31]
1 I say that some things can be said to belong to the law of nature in two ways. One way
2 is as first practical principles known from their terms or as conclusions necessarily
3 entailed by them. These are said to belong to the law of nature in the strictest sense,
4 and there can be no dispensation in their regard. ... The precepts of the first table of
5 the decalogue regard God immediately as their object. Indeed, the first two, if they be
6 understood in a purely negative sense – viz. 'You shall have no other gods before me'
7 and 'You shall not take the name of the Lord your God in vain' (i.e. you should show
8 no irreverence to God) – belong to the natural law, taking law of nature strictly, for this
9 follows necessarily: 'If God exists, then he alone should be loved as God'. It likewise
10 follows that nothing else must be worshipped as God, nor must any irreverence be
11 shown to him. Consequently, God could not dispense in regard to these so that
12 someone could do the opposite of what this or that prohibits.[120]

God is the ultimate goal of all activity – even his own. The key claim is that the inference from God's existence to God's alone being such that he should be loved as God is logically necessary **[31.1–3, 9–11]**. Here a factual claim straightforwardly entails an evaluative one, as on standard natural law theories; hence the commands of the first table of the decalogue 'belong to natural law, taking law of nature strictly' **[31.3–4, 8]**.

Scotus holds, then, that the content of all moral precepts and prohibitions other than those contained in the first table of the decalogue is (or can be) wholly determined by God. This basically deontological line of thought does not help deal with the problem of God's cooperation with sin. Given that God has determined that certain courses of action are sinful (e.g. indiscriminate killing of the innocent), and given that God is an immediate partial cause of all free human actions, how can we avoid the claim that God, in partially causing (e.g.) indiscriminate acts of killing the innocent, thereby sins? As we saw above, Scotus wants to be able to say that God's action is necessary but not sufficient for the sin. As Scotus sees it, God permits sinful actions, and actively wills this permission even though the sinful action is something that God actively wills against. And this active willing (of his permission) is a good that 'trumps' God's willing against the sinful action.[121] Antonie Vos and his 'Research Group Duns Scotus' have argued, plausibly, that the reason why permission of a sinful action is a good is the preservation of human freedom.[122]

---

[120] Scotus, *Ord.* 3.37.un., n. 6 (Wadding, VII, 645; *WM*, 277); see also Ibid., 3.27.un., n. 2 (Wadding, VII, 645; *WM*, 425).

[121] Scotus, *Ord.* 1.47.un., nn. 7–9 (Vatican, VI, 383–4; *DSDL* 181–3).

[122] See A. Vos and others, *Duns Scotus on Divine Love: Texts and Commentary on Goodness and Freedom, God and Humans*, 188–9.

Chapter 5

Divine Infinity

Generally, Scotus prioritizes the notion of infinity over that of simplicity: that is to say, he believes that divine infinity explains divine simplicity. But some of his proofs for divine infinity require one claim about divine simplicity, namely that there is some sense in which the attributes of the supreme nature are the same as it is: specifically, as Scotus sees it, God's knowledge needs to be identical with his essence. I explained this requirement at the end of the previous chapter. Scotus refrains from labelling the first being 'God' until the proof of the infinity of this being: again, I take it, a sign of the importance Scotus accords to this notion.[1] As we shall see in chapter 6 §4, a great deal of Scotus's distinctive account of divine simplicity is argued for on the basis of divine infinity too.

1 Arguments for Divine Infinity

Scotus proposes no fewer than seven very detailed and complex arguments for divine infinity, the ninth conclusion of book 4 of *De primo principio*, and by far the largest single portion of book 4. Scotus thinks of this ninth conclusion as 'most fertile', because it 'would have made evident many of the conclusions mentioned earlier'[2] – and, indeed, entails 'every kind of simplicity', as the tenth conclusion of *De primo principio*, chapter 4, has it.[3] I discuss here the two arguments that seem to me most significant, namely the first and the last.

The key first argument reasons from the omniscience of the first cause:

[1]
1 Are there not ... infinite intelligibles, and [are these not] actually in an intellect that
2 actually understands everything? Therefore that intellect that actually understands all
3 things at once is infinite. Such, our God, is your [intellect]. ... Therefore the nature
4 with which the intellect is the same is infinite.
5 I show the antecedent and the consequent of this enthymeme. The antecedent:
6 there can be no end of whatever things are potentially infinite (that is, taking one after
7 the other); if all those things are actually simultaneous, they are actually infinite [in
8 number]. But intelligibles are like this with respect to a created intellect, as is clear,
9 and in your [intellect] all things – which are intelligible by a created [intellect]

---

[1] See e.g. Scotus, *DPP* 4, n. 36 (Wolter, 143 (¶ 4.84)), and **[1.3]** below. For helpful accounts of Scotus on infinity, see William A. Frank and Allan B. Wolter (eds and trans.), *Duns Scotus, Metaphysician*, 151–5, and Francis J. Catania, 'John Duns Scotus on *Ens Infinitum*'. Catania gives a useful bibliography on the topic.
[2] Scotus, *DPP* 4, n. 15 (Wolter, 103 (¶ 4.47)).
[3] Ibid., n. 31 (Wolter, 135 (¶ 4.75)).

10 successively – are actually simultaneously understood. Therefore there are there [viz. in your
11 intellect] actually infinitely many things understood.
12 I prove the major of this syllogism, though it seems sufficiently evident, for all
13 such things that can be taken, when they are existent simultaneously, are either
14 actually infinite, or actually finite. But if they are actually finite, then by taking them
15 one after the other, at some time all can be taken. Therefore, if they cannot all be
16 actually taken, then if they are actual simultaneously, they are actually infinite.
17 I thus prove the consequent of the enthymeme: when a greater number requires
18 or entails greater perfection than a lesser one, then numerical infinity entails infinite
19 perfection. An example: to be able to carry ten things requires greater perfection of
20 motive force than to be able to carry five things [does]; therefore to be able to carry
21 infinite things entails infinite motive force. Therefore in the case at hand, since to be
22 able simultaneously to understand two things distinctly entails a greater perfection of
23 the intellect than to be able to understand just one, the proposed conclusion follows.
24 I prove this last: in order to understand distinctly some intelligible, application
25 is required, and the determined conversion of the intellect; therefore, if [the intellect]
26 can be applied to many, it is not limited by any of them; and thus if applicable to
27 infinitely many is not at all limited.[4]

As Scotus has already made clear, the intellect that actually understands everything at once is God's [**1.3**].[5] The point of the claim is that God's knowledge is all occurrent: he thinks of (and understands) everything all at once. The 'enthymeme' that Scotus refers to in [**1.5, 17**] is this:

Antecedent: God's intellect simultaneously understands infinitely many intelligible objects [**1.1–2**].
Consequent: God's intellect is infinitely perfect [**1.2–3**].

[**1.5–16**] is taken up with a proof of the antecedent; [**1.17–27**] with showing what further premiss needs to be added in order to entail the consequent. Proving the antecedent is, for Scotus, entirely a matter of showing that there are actually infinitely many intelligibles. The relevant contrast is with the *potential* infinite. According to Aristotle, an *actual* infinity is impossible: however many things we count, we can always count more.[6] But the fact that we can always count more means that there is no limit to the number of things we can count: in this sense, the infinite is *possible*. Scotus starts from the fact that the potential infinite means that there are no limits to what can be counted, and supposes – against Aristotle – that it makes sense to think of the set of such things as completed, and thus as actually infinite [**1.5–8**]. The number of things that can be understood is infinite, and if potentially so by a created intellect, then actually so by the divine intellect [**1.8–11**].
There is a problem here, getting from the potential to the actual infinite [**1.6–8**] (the 'major premiss' [**1.12**] of the proof of the antecedent in [**1.1–2**]; the minor premiss is [**1.8**], that intelligibles are (at least) potentially infinite). Scotus attempts to deal with the problem by raising the following consideration. Take the whole set

[4] Ibid., n. 15 (Wolter, 103 (¶ 4.48)).
[5] Ibid., n. 11 (Wolter, 97 (¶ 4.33)).
[6] See chapter 3 above on this, and below for a more detailed discussion.

of potentially infinite things. Either this set contains finitely many or infinitely many members **[1.12–14]**. But the test of finitude is that the process of counting can come to an end **[1.14–15]**. If such a process could not come to an end, then there are infinitely many members of the set **[1.15–16]**. What Scotus is trying to get at is that the fact that there is no process of counting an infinite set that could be completed is not itself an argument against the possibility of an infinite set. All it shows is that, if for some given set there is no such completable process, then that set has actually infinitely many members.

How does Scotus get from the antecedent of his enthymeme to its conclusion? He supposes that it is possible to speak in quantitative terms about qualitative perfections, and that a power is more perfect if it is capable of doing more things – indeed, he supposes that a power capable of doing infinitely many things (at once) is infinitely perfect. A cognitive power that knows infinitely many things is infinitely perfect **[1.17–23]**, and this is because its power is not determined or limited to a finite number of intelligible objects **[1.24–7]**. So any intellect which understands infinitely many objects is infinitely perfect, since the number of things actually understood is proportionate to the perfection of the intellect.

If there is a problem here it is that Scotus's inference of divine infinity from his quantification of qualitative powers requires these quantities to be globally proportional to each other (that is to say, every such quality must be proportional to every other such quality). It is hard, otherwise, to see what the force of calling divine attributes *infinite* might be. Scotus does not just mean 'unsurpassed', but 'unsurpassable', and in a very particular quantifiable way. I take it, too, that the infinity of the divine intellect entails that it is logically unsurpassable, since it would be logically impossible (according to Scotus) for anything to be greater than the infinite.

Setting this worry aside, Scotus does not deal with what strikes me as the most problematic inference: that from the infinite perfection of God's knowledge to the (unqualified) infinite perfection of the divine nature **[1.3–4]**. Scotus clearly thinks this inference is just obvious. But it seems to me that the metaphysics here is being made to do too much work. Suppose that God is the same as his attributes. What we mean, in this context, is that his attributes are not things over and above God. But the perfection of one of his attributes does not entail his unqualified perfection, and neither, on the face of it, does the infinity of one of his attributes entail his unqualified infinity.

The final argument for infinity proceeds from the notion of divine power. The starting point is Aristotle's attempt to prove the infinite power of the prime mover. According to Aristotle, the infinite power of the first mover can be inferred from its infinite (i.e. beginningless and endless) motion.[7] Scotus rejects this argument as it stands, since it does not follow from the fact that an agent can do the same thing a limitless number of times that its power at any one of those times is limitless: it could simply possess finite power for an indefinite period.[8] Scotus's preferred argument runs as follows:

---

[7] Scotus, *DPP* 4, n. 26 (Wolter, 125–7 (¶ 4.67)), referring to Aristotle, *Ph.* 8.10 (266ᵃ10–24, 266ᵇ6–20); *Metaph.* Λ.7 (1073ᵃ3–13).

[8] Scotus, *DPP* 4, n. 26 (Wolter, 127 (¶ 4.68)).

[2]
1 [The first cause] has eminently the causal power of any second cause, even proper to it
2 (though it is not proved that that [power] as possessed formally adds nothing to the
3 power as possessed eminently). Therefore [the first cause] simultaneously possesses
4 eminently all causality with respect to everything that can be effected, even infinitely
5 many – even though these be brought about successively. ... From this, I prove
6 infinity thus: if the first [cause] had all causality formally and simultaneously, it would
7 be infinite, even if all causable things could not be made to exist simultaneously, for
8 in so far as it is in itself, it could simultaneously [bring about] infinitely many. And to
9 be able to bring about many things simultaneously entails intensively greater power.
10 Therefore if it had [a power] more perfectly than if it had all causality formally,
11 intensive infinity would be more greatly entailed. But it has all [causality] totally,
12 which is in it more eminently than if it were in it formally. Therefore it is of
13 intensively infinite power.[9]

The basic claim here derives from Scotus's analysis of essentially ordered causal series. The second feature of such a series, as outlined in passage **[1]** of chapter 1, is that higher causes are more perfect than lower ones, in the sense that higher causes possess whatever is required in order to allow them to activate lower causes. And it is this relationship that Scotus is talking about when referring to the first cause possessing some power 'eminently' **[2.**1, 3, 4, 12**]**. Possessing a causal power 'formally' is simply possessing it, and Scotus's proof here does not require that the first cause actually *possess* all the causal powers of lower-order causes. What it does require is that possessing a causal power eminently is more perfect – or at least as perfect as – possessing it formally: it is more perfect for an agent *a* to be able to make something bring about an effect *e* than it is for *a* itself to be able to bring about *e* **[2.**10–12**]**. The first cause possesses all creaturely power eminently (since it stands at the head of every causal chain) **[2.**12**]**. Its power does not change as its circumstances change (it is wholly unconditioned). So it must always possess eminently all the powers ever possessed formally by creatures – even infinitely many, supposing that there will be infinitely many (possible kinds of?) creatures **[2.**3–5**]**. Now, it is clear that something that actually (formally) possessed all the infinitely many possible kinds of causal power would be infinitely powerful **[2.**5–7**]**. But possessing such powers eminently does not detract from the perfection of the power **[2.**10–11**]**. So something possessing such powers eminently is infinite in power **[2.**11–13**]**.

2 Omnipotence and Divine Infinity

The clarifications in **[2.**5, 7–8**]** have to do with the widespread Aristotelian assumption, mentioned above, that infinitely many things cannot exist at once. Scotus's point is that even if this is granted, it does not affect the argument. For his position is that God has the power sufficient to produce infinitely many effects at once, even though that power cannot, on the relevant Aristotelian assumption, ever be exercised. The points about formal possession of a power have to do with

---

[9] Ibid., n. 27 (Wolter, 129–31 (¶ 4.70)).

omnipotence. For Scotus's argument does not rely on the assumption that God *formally* possesses every causal power. Such a God would, as Scotus sees it, be omnipotent: able to bring about any effect directly, independent of any secondary cause. Scotus believes that God is omnipotent in this sense. But he does not believe that this omnipotence can be shown apart from revelation. First, we cannot infer omnipotence from some *a priori* understanding of the divine essence, since we have no such understanding.[10] Neither can we infer omnipotence from any of the conclusions of Scotus's cosmological argument. The basic reason is a perfect-being one. It is not clear that omnipotence, thus understood, is a perfection. Scotus considers an argument for omnipotence from God's eminent possession of all causal powers – an argument, in other words, from eminent to formal possession of power. Underlying the inference is the belief that lack of such formal power would entail imperfection: if eminent possession were inconsistent with formal possession, then eminent possession would entail imperfection. But imperfection cannot be a necessary condition for causal action as such; so perfect eminent possession of the power must entail formal possession of the power, and thus the power to cause immediately whatever the agent can cause mediately.[11] Scotus notes, however, that Aristotle would not accept this argument,[12] and offers on his behalf a reply:

[3]
1 When it is argued that imperfection is not required for causing, he would say that,
2 when I say 'cause immediately', I say two things, namely, causation (and that requires
3 perfection), and the mode or immediacy of causing (and that requires some added
4 imperfection). Therefore imperfection is required for immediately causing – not as the
5 basis for causing, but as a necessary condition in the agent. For where there is an
6 essential order, only what is in some way imperfect can be next to the least perfect, for
7 if the perfect were next to the least perfect it would be equally immediate to every
8 [member of the essential order] other than itself: and then there would be no essential
9 order, just as there would not be an essential order in the kinds of number if each
10 equally immediately succeeded unity.[13]

In short, we cannot tell merely from considerations engendered by a cosmological argument whether immediate causal contact with lowest effects is or is not a perfection. It is revelation that tells us that it is. The claim in [3] is that imperfection is not a necessary condition for causing as such; but that it may be a necessary condition for immediate causation [3.1–4]. Claiming that imperfection is not the 'basis' for causing is just a way of claiming that possession of a causal power is not itself an imperfection [3.4–5]. But this does not mean that immediate causation does not require some other imperfection in the agent: on the contrary, this 'Aristotelian' argument insists that it does [3.5]. [3.5–10] outlines the argument in favour of the Aristotelian view. The presupposition is that ordering in an essential order must be necessary, analogous to the way that the order of numbers is necessary. For the

---

[10] Scotus, *Quod.* 7, n. 11 (Wadding, XII, 175; Alluntis and Wolter, 169–70 (¶ 7.29)).
[11] Ibid., n. 19 (Wadding, XII, 179; Alluntis and Wolter, 175 (¶ 7.53)).
[12] Ibid. (Wadding, XII, 179; Alluntis and Wolter, 175 (¶ 7.54)).
[13] Ibid., n. 20 (Wadding, XII, 179; Alluntis and Wolter, 175–6 (¶ 7.55)); see too Ibid., n. 16 (Wadding, XII, 178; Alluntis and Wolter, 172–3 (¶ 7.43)).

argument in [**3.5–9**] is *modal*, not factual: if the first member of an essential order *could* be immediate to the final effect, then there would be, against the hypothesis, no essential order – just as there would be no numerical order if all numbers were (i.e. could be) equally close to the number one [**3.9–10**]. Of course, if God were omnipotent, then there would be no essential orders in the case that God exercised his power to cause directly. Scotus does not offer a reply to this potentially damaging argument.

An omnipotent God is one who could run a universe along entirely occasionalist principles, bringing about all effects directly. Scotus makes an important clarification: God could not bring about all effects directly in the sense that he could bring about any effect in the absence of every other effect. *Relations*, as Scotus notes, are effects that require other effects for their existence.[14] This doubtless places some constraints on the range of God's occasional power: God can sustain me directly, but he cannot cause breathing in me without air (breathing requires a relation between me and air); neither can God cause me to be sustained by air.

3 Infinity as an Intrinsic and Non-negative Feature of a Thing

Part of the significance of Scotus for the doctrine of divine infinity lies in his development of a novel account of what it is for something to be infinite. Aquinas, for example, proposes that infinity is simply the negation of intrinsic and extrinsic limits. Scotus rejects this view:

[4]
1 The proposed conclusion is demonstrated [by others] from the negation of an intrinsic
2 cause: for form is limited by matter; therefore that which cannot be in matter is
3 unlimited. I think this to be invalid, for according to them [viz. the defenders of this
4 argument] an immaterial angel is not unlimited. And existence (*esse*) – according to
5 them posterior to essence – will never limit essence. Whence any entity has an
6 intrinsic degree of perfection, not through some other thing. And there is [in this
7 argument] a fallacy of the consequent: if form is limited by matter, then it is not
8 limited without it [matter]. This is the fallacy of *Physics* III: body is limited by body;
9 therefore if [a body is] not limited by it [viz. body], it is unlimited; therefore the
10 outermost heaven will be infinite.[15] Because a body is primarily limited in itself, so
11 too a limited form is primarily limited in itself – that is, because such a nature is
12 among beings prior to its being limited by matter. For the second limitation
13 presupposes the first; it does not cause it. Therefore in some instant of nature the
14 essence is limited; therefore it cannot be limited by existence; therefore in the second
15 instant of nature it is not limited by existence.[16]

The term that I translated as 'unlimited' is '*infinitum*', and likewise for 'limited' ('*finitum*'); I do this since we do not use 'finite' and 'infinite' as verbs, and verbal senses are required to make sense of the passage. That Aquinas is the target is made

---

[14] Ibid., n. 15 (Wadding, XII, 177; Alluntis and Wolter, 172 (¶ 7.41)).
[15] Aristotle, *Ph.* 3.4 (203ᵇ20–2).
[16] Scotus, *DPP* 4, n. 30 (Wolter, 133–35 (¶ 4.74)).

clear by [**4**.4–5, 13–15], where Scotus clearly intends to talk about the limitation that is distinctively ascribed by Aquinas to angels.[17] The basic argument in [**4**.1–3] is closely parallel to Aquinas's argument for divine infinity. According to Aquinas, the fact that form is limited by matter entails that an immaterial form is unlimited.[18] Scotus rejects this for two reasons: first, it seems to entail that any immaterial substance is infinite [**4**.3–4]. Secondly, the argument is invalid, of the form (p→q) → (not-p→not-q) [**4**.6–8]. Scotus goes on to give an example of a similarly fallacious argument diagnosed by Aristotle [**4**.8–10]. Scotus rejects too the position that he ascribes to Aquinas, that existence could limit essence [**4**.4–5, 13–14]. Scotus does not, of course, accept that an individual essence is in any way prior to existence: his argument is entirely *ad hominem*.[19] Suppose we hold that individual essence is prior to existence. Scotus's claim is that, in this case, essence is limited (individuated) prior to the very entity – existence – that is supposed to limit it [**4**.13–15]. The priority here is not temporal, of course; all that Scotus is asserting is a causal or explanatory priority. But this is sufficient for his purposes: on the view he is describing, the thing to be explained is prior to its explanation.

Scotus's preferred view is that limitation and its lack must be somehow intrinsic to the limited or unlimited things themselves: the explanations for these features must be simply the things themselves [**4**.10–12]. In line with this, Scotus proposes a new way of understanding infinity (and finitude) as an *intrinsic mode* of a substance or attribute. I deal with the general notion of intrinsic modes in chapter 6 below. But – relevant to the discussion here – Scotus's understanding of infinity as a (positive) intrinsic mode entails that he reject Aquinas's view that infinity is best thought of as a *lack* of limits.[20] Scotus's starting point is an Aristotelian account of the infinite as something only potentially real. The idea is that, however many things you have, or parts you have identified, there are always more to have or identify.[21] Scotus conducts a thought-experiment to try to spell out the notion of an actual infinity: all the parts taken at once:

[5]
1 Let us change the idea of the potentially infinite in quantity into the idea of the
2 actually infinite in quantity, if it could there be actual. For if the quantity of the

---

[17] See Aquinas, *ST* 1.7.2 c (I/1, 33ᵃ⁻ᵇ). In fact, Scotus's account here is hardly an accurate portrait of Aquinas's position, since Aquinas holds that essence limits *esse*, and not *vice versa*. On this, see n. 19 below.

[18] Aquinas, *ST* 1.7.1 c (I/1, 32ᵇ).

[19] It is of course a hugely moot point whether Aquinas held that there is a distinction between *individual* essence and existence, and if he did, in what sense he would accept that essence is *prior* to existence. I try to describe some of the difficulties in *The Metaphysics of the Incarnation*, 250–6. Whatever Aquinas's position, it is clear that an attempt to argue that subsistent *esse* is unlimited on the grounds that it is not limited by essence would admit of just the same criticism on *formal* grounds (namely, affirming the consequent) as the argument in [**4**.2–3].

[20] Though note that, early in his life, Scotus is happy to accept this view of the infinite: see Scotus, *In Metaph.* 2.4–6, n. 18 (St Bonaventure, III, 244).

[21] Scotus quotes Aristotle: 'The infinite is that whose quantity is such that, whatever is taken away, there is always more to take' (Scotus, *Quod.* 5, n. 2 (Wadding, XII, 118; Alluntis and Wolter, 108 (¶ 5.5))). I deal with the potential infinite in Scotus in my *The Physics of Duns Scotus*, ch. 7.

3 [potentially] infinite necessarily grew by taking part after part, so too we could
4 imagine taken at once (or to remain at once) all the parts that can be taken, and we
5 would have an actually infinite quantity, for it would be as great actually as it is
6 potentially.[22]

As Scotus understands it, an actually infinite magnitude is one that can be neither subtracted from nor added to [5.3–5]. Still, even such a quantitative infinite would be imperfect, in the sense that each part would be less than the whole. Since there is some sense in which a quantitative infinite is composed of its parts, it follows that such an infinite is composed of imperfect parts. Scotus thus proposes a further thought-experiment:

[6]
1 If we were to understand there to be, among beings, something actually infinite in
2 entity, that should be understood proportionately to the imagined actual infinite in
3 quantity, such that that being is said to be infinite that cannot be exceeded in entity by
4 anything, and that truly will have the feature of a whole, and of something perfect:
5 whole, for although the whole actually infinite in quantity lacks none of its parts, or no
6 part of such a quantity, nevertheless each part is outside the other, and thus the whole
7 is from imperfect things. But a being infinite in entity has nothing entitative 'outside'
8 in this way, for its totality does not depend on things imperfect in entity: for it is
9 whole in such a way that it has no extrinsic part (for then it would not be totally
10 whole). So although the actually infinite could be perfect in quantity – for it is lacking
11 nothing of the quantity, according to itself – nevertheless each part is lacking some of
12 the quantity, namely, that which is in another [part]: neither is it perfect in this way
13 [viz. quantitatively] unless each [part] of it is imperfect. But an infinite being is
14 perfect in such a way that neither it nor any of its [parts] lacks anything.[23]

Scotus proposes that we can assign quantitative measures to the degrees of perfections, and [6] describes what an infinite degree of a perfection would be like.[24] The infinity of an infinite being, for example, is analogous ('proportionate') to the infinity of an infinite quantity [6.1–3]: logically unsurpassable [6.3–4]. But it is unlike the quantitative infinite in various ways too: a quantitative infinite is made up of (infinitely many) parts finite in extent [6.6–7, 11–12]. This means that a quantitative infinite is neither fully perfect (since composed of quantitatively imperfect things [6.9–14]) nor fully 'whole' (for it has part outside part) [6.6–10]. An entitatively infinite thing, contrariwise, is fully perfect and fully whole [6.6–10, 13–14]. And there is a more general disanalogy between strictly quantitative and non-quantitative measures too: the degrees of a perfection are not additive. Rather, they are proportional to each other only in the sense that there is an order between the various degrees.[25] What this means is that God's infinity, as spelled out by Scotus, really amounts to no more than his logical unsurpassability.

---

[22] Scotus, *Quod.* 5, n. 2 (Wadding, XII, 118; Alluntis and Wolter, 109 (¶ 5.6)).

[23] Ibid., n. 3 (Wadding, XII, 118; Alluntis and Wolter, 109–10 (¶ 5.7)).

[24] For the degrees of a perfection or quality in Scotus, see my *The Physics of Duns Scotus*, ch. 10.

[25] Scotus, *Quod.* 5, n. 4 (Wadding, XII, 118–19; Alluntis and Wolter, 110–11 (¶ 5.9)).

Chapter 6

Divine Simplicity

The doctrine of divine simplicity is intended to rule out composition in God. Of course, what is ruled out very much depends on prior metaphysical assumptions about the ways in which things can be composed. For example, material substances are, on medieval views, composed of matter and substantial form; they are composed of extended bodily parts; and they can, according to medieval accounts, enter into composition with accidents. Equally, they seem to have various necessary or essential attributes that are in some way distinct from each other, and they seem subject to temporal processes that in at least some metaphysical analyses are understood to entail that material substances are composed of temporal parts. In what follows, I examine quickly Scotus's refutation of the claims that God could be composite in any of the first three ways, and then devote most of the rest of the chapter to the question of God's distinction from his necessary attributes. In chapter 8 I examine the question of God's timelessness.

As I noted in chapter 5 above, Scotus holds that divine simplicity is entailed by divine infinity. In the *Ordinatio*, Scotus concludes his discussion of divine simplicity with two general arguments from infinity and necessity, respectively. Every part can be exceeded. What is infinite cannot be exceeded. So God cannot be a part.[1] Neither can God be composed of parts, for these parts cannot be infinitely perfect (since then they could not be exceeded and thus could not be parts); neither can they be finitely perfect, for anything composed of finitely perfect parts can be exceeded (i.e. by something lacking parts merely finite in perfection).[2] Equally, a necessary being cannot necessarily include contingent parts, since if it did it would be contingent – against the hypothesis; neither could it include necessary parts, for then – absurdly – its necessity would be over-explained. The argument parallels that for (C6) in chapter 2 §4 above.[3]

1 God's Lack of Material Parts

In all the accounts, Scotus begins with God's lack of essential parts – his failure to be composed of matter and form. In *De primo principio*, Scotus proposes one very simple argument for this: if God were composed of essential parts, each one would either be finite or infinite. If finite, then God would be finite: as Wolter notes *in loc.*, 'According to Scotus' definition of infinity the infinite exceeds the finite by a non-finite measure. Thus, no matter how many the parts, they do not add up to

---

[1] Scotus, *Ord.* 1.8.1.1, n. 17 (Vatican, IV, 160).

[2] Ibid. (Vatican, IV, 161).

[3] Ibid., n. 16 (Vatican, IV, 160).

infinite.'[4] If infinite, then – absurdly – the parts would not be less than the (infinite) whole.[5] Elsewhere, Scotus appeals to the fact that composition of matter and form requires a causal explanation (an efficient cause),[6] and the causal interrelation of the parts themselves, considered as potency and act.[7]

Neither can God be composed of extended parts. He cannot, in other words, be a body. The basic reason here derives from an Aristotelian argument: no infinite perfection can be the perfection of a body, for if so, then (absurdly) the more of the body there was, the greater the perfection.[8] This argument seems open to an obvious objection that Scotus himself raises: if the perfection is, as it were, the same 'all over', the same in each part of the body in which it inheres, then why suppose that more body entails more perfection?[9] The idea is that a perfection of a body does not itself need to be extended in the way that the body is. Scotus thus proposes the following 'colouration' to Aristotle's argument, restricting its scope to powers: greater magnitude entails greater causal efficacy, though not greater intensive perfection. A small fire is as perfect, *qua* fire, as a large fire; but a large fire is certainly a more effective tool of heating. (A small patch of red is just as red as a large patch of red; a large patch of red may well be more visible.) From this, Scotus infers that no infinitely perfect power is extended. For any infinitely perfect power must be infinitely efficacious. But any bodily power can be made more efficacious by greater extension; thus no bodily power could be infinitely efficacious. Since no body could be infinite in extension,[10] it follows that no bodily power can be infinitely perfect.[11]

Does this conclusion not compromise the claim that a greater magnitude does not entail greater perfection in the power? Not according to Scotus, for if the power is such that it is equally perfect in every part of the body, the power is not extended along with the body.[12] What I think we need to keep in mind here is that the claim that an increase in efficacy does not entail an increase in perfection does not itself mean that infinite power does not require infinite efficacy.

In *De primo principio*, Scotus offers a further brief argument in favour of divine simplicity. Something which understands cannot be extended. The first nature understands. So it cannot be the subject of extension.[13] This argument relies on an immaterialist understanding of thinking. But this understanding is one that Scotus elsewhere hesitates to affirm without revelation.[14]

---

[4] Scotus, *DPP* (Wolter, 353).

[5] Scotus, *DPP* 4, n. 31 (Wolter, 135 (¶ 4.76)); in accordance with two of the MSS, I read the relevant passage as follows (added variant indicated in angle brackets): '*Prima, intrinseca in essentia, quia aut componeretur ex finitis in se aut ex infinitis; si primum, igitur finitum; si secundum, igitur pars <non> minor toto*', as clearly required by the sense.

[6] Scotus, *Ord.* 1.8.1.1, n. 9 (Vatican, IV, 155–6).

[7] Ibid., n. 7 (Vatican, IV, 155).

[8] Scotus, *DPP* 4, n. 31 (Wolter, 135 (¶ 4.77)), referring to Aristotle, *Ph.* 8.10 (226^{a}24–^{b}6); *Metaph.* Λ.7 (1073^{a}3–11).

[9] Ibid. (¶ 4.78).

[10] Scotus, *Ord.* 1.8.1.1, n. 13 (Vatican, IV, 158).

[11] Scotus, *DPP* 4, n. 31 (Wolter, 135–7 (¶ 4.78)).

[12] Ibid., n. 32 (Wolter, 137 (¶ 4.78)); see *Ord.* 1.8.1.1, n. 14 (Vatican, IV, 158).

[13] Ibid. (Wolter, 139 (¶ 4.79)).

[14] On this, see my 'Philosophy of Mind', 263–7.

According to these arguments, then, God lacks among other things a body. This lack entails that God is spaceless. Scotus proposes a rather curious account of divine spacelessness. According to Aquinas, for example, God's omnipresence is reducible to the conjunction of two characteristics: God's creative and sustaining action, and God's cognitive access to everything that there is.[15] For convenience I call this kind of presence 'causal' presence. Scotus's view is very different from this. At one point, Scotus wonders whether God's omnipresence could be inferred from his omnipotence. Scotus rightly holds that, in the absence of any material universe, it makes no sense to think of God being omnipresent or immense at all, 'as though God were present according to his essence [in] an imagined infinite vacuum'.[16] But Scotus holds too that God's presence in the universe is more than just causal:

[1]
1 If omnipotence is the will on whose willing it follows that a thing exists, then since a
2 will can will equally what is distant as well as what is close, it seems that if the
3 omnipotent were, *per impossibile*, in some determined place and not everywhere, it
4 could will something to be in another place [in which] it is not impossible for it to be,
5 and consequently that thing would have existence in that place by its [viz. the
6 omnipotent's] willing, and consequently that would be brought about by the
7 omnipotent without the omnipotent's being present there according to essence.[17]

Now, it is admittedly the case that Scotus's reasoning here proceeds under an impossible assumption (that God is not essentially omnipresent) [1.3]. But the gist is that even in such a case God would still be *causally* omnipresent [1.3–4, 7]: God's not being essentially omnipresent does *not* entail that he is not causally omnipresent. I take it that the point Scotus wants to make is that essential omnipresence is something over and above causal omnipresence. This does not mean that God's omnipresence is any sort of spatial presence, though since spatial presence and causal presence seem to exhaust the possibilities, it is hard to see what Scotus has in mind. The claim about God's existing in some determined place should not be understood to imply any kind of spatial existence: again, like the presence of an angel at a place, this presence can be both limited and non-spatial without being reducible merely to (finite) causal presence. A 'determined place' [1.3] is contrasted with ubiquity, and what Scotus means is simply location in one place of finite dimension, without any implication that the place and the body it locates have the additional relation of being such that each part of the place corresponds to one part of the located body – the relation that Scotus labels 'commensuration' or 'position'.[18]

---

[15] See Aquinas, *ST* 1.8.3 c (I/1, 38ᵃ⁻ᵇ). In his *ex professo* discussion Aquinas adds too a further way in which God can be present in the universe: God is present by being the object of creatures' cognitive and appetitive activity: *ST* 1.8.3 c (I/1, 38ᵃ). Data from Christian revelation about the Incarnation would doubtless provide Aquinas with a further way in which a divine person is present in the universe. But this is not relevant for the discussion here.

[16] Scotus, *Ord.* 1.37.un., n. 9 (Vatican, VI, 302).

[17] Ibid. (Vatican, VI, 301–2).

[18] On this, see Scotus, *Ord.* 2.2.2.1–2, n. 216 (Vatican, VII, 253), and my discussion in *The Physics of Duns Scotus*, 194–202.

It seems likely to me that there is some kind of background here, namely the account of angelic presence suggested by the 1277 Condemnations. For amongst the propositions condemned by the Archbishop of Paris, Stephen Tempier, is included the following: that an angelic substance cannot be at a place without acting at that place.[19] Angelic presence, then, cannot be merely causal, and it may be that a cursory reading of this condemnation, coupled with the intellectually refined drive to generalization, could have led to the kind of view that Scotus defends here. It is not an agreeable view, in the sense that it is hard to understand, does not seem to add anything substantive to the simpler and more elegant account of (say) Aquinas, and seems to represent something of a minority view in the theological tradition (at least until recent times; but what modern theologians want to say on the subjects of divine omnipresence and immanence seems to me more than usually obscure and confused).

2 God's Lack of Accidents

Scotus's final claim in *De primo principio* about divine simplicity concerns God's inability to be the subject of accidents:

> **[2]**
> 1 Anything that can be perfected lacks in itself some entity of the perfection, otherwise
> 2 it would not be in potency to it. For this reason the perfection is added to what can be
> 3 perfected, and the whole is something more perfect than either of the things united.
> 4 Nothing is lacking from the infinite; nothing that can be united to it adds perfection,
> 5 for then something would be greater than the infinite. Secondly, because it is not
> 6 extended, no material accident can be in it. Immaterial accidents pertaining to the
> 7 intellect and will are not in it, for the things which most seem to be accidents there –
> 8 such as understanding and willing – are the same as it, from the sixth [conclusion] of
> 9 this [fourth chapter].[20]

Central here is divine infinity. For nothing can be greater than what is infinite [2.5]. Suppose that God could gain or lose certain attributes. In this case, God considered with each attribute is greater than God alone: each attribute is a (different) perfection of God [2.1–3]. But it is God alone – the divine essence – that is infinite and thus unsurpassable [2.4–5]. So God considered with different attributes cannot be greater than the divine essence as such. So God cannot be the subject of accidents. The argument in [2.5–8] simply attempts to exclude all possible sorts of accidents. Material accidents (colour, size) are excluded by God's immateriality [2.5–6], and immaterial accidents (knowledge, willing) are excluded by Scotus's prior attempt to show that these attributes are simply identical (in a sense to be spelled out in a moment) with the divine essence [2.6–8]: see above, chapter 4 §8. God's infinite perfection entails straightforwardly that he cannot enter into composition with anything else. If God were a component of something else, that

---

[19] Article 204 (*Cartularium universitatis Parisiensis*, ed. H. Denifle and E. Chatelain, I, 554). Scotus cites it at *Ord.* 2.2.2.1–2, n. 200 (Vatican, VII, 244).

[20] Scotus, *DPP* 4, n. 33 (Wolter, 139 (¶ 4.80)).

thing would be greater than he is; but nothing can be greater than an infinite God.[21]

God's inability to be a subject of accidents entails *a fortiori* that God cannot be subject to relational accidents. If we couple this with the contingency of all external divine activity, it entails that God cannot be really related to any of his creatures. Scotus understands all relational accidents to be inherent items,[22] and in denying that God is contingently really related to his creatures, Scotus is denying that there is such an item inherent in God. The alternative for any contingent relation is a merely rational relation. And, on Scotus's understanding, a merely rational relation does not pick out any real feature of the thing thus related at all:

[3]
1 If *per impossibile* God were not an intellectual nature ... and he produced a stone,
2 then the stone would be really related to God, and nevertheless there would be no
3 relation of reason in God to [the stone].[23]

This does not mean that the stone would not be really related (as creature) to God (as creator). Neither does it mean that it would not be the case that God is (really) creator. But the extramental truth-maker for claims about God's being the creator is not any real relation in God to his creatures. It is merely something intrinsic to the creature (namely, its real relation of *being created*). A rational relation *requires* the operation of a mind.

3 Distinctions Between the Divine Attributes

In the rest of this section I shall consider material that Scotus's contemporaries would have regarded as far more contentious than the largely commonplace conclusions recounted above. The issues all have to do with the relationship between God and his attributes, and it seems to me that there are at least three relevant questions:

(i)   Does God have real attributes?
(ii) Are God's attributes all the same as each other?
(iii) Are they all just God?

Someone who answers (i) negatively, denying that God has real attributes, is likely to talk as though God is just identical with one 'super-attribute' – divinity or whatever – thus apparently wanting to answer (ii) and (iii) positively. Aquinas, for example, distinctively claims that God is just the super-attribute of his own *esse* or existence: I will return to this briefly below. But a negative answer to (i) does not

---

[21] Scotus, *Ord.* 3.1.1, n. 16 (Wadding, VII, 25). Clearly, the infinite perfection of God is compatible with there being more things than just God; God's infinite intensive perfection, then, does not place any blocks on there being extensively more things than God, or on there being aggregates of things that include God.

[22] On this, see Mark G. Henninger, *Relations: Medieval Theories 1250–1325*, ch. 5, and my *The Physics of Duns Scotus*, 107–15.

[23] Scotus, *Ord.* 1.30.1–2, n. 39 (Vatican, VI, 186).

entail a positive answer to (iii): God could neither be nor have any attributes at all.
I shall consider below the position of Thomas of Sutton, whom Scotus presents as
adopting something like this position. A motivation for this sort of position would
be some sort of nominalism about properties – that is to say, claiming that our talk
about properties involves no ontological commitment at all, such that properties are
not in any sense real, or in any sense constituents of things.

Scotus believes that God's attributes are real (constituents of God), that they are
in some way distinct from each other, and that each one is in some way distinct from
God too. According to Scotus, there is some sort of distinction between the different
properties of any given thing. Scotus holds that one way (not the only way) of
inferring this is by appealing to the fact that properties fail to be coextensive: more
things, for example, are white than are wise, or animal than man.[24] This extensional
distinction entails an intensional one for Scotus: whiteness is not wisdom; animality
is not humanity. But intensional distinction does not entail extensional distinction,
and another way of telling that there are distinctions between properties is simply
by noting that we truly form different concepts of one and the same object. To do
this, the properties from which we abstract the concepts must be in some sense or
another distinct: whiteness in Socrates, for example, is not wisdom in Socrates.

This much is perhaps uncontroversial – though Scotus, following some
suggestions made by thirteenth-century scholastics, proposes a detailed way of
talking about and analysing this distinction between properties, and I shall discuss
this below. More controversial in the context of thirteenth-century theology is
Scotus's attempt to show that similar distinctions must obtain between the various
divine attributes. According to Scotus, if wisdom in Socrates is distinct from (say)
goodness in Socrates, then it must be the case that wisdom in God is distinct from
goodness in God. Aquinas, for example, disagrees. Thus, while he denies that the
words we use about God are synonymous, he denies that this entails that there are
extramental distinctions in the thing to which we ascribe the various properties
signified by the words.[25] Scotus's position is that, if nominalism about properties is
false, then it must be so globally. Thus, if there are extramental distinctions between
relevant creaturely properties, then there must be such distinctions between
corresponding divine properties too.

On the face of it, it is true that, if nominalism about properties is false, then it
must be so globally. That is to say, someone accepting nominalism in just a
particular case needs to provide a good reason for doing so. One reason for
accepting nominalism for a certain kind of substance would be if it should turn out
that all the predicates of that substance are coextensive, or (perhaps) necessarily
coextensive, and this is clearly true of God.[26] This move would not require accepting
extensionalist accounts of properties in general, just in the particular case where the
predicates are all coextensive or necessarily coextensive. And we could guarantee
that all divine predicates (for example) are necessarily coextensive by asserting that
there is a particular kind of goodness, wisdom, and so on, proper to God, and that
these kinds of property are had by God, and only by God, as a matter of necessity.

---

[24] On this, see the discussion of **[5]** in Part II, chapter 17 below.

[25] Aquinas, *ST* 1.13.4 c (I/1, 66ᵃ).

[26] For a move like this, see William E. Mann, 'Divine Simplicity'.

This clearly requires that the intensions of the divine properties are sufficiently different from their creaturely counterparts to allow that the divine properties are simply one and the same. As we shall see, Scotus sees this requirement as counterintuitive. How can a property φ be the same property in God and in Socrates, and yet be identical (in every way) with any other property ψ in God, but not in Socrates? Can the intensional features of wisdom *ever* be such as to allow it to be identical with (the intensional features of) every other property had by God? Contrariwise, if φ is not the same property in the two cases of God and Socrates, then (at the very least) we need a theory to show how it is less distinct in these two cases than it is from any case of another property – how it can be that God's wisdom and Socrates' wisdom have more in common than (say) God's wisdom and Socrates' goodness, or God's goodness and Socrates' wisdom? Scotus's approach is simple: no such theory is required, because it is possible to make sense of the demands of divine simplicity without asserting that God's wisdom and God's goodness are identical.

Scotus's spokesman for the nominalist strategy is Thomas of Sutton. According to Sutton, the distinction between, and reality of, the various attributes in God is simply the result of the way in which creatures understand God:

[4]
1 In God, unity of essence corresponds to the notions of all the attributes (viz. which
2 imply perfection in God and creatures), not according to the existence which it has
3 absolutely ... but according to the relation which it has to creatures ... in so far as the
4 divine essence is compared to creatures as formal cause, containing in itself the
5 wholeness of every perfection which is separately and imperfectly in creatures. It is
6 by this that the essence is imitable by everything, in different ways. Furthermore, the
7 plurality of attribute-perfections ... is conceived by the intellect *a posteriori*,
8 understanding by natural light, in so far as it forms, from really diverse perfections in
9 creatures, corresponding proportional conceptions and perfections in God.[27]

The gist here is that there is no extramental distinction of divine attributes, and the reason is quite simply that there are no divine attributes distinct in any way from God. More precisely, divine attributes are just ways in which God can be resembled [4.3–6], and thus are merely rational relations in God to the creatures that really resemble him [4.3]. The point is not that God is just an attribute, but that he is just a completely simple concrete object.

Scotus's arguments against nominalism are generally combined with arguments about the distinction of attributes. The basic structure is that extramental *distinction* of attributes entails the extramental *existence* of attributes – and thus the falsity of nominalism. So a negative answer to my second question above entails a positive answer to the first question. The main argument has a complex theological nature, presupposing the truth of the doctrine of the Trinity. In fact, since, as we shall see in Part II, Scotus holds that the Trinity can be shown by natural reason, and since nothing about the argument up to that point presupposes anti-nominalism about the

---

[27] This passage from Scotus, *Ord.* 1.8.1.4, n. 162 (Vatican, IV, 233–4), is a medley of various passages from Sutton's *Quodlibeta*, outlined in the footnote in apparatus F of the Vatican edition *in loc.*: see Sutton, *Quod.* 2.2 (167, l. 80–p. 169, l. 129).

divine attributes, it is legitimate to appeal to Trinitarian doctrine, though it looks a bit odd. (In any case, as we shall see, Scotus has some non-theological arguments too.)

[5]
1 The distinction of attribute-perfections is the basis in relation to the distinction of
2 emanations. But the distinction of emanations is real, as is evident. But no real
3 distinction presupposes of necessity a distinction which is merely of reason, just as
4 nothing truly real presupposes something which is merely a being of reason.
5 Therefore the distinction of attributes is not merely rational, but in some way real (*ex*
6 *natura rei*). The assumption is clear for real being, as distinguished from being of
7 reason, is that which has existence of itself, in circumscription from every act of
8 intellect as intellect. But whatever depends on a being of reason, or presupposes it,
9 cannot have its existence in circumscription from every act of intellect. Therefore
10 nothing which presupposes a being of reason is truly a real being.[28]

The emanations that Scotus has in mind [5.2] are the processions of Son and Spirit, and he holds (as we shall see in Part II) that what distinguishes these emanations is that one (the Son) springs from intellect, and the other (the Spirit) springs from will. Intellect and will, then, are the relevant attribute-perfections that Scotus has in mind [5.1]. The argument is that the extramental distinction of attribute-perfections is a *necessary condition* for the distinction of emanations [5.1–2], and that no merely mind-dependent distinction can be a necessary condition for any real distinction [5.2–4]. Since the emanations of Son and Spirit are really distinct [5.2], the distinction of attributes must be real too [5.5–6].

The point of this stage of the argument is that an *irreducible* distinction between different sorts of causal activity entails real causal powers. Scotus does not suggest here that this argument is generalizable to cover all sorts of causal power. For example, many distinctions between different sorts of causal activity can be explained by a prior difference in the kind of thing affected – the *patient* to which the causal agency is directed. The point about the emanations of Son and Spirit in God is that there is nothing affected: there is no pre-existent substrate that is somehow changed by the action; there is, in other words, no patient.[29] The argument is that, if causal powers in God are to be really distinguished (as they must be, since they have irreducibly distinct kinds of effect), then nominalism – at least about causal powers – must be false. On nominalism, the only distinction between different powers is mind-imposed – in this case, the mind's considering the different ways in which God can be imitated – and thus not sufficient to ground the distinction of effect.[30]

---

[28] Scotus, *Ord.* 1.8.1.4, n. 177 (Vatican, IV, 246).

[29] Henry of Ghent, as we shall see in Part II, chapter 13 §3 below, holds that there is a sense in which the divine essence is the patient, receiving the forms of filiation and passive spiration. But even in this case the substrate – the divine essence – is the same for both emanations. So even if we accept that there could be a substrate for the divine emanations, the substrate will be the same in both cases, and thus not sufficient to distinguish the kinds of causal activity.

[30] Although this argument is specifically directed to the question of irreducibly distinct causal powers, it is worth keeping in mind that Scotus accepts arguments to the effect that nominalism is false for any causal power. His opponent is Henry of Ghent, who holds that talk of different causal powers is just a way of talking about the ways in which different effects are related to their cause: see Henry, *Quod.* 3.14 (Paris, I, fo. 66ʳ–71ʳ), and Scotus's discussion in *Rep.* 2.16.un., nn. 10–13 (Wadding, XI, 347ᵃ–ᵇ).

Underlying this argument is a further stage, namely that nothing merely mind-dependent can be a necessary condition for anything real. Clearly, this general claim, if true, entails the claim in [5.2–3]. But the general claim may not be true if it is understood to buttress a straightforward inference from the reality of an emanation to the reality of the relevant causal power (intellect or will, respectively). Scotus at one point reports favourably the following argument from Henry Harclay: 'Intellect, as existent, according to its proper formal notion is really in God ... because it is a principle of real production'.[31] This is not obviously true. The reality of an effect does not evidently entail the reality of causal powers. All it requires is the reality of the cause. The rest of the argument in [5] seems committed to a similar mistake.[32] Of course, this in no way vitiates the argument in [5.1–5], which is that an irreducible distinction in *kinds* of causal activity requires a real (extramental) distinction of causal powers. In other words, even though the reality of a causal power cannot be inferred from the reality of the effect (though the reality of the agent doubtless can be), nevertheless the reality and distinction of various causal powers can be inferred from a distinction in the kinds of effects produced. So one way to salvage the second stage of the argument would be to substitute the word 'distinction' for every instance of the word 'being' in [5.6–10]. The point would be that no real distinction (of kinds of effects) can presuppose no more than a rational distinction (of causal principles), and [5.6–10] would then amount to no more than [5.1–5].

Scotus's main argument is straightforwardly metaphysical. Basically, the argument is that if nominalism is false for creatures, and if the divine attributes are intensionally the same as (or intensionally overlapping with) creaturely attributes, then distinctions between creaturely attributes entail distinctions between divine attributes too:

[6]

1 There is therefore a distinction [between essential divine perfections] preceding in
2 every way the intellect, and it is this: that wisdom really exists in reality (*est in re ex*
3 *natura rei*), and goodness really exists in reality, but real (*in re*) wisdom is not real
4 goodness. Which is proved, for if infinite wisdom were formally infinite goodness,
5 then wisdom in general would be formally goodness in general. For infinity does not
6 destroy the formal notion of the thing to which it is added, for in whatever degree
7 some perfection is understood to be (which degree is a degree of the perfection), the

---

[31] Scotus, *Ord.* 1.8.1.4, *text. int.* (Vatican, IV, 253, ll. 16–17, p. 255, l. 6). On the identity of the MSS's 'Arcl'inus', see the editors' introduction to Scotus, *Opera Omnia* (Vatican, IV, 28*–39*), where they cite relevant passages from Harclay, *In Sent.* 1.35 (MS Vat. Lat. 13687, fo. 82ʳ⁻ᵛ). It should be borne in mind, however, that Harclay's *Sentence* commentary is usually thought to post-date all parts of Scotus's *Ordinatio*.

[32] Related difficulties seem to surround other arguments Scotus proposes. For example, he suggests at one point that nominalism must be false for divine perfections, otherwise the perfections would 'not be perfectly in God'. The reason is that nominalism makes perfections simply mind-dependent, and thus merely thought-objects, and a thought-object 'as distinct from an existent thing is diminished in being' (Scotus, *Ord.* 1.8.1.4, n. 185 (Vatican, IV, 252–3)). This argument seems to beg the question: nominalism does not mean that God is not really perfect, merely that it is not in virtue of some real feature of his – somehow distinct from, and a constituent of, himself – that he is perfect.

8 formal notion of that perfection is not removed by the degree, and thus, if [this
9 perfection] *as in general* does not formally include [that perfection] *as in general*,
10 neither [does this perfection] *as in particular* [include that perfection] *as in particular*.
11   I show this, because 'to include formally' is to include something in its
12 essential notion, such that if there were a definition of the including thing, then the
13 thing included would be the definition or a part of the definition. Just as, however, the
14 definition of goodness in general does not include wisdom, neither does infinite
15 [goodness include] infinite [wisdom]. There is therefore some formal non-identity
16 between wisdom and goodness, inasmuch as there would be distinct definitions of
17 them if they were definable. But a definition does not only indicate a concept caused
18 by the intellect, but the quiddity of a thing: there is therefore formal non-identity from
19 the side of the thing, which I understand thus: the intellect forming this [sentence]
20 'wisdom is not formally goodness' does not cause, by its act of combining, the truth of
21 this combination, but it finds the terms in the object, and a true act is made by their
22 combination.[33]

Much is contained in this extremely rich passage. The crucial material on the formal distinction [6.11–13] I will deal with below, in this chapter and in Part II, chapter 17 §2. Suffice it to note for now that the formal distinction is the kind of distinction that obtains between (inseparable) properties on the assumption that nominalism about properties is false. The first stage of the argument is stated secondly [6.11–22]: namely, that there are extramental distinctions between some creaturely properties. The anti-nominalist position is stated in [6.17–18]: properties have definitions, or descriptions that do duties for definitions [6.16–17]. But things that have such descriptions are not merely thought-objects or concepts, but real things – things with 'quiddities' [6.17–18]. Scotus does not offer an argument for this claim (which is in any case intended here to be merely explanatory), but how he is thinking is made clear in the next few lines: statements about the identity or distinction of different attributes are not just automatically true, and are not simply analytic [6.19–21]: they require truth-makers ('terms' found by the intellect 'in the object' – i.e. in extramental reality) [6.21–22]. Talk about 'definitions' and 'quiddities' in [6.11–22] is a way of affirming an intensional, not merely extensional, account of properties, and Scotus's basic point is that if the intensions of the various properties are distinct, there must be some extramental explanation for this.[34] And the explanation will not be just extensionalist. Given this, of course, it is hard to see just how nominalism could possibly be true. But what is lacking is an argument that extensionalist accounts of properties are false.

The rest of the passage reasons from this distinction amongst creaturely properties (roughly, the property 'in general') to a distinction amongst divine properties. The assumption is that a property had by God is the same as, or overlaps with, a creaturely property. The reason offered is that the notion of a degree of a

[33] Scotus, *Ord.* 1.8.1.4, nn. 192–3 (Vatican, IV, 261–2).

[34] Scotus accepts as a corollary of his account of this that simplicity is not proper to God. There are irreducibly simple created properties of things – specific differences and haecceities, for example (rationality as such, for example, or Socrateity) (Scotus, *Ord.* 1.8.1.2, n. 31 (Vatican, IV, 165)). What distinguishes the simplicity of these created properties from God's simplicity is that (1) every created property is such that it can enter into composition with something else, and (2) every created property is subject to some kind of privative limitation (Scotus, *Ord.* 1.8.1.2, nn. 32–4 (Vatican, IV, 165–7)).

perfection does not entail that the basic account or definition of the perfection is altered [6.5–8].[35] God and (say) Socrates are both wise, though this does not mean that they are both wise in just the same way. Scotus does not believe his account to entail that there are properties really shared by both God and creatures (on this, see the Appendix below). The commonality is not that of a universal. But this nominalism about universal concepts covering both God and creatures does not entail nominalism about properties. Neither does it undermine the claim that the two properties share key intensional features. Talk of definitions and quiddities does not entail that nominalism about universals is false – though given that realism in this context is false, Scotus will need some way of guaranteeing that the two properties – God's wisdom, say, and Socrates' wisdom – fall under the intension of one and the same concept. I deal with part of Scotus's explanation for this in a moment.

Given that there is some intensional commonality between divine and creaturely perfections, and given that the intension of each creaturely perfection is distinct from those of certain other creaturely perfections, it follows that the intensions of the corresponding divine perfections are distinct, and thus that there are formal distinctions between the various divine perfections. The reason is that this intensional commonality includes the basic definition of each perfection, and the basic definitions of the various perfections are simply and irreducibly distinct [6.2–5]. This distinction is extramental, and this entails that the properties themselves have some sort of extramental reality – and thus that nominalism about divine properties is false (see [6.1–4]).

So there is a formal distinction between the various divine attributes. How does this formal distinction relate to real distinction? Basically, Scotus believes that really distinct things are separable,[36] or at least are the kinds of thing that either are capable of being independent *supposita* (absolutely non-instantiable or non-exemplifiable non-relational subjects of properties) or are uniquely properties of such things.[37] Formal distinctions obtain between the necessary properties of any one such *suppositum*. In this context, Scotus presents the distinction as one that obtains between not things but *formalities* – little or diminished things – and the sort of distinction is not real but somehow diminished too.[38] These formalities are inseparable, and thus really identical with each other. Their formal distinction results from the fact that they are different properties: not sharing the same definition, even if in some cases interdefinable – see [6.11–13]. The relation of real identity is what explains the unity of these properties with each other, and the real

---

[35] On this, see too the discussion of intrinsic modes below: modes of an attribute that do not affect its formal content.

[36] See e.g. Scotus, *Quod.* 3, n. 15 (Wadding, XII, 81; Alluntis and Wolter, 73–4 (¶ 3.46)) for the necessity of separability for real distinction; Scotus, *Ord.* 2.1.4–5, n. 200 (Vatican, VII, 101) for the sufficiency of separability for real distinction. As I immediately make clear here, Scotus in fact restricts this first criterion to the created realm.

[37] As we shall see, Scotus holds that the divine persons are inseparable and yet really distinct. I deal with this issue in Part II, chapter 12 § 1 and chapter 13 §1 below.

[38] For the diminished character of the distinction, see e.g. Scotus, *Ord.* 1.2.2.1–4, nn. 400–4 (Vatican, II, 355–7). I deal with the different ways in which Scotus presents his distinction in my 'Scotus's Parisian Teaching on Divine Simplicity'. The applicability of the teaching to the question of divine simplicity at hand is, of course, made clear in [6] above.

identity itself is (in normal cases) explained by the identity of the *suppositum* whose properties they are. Thus, what explains the real identity of my necessary properties with each other is just that they are properties of me. Considered in abstraction from their unity in me, they would not be unified with each other.[39]

Still, all of this presupposes that Scotus has a good reason for rejecting nominalism for creaturely properties. One reason for so doing is to allow for the reality of accidental modifications. Scotus's basic reason is that he believes attributes to have some causal or explanatory role in the world.[40] This, of course, would be unlikely to convince Scotus's opponent, who would hold that it is substances, not their attributes, that have a causal role in the world. Still, it seems to me that a case can be made that even Aquinas – who is about the most careful of all medieval thinkers on this sort of issue – tends to reify accidental properties,[41] so Scotus's arguments in favour of the extramental reality of divine attributes may have some *ad hominem* success.

Scotus's attack on global nominalism largely takes place within the context of his theory of religious language – in order to support a certain semantic theory, Scotus requires the global rejection of nominalism. Basically, Scotus believes that there are certain concepts under whose extension both God and creatures fall. Our words can successfully signify such concepts – indeed, they must do so if (as Scotus and others believe) theology is to be genuinely scientific (in the sense of employing valid deductive arguments). Thus Scotus holds that this kind of semantic theory is entailed by the 'scientific' and argumentative theological practice of the Christian tradition. (I discuss his arguments in favour of this 'univocity' theory of religious language in the Appendix.) Scotus believes that, in order for God and creatures to fall under the extension of the same concepts, the various divine and human features in virtue of which the same concepts are applicable must be, at root, the same. If, for example, wisdom and power are distinct in Socrates (as most agree to be the case), then they must be distinct in God too. A formal semantic theory here entails a material theological conclusion. But Scotus's reason for believing the semantic theory to be true is itself theological – that the Christian tradition presupposes the semantic theory. As Scotus sees it, it is not he but his opponent who is the innovator.

The claim that Scotus's account of divine simplicity is generated by coupling (standard) realism about creaturely properties (not, in this context, universals) with some thoroughly traditional theological insights is strengthened by a further consideration. Scotus distinguishes the relation of *imitation* or *representation* from the similarity of univocity.[42] Univocity is the commonality of a concept. Imitation is the similarity of the creatures to their exemplar cause, their being 'measured' by it. It is asymmetrical, and (in scholastic jargon) non-mutual (real only in the creature).[43] The exemplar cause of creatures is nothing other than the divine essence: all creatures imitate, in certain respects, the divine essence. Scotus's argument is that the similarity between creatures and God which grounds univocity cannot be

---

[39] On all this, see **[8]** below.

[40] See e.g. Scotus, *Ord.* 4.12.1, n. 16 (Wadding, VIII, 720).

[41] On this, see my *The Metaphysics of the Incarnation*, 40–3.

[42] Scotus, *Ord.* 1.3.1.1–2, n. 56 (Vatican, III, 38–9; *PW*, 26; Frank and Wolter, 114).

[43] Ibid. 1.3.2.un., n. 297 (Vatican, III, 180).

connected in any way to the divine ideas as such, otherwise we would have as much warrant for calling God a stone as for calling God wise.[44] This suggests that Scotus's account of the extramental basis for univocity is ultimately the asymmetrical relationship of imitation. Hence, the reason why God's wisdom and Socrates's wisdom fall under the same concept is that Socrates imitates God, or participates in God (or in an attribute had by him), in the relevant respect.[45]

4 God as a Collection of Really Identical Attributes

For Scotus, then, God's properties are fully real. Does Scotus believe that these properties themselves inhere in some substrate or substance with which the collection of formally distinct properties fails to be identical? This is the third of the questions I raised above. Scotus does not believe so, and (indeed) it is not clear to me that he would believe in a substrate for any collection of properties.[46] (Matter for Scotus is a physical – not a metaphysical – subject, and haecceity is a property that is somehow tied in to the collection of individualized common properties that a thing is without being the subject of these properties.) As Scotus understands his account of the formal distinction between the divine attributes, it admits of an objection to the effect that the properties will be 'acts and forms with respect to the divine essence'.[47] Scotus interprets his position as entailing simply that the divine essence consists of the various divine properties really (though not formally) identical with each other:

[7]
1 A form in creatures has imperfection in two ways: namely, because it is an informing
2 form, and because it is a part of a composite; and it has something which fails to be
3 imperfect and which follows the [form] according to [the form's] essential nature,
4 namely that [the form] is that in virtue of which something is such-and-such. For
5 example: wisdom in us is an accident, and this is an imperfection. But [the fact] that
6 [wisdom in us] is that in virtue of which something is wise is not an imperfection, but
7 pertains to the essential nature of wisdom. In God nothing is a form according to the
8 twofold sort of imperfection, for [it] neither informs, nor [is] a part. There is
9 wisdom there, however, in so far as it is that in virtue of which that which it is in is
10 wise. And this is not from any composition of wisdom with any quasi-subject, nor as
11 though that wisdom were part of some composite, but by real identity, by which
12 [divine] wisdom, on account of its perfect infinity, is perfectly the same as anything
13 with which it is naturally found [viz. any other divine attribute].[48]

---

[44] Ibid. 1.8.1.3, n. 74 (Vatican, IV, 186–7). I dealt with this in chapter 4 above.

[45] For participation, see e.g. Scotus, *Ord.* 1.8.1.3, n. 86 (Vatican, IV, 193–4).

[46] On this, see my *The Metaphysics of the Incarnation*, 20–1.

[47] Scotus, *Ord.* 1.8.1.4, n. 210 (Vatican, IV, 270), referring to n. 198 (Vatican, IV, 264), where Scotus claims that his anti-nominalist strategy on the divine attributes is necessary to make sense of a distinction, posited by John of Damascus, between the divine essence and the divine attributes as 'circumstances' of the essence ('peri tēn phusin'): see John of Damascus, *Exp. fid.* 4 (Kotter, 13, ll. 34–6; Buytaert, 21, ll. 43–5).

[48] Scotus, *Ord.* 1.8.1.4, n. 213 (Vatican, IV, 271).

The key idea – **[7.4]** – is that a form is, roughly, what we might call a truth-maker: a form φ-ness is something that explains why statements of the form '*x* is φ' are true. More precisely (since Scotus does not always mention the notion of truth in this context), a form is that *structural* fact about *x* which explains *x*'s being φ. This basic function of a form is associated, in creatures, with one or both of two imperfections: informing (actualizing passive potency in the thing that the form belongs to) **[7.1–2]** and being a part of a composite **[7.2]**. What Scotus means in this second case is that creatures are really separable from some of their forms, and indeed matter is really separable from every form. This separability entails for Scotus that there is some real kind of distinction between substances and their forms: a creature is, to a greater or lesser extent, an entity that is independent of its forms. Composite things are such that they can be disintegrated.[49] In the case of the divine attributes, neither of these imperfections obtains **[7.7–8]**. Nevertheless, the explanatory function of an attribute remains: God's wisdom, for example, explains that fact that God is wise **[7.8–10]**. How, from a structural point of view, does God's wisdom do this? Scotus holds that it does this not by actualizing any passive potency in God – by God's being a subject distinct from all of his properties (a 'quasi-subject') **[7.10]** – nor by being a separable component of a destructible whole **[7.10–11]**, but simply by being really identical with all of the other divine attributes – attributes from which divine wisdom is formally distinct **[7.11–13]**.

The rest of the passage is devoted to explaining just how the relation of real identity is relevant here. The problem Scotus is interested in here is the question of the truth of predications where subject and predicate are both *abstract* terms, abstracted not only from the subject in which the referents of these terms inhere but from anything external to the definition of the quiddity or essence referred to:

[8]
1 In creatures ... if we abstract those realities which are in the same thing (for example,
2 the reality of genus and difference), and consider them most precisely, each is finite
3 and neither is perfectly the same as the other. For they are the same as each other only
4 because of a third with which they are the same. For this reason, if they were
5 abstracted from the third, the cause of their identity does not remain, and for this
6 reason neither [would there remain] the cause of the truth of a proposition uniting those
7 extremes. Therefore this is false: 'animality is rationality', and *vice versa*, and this by
8 any kind of predication, because not only are the extremes not formally the same, but
9 neither [are they] truly the same: for this quiddity is precisely potential to that
10 quiddity, and it is the same as that [quiddity] only on account of the identity with the
11 third from which they are abstracted. Therefore the abstraction destroys the truth of
12 the affirmative [proposition] uniting them.
13   The opposite holds in God, for if we abstract wisdom from anything which is
14 outside the notion of wisdom, and likewise if we abstract goodness from anything
15 which is formally outside its notion, each quiddity will remain, understood precisely,
16 formally infinite. From the fact that the cause of their identity in this very precise
17 abstraction is infinity, the cause of the identity of the extreme terms [in a proposition]
18 remains. For these were precisely the same not on account of their identity with some
19 third thing from which they are abstracted, but on account of the formal infinity of
20 each.[50]

---

49 I deal with these various issues in *The Physics of Duns Scotus*, chs 2, 3, and 6.
50 Scotus, *Ord.* 1.8.1.4, nn. 219–20 (Vatican, IV, 274–5).

Here, Scotus contrasts infinite and finite cases of the same sort of attribute. [**8**.1–12] deals with the finite case. What unites formally distinct attributes in a creature is the identity of their *suppositum*. Scotus makes the point by considering the (individualized) attributes in abstraction from their *suppositum*. We refer to such abstracted attributes by using abstract nouns: rationality, for example, is an (individualized) property considered in abstraction from its *suppositum*. The kind of identity Scotus is talking about in [**8**] is *real* identity, and the various predications he talks about in [**8**] are ways of asserting real (numerical) identity, or real distinction. What unifies formally distinct finite attributes with each other is their unity with their *suppositum* [**8**.3–4]. If, therefore, the attributes were abstracted from their *suppositum*, the cause of their real identity with each other would be lacking [**8**.4–5], and likewise the cause of the truth of propositions asserting the identity of the attributes with each other [**8**.6–12]. Since, as I suggested above, Scotus probably rejects the notion of a substrate for any collection of properties, I suspect that what he has in mind is that, in the case of creaturely attributes, their *suppositum* somehow 'emerges from', or 'supervenes on', their unity, such that, if somehow this supervenience relation were lacking, the attributes would not be united to each other. I deal with the notion of a *suppositum* in Part II, chapter 12 §3 below.

The case of divine attributes is not like this. Scotus holds that the real identity of essential divine attributes can be inferred simply from their essential infinity. Each divine attribute is infinite [**8**.15–16]. And each is formally distinct from any other [**8**.13–15]. But infinity guarantees real identity without the need to appeal to any third thing or *suppositum* in which they are united [**8**.16–20]. If a divine attribute could be part of a composite, it would not itself be infinite.[51] The reason for this goes back to those arguments that derive simplicity from infinity, mentioned at the very beginning of this chapter. Things that can enter into composition are finite, since being a component entails being less than the whole made up of components. Infinite attributes are such that they cannot be exceeded, and therefore such that they cannot enter into composition with each other. They are therefore really identical. Thus, considered even in the 'most ultimate abstraction'[52] – that is to say, in complete abstraction from their subject (in this case, the divine essence) – divine attributes can be predicated of each other 'by identity', as Scotus puts it. Infinity guarantees numerical identity, and thus occupies a key role in the most characteristic Scotist teaching on divine simplicity, namely the real identity of, and formal distinction between, the various divine attributes.

The result of this is that the divine essence is nothing more than a collection of really identical and formally distinct attributes.[53] It is not, for example, anything underlying those attributes. Like Thomas of Sutton, Scotus accepts a one-category analysis of the divine essence. But whereas Sutton's one category is nothing at all like a property, Scotus's one category is entirely properties.

---

[51] Thus in *Ord.* 1.8.1.4, n. 221 (Vatican, IV, 276), Scotus notes that the infinity of just one of two attributes considered in ultimate abstraction is sufficient to guarantee their real identity.

[52] For ultimate abstraction, see Scotus, *Lect.* 1.5.1.un, n. 21 (Vatican, XVI, 417); *Ord.* 1.5.1.un., n. 19 (Vatican, IV, 19); *Rep.* 1A.5.1 (MS M, fo. 45ʳ, abbreviated in Wadding, XI, 59ᵇ (n. 5)).

[53] I have shown in 'Scotus's Parisian Teaching on Divine Simplicity' that, even though there is no *ex professo* discussion of the formal distinction of the divine attributes from each other in the manner of dist. 8 of *Ord.*, Scotus's teaching in the late *Rep.* is fundamentally the same as his earlier, more extended, treatment.

5 Divine Attributes and Intrinsic Modes

The question of the infinity of the divine essence and attributes raises a further difficulty. As we saw in chapter 5 §3 above, Scotus holds that infinity is a real mode of an essence or attribute. What is such a mode, and how – in terms of composition – does it relate to the entity of which it is a mode? Does, for example, it add anything real to the entity of which it is a mode? Scotus's basic answer is that, although the entity and the (entity + mode) are not in every way the same, this distinction is not the result of the fact that the mode adds something real to the entity (see **[6**.5–10] above). A mode is, as Scotus sees it, something like an 'amount' or 'quantity' of the entity. Scotus distinguishes between the concept of the entity and the concept of the (entity + mode) as a distinction between imperfect and perfect understandings of the same reality – that is, of the (entity + mode), as the sole reality there.[54] Having a (perfect) understanding of the entity entails having a perfect understanding of the (entity + mode).[55] It is hard to know just how to assess this teaching relative to divine simplicity. Suffice it to say that, in terms of every real entity, there is no distinction whatever between wisdom in God and infinite wisdom in God. Modes are less than formalities, and on this view do not count as even minimal constituents of reality. Among God's attributes, then, we should not count *infinity*, since infinity is simply a mode of an attribute.

How far the doctrine of modes should be taken to extend is left unclear. It may be that Scotus intends 'infinity' to be the only such thing. But it may be that the list of intrinsic modes of attributes includes the 'higher' of each of the so-called disjunctive transcendentals coextensive with being – the first of each pair (or perhaps merely of some of these pairs; Scotus is not clear) of disjuncts in the following list: necessary-or-contingent, actual-or-potential, infinite-or-finite, cause-or-caused, prior-or-posterior, independent-or-dependent, absolute-or-relative, goal-or-goal-directed, simple-or-composite, one-or-many, exceeding-or-exceeded, substance-or-accident, same-or-diverse, equal-or-unequal.[56]

---

[54] Scotus, *Ord.* 1.8.1.3, nn. 138–9 (Vatican, IV, 222–3); for a discussion of the whole passage, see Peter King, 'Duns Scotus on the Common Nature and Individual Differentia', 60–4, 70–1); see too Allan B. Wolter, *The Transcendentals and their Function in the Metaphysics of Duns Scotus*, 24–7; and on the whole issue of the degrees of an entity, my *The Physics of Duns Scotus*, ch. 10.

[55] Scotus, *Ord.* 1.8.1.3, n. 140 (Vatican, IV, 223).

[56] For this list, see Wolter, *The Transcendentals*, 138; for a discussion of the disjunctive transcendentals, see 138–61. One famous medieval teaching – Aquinas's view that God is identical with his *esse* – is not explicitly discussed by Scotus at all. But it is not hard to see what he would say about it. Scotus certainly accepts that God is a necessary existent. Indeed, he is happy to talk about a necessary being (*ens per essentiam*) using the traditional Augustinian language about such a thing being *de se esse*, understood as 'having every condition necessarily required for existence' (Scotus, *Ord.* 1.8.1.3, n. 149 (Vatican, IV, 227); see Augustine, *De Trin.* 7.1.2 (CCSL, 50, 249)). But he does not believe that, in order to capture this sort of claim, it is necessary to hold that anything other than God includes an existence over and above its (individual) nature: as he puts it, 'I do not know that fiction according to which existence is something that supervenes on an essence' (*Ord.* 4.11.3, n. 46 (Wadding, VIII, 649)). Causing an individual, for example, and causing its existence are just one and the same thing. In this sense, there is no distinction between individual and existence in anything, and *a fortiori* not in God. What precisely Aquinas intends is, of course, a matter of huge and sometimes acrimonious dispute. It is certainly clear that, whatever the teaching is supposed to be, Scotus is just not interested in it.

Chapter 7

Divine Unicity

Infinity is the key attribute in the derivation of divine unicity. Thus Scotus proposes five arguments for unicity, from (1) infinite intellect, (2) infinite will, (3) infinite power, (4) necessary existence, and (5) infinite goodness. I discuss the first and third of these in detail in this chapter. The fourth, from necessary existence, closely resembles the argument for (C6) outlined in chapter 2 §4 above: if there were more than one necessary existent, then necessary existence would be a species, and the necessary existents would thus both include some entity that is not itself necessary, and thus each necessary existent be such that it fails to be 'primarily necessary': necessary in such a way that no explanation of its necessity is required.[1] The argument seems to me to admit of similar comment to that for (C6) above.

The argument from infinite intellect runs as follows:

[1]
1 An infinite intellect perfectly understands everything, that is, to the extent that
2 [everything] is intelligible, and in understanding it depends on nothing else, for then it
3 would not be infinite. If there were two infinite intellects – call them A and B – in
4 each there would be lacking perfect independent intellection. For A, if it understood
5 B through B, would, in understanding B, depend on B as an act [depends] on [its]
6 object when it is not the same [as its object]. If A understands B through itself, and
7 not through B, it does not understand B as perfectly as B is intelligible, for nothing is
8 perfectly present other than in itself or in something eminently containing [it]; A itself
9 does not contain B. If you say that it is similar to [B], against this: knowledge through
10 what is similar is only knowledge in a universal, to that extent that [the things] are
11 similar. The proper features by which they are distinguished are not known through
12 this [universal]. And this knowledge in a universal is not intuitive but abstractive; and
13 intuitive is more perfect. Again: the same act cannot have two adequate objects; A is
14 adequate to itself; therefore it does not understand B.[2]

The point of **[1]** is to show that perfect understanding of some external object requires the presence of the object in some way **[1.6–7]**. An external object can be present to a mind in one of two ways: either in itself, or as somehow contained eminently in an object really present to this mind **[1.7–8]**. And this gives Scotus two horns of a dilemma. Suppose there were two infinite minds. One would know the other either directly or as a result of its own self-knowledge. As we saw in chapter 4 §3 above, creatures are present to the divine mind by being virtually or eminently contained in the divine essence. But one infinite mind could not be present to another in this way **[1.8–9]**, because the relation of eminent containment is

---

[1] See Scotus, *Ord.* 1.2.1.1–2, n. 177 (Vatican, II, 233–4; *PW*, 89).
[2] Scotus, *DPP* 4, n. 38 (Wolter, 149 (¶ 4.89)).

standardly understood by Scotus to obtain between a more perfect being somehow including the perfection of a less perfect one, and on the hypothesis the two intellects are equally perfect. But, taking the other horn of the dilemma, if one of the infinite intellects – A – understood B in virtue of B's presence, with B as the object of its understanding, then A's understanding would depend on B, and thus A's understanding would be somehow imperfect [1.4–6]. Presumably an intellect infinite (unlimited) in every way does not depend on anything else when it understands, for its dependence will count as some kind of limitation [1.2–3]. So the existence of two infinite intellects would entail that the understanding of each one of them was either dependent or imperfect. But the understanding of an infinite intellect can be neither of these [1.3–4].

The kind of understanding that Scotus is talking about is *intuitive*: the direct, non-representational, intellectual understanding that it is possible to have of an individual. [1.9–13] explains further the horn of the dilemma outlined in [1.8–9], and shows that, if A's understanding of itself is to give it any understanding of B – perhaps in virtue of some similarity between A and B – this understanding would be of a universal, and thus abstractive and representational (since a genuine universal is not a real existent, but at best a representation of real particular existents) [1.9–11].[3] This would leave A in ignorance of the individual features of B. Knowledge of such individual features is, however, necessary for a full understanding of B [1.11–12]. This kind of knowledge is less perfect than one which would give A knowledge of B's individual features [1.12–13]. Scotus appends a brief additional argument at the end: the self-knowledge of an infinite intellect would exhaust its capacity for knowing such infinitely perfect objects [1.13–14].

The third argument in favour of divine unicity – the other one that I discuss in this chapter – makes use of the notion of infinite power:

[2]
1 If there were two infinite powers, each would be first with respect to the same
2 [effects], for essential dependence is on a nature, and equally to everything in the
3 nature. The same thing cannot depend on two first [causes], from the sixteenth
4 [conclusion] of the third [chapter]. Therefore plurality of rule is not good, for either
5 [it is] impossible, or each ruler will be diminished and partially ruling, and then we
6 need to ask in virtue of which one thing they are joined in ruling.[4]

The basic worry is causal over-determination: each of two infinitely powerful beings would be a sufficient cause for all effects – or at least, for some of the same effects. And this is impossible [2.3–4]. The justification for the claim that the two causes will necessarily produce the same effects (or even just some of them) is one touched on in chapter 2 above: one causal order is directed to one determined kind of cause, and within that kind to one individual thing. Someone could presumably deny this, and the second disjunct in [2.4–6] ('each ruler will be diminished ...') is supposed to make it hard nevertheless to claim that there could be two first principles. For suppose that the two first principles were merely *jointly* sufficient for an effect. A

---

[3] On universals as such in Scotus, and the contrast with common natures, see my 'Divisibility, Communicability, and Predicability in Duns Scotus's Theories of the Common Nature'.

[4] Scotus, *DPP* 4, n. 39 (Wolter, 151 (¶ 4.91)).

further explanation would still need to be given of the fact that the agents are (indefectibly and inerrantly?) united in their causal activity [**2.5–6**].

Scotus develops this last point further in the fuller treatment in the *Ordinatio*. There, he adds an additional argument from divine omnipotence that addresses the question of the united action of two causes. The point about omnipotence, as Scotus understands it, is that an omnipotent agent is able to bring about any effect directly. If there were two such beings, then one could frustrate the activity of the other: the first could bring about some state of affairs *s*, and the second could bring about not-*s*.[5] Scotus suggests a 'sophistical' objection: could not the two agents voluntarily agree to act consistently with each other?[6] Scotus's reply is that, in effect, such a pact between the two agents would not deal with the *logical* possibility of contradictory effects on the supposition of two omnipotent Gods. For the two agents would still be infinitely powerful, and would thus over-determine their effects. But over-determination of this kind entails (absurdly) the possibility of contradictory effects.[7] Still, as we saw above, Scotus does not regard omnipotence as demonstrable by natural reason. So this argument from the *Ordinatio* is no help in Scotus's metaphysical project here.

---

[5] Scotus, *Ord.* 1.2.1.1–2, n. 180 (Vatican, II, 235; *PW*, 90).

[6] Ibid., n. 181 (Vatican II, 235; *PW*, 90).

[7] Ibid. (Vatican, II, 236; *PW*, 90–1).

Chapter 8

Divine Immutability and Timelessness

1 Divine Immutability

One well-known argument for divine immutability, of Aristotelian inspiration, argues from the impossibility of self-motion to the existence of an unmoved prime mover of all physical processes.[1] I gave Aquinas's version of the argument in chapter 1 above. Scotus is hesitant about arguments of this nature: 'if perhaps they are valid, they nevertheless have a restricted conclusion'.[2] The reason is that Scotus believes self-motion to be a widespread feature of the physical universe;[3] at best, then, Aristotle's arguments could show that 'the first mover does not move as a body does, or as an embodied power, as the soul is moved accidentally in moved body'.[4] Scotus believes, however, that it is an easy matter to demonstrate God's immutability from his simplicity:

> [1]
> 1 Because God is perfectly simple (as was proved from his infinity), he cannot be
> 2 changed to some form which is received in him; because he is necessary existence (as
> 3 was proved from the primacy of efficiency ...), he cannot be changed from existence
> 4 to non-existence, or from non-existence to existence. ... God is said therefore to be
> 5 simply immutable in every [kind of] mutation, substantial or accidental.[5]

Every change is either substantial or accidental. Substantial changes are coming into existence and going out of existence; accidental changes are the changes that a persisting substance undergoes during its existence. The claim about accidental change [1.1–2] is straightforward enough, given Scotus's proof that a wholly simple being cannot be the subject of accidents. The point about necessary existence [1.2–4] is a little more complex. As we saw in chapter 2 §1 above, Scotus holds (in this sort of context) that a necessary existent is one that is necessarily uncaused. Given that no causal condition extrinsic to the nature of such a thing could account for its existence, it seems plausible enough to assume that no causal condition extrinsic to the nature of the thing could cause its demise. Scotus infers, then, that

---

[1] Scotus, *Ord.* 1.8.2.un., nn. 226–7 (Vatican, 280–1), referring to Aristotle, *Ph.* 7.1 (242^{a}13–20, 242^{b}18–19); *Ph.* 8.4–5 (255^{b}31–256^{a}21).

[2] Ibid., n. 228 (Vatican, IV, 281).

[3] On this, see in particular King, 'Duns Scotus on the Reality of Self-Change'; see too Scotus, *Ord.* 2.2.2.6, n. 470 (Vatican, VII, 366–7) for Scotus's discussion of the sense in which the '*omne quod movetur ab alio movetur*' principle is true (namely, as a claim about the efficient causes of substances, not about motion as such).

[4] Scotus, *Ord.* 1.8.2.un., n. 228 (Vatican, IV, 281).

[5] Ibid., n. 229 (Vatican, IV, 281).

such a being could not come into existence or pass out of existence [**1**.3–4]. Since it is the *nature* of the thing that is supposed to explain indestructibility, I take it that such a being could not voluntarily destroy itself.[6]

2 Immutability and Divine Freedom

As we saw in chapter 4 §1 above, Scotus holds that God is free in what we would describe as a contra-causal way. How can the notion of contra-causal freedom have any purchase in the context of complete immutability? Scotus spends some time worrying about divine action in the light of this problem. As outlined in chapter 4 §1 above, Scotus identifies contingency with freedom. Freedom, as Scotus understands it, requires the notion of choice at an instant: the claim that an agent willing *a* at time *t* retains its *power* at *t* to will not-*a*.[7] The notion of choice at an instant is a necessary presupposition in any account of the freedom of an immutable God. But it is not sufficient to deal with the problem. For the synchronic power for opposites is about a *power*: a power at one and the same time to do *a* or not-*a*. But an agent who, for example, wills *a* at *t* does not retain its *opportunity* at *t* to will not-*a*. So the notion of choice at an instant entails merely that an immutable God has the power to will all sorts of thing that he does not in fact will; it does not entail that he ever had the opportunity to will these things. As Scotus states the problem relative to divine action, 'both the will and the effect are invariable'.[8] Scotus attempts to deal with the issue by distinguishing an act of will from the objects and effects to which the act tends. In created wills, each object or effect is the object or effect of a distinct act of will. Each time I, for example, deliberately bring about some state of affairs, I have to will specifically *that* state of affairs. Hence my acts of will are constantly changing, as I successively will different things. At each stage in the succession, I lose the opportunity (though not of course the power) to will other than I do. To be able to range over different objects and effects is just what it is for the will to be free. But Scotus believes that the kind of mutability in the will entailed by successive and distinct acts of will is an imperfection. Thus, in God, there is one act of will directed to all actual effects God brings about:

[2]
1 Let us take those things which pertain to imperfection away from the divine will,
2 which is not indifferent to the acts through which it relates to diverse objects (for this is
3 an imperfection in us); rather its (viz. the divine will's) act is one and simple and
4 indifferent to diverse objects. It is both related necessarily to its first act, and related
5 contingently through that act to other [objects]. Thus therefore the divine will is not

---

[6] Unlike many of his contemporaries, Scotus does not hold that immutability is proper to God. He believes that there are many completely simple properties that cannot be subject to further properties or modifications. But such things are immutable as a result of their imperfection, and in any case are such that they come into existence and pass out of existence. So their immutability is of a different kind and order from God's: see *Ord.* 1.8.2.un., nn. 292–3 (Vatican, IV, 321–2).

[7] Scotus, *Lect.* 1.39.1–5, nn. 49–51 (Vatican, XVII, 494–6; Vos 116–20); see *Rep.* 1A.39–40.1–3, nn. 58–9 (Söder, 255–6).

[8] Scotus, *Rep.* 1A.39–40.1–3, n. 39 (Söder, 250).

6 indifferent to opposite acts, but is indifferent [to opposite objects] through one act (as
7 it is formally actually willing), for [it is] an unlimited and infinite [act]. So, on
8 account of unlimitedness, indifferently, it can will *a* and can will not-*a* in one unique
9 simple act, just as I [can do so] in many acts, since in us willing and nilling with
10 respect to the same object are diverse acts.[9]

Once I elicit an act of will for *a* at *t*, I lose my opportunity to will not-*a* at *t*. The reason is that willing *a* and willing not-*a* (nilling *a*, in Scotus's terminology) are two distinct and incompatible acts **[2.9–10]**. The problem does not arise in the case of God: his act is such that whichever of *a* or not-*a* God wills, he does so in just the same act. Willing *a* immutably thus does not mean that God could not immutably will not-*a* – although, of course, God cannot in fact will both *a* and not-*a* **[2.7–8]**. The rest of the passage is more straightforward. God's immutable willing means that he cannot go through any sort of *process* when he acts, and his possession of just one unlimited act of will is a way of denying process in God's activity **[2.3–4, 5–7]**. It is necessary that God's will is active, and in that act of will he indifferently wills all contingent states of affairs **[2.4–5]**. So acting on this account does not entail fixity to different objects – the opportunity to will different objects is in some sense not lost through the act itself.

3 Divine Timelessness

An intrinsically immutable God need not be timeless. Such a God could be everlasting. For mere changes in temporal location are not intrinsic changes, but merely changes in relation – merely Cambridge changes, as we would now say. A timeless God presumably could not undergo even such minimal changes. We have to say of a timeless God that it is not the case that he exists 'at' any one or more times at all: whatever his relation to time, it is not such as to include this sort of relation. It seems clear enough to me that a thinker like Aquinas, who wants to give God eternal cognitive access to the future (as much as to the past and the present), is committed to the notion that God is timeless. It must be admitted, however, that Aquinas is not always as clear as he might be. Because he wants to give God access to all times, he sometimes speaks as though God exists 'at' all times,[10] or (in similar vein) that all of time is 'present' to him.[11] A view like this makes it hard to sustain the reality of the distinction between past, present, and future. The whole of time is equally actual, and is equally present to God. Since distinctions between past, present, and future rely on their not all being equally actual – or equally present to anything – past, present, and future on Aquinas's view all turn out to be identical.[12]

Scotus criticizes Aquinas's view on the question of God's cognitive access to the future. It is often held that the burden of Scotus's critique is a denial of divine

---

[9] Ibid., n. 40 (Söder, 250–1).

[10] For a helpful list of references, see Brian Davies, *The Thought of Thomas Aquinas*, 108.

[11] See e.g. Aquinas, *ST* 1.14.13 c (I/1, 86^b–7^a).

[12] This does not mean that all events are simultaneous. Some events can be before others, but not in such a way as to be past, present, or future.

timelessness. For one obvious way of arguing that God cannot have cognitive access to the future is by claiming that he is temporal (though everlasting).[13] I doubt that this is the right way of reading the critique of Aquinas. For, as I noted above, what Scotus seems to want to do is sever God's immediate cognitive link with time, and it seems to me that the reason that he does so is that he sees that a failure to do so results in the breakdown of the distinction between past, present, and future – a distinction to which Scotus is evidently firmly committed.[14] I have argued this point above, and will not repeat the material here.

Scotus, then, if I am right, gives a way in principle for the existence of a timeless God to be consistent with the reality of what philosophers sometimes call 'A-series' time: that time which is perceived as passage from future to past. But what is the evidence that Scotus's God is timeless? After all, one of the more powerful reasons for supposing that Aquinas's God is timeless is that Aquinas's God has cognitive access equally to the whole of time. The position in Scotus is somewhat complex. Scotus quotes Boethius's famous definition of God's eternity: 'Eternity is endless life, possessed perfectly and all at once'.[15] And he makes it clear too that we should accept talk of a 'static' now: God's existence is all at once, and without ceasing.[16] But we need to treat this definition with caution. For life is, usually, a process – a successive thing, in the medieval jargon – and processes, as the medievals noticed, do not have all their parts at once.[17] Boethius's definition might just be a way of asserting that God's life is not a process. He possesses all his parts or intrinsic properties at once. But the same could be true of a completely intrinsically static but everlasting item, and perhaps even of substances in general, provided that we distinguish a substance from its life-story. For a substance may not be a process even if its life-story is. Temporal items do not have to have temporal parts. On many – indeed, most – views of substances, not only ancient and medieval but also modern, a material substance is not a four-dimensional object, but a three-dimensional object that, for any time that it exists, exists as a whole.

Much the same considerations should prevent us from taking Scotus's account of the notion of divine, immutable, choice at an instant as evidence in favour of God's timelessness. As we saw above, Scotus holds that God's will differs from ours by (among other things) being immutable. Now a choice made by an immutable agent is not a choice that can take time: God's choice must simply always have been determined by him.

Still, it seems to me that there is some unequivocal evidence that Scotus believes God to be timeless. Scotus holds that, when producing temporal effects, God, as an infinitely powerful disembodied Spirit, does so merely by willing such effects. And willing does not require undergoing any further process at the time that the effect comes about. God's causal activity could be at least temporally 'telekinetic':

---

[13] Craig, *The Problem of Divine Foreknowledge*, 130.

[14] I mention Scotus's attempts to deal with the distinct reality of past, present, and future in chapter 4 §§ 6–7 above.

[15] Scotus, *Quod.* 6, n. 14 (Wadding, XII, 150; Alluntis and Wolter, 141 (¶ 6.34)), quoting Boethius, *Cons.* 5.6, n. 4 (Moreschini, 155).

[16] Scotus, *Ord.* 1.9.un., n. 11 (Vatican, IV, 332–3).

[17] See my *The Physics of Duns Scotus*, 215–16.

[3]
1 A new effect can be made by an old act of the will without a change of will. Just as I,
2 by means of my continuous volition (by which I will something to be done), will then
3 do it just for the 'when' for which I will to do it, so God in eternity willed something
4 other than himself to be for some time and then created it for the 'when' for which he
5 willed it to be.[18]

The idea here is that an act of will need not be temporally simultaneous with the effect that is ultimately brought about as a result of that act of will. Scotus gives an example: I can today will something to take place tomorrow [**3**.1–3]. The point about my willing being continuous is that I cannot bring something about tomorrow without willing and doing something tomorrow – my causal activity inevitably involves (physical) process. But God's willing is causally sufficient for its effect, and God does not need to go through any such process. So God can bring about an effect tomorrow just by willing (today) that that effect occur (tomorrow) [**3**.3–5]. Scotus carefully attaches the time index (the 'when') to the effect, not to the act of will which brings that effect about [**3**.4].

Still, Scotus makes a further point here. Unlike me, or some agent who really acts telekinetically 'from the past', God does not have to wait for his effect. Not having to wait clearly entails being timeless:

[4]
1 [God's] will is not impotent; neither does it have existence in time, such that it would
2 wait for the time for which it produces what it wills. It does not will this [willed
3 thing] then to exist necessarily when it wills. Rather, it wills [it] to exist for some
4 determined time – for which, however, it does not wait, for the operation of [God's]
5 will is not in time.[19]

Again, the time indices are scrupulously attached to the effect, not to the causal or volitional activity in God [**4**.3–4]. But God's causal activity is in fact not *temporally* prior to its effect at all. God's effects are not willed telekinetically 'from the past'. God's effects are willed *timelessly*, and God's willing lacks any and every temporal location. God is thus not only immutable, but also timeless.

---

[18] Scotus, *Ord.* 1.8.2.un., n. 294 (Vatican, IV, 322).
[19] Ibid., n. 297 (Vatican, IV, 324).

PART II

THE TRINITARIAN NATURE
OF THE ONE GOD

Chapter 9

The Trinity and Scientific Demonstration

1 Demonstration and Self-evidence

In the early *Lectura*, Scotus claims that there are arguments for the Trinity that are 'more demonstrative than many demonstrations posited in metaphysics'.[1] As far as I can see, Scotus never diverges from his early view that the arguments in favour of the Trinity are demonstrative in this way. In the *Ordinatio*, for example, he criticizes some of the arguments offered by his predecessors – notably Henry of Ghent – on the grounds that the arguments fail 'if he [Henry] wants to *persuade* the unbeliever'.[2] Still, the *Ordinatio* makes it clear that, while persuasive, Scotus's arguments do not count as demonstrations: 'According to the Canterbury articles, it is necessary that the reasons used to solve this question [viz. whether there can be productions in God] are not demonstrations.'[3] The Vatican editors rightly query this, since there is no extant evidence of any such claim in the Oxonian condemnations of 1277 under Robert Kilwardby, or the Canterbury condemnations of 1286 under John Pecham.[4] But what, in any case, is the distinction intended between a 'demonstration' and a 'persuasion'? As Antonie Vos has noted, the claim that the arguments are intended to be no more than 'persuasions' does not mean that they are not proofs in the modern sense (i.e. true and valid deductive arguments).[5] Scotus restricts the domain of demonstrations to just two kinds of deductive argument: arguments *propter quid*, and arguments *quia* – technical terms translating Aristotle's '*dioti*' and '*hoti*'.[6] A *propter quid* demonstration is, in Scotus's account, one that satisfies the very stringent conditions laid out in the Introduction and Part I, chapter 2 §1 above: an argument whose premises are (1) certain, (2) necessary, (3) self-evident, and (4) explanatory of their conclusion. I dealt with the first two of these in chapter 2 §1 above. The explanatoriness condition is simply that the premises must offer the *reason why* the conclusion is true. Demonstrations *quia* are not explanatory in this way: *propter quid* demonstrations reason from causes to their effects; *quia* demonstrations from effects to their causes. (On this, see the Introduction above.)[7]

Self-evidence is more important, and, unlike necessity and explanatoriness, it is in Scotus's account a feature shared with demonstrations *quia* too. Basically, a claim

---

[1] Scotus, *Lect.* 1.2.2.1–4, n. 165 (Vatican, XVI, 167).

[2] Scotus, *Ord.* 1.2.2.1–4, n. 252 (Vatican, II, 277).

[3] Ibid., n. 242 (Vatican, II, 274).

[4] See Scotus, *Opera Omnia* (Vatican, II, 274, n. T 1).

[5] See Antonie Vos, 'The Scotian Notion of Natural Law', 210.

[6] See Aristotle, *An. post.* 1.13–14 (78ᵃ22–79ᵃ33).

[7] Scotus, *Quod.* 7, n. 3 (Wadding, XII, 169; Alluntis and Wolter, 160 (¶ 7.7)). These claims are just commonplaces in the Aristotelian tradition.

128   *Duns Scotus on God*

is self-evident if it can be known non-inferentially, and such claims are of two types: necessary and contingent, respectively the premises in *propter quid* and *quia* demonstrations. Typically, necessary and self-evident claims are knowable simply from the definitions of their terms, and these sorts of claims are the premises in *propter quid* demonstrations.[8] Examples of such claims would be *a priori* claims: indeed, Aristotle's examples are precisely such – the law of non-contradiction and the claim that a part is always less than a whole – and Scotus cites these too.[9] It is not clear to me, however, that all such underivable claims are *a priori*. As a good essentialist, Scotus holds in effect that there are analytic *a posteriori* statements, and definitions and various sorts of other broadly logical truths fit this description. At least some of these, according to Scotus, will be *per se nota*: so-called 'immediate' truths, such as 'man is a rational animal'.[10] The contingent, empirical premises of a demonstration *quia* are likewise in some sense self-evident: known directly and non-inferentially:

[1]
1 Although [the statement that something is effected] is contingent with relation to God,
2 it is a most evident contingent [statement], such that someone who denied that some
3 being exists that is not eternal needs both sense faculty and punishment.[11]

Coming from Scotus's proof for the existence of a first being (dealt with above in Part I, chapter 2), the problem here is how to derive the (necessarily true) claim that God exists from the contingent claim that something is effected, since on the face of it necessary claims should be more evident than contingent ones **[1.1–2]**. Scotus's argument is that the contingent claim that there exist beings that are not beginningless is 'most evident', such that denying it could result only from a complete lack of all sense faculties, or else wilful stubbornness **[1.2–3]**.[12] I take it that, for Scotus, the point of distinguishing both of these sorts of demonstration (*propter quid* and *quia*) from other probative arguments is that both forms, since they are based on evident truths, guarantee a greater degree of certainty than other sorts of argument.

2 The Trinity and Demonstration

The claim, then, that the proofs of the Trinity are not demonstrations simply means that they are not based on premises that have the strong degree of *evidence* (i.e. either inferential underivability or empirical undeniability) required for a

---

[8] Scotus, *Lect.* 1.2.1.1–2, n. 14 (Vatican, XVI, 114–15); see too *Ord.* 3.24.un., n. 14 (Wadding, VII, 483). The whole position is recounted in Vos, 'Scotian Notion', 205–11, summarized at 209.

[9] For the first, see e.g. Scotus, *Super praed.* 4, n. 12 (St Bonaventure, I, 276); for the second, *In Metaph.* 6.3, n. 56 (St Bonaventure, IV, 76); *Ord.* 3.24, n. 19 (Wadding, VII, 486).

[10] See e.g. Scotus, *Ord.* 3.7.1, n. 7 (Wadding, VII, 192).

[11] Scotus, *Lect.* 1.2.1.1–2, n. 56 (Vatican, XVI, 131).

[12] Elsewhere, Scotus notes that this sort of experiential knowledge is a necessary part of all sorts of scientific reasoning: see e.g. Scotus, *Quod.* 7, n. 3 (Wadding, XII, 169; Alluntis and Wolter, 160–1 (¶ 7.7)), citing Aristotle, *Metaph.* A.1 (980^{b}28) and *An. post.* 2.19 (100^{a}3–12).

demonstration. In point of fact, I take it that the premisses are necessary but derivable. So the proof will be strongly deductive, though not demonstrative in the strict sense. In the *Quodlibet*, Scotus goes into some detail on the question of the failure of the proofs to count as demonstrations. In this work, he makes it clear that his objection to the demonstrative nature of the arguments is not simply fideistic, based on the alleged ruling of John Pecham. But the discussion makes it clear too just how little Scotus is denying in claiming that the arguments are not demonstrations, and the reasons he gives for his position are often of a highly specialized nature, as we shall see. The whole of question 14 of the *Quodlibet* is devoted to the discussion, and Scotus includes a consideration of various varieties of faith that, although interesting, is irrelevant to my purpose here. Equally, Scotus includes a long disquisition on the impossibility of natural knowledge of the quiddity or defining features of God that is beyond my immediate aim, though I return to it in the Appendix below.

Basically, Scotus claims that a *propter quid* demonstration for God's Trinitarian nature would require immediate knowledge of those features of the divine essence that *explain* God's being a Trinity, knowledge that we clearly do not have in the normal run of things.[13] The reason is that God's self-revelation is a voluntary matter: we cannot have intuitive knowledge of his essence unless he shows himself to us. Neither can we have abstractive knowledge, because no created representation is such that we can abstract knowledge of the divine essence from it in any non-inferential way.[14]

Scotus reasons similarly about a demonstration *quia* of God's Trinitarian nature. There are no empirically evident facts – facts that could not intelligibly be denied – sufficient to ground the claim that God is a Trinity. The relevant empirically evident facts lead simply to the existence of one God, not to a Trinity of persons:

[2]
1 Concerning knowledge *quia*, I say that no one can now attain, merely by natural
2 means, understanding of the Trinity in God in this way, for he cannot know about a
3 cause, by a demonstration *quia* through an effect, something such that, if it were
4 eliminated, there would remain in the cause whatever is necessary for causing. But if,
5 *per impossibile*, the Trinity were eliminated, whatever is necessary in God for causing
6 a creature would still be possessed, for [there would be] both a perfect and complete
7 formal principle of causing, and a *suppositum* having that formal perfect principle. ...
8 But a perfect *suppositum* having a perfect formal principle seems to be sufficient for
9 causing.[15]

---

[13] Scotus, *Quod.* 14, n. 9 (Wadding, XII, 356; Alluntis and Wolter, 323–4 (¶ 14.35)). 'In the normal run of things' = '*de lege communi*': see Wolter's helpful comment at Alluntis and Wolter, 163, n. 11.

[14] Ibid., nn. 10–11 (Wadding, XII, 369; Alluntis and Wolter, 324–5 (¶ 14.36–14.37)); see too *Ord.* 1.3.1.1–2, n. 57 (Vatican, III, 39; *PW*, 26; Frank and Wolter, 114–16). Scotus holds that God can give, by revelation, perfect abstractive knowledge of his essence, but that we cannot have such knowledge naturally. On the possibility of perfect abstractive knowledge of the divine essence, see Stephen D. Dumont, 'Theology as a Practical Science and Duns Scotus's Distinction between Intuitive and Abstractive Cognition', discussing relevant parts of the prologue of *Rep.*

[15] Scotus, *Quod.* 14, n. 9 (Wadding, XII, 359; Alluntis and Wolter, 323 (¶ 14.34)).

The general principle is that a demonstration *quia* will not yield knowledge of features of the cause that are not necessary for the production of the effect [**2.2–4**]. What is required for causing a creature is (i) a *suppositum* and (ii) the *suppositum*'s possession of the relevant causal power [**2.6–7**], and indeed these two conditions are jointly sufficient too [**2.8–9**]. But these two criteria would be met even if Unitarianism were true [**2.4–6**].[16] So arguments from evident effect to cause will not yield the existence of God's Trinitarian nature [**2.1–2**].[17]

Having said this, it is clear that Scotus regards his own arguments as stronger than those of his opponents, who appeal to arguments of the 'good is self-diffusive' kind, rejected by Scotus because 'it would be necessary to show that communication of the same thing or nature is possible, for there is no power or communication of goodness to the impossible including a contradiction'.[18] Bare appeal to this principle is, according to Scotus, weaker than his own argument, since his own argument can – and his opponents' cannot – show that the relevant communication is possible. Scotus's argument appeals to what he believes is a different but familiar example – the generation of a thought-act, in this case. But the appeal is not sufficient for a demonstration, for 'it is not evident that perfect memory is a principle of production':[19] the philosophy of mind is not overwhelmingly, undeniably, evident, in the way that *a priori* claims and many empirical claims are. I give in footnotes as I proceed some of the clarifications that Scotus makes to his arguments against someone who would argue that they would amount to demonstrations.

[16] On the existence of a divine *suppositum* given Unitarianism, and more generally on the question of the distinction between *suppositum* and nature, see chapter 12 §§2 and 3, and chapter 13 §1, respectively, below.

[17] Elsewhere, Scotus suggests that the presence of the image of the Trinity in the mind is 'valid for someone who believes in the Trinity to persuade how [the Trinity] can be, but [does] not prove (*concludunt*) that [the Trinity] exists, for that whole conjunction of many things in the mind – in which the image consists – could be, and is, [possessed] by one person. For this reason, it cannot be shown that it is an image of the Trinity by a demonstration *quia*': Scotus, *Ord.* 1.3.3.4, n. 597 (Vatican, III, 352). This claim is not made about arguments for the Trinity in general, but merely for an argument directly from the image to the Trinity.

[18] Scotus, *Ord.* 1.2.2.1–4, n. 256 (Vatican, II, 279), rejecting the argument proposed in Bonaventure, *In Sent.* 1.2.un.2, arg. 1 (I, 53a).

[19] Ibid. 1.2.2.1–4, n. 245 (Vatican, II, 275).

Chapter 10

Internal Divine Productions

As we saw in Part I, Scotus's argument for God's existence arrives at the existence of an individual substance. Scotus believes that – with the caveats mentioned in chapter 9 above – it is possible to provide arguments to show that this divine substance is a Trinity of persons. The argument, in its first stages, goes more or less like this: there are internal divine productions; there are just two such productions, and one producer; the producer and the products are all persons. This yields the conclusion that there are just three divine persons. In chapters 10–12 I present these three stages of the argument. In chapter 13 I deal with the relationship between the persons and the divine substance.

1 A General Proof of Internal Divine Productivity

Scotus offers four arguments in all in favour of the existence of internal productions in God. I will consider two of these arguments: the first and the third. The third, with which I begin, is a general argument to show that there are productions internal to God. It does not specify just what these productions are:

> **[1]**
> 1 In every state of being which is not by nature imperfect, necessity is simply a
> 2 perfection. Therefore [it is so] also in production, for that [i.e. production] does not
> 3 imply imperfection in itself. Proof of the antecedent: just as the necessary is a state of
> 4 perfection in being as being, so too it belongs to the perfection of anything dividing
> 5 being, provided that [the thing] is not in itself imperfect and limited. For just as when
> 6 being is divided by opposed [objects], one of the dividers is perfect in being, and the
> 7 other imperfect, so in anything which is perfect, in any division of [this thing], one
> 8 member is possible – which is an imperfection – and the other necessary – which is a
> 9 perfection. But a producer as such does not include imperfection; therefore any
> 10 producer perfect in the nature of producing is a producer necessarily. But the first
> 11 producer cannot be necessarily productive of anything external, other than itself, as is
> 12 said in distinction 8. Therefore [it is necessarily productive] internally. The same is
> 13 argued about natural production, for natural production is the first production.
> 14 Therefore it pertains to the first producer. But it cannot belong to the first producer
> 15 externally, as will be shown elsewhere. Therefore [the first producer is naturally
> 16 productive] internally.[1]

The argument here is that *being productive* is not an imperfection **[1.2–3]**, and that necessity is a perfection of any attribute that is not imperfect **[1.1–2]** – such as *being*

---

[1] Scotus, *Ord.* 1.2.2.1–4, n. 239 (Vatican, II, 271–2), referring to *Ord.* 1.8.2.un., nn. 259–68 (Vatican, IV, 300–5).

productive. So for anything that is productive it is a greater perfection to be so necessarily than merely contingently, and anything perfectly productive – anything which is a perfect producer – produces necessarily [**1.9–10**]. But this necessary production cannot be external, since, as we saw in Part I, chapter 4 §1 above, Scotus argues that creation is contingent, and he does so by appealing not to Christian revelation but simply to reason [**1.10–11, 14–15**]. Since the only alternative to external production is internal production, God is necessarily internally productive [**1.11–12**]. Most of [**1**] is taken up with the proof of the controversial premiss in [**1.1**] that necessity is a perfection of anything not imperfect. The premiss is that necessity is a perfection of being [**1.3–4**], and the thought behind this is simply that being necessary is more perfect than being contingent. Scotus argues that this must, *pari passu*, be true too of any perfection: it is more perfect for a perfection to be possessed necessarily than for it to be possessed contingently [**1.4–9**]. Actual production, however, is not an imperfection, and as such is possessed necessarily rather than contingently in anything perfectly able to produce [**1.9–10**].

Natural production [**1.13**] is a particular sort of production, contrasted with *voluntary* production; the point here is that any voluntary production presupposes an involuntary production, and hence that – given that God is contingently creative – a natural production must belong to God [**1.14**]. And again this production must be internal, not external [**1.14–16**]. Scotus holds that any act of will (any voluntary production) presupposes a cognitive act. Cognitive acts are natural; hence every voluntary act presupposes a natural act. (Scotus believes that there is an internal voluntary production in God too; I will deal with this below.)

The argument in [**1**], as are many of the ones that Scotus uses in his deduction of God's Trinitarian nature, seems an unashamed piece of perfect-being theology. And as we saw in Part I, chapter 3, Scotus is somewhat ambivalent about this principle. When criticizing the probative nature of some of his arguments in favour of the Trinity, Scotus worries that at least one of the perfection claims that he relies on is insecure.[2] But I get no sense that he is troubled by the whole perfect-being project in this context.

2 Internal Production by Memory

The first argument in favour of internal productions in God – by far the most complex – makes use of Scotus's account of the formation of an occurrent mental act described briefly in Part I, chapter 4 §3 above. Basically, occurrent mental acts in creatures are caused jointly by the object of cognition and the memory (the storehouse for mental objects of cognition). Scotus splits the argument into sections, and I follow his divisions:

[**2**]
1 Whatever is, in its formal nature (*de ratione sua formali*), a productive principle, is a
2 productive principle in anything in which it exists without imperfection. But
3 perfected memory, or (which is the same thing), this whole: *the intellect having an*

---

[2] See Ibid., 1.2.2.1–4, n. 243 (Vatican, II, 275).

4 *intelligible object present to it*, is, in its formal nature, a principle productive of
5 generated knowledge. And it is clear that this sort of memory is in some divine
6 person in itself, because there is some unproduced [divine person]. Therefore this
7 [person] will be able perfectly to produce by means of such a perfect principle.[3]

'In its formal nature' means basically 'by definition', and the first premiss of the
argument, in [2.1–2], is that something that is by definition a productive principle is
not prevented from being so by existing in something perfectly. The rest of the
argument is a little compressed, but Scotus means us to understand that part of the
'formal nature' of memory is to be productive – memory is, among other things, the
faculty responsible for the formation of an occurrent mental act ('generated
knowledge') and that memory exists perfectly in some subject when it has an
'intelligible object present to it' [2.2–5]. So memory, in such circumstances, is
productive: it forms mental acts (recall the distinction between production and
operation outlined in Part I, chapter 1 §1 above). The 'intelligible objects' that
Scotus is talking about can be either internal representations (intelligible species),
or external objects, in the case that such objects are directly accessible to memory –
as in intuitive cognition, discussed in Part I, chapter 4 §2 above. As Scotus makes
clear in passage [3] below, he believes that the divine essence is an intelligible object
immediately present to the divine memory, and [2.5–6] assert that such memory –
with an object present to it – is in some person. Such a person, then, will be able to
produce [2.6–7]. (I discuss the identity of the divine producer as a *person* in chapter
4 §2 below.)

Having established this much, Scotus goes on to show two further points
necessary for his argument: first, that the thing that can be produced is infinite, and
thus (since only God is infinite) internal to God somehow; and secondly that a thing
that can be produced in the way described will be produced:

[3]
1 I argue further: no production through perfect memory is perfect unless it is [the
2 production] of knowledge equal (*adaequatae*) to the memory or the intellect with
3 respect to such an object. But only infinite knowledge is equal to the memory or
4 intellect of an infinite divine person with respect to the divine essence as intelligible,
5 for that intellect is able to comprehend that infinite object. Therefore, some divine
6 person can produce, through memory, infinite knowledge. Furthermore, this
7 [knowledge] can be only in the divine nature, for this alone is infinite. Therefore,
8 there can be, through memory, an internal production in God. Furthermore, if it can
9 be so, it therefore is, both because what is possible [in God] is necessary, and because
10 that principle is naturally productive, and therefore necessarily so. The consequence
11 is proved, because it can neither be prevented, nor depend on some other in its action:
12 for every agent [that acts] from the necessity of nature acts unless it is either prevented
13 or dependent on some other in its acting.[4]

To understand the point that knowledge could be 'equal' to a power [3.2–3], we need
to keep in mind various things. The first is that the apparently quantitative measure

[3] Ibid., n. 221 (Vatican, II, 259–60).
[4] Ibid., n. 222 (Vatican, II, 260–1).

Scotus is applying here is simply an assertion of a degree of perfection: infinite perfection in the case at hand. (I dealt with Scotus's account of infinity in Part I, chapter 5 above.) We need to keep in mind too that, according to Scotus, knowledge is an act of the intelligence, and an act of the intelligence is a quality. Scotus's ontology, as I mentioned above, tends to reify properties such as qualities, and in some sense for Scotus qualities are as real as substances (substances themselves being complexes of properties). In this sort of ontology, it is not entirely senseless to think that, if substances admit of degrees of perfection, qualities can do too. The argument in [3.1–3] is that perfect memory – memory with an object present to it – produces an act that is just as perfect as the memory is in relation to its object.

The perfection of memory in relation to its object is meant to cover various different things: the degree of memory's capacity to grasp its object, and the degree of perfection of the object thus grasped. Scotus clarifies the first of these as follows:

[4]
1 Just as there is no perfect memory in relation to some intelligible thing unless that
2 object is present in the reason as actually intelligible to the extent to which it can be
3 intelligible to that [reason], so there is no perfect product (*proles*) of that memory
4 unless it is an actual knowledge of that object that is of as great an extent as can
5 pertain to such an intellect in relation to such an object. And this I call 'equal' to that
6 intellect in relation to such an object.[5]

Clearly, a perfect product is relative to the power of the intellect knowing it: I have a perfect cognitive product on this view if I have a knowledge that is as great a knowledge of some object as a human person ('such an intellect') could have [4.3–5]. This does not mean that, considered absolutely, there could not be – in another mind – a more perfect product. God has a more perfect knowledge of the nature of human DNA than any scientist; a clever scientist could still have knowledge that is perfect relative to human cognitive capacities. And 'knowledge of [an] object that is of as great an extent as can pertain to such an intellect in relation to such an object' is Scotus's 'equal' knowledge: 'equal to that intellect in relation to such an object' [4.5–6].

On the face of it, the point is that the *contents* of the mental act – the concept – are as perfect as the object of the concept, but that imperfection can arise both in the nature of the object and in the ability of the mind to form an act equal to the object of the act. (I introduced the distinction between an act (a real qualitative accident) and its contents (non-real or intentional) in Part I, chapter 4 §3 above.) Indeed, it is clear that it is the contents of an occurrent mental act that are at issue in [4], since it is the extent of the 'knowledge' had by a cognizer that is at stake – and the perfection of someone's knowledge is centrally determined by how well the contents of that person's mental acts correspond to the objects that they represent. In the case of a mind able fully to grasp an object of infinite perfection, there is no reason why the contents of the act are not infinitely perfect, and this is Scotus's point in [3.3–5]. Nevertheless, there seems to be an ambiguity here, for the conclusion seems to be not that the contents of the act are infinitely perfect, but that

---

[5] Ibid., n. 225 (Vatican, II, 263).

the act itself is – the entity that would, in the case of a finite intellect, be an inherent quality, and that in the case of God is (as we shall see) a subsistent entity. Scotus feels warranted in concluding, given the conclusion in the argument in [2.6–7] (namely that a divine person can produce a mental act), that a divine person can produce some act that is infinitely perfect (the 'infinite knowledge' of [3.6]), and this is his point in [3.5–6]. Perhaps Scotus thinks it obvious that an act whose contents are perfect, and which is had by an infinitely perfect agent, will itself simply be infinitely perfect. The infinite nature of the act allows Scotus to conclude that the possible act will be internal to God, since only God is infinite [3.6–7]. Since acts are produced, it follows that any such production is internal to God [3.7–8].

The conclusion at this point in the argument is that it is possible that there is an internal production in God. Scotus offers two distinct arguments to show that, if it is possible that there is an internal production in God, then there will be such a production in reality [3.8–10]. The first is that 'what is possible [in God] is necessary' [3.9]. We encountered this principle in Part I, chapter 2 §1 above. The second argument – very similar to this – has to do with the nature of a 'natural cause'. The distinction between natural and rational (free) causes, modified from Aristotle's account in *Metaphysics* Θ, is fundamental in Scotus's account of causality, as we have seen. Here the argument is that memory, as had by an unproduced divine person, is a 'principle [that] is naturally productive, and therefore necessarily so' [3.10], and Scotus's proof of this simply draws on the definition of a natural cause as one that 'acts unless it is either prevented or dependent on some other in its acting' [3.12–13]; perfect memory, had by an unproduced divine person, is such that it is neither preventable (by some prior agent) nor causally dependent (on some prior agent) [3.11]. So this memory is necessarily productive, and there is a necessary production in God.

There are some obvious difficulties raised by the complex discussion in [2] and [3], and Scotus gives detailed arguments in favour of various premises that could be regarded as not obviously true. I have discussed one such case in relation to [3] above. Perhaps the most dubious premiss in [2] is that 'perfected memory ... is, in its formal nature, a principle productive of generated knowledge' [2.3–5]. For it could be argued that while memory in creatures is productive of mental acts, it makes little sense to speak of *God's* memory as being productive of such acts. God does not need to call things to mind; if he always and necessarily knows what he knows, what need is there to think of God's memory as productive of occurrent acts of thought? Worries of this nature clearly caused Scotus some difficulty, and he formulates various related objections to his view. Central is the objection that the divine intellect does not – indeed cannot – form mental acts, because such production implies that the intellect's acts are somehow distinct from it, and thus that they perfect it. But the divine intellect is not like this. It knows necessarily, and its acts are not thus distinct from it.[6]

Scotus's discussion includes various attempts at identifying a coherent response. If the divine intellect were to be perfected by episodic mental acts, this would imply that the formation of such acts requires the intellect to have a passive capacity to receive them. The reply attempts to show that this is not necessarily so:

---

[6] Ibid., nn. 227–9 (Vatican, II, 264).

[5]

1 I say that our intellect has a receptive potency in relation to produced knowledge, and
2 this potentiality is an imperfection, since it is a passive potentiality. But this has no
3 direct bearing on the nature (*ratio*) of a productive principle, especially when the
4 productive principle can be perfect in itself. For our intellect has the nature of a
5 productive principle in relation to produced knowledge, and this derives from its
6 perfection, to the extent that a first act virtually contains a second act.
7 It is clear that the first of these – namely, the reception of an intellection –
8 pertains to the passive intellect. About the second, it is not thus certain whether it
9 belongs to the passive or the active intellect – this will be discussed elsewhere. Now,
10 however, if we accept indistinctly about the intellect that it is a principle that is
11 productive of knowledge (which I think sufficiently true, and which will be shown in
12 distinction 3), and intellect is in God in this way (for he has intellect in every way
13 which does not imply imperfection), then I argue thus: whenever two things are
14 accidentally connected in something – namely, the notions of acting and of undergoing
15 – and the thing which is the basis for acting is *per se*, it is no less the basis for acting:
16 this is clear from *Physics* 2, about the doctor healing himself. If medicine is separated
17 from infirmity, no less will there remain the notion of healing. Therefore if these two
18 are separated from each other in the intellect, the nature of producing will remain if
19 the thing that was the *per se* basis for producing remains, even if there is no passive
20 receptive potentiality there.[7]

In [5.2–6, 13–20] Scotus argues that the notion of production does not require the
notion of a form somehow impressed on, or made to inhere in, some patient – a
notion central to Aristotle's understanding of causation. [5.2–4] suggests that the
notion of passive receptivity is distinct from that of production, and more so 'when
the productive principle can be perfect in itself'. The crucial claim is [5.4–6]: for
first act virtually to contain second act is a complex way of saying that some entity
(first act) is able to operate or cause (second act). As we have seen, Scotus's standard
cognitive theory requires that memory brings about (produces) an operation that
perfects (inheres in) the intelligence (intelligence is part of the passive intellect:
hence the claim in [5.7–8]).[8] [5.9–13] makes it clear that God has memory: the
relevant active power – the productive aspect of intellect – and that production does
not require passivity.

[5.13–17] rather unsuccessfully attempts to relate the issue specifically to the
question of reflexive action. For the intellect is supposed to act on itself in the
formation of occurrent acts of knowledge, and in [5.13–17] Scotus tries to come up
with an Aristotelian example to show that even in the case in which action and
passion are linked in some one agent, the active power is no less an active power
than it would be in the case in which action and passion belong to really distinct
items. He considers Aristotle's example of a doctor who heals himself. The doctor's
active power of healing is no less an active power in this case than it is in the case
that he heals someone other than himself. *Pari passu*, Scotus reasons, the notion of
the production of a mental act remains even in the absence of an intrinsic recipient

---

[7] Scotus, Ibid., nn. 231–3 (Vatican, II, 265–6), referring to Aristotle, *Ph.* 2.1 (192ᵇ23–7).

[8] Scotus is unsure whether the aspect of the memory that is responsible for producing occurrent acts
of thought should be classified as active or as passive intellect: for the whole discussion, see *Quod.* 15,
nn. 13–20 (Wadding, 425–33; Alluntis and Wolter, 355–63 (¶¶ 15.40–15.62)).

of the formed concept [5.17–20]. The argument can hardly be counted a success. The doctor's healing agency does not have to relate to himself as recipient, but it certainly has to relate to *some* recipient; the argument does not show that the notion of agency could survive the lack of *any* recipient.

Still, it is easy enough to see what Scotus is trying to say: the notion of the production of occurrent mental acts does not require, other than *per accidens*, the notion of a recipient for the act. The purely active divine mind needs no recipient: it simply, actively, produces an act. The notion of the active production of an act, without any corresponding passion, is a perfection. This may make it look as though the relevant production amounts to creation. Scotus holds, however, that the act produced remains internal to God; indeed, as we shall see in chapter 12 §1 below, he holds that the act is a further exemplification of the divine essence, and as such certainly not a creature.

Scotus must be right in thinking that it is not obvious that the production of mental acts is in any way the result of the imperfection of creaturely existence, or of our cognitive mechanisms. There is an obvious contrast here: the abstraction of intelligible species from phantasms. God does not know by abstraction, and does not require an active intellect. God's nature gives him immediate access to all possible objects, without the need to abstract representations from particular instances. God does not need intelligible species in his thinking. But he needs acts of thought (even if in some way these have to be identical with his essence).

One other significant point is the claim in [2.6] that there is an unproduced divine person. Since there is at least one unproduced item in God, the only way in which there could fail to be at least one unproduced divine item would be if there is an infinite regress of such items, each one produced by one or more others in a causal sequence. As we saw in Part I chapter 1 above, Scotus rejects the possibility of such an infinite causal sequence, and he applies his reasoning in the case of divine things too, specifically claiming that one divine person must have memory without in any way being produced: 'Unless some person in God had perfect memory *a se*, there would be an infinite regress.'[9] (I will return to the number of such unproduced persons below.)

3 Internal Production by Will

Scotus believes that an argument comparable to that in [2] can be given to show the necessity of the production of some further, non-cognitive, act, corresponding to another sort of power that Scotus has shown God to have, namely, will:

[6]
1 The same can be argued about the will, for the will having an actually cognized object
2 present to it, is by its nature productive of love for such a produced object.[10]

This is the final stage in Scotus's first argument in favour of productions in God. Elsewhere, he goes into rather more detail:

---

[9] Scotus, *Ord.* 1.2.2.1–4, *text. int.* (Vatican, II, 262, ll. 11–13).
[10] Ibid., n. 226 (Vatican, II, 263).

[7]

1 There is will in God (as is clear from question 1 of the second distinction and also
2 from the question 'On the attributes' in distinction 8).
3 It is also clear from this, that God is in his nature blessed. But blessedness
4 cannot exist without will, or without an act of will. ...
5 And from these [claims], furthermore: in anything in which there is some
6 principle which is in its nature a productive principle, that [principle] will be for [that
7 thing] a principle of producing, if it is in it without imperfection, and is not
8 understood already to have some product that is simply equal [to it]. In God, as has
9 been proved, will formally exists by nature, and as (*sub ratione*) a free productive
10 principle with respect to love, and it is clear that it is there without imperfection.
11 Therefore there will be in God a principle for the production of love, in proportion to
12 his perfection, such that, just as a created will is the principle for the production of a
13 love as great as the love by which it can love an object (which is called 'equal love'
14 (*amor adaequatus*)), so this [viz. divine] will is a principle for the production of a love
15 as great as the [will] can love an infinite object. But [the divine will] by nature loves
16 an infinite object with infinite love. Therefore the will by nature is a principle for the
17 production of infinite love.[11]

Will is by nature productive of acts of love – producing acts of love is, in other words, simply the sort of thing that will does [7.5–6]. If something that is by nature productive exists without imperfection in some entity, then it will be by nature productive in that entity [7.6–7]. But will exists in God [7.1–2], without imperfection [7.8–10]. So will in God is by nature productive [7.11–12]. In fact, God is by nature blessed, and thus by nature productive of an act of love [7.3–4]. Acts of love increase in value in proportion to the value of the object, up to whatever intrinsic ceiling or limit there is in the capacity of the relevant power [7.11–13]. But the capacity of the divine will is infinite – there is thus no intrinsic limit to its perfection – and the perfection of the object is infinite [7.15–16]. Therefore the love produced is infinite too [7.17].[12]

This raises an obvious question. If the divine will is naturally productive of an act of love, how can its act of love be free? For something that is naturally productive is – assuming no external block – necessarily productive. And we might be forgiven for thinking that something that is necessarily productive is not freely productive.

---

[11] Ibid., 1.10.un., nn. 6–7, 9 (Vatican, IV, 341–2), Ibid. 1.2.1.1–2, nn. 75–88 (Vatican, II, 175–80; *PW*, 52–6); Ibid. 1.8.1.4, nn. 177–217 (Vatican, IV, 246–74). On the whole question discussed in this section, see too the comments in A. Vos and others, *Duns Scotus on Divine Love: Texts and Commentary on Goodness and Freedom, God and Humans*, 208–22.

[12] Scotus does not devote much space to the question of the production of an act of will in creatures. But it is clear that he sees something very analogous to the sort of structure proposed for the act of understanding or intellection. Thus he suggests that the will has productive and operative potencies in much the same way as intellect is divided into memory and intelligence – though he does not give these potencies names (see Scotus, *Lect.* 2.25.un., nn. 87–8 (Vatican, XVI, 258); for a useful discussion of a slightly defective text that contains much the same teaching, see King, 'Duns Scotus on the Reality of Self-Change', 262 n. 56). An elicited or produced volition inheres in the will, such that 'the will is said to be perfect in so far as it is the subject of a perfect act of willing', just as the intelligence is perfect 'as it is the subject of generated knowledge' (Scotus, *Ord.* 1.3.3.4, n. 580 (Vatican, III, 343)). In short, a 'volition' is produced by the 'productive' will, and is made to inhere in the 'operative' will. In the divine processions, of course, as we have seen, there is no passive subject for the operation itself.

Scotus considers a rather different objection from this. For him, the problem is not in explaining how a free power is (sometimes) necessitated in its act. Rather, it lies in explaining what the source of this necessity is: 'how can the will be necessarily a principle of production, and which necessity is necessarily required in this production?'[13] The presupposition in the discussion is that necessity is compatible with the notion of willing:

[8]
1 A perfect productive principle can give to its product every perfection that is not
2 incompatible with it [viz. the product]. An infinite will is a perfect productive
3 principle. Therefore it can give to its product every perfection that [can] belong to it
4 [viz. the product]. Necessity is not incompatible with [an infinite product]. (Rather,
5 [necessity] necessarily belongs to it, because nothing infinite is [merely] possible [viz.
6 contingent], and not necessary.) Therefore this principle, which is an infinite will, is a
7 sufficient principle for giving necessity to this product.[14]

Scotus sees this as an '*a posteriori*' argument in favour of the necessity of the will's production of any perfect act of love.[15] ('*A posteriori*' because it does not explain how it is that the will gives necessity to its product; it merely alleges that the will must do so because its product is infinite, and thus necessary.) I have glossed 'possible' with 'contingent' ([8.5–6]) in the light of comments Scotus makes in the *textus interpolatus*, where he uses the happier modal term.[16] The product of an infinite will is itself infinite, as we shall see in a moment. While not analytic, the premiss in [8.1–2] looks to have a strong claim to be necessarily true, and Scotus could appeal to his discussion of the perfect nature of any real infinite, recounted in Part I, chapter 4 above, to defend the second premiss [8.2–3]. Necessity is a perfection, and it does not seem to be incompatible with the notion of an infinite product of the will [8.4]. So the will is a sufficient principle for the necessity of any perfect product of itself [8.6–7]. Indeed, the infinity of the product entails its necessity, since everything infinite is necessary [8.4–6] – a principle entailed by Scotus's natural theology.

So necessity is compatible with the notion of an act of will. This presupposition, it should be noted, is in fact distinct from the view that freedom and necessity are compatible. At issue here is not the capacity to make a *choice*.[17] Scotus's point is that the notion simply of wanting something is wholly compatible with the notion that what we want we necessarily want. But the question arises, just what could make it that some agent necessarily wants something? What could explain this sort of state of affairs? And answering this question would, according to Scotus, give us

---

[13] Scotus, *Ord.* 1.10.un., n. 11 (Vatican, IV, 344).

[14] Ibid., n. 39 (Vatican, IV, 355–6).

[15] Ibid., n. 40 (Vatican, IV, 357).

[16] Ibid., *text. int.* (Vatican, IV, 356, ll. 19, 21–p. 257, ll. 19–20). 'Possible' in the non-logical sense of 'can be caused' is of course legitimate here; the *textus interpolatus* pushes away from a statistical, and towards a logical, understanding of the relevant modal concepts.

[17] We should note, however, that Scotus believes too that even the notion of freedom is compatible with that of necessity – see e.g. my brief discussion of the beatific vision in *Duns Scotus*, 149–51. But this does not mean that he believes every free act to be necessitated. I shall return to this in a moment.

an *a priori* argument in favour of the compatibility of the necessity and voluntariness.

Scotus is adamant that the answer to this question can neither lie simply in the nature of the thing wanted, nor simply in the nature of the thing that does the wanting:

[9]
1 If an *a priori* or explanatory (*a causa*) reason is sought for what it is through which this
2 will gives necessity to this production, I reply that neither does the infinite will, by
3 itself alone ([i.e.] relating this [will] to any object), give necessity to the produced
4 love, nor does the loved object – which is the goal – alone ([i.e.] related to any will)
5 give necessity to the act of willing or to the production of love.[18]

The search is for an explanatory reason, an argument *propter quid* [9.1], and the point is that the notion of an infinite will's production is not alone sufficient for the necessity of the product – namely, the act of love [9.2–4] (as Scotus puts it, 'relating this will to any object': prescinding from the love directed towards an infinite object, and simply considering the will as productive) – just as the notion of an infinite object loved by the will – its goal – is not alone sufficient for the necessity of the produced act of love [9.4–5]: after all, the goal of many finite, creaturely acts of love is infinite – namely, God – but this does not make these creaturely acts of love necessary.

The claim in [9.2–4] is proved by considering the contingency of God's love for creatures. If the infinity of the divine will were sufficient for the necessity of every divine act of love, then God's love for creatures would, counterfactually, be necessary.[19] And [9.4–5] is proved by the fact that the necessity of human acts of love for God does not spring from the nature of the goal itself: Scotus holds that even the clear vision of the divine essence is not sufficient to guarantee impeccability. Someone with the beatific vision could, in principle, will against God. Impeccability, for Scotus, is explained by some *further* divine causal activity relative to the saints in heaven.[20]

Rather, Scotus posits that necessary and jointly sufficient for the necessity of some product of the divine will are the infinity of the will coupled with the infinity of the object:

[10]
1 Therefore I say that the necessity of this production of equal love ... is from the
2 infinity of the will and from the infinity of the goodness of the object, since neither
3 without the other is sufficient for necessity.[21]

And this in turn entails that the will coupled with the object are joint causes of the necessarily produced act of love.[22] Scotus goes on to explain in some detail just how this necessity arises:

---

[18] Scotus, *Ord.* 1.10.un., n. 40 (Vatican, IV, 357).
[19] Ibid. See above, Part I, chapter 4 §§ 1 and 9, for the proof that all external divine acts are contingent.
[20] See my *Duns Scotus*, 149–51.
[21] Scotus, *Ord.* 1.10.un., n. 47 (Vatican, IV, 359).
[22] Ibid., n. 49 (Vatican, IV, 359–61).

[11]
1 These two are sufficient in the following way. An infinite will cannot fail to be right
2 (*recta*); neither can it fail to be in act, for then it would be potential. Therefore it is
3 necessarily in a right act. But not every willing is right precisely on the grounds that it
4 is from that will alone – as though nothing were to be willed in itself but only [to be
5 willed] on the grounds that it is willed by that will. For the divine essence, which is
6 the first object of that will, is to be willed in itself. Therefore that will is of necessity
7 in a right act of willing that object which is in itself rightly to be willed; and just as of
8 necessity [the divine will] is the principle of willing, so of necessity is it the principle
9 of producing love of [the divine essence].[23]

The point here is that, as we saw in Part I, chapter 4 §9 above, God's will tends to
everything other than himself contingently. But it tends to himself of necessity: he
cannot fail to love himself, and the reason for this is that God's nature is to be loved.
God is good in himself, and it is right for God to love himself for precisely this
reason [**11.3–6**]. Now, if it is right for God to do this, then he cannot do the opposite,
since he cannot fail to act rightly. But God is pure actuality, lacking any potentiality.
And this means that he cannot be neutral with regard to the right act of divine self-
love [**11.1–2**]. So he necessarily loves himself [**11.2–3**]. And this in turn means that
he necessarily produces an act of love for himself [**11.6–9**].

The step in [**11.1–2**] about the impossibility of God's being neutral, failing to
elicit either an act of love or an act of hate for himself, does not seem to be
sufficiently established here. In the *textus interpolatus*, Scotus tries to show how
God's pure actuality entails the necessity of his act of will:

[12]
1 An infinite will – adding absolutely nothing there of the object present – is necessarily
2 in an act of willing, such that it is not in potency of contradiction to any act of willing,
3 for then it would admit of composition (*componibilis*).[24]

The problem here is that the argument seems to prove too much. God's pure
actuality is inconsistent with his having liberty of indifference ('is not in potency of
contradiction': [**12.2**]), for such freedom entails composition (God could be other
than he is), and composition is incompatible with pure actuality. It is clearly true
that, if God really lacks the liberty of indifference, then whatever he wills, he does
so necessarily.[25] But this conclusion means that no divine action is free. (As Scotus
notes, he is prescinding from the question of any particular object present [**12.1**].)
Still, the *a posteriori* argument in favour of a necessary production of love in God
is not affected by this defect.

Things that Scotus says elsewhere clear up remaining issues and difficulties. The
first is that the notion of necessity here does not amount to any sort of psychological
need on the part of God. Thus Scotus is careful to show that the production is the
result of divine liberality.[26] But there is a more pressing concern. Scotus believes

---

[23] Ibid., n. 48 (Vatican, IV, 359).

[24] Ibid., *text. int.* (Vatican, IV, 360, ll. 13–15).

[25] Assuming that liberty of indifference is necessary not merely for being able, in one and the same set
of circumstances, to will *a* or not-*a*, but also to will *a* or not to will *a* (refraining from willing anything).

[26] See Scotus, *Ord.* 1.2.2.1–4, n. 235 (Vatican, II, 268–9).

that intellect and will are irreducibly distinct powers, on the grounds that will is capable of choice in a way that intellect is not. (I will return to this in the next chapter, since it is a claim that forms an integral part of Scotus's argument for exactly two divine productions.) It might be thought that Scotus's claim that a perfect will is necessarily productive undermines this. But it does not. Scotus maintains that a free power – unlike a natural power – is such that its exercise is incompatible with *natural* necessity. That is to say, the exercise of a free power is such that no antecedent condition, extrinsic to itself, can be causally sufficient for its exercise:

[13]
1 It is consistent with liberty that [the will] is determined to operating with respect to
2 [some object that is essentially perfective of the will], and consequently to acting in
3 relation to that operation.[27]

Without going into too much detail on what is a complex and difficult subject, the point here is that the determination of the will **[13.1]** is (at least in part) *intrinsic*. The object does not exercise any sufficient causality over the will's operation.[28] The intellect is not like this: in the presence of its object, it operates automatically.[29]

4 The Productions as Eternal

A further issue that Scotus takes care to discuss is that the productions are eternal: that is to say, the products have neither temporal beginning nor end, and are in fact timeless. Scotus focuses on the production of a mental word, but precisely the same considerations would obtain in the case of the production of an act of love too:

[14]
1 I show that it is eternal, because a sufficient agent (that is, one dependent on nothing),
2 that produces in the manner of nature has – if it does not produce by motion – a
3 production, and also a perfect product, coeval with itself. The generating Father is
4 such an agent. Therefore he has a generation, and also a generated thing, coeval with
5 himself.[30]

Scotus seems to regard the complex major premiss **[14.1–3]** as necessarily true. For, he reasons, the correct question to ask in a case where an agent precedes its effect is: what are the conditions necessary for an agent to precede its effect? And as

---

[27] Ibid. 1.13.un., n. 57 (Vatican, V, 95).

[28] On this, see too e.g. Scotus, *Ord.* 1.10.un., nn. 47–8 (Vatican, IV, 359); *Ord.* 1.13.un., nn. 46–7 (Vatican, 89–90); *Quod.* 16, n. 16 (Wadding, XII, 457; Alluntis and Wolter, 385 (¶ 16.44)). For a helpful discussion, see Tobias Hoffmann, 'The Distinction Between Nature and Will in Duns Scotus', 205–8.

[29] On this distinction between intellect and will, see e.g. Scotus, *In Metaph.* 9.15, n. 36 (St Bonaventure, IV, 684–5), a passage where Scotus explicitly links the distinction to the two internal divine productions.

[30] Scotus, *Ord.* 1.9.un., n. 7 (Vatican, IV, 331); see too in particular *Ord.* 1.10.un., *text. int.* (Vatican, IV, 370, ll. 2–4, 10).

Scotus sees it, there are only three disjunctively necessary conditions: (1) the agent is free (in a sense incompatible with any causal necessity); (2) the agent is dependent on prior causal conditions; (3) the agent's activity involves motion or change or some kind.[31] And the major premiss simply states that, if none of these conditions applies, the agent does not precede its effect. In the case of the production of a mental word in God, none of the three conditions applies. For, as we have seen, (1) the production is necessary, and (2) the agent is not dependent on any prior causal conditions. Scotus proves (3) – that God's necessary production of a mental word does not involve any change – by ruling out the possibility of the production's involving the actualization of any passive potency.[32] Since the actualization of passive potency is necessary for motion or change on standard Aristotelian understandings of causality, it follows that the production does not involve any such motion or change. Hence, none of the disjunctively necessary conditions for the temporal priority of an agent over its effect apply in the case of God's production of a mental word. Since none of the conditions necessary for temporal priority are satisfied, the effect is 'coeval' with the cause. So the divine Word is eternal, just as the agent is.[33]

---

[31] Ibid. 1.9.un., n. 8 (Vatican, IV, 331).

[32] Scotus, *Ord.* 1.9.un., n. 6 (Vatican, IV, 330–1), referring to *Ord.* 1.5.2.un., n. 97 (Vatican, IV, 61–2); see too *Ord.* 1.2.2.1–4, n. 266 (Vatican, II, 285): 'In generation, even in creatures, there occur together two notions: viz. that there is a mutation, and that there is a production. As there is a mutation, there is a form of a changed subject; as there is a production, there is – as a way [to the end term] – the produced end term. These notions do not include each other essentially, even in creatures, for they primarily relate to diverse things. Therefore without contradiction the notion of production can be understood without the notion of mutation, and thus generation is transferred to God under the description of production, though not under the description of mutation.'

[33] Scotus, *Ord.* 1.9.un., n. 9 (Vatican, IV, 331). The argument about productions just outlined relies on taking the notion of memory and will as the principles of divine production quite literally, and I will return to this – about which Scotus is explicit – in chapter 14 §3 below.

Chapter 11

The Number of Productions

In the previous chapter, I discussed Scotus's argument to the effect that there are productions in God, that (at least) one is by intellect, and (at least) one by will. This does not give us an argument in favour of exactly two productions, and exactly one unproduced agent. But Scotus provides such an argument.

1 Only Two Productions in God

The first step is simply to try to show that there can be only two productions in God:

> **[1]**
> 1 There are only two productions there, distinct according to the formal natures of the
> 2 productions, and this is because there are only two productive principles having
> 3 distinct formal natures of producing.[1]

The antecedent is that there are only two productive principles **[1.2]**, and according to Scotus it entails that there are only two productions **[1.1]**. Scotus devotes considerable space to a multi-staged proof of the antecedent, showing first that the sorts of productive principle in God must be reduced to at most two, and secondly that they must be reduced to at least two.

> **[2]**
> 1 All plurality is reduced to unity, or to as small a number as it can be reduced.
> 2 Therefore, the plurality of active principles should be reduced to unity, or to as small a
> 3 number as it can be reduced. But it cannot be reduced to some one productive
> 4 principle. Proof: for that would have determinately the manner of causing of one or
> 5 other of these: either it would be productive from itself determinately in the manner of
> 6 nature; or [it would be productive] not from itself determinately, but freely, and thus
> 7 in the manner of will. Therefore they cannot be reduced to some principle, as it were
> 8 a third [distinct] from these, which would have the nature of neither of these in
> 9 producing.
> 10 Neither is the one reduced to the other, for then one according to its whole
> 11 genus would be imperfect, which is false, for since it pertains to each from the same
> 12 perfection to be an operative and a productive principle ... and neither one is in
> 13 itself imperfect in so far as it is operative (for then it would not be in God), therefore
> 14 neither is it imperfect in so far as it is productive. Therefore the productive principles
> 15 cannot be reduced to a number less than a duality of principle, that is to say,
> 16 productive in the manner of nature and productive in the manner of will.[2]

---

[1] Scotus, *Ord.* 1.2.2.1–4, n. 300 (Vatican, II, 305).
[2] Ibid., nn. 301–2 (Vatican, II, 305–6); see Ibid. 1.10.un., n. 8 (Vatican, IV, 341).

[2.1] – the principle of parsimony – is presented as a general claim: that the universe is as simple as it can be. (Thus, the principle here is not just a methodological canon, but a metaphysical criterion.) Scotus clearly understands this principle to hold of God too: the supremely simple God is neither metaphysically extravagant, nor constituted in some needlessly lavish way. The application of parsimony – understood metaphysically – in the case at hand means that the number of (kinds of) productive principles is reduced to as few as it can be, and thus that the supreme cases of such kinds are as few as can be consonant with the explanation of the existence of such principles at all **[2.**2–3]. But there is a fundamental division of productive principles into two kinds: natural and free **[2.**4–7], and hence parsimony cannot reduce the principles to just one **[2.**3–4]. The point in **[2.**7–9] is, I take it, that there are no productive principles that exhibit neither one of these two characteristics – presumably something that would be a genus of which the two characteristic modes of causing are species. *Being a cause* would be an example. But such a genus would be a vicious abstraction: nothing is just a cause without being either a natural or a voluntary cause, and what Scotus is interested in are *real* powers, not mere abstractions. In line with this, **[2.**10–11] requires us to suppose that one or other of the two kinds of principle could be somehow explanatory of the other, in the sense that one of the principles would be responsible for *producing* the other. Hence **[2.**13–14] excludes the notion that one of the principles could be productive of the other. The argument for this is complex, relying on the premiss that, if it is a perfection of a power to be operative, it is a perfection of that power to be productive **[2.**11–12]. I discussed the distinction between operation and production in Part I, chapter 1 §1 above. The point of the claim in **[2.**11–12] is that a power's being (immanently) operative requires that it *produce* its operation. It is certainly a perfection for a divine power to be operative **[2.**12–13], and the implicit premiss here is that, for a perfect power, it is a perfection to be operative. (How could a power be perfect, and yet it not be a perfection for that power to operate? Operation is just what powers are fundamentally for.) If, then, it is a perfection of a divine power to be operative, it is a perfection of a divine power to be productive **[2.**13–14]. And this excludes the possibility of one power being dependent on another, since the way in which the operation of one power would be dependent on another would be if the operation of the first power were produced by the other. So there are exactly two productive principles in God **[2.**14–16].

Scotus believes that he needs to do more than simply show there to be such principles in God. He tries to show that the principles are actually productive of objects equal to themselves. This step is important, for the attempt to show that there can be only one internal production of each kind relies on the fact that the products are equal to the principles. But the additional step here simply repeats arguments that I examined in chapter 11 above (see e.g. passage **[1]** there). More important is the attempt to defend the inference in **[1]** above:

[3]
1 If there are only two productive principles of either kind, then there are only
2 numerically two productions. Proof: for each productive principle has a production
3 equal to it and coeternal [with it]; therefore once that exists, it cannot have another.[3]

---

[3] Ibid., 1.2.2.1–4, n. 303 (Vatican, II, 308–9).

The thought here, I believe, is roughly that an equal production 'exhausts' the possibility of a power to cause other such productions – other productions that are equal to it [3.2–3]. But putting the point in this way is something that Scotus finds somewhat objectionable, as I will show in a moment.

The whole argument from [1] to [3] raises a number of questions, all of which Scotus promises to deal with. Perhaps the most obvious of all is simply this: why suppose that there could not be another basic kind of causal principle? Clearly, the distinction into natural and free causal powers is intended by Scotus to represent the most basic and fundamental division of causality that there is. But, he reasons, could there not be some other equally basic division, or could not this division just itself be reduced yet further – perhaps just to the notion of a causal power? The point, in other words, is that there is something arbitrary about the proposed distinction.[4] It is important to keep in mind that Scotus does not believe it to be even a *prima facie* objection to his position that there could be other natural productions in God than the production of a mental word. The structure of the argument is that there is a natural production – the production of a mental word – and that the existence of this production exhausts God's power to be naturally internally productive. Of course, one way of attacking this argument would be to try to locate rival candidates for natural internal production. This is not a way that Scotus attempts; perhaps, given his propensity for defending his position against as many refutations as possible, he simply could not think of any suitable candidates. In any case, the notion of internal production seems applicable most obviously in the case of intellectual and intentional acts.

Rather, what fundamentally worries Scotus is that the notion of the two sorts of power is itself parasitic on some more basic sort of thing: just a causal power. The reply is that if the powers could somehow be reduced to some common sort of power that they are or have in common, then each would be somehow imperfect, presumably since each would somehow depend on this anterior entity or form. The notion of a causal power, abstracted from the notion of a natural power or a voluntary power, is just an abstraction, and no more than that. Thus, as Scotus reasons:

[4]
1 This third [power] would be a principle according to the nature of one of these two
2 [viz. natural or free], because between these two there is no middle state of causing,
3 and thus if both were reduced to some third, one would be reduced to the other, and
4 the other [would be reduced to] itself.[5]

The point here is that there is no bare 'causing', neither natural nor free [4.2]. Thus, if one or other of these sorts of causing were reduced to the other, then it would follow that there would be only powers that were fundamentally natural, or fundamentally free [4.1, 3–4].

As I noted above, Scotus is not happy with the notion that the production of an equal product somehow 'exhausts' the capacity of the power to produce other such equal products, a position that is defended by Henry of Ghent:

---

[4] For the objection, see Ibid., nn. 304, 306 (Vatican, II, 310–11).

[5] Ibid., n. 315 (Vatican, II, 316).

[5]
1 To be exhausted signifies, in bodily things, that the [fecundity] does not remain in that
2 from which it is exhausted; it cannot be understood in this way, but that [the
3 fecundity] does not remain for any further act.[6]

The point about exhaustion is that the power (the 'fecundity') for some action no longer remains [5.1–2]. In God, the relevant power remains; what does not remain is its opportunity to elicit any further operation [5.2–3]. To this extent, my characterization of the arguments about equality as being fundamentally about the 'exhaustion' of the relevant power, is not exactly the correct way to understand the claim.

In the very late *Quodlibet*, Scotus tries an altogether different approach. He proposes two fundamentally equivalent arguments, of which I consider the first here:

[6]
1 If many productions of the same kind (*ratio*) can exist, then infinitely [many can
2 exist], and if they do, then it is necessary that there are infinitely [many], for nothing
3 can be in there [i.e. in God] other than the necessary. The last consequent is clearly
4 impossible; therefore also the first antecedent [is impossible].[7]

The point of the odd-sounding inference in [6.1–2] is that if something can be exemplified more than once, then, provided there are no extrinsic blocks on its being exemplified by an indefinite number of things,[8] it can in principle be exemplified by an indefinite number of things.[9] But there are no extrinsic blocks on the possibility of infinite exemplifications in the case of a divine production. So either there are no blocks on the infinite exemplification of a divine production, or else the relevant kind of production can, of its very nature, be exemplified just once. The rest of the passage draws the conclusion that the relevant kind of production can be exemplified just once, and I return to it in a moment.

Why suppose that there are no extrinsic blocks on the possibility of infinite exemplifications in the case of a divine production? Such a block could not be anything logically *posterior* to the thing, for obvious reasons of explanatory ordering. Neither could it come from anything logically *simultaneous* with the production, for, Scotus argues:

[7]
1 For the reason that a production which is of one kind is not determined of itself to a
2 certain number, for the same reason neither [is] that which is naturally simultaneous
3 [determined to a certain number].[10]

---

[6] Ibid. 1.7.1, n. 93 (Vatican, IV, 148–9), against Henry, *SQ* 54.8 (II, fo. 101E–F).

[7] Scotus, *Quod.* 2, n. 16 (Wadding, XII, 51; Alluntis and Wolter, 44 (¶ 2.47)).

[8] Ibid., n. 17 (Wadding, XII, 52; Alluntis and Wolter, 45–6 (¶ 2.50)); I summarize in one inadequate sentence a far more complex and nuanced argument.

[9] Ibid., n. 16 (Wadding, XII, 51; Alluntis and Wolter, 45 (¶ 2.49)).

[10] Ibid., n. 17 (Wadding, XII, 52; Alluntis and Wolter, 46 (¶ 2.50)).

And it could not come from anything *prior*:

[8]
1 The determination cannot come from the formal productive principle ... for a
2 productive principle of the same kind does not determine itself to a certain plurality of
3 productions of the same kind. Neither can it be determined by a producing
4 *suppositum*, for a *suppositum* can have as many productions as the productive
5 principle which is in the *suppositum* extends itself to. If therefore there is no
6 determination on the part of the formal productive principle, neither is there on the
7 part of the producer.[11]

The point here is that the relevant entity prior to the production is the person (*suppositum*) with his productive principle. The productive principle cannot be the entity extrinsic to the production that is responsible for limiting the possible number of productions, for the productive principle can in principle produce as many times as it will [8.1–3] – presumably unless it itself is limited by something extrinsic to it (e.g. scarcity of required resources). Neither can the person be the entity responsible for limiting the possible number of productions, for the person can produce as often as his productive principle allows him [8.3–5], and the productive principle in God is not thus limited [8.5–6]. So, 'if many productions of the same kind can exist [in God], then infinitely many can exist' in him [6.1]. Now, everything that can be so in God is so [6.2–3]; so if there can be infinite productions of the same kind, there will be such productions [6.2]. But there are not and cannot be infinite productions of the same kind in God [6.3]. So there cannot be more than one production of the same kind in God [6.4]. And this is, according to Scotus, just a basic fact, one for which there can be no further explanation. The argument requires it to be factually false that there are not infinitely many productions of the same kind in God. But nothing about Scotus's account of the intensive infinite requires him to abandon the standard Aristotelian belief that there cannot be an infinite multitude of things.

What Scotus is talking about here is kinds of production, and it does not matter whether the kind of restriction he is talking about is specific or numerical: that is to say, the idea is that if a kind can be divided into various species, then this sort of division can in principle be infinite (he is supposing that there is no intrinsic limit on the variety of, for example, animal species that there can be); if a species can be divided into various numerically distinct instances, there is no intrinsic limit on the number of individuals into which the species can be divided. The point here is that the relevant kinds are 'natural internal production' and 'voluntary internal production', and the argument does double duty for both specific and numerical division.

2 Only One Unproduced Producer in God

Thus far, if successful, Scotus's arguments will have shown that there are exactly two productions in the Trinity. The arguments will in fact have shown, further, that

[11] Ibid.

there are only two necessary divine productions. This, of course, is not sufficient to show that there is a Trinity of persons, for – setting aside the question of the status of the relevant entities as persons (which I return to in the next chapter) – it leaves it open whether there may be more than one unproduced thing. So Scotus's next move is to attempt to show that there must be exactly one unproduced thing. The arguments talk of just one unproduced 'person' or '*suppositum*' here, and I follow them for convenience, noting that I will deal with the question of persons as such in the next chapter.

Henry of Ghent proposed what is on the face of it a very appealing argument in favour of the existence of just one unproduced thing. Scotus summarizes:

[9]
1 Many absolute *supposita* cannot be in this [i.e. divine] nature, because a nature is not
2 in many absolute *supposita* without the division of the nature. There will be,
3 therefore, many relative *supposita*. Therefore, they [are distinguished] either by
4 mutual relation between themselves, or [by relation] to other things. But if there were
5 many unproduced *supposita*, they would not be distinguished by relation to other
6 *supposita*, because [they would] not [be distinguished] by relation to producing
7 *supposita* (because there are none on the hypothesis); neither [would they be
8 distinguished by relation] to produced *supposita*, because they share the same relation
9 to [the produced *supposita*], just as the Father and Son now have the same relation of
10 active spiration to the Holy Spirit. Therefore they would be distinguished by relations
11 between themselves, and this by relations of origin – which is what is proposed.[12]

Henry's argument, here presented by Scotus, presupposes an important point, rejected by Scotus, that I discuss in chapter 14 §4 below, namely that *supposita* that are distinguished by non-relational features can be instantiations of a nature only if the nature is divided between them such that the nature in its different instantiations fails to be numerically one **[9**.1–2**]**. So if there could be more than one unproduced person, Henry reasons, what distinguishes the persons must be a relation **[9**.2–3**]**. But, Henry reasons, the only possible sorts of relation are either relations between the unproduced persons, or relations to entities other than these persons **[9**.3–4**]**. Taking the second horn first, Henry makes a further distinction: the entities other than the unproduced persons, to which these unproduced persons could be related, are persons, and divine persons are either unproduced or produced. But the unproduced persons could not be distinguished by relation to other unproduced divine persons (what Scotus here calls 'producing *supposita*') because on the hypothesis there are none: the argument presupposes that the set of unproduced persons whose individuation is being asked about is the complete set of such persons **[9**.5–7**]**. Neither could the unproduced persons be distinguished by their relations to produced divine persons, because they would all share the same relation to these persons **[9**.7–9**]** – just as Father and Son in the Trinity share the same relation to the Holy Spirit **[9**.9–10**]**. So the only thing which can distinguish divine persons are their mutual relations between themselves **[9**.10–11**]**. But the only real relations which obtain between divine persons are relations of origin **[9**.11**]**. If therefore the only relations between the various divine persons are relations of origin, then it

---

[12] Scotus, *Ord.* 1.2.2.1–4, n. 366 (Vatican, II, 339), referring to Henry *Quod.* 6.1 (Macken, X, 7–11).

follows that there cannot be more than one unproduced person, since such persons could not be related *to each other* by relations of origin [**9**.11].

Clearly, this argument makes various crucial unsupported presuppositions, and Scotus criticizes the argument for precisely this reason:

[**10**]
1 When [Henry] accepts in his argument that there cannot be many absolute persons in
2 the same nature: how is this more evident than the conclusion? For someone who
3 posited many ungenerated persons would not say that they are formally constituted by
4 any relations; therefore, to accept – against him – that there cannot be many absolute
5 persons, seems to be to accept something less manifest than what is concluded.
6   When further he says that they are not distinguished by relations between
7 themselves, because this would not be other than by relations of origin, it is necessary
8 to prove this consequence: {though if it is granted that there is no distinction other
9 than by relation of origin, he would immediately have what is proposed}.[13]

Scotus here does not take issue with the contentious claim in [**10**.1–2], though he does not believe that it is true, and in fact holds that there are no logical difficulties in maintaining that the divine persons could be distinguished by non-relational features – something I discuss in chapter 14 §4 below. But here he clearly concedes the presupposition for the sake of argument. Rather, his criticism is more straightforward: it is not obvious that the claim that there cannot be more than one non-relational person is any more evident than the claim that there cannot be more than one ungenerated person [**10**.1–2]; indeed, someone who accepted that there could be more than one ungenerated person would doubtless deny that there cannot be more than one non-relational person [**10**.2–4]. Thus – worse still for Henry's argument – the claim that there cannot be more than one absolute person is less obvious than the claim that there cannot be more than one ungenerated person [**10**.4–5]. The other obviously contentious step in Henry's argument is the claim that the only relations that can obtain between divine persons are relations of origin [**9**.10–11], and Scotus's criticism is simply that this claim is unsupported [**10**.7–8]. It is easy to see what would motivate Scotus to make the suggestion that I have placed in curly brackets [**10**.8–9]: if the only possible relations between divine persons are relations of origin, then it will follow straightforwardly that there cannot be more than one unproduced person. But we will see below, when discussing Scotus's treatment of the divine personal properties, Scotus is ambivalent about the view that the divine persons are just subsistent relations. So perhaps for this reason he decided to delete the claim in [**10**.8–9].

Scotus's own argument resembles that in [**7**]; perhaps Scotus, when editing the *Quodlibet*, realized the possible applicability of the reasoning in [**11**] in the case too of the argument for just one production of each type in God:

[**11**]
1 Whatever can be in many *supposita* and is not determined to a certain number by
2 something other than itself, in so far as it is in itself can be in infinitely [many

---

[13] Ibid., nn. 368–9 (Vatican, II, 340); I place in curly brackets an interesting text that Scotus later cancelled (Vatican, II, 340, ll. 17–18).

3 *supposita*]; and if it is necessary being, it is in infinitely [many], because whatever can
4 be there, is. But if *ungenerated* can be in many *supposita*, it is not determined by
5 something else in how many *supposita* it is, because to be determined by something
6 else to exist in a *suppositum* or *supposita* is against the nature of *ungenerated*.
7 Therefore by its nature it can be in infinitely [many *supposita*]; and if it can be, then it
8 is, for everything ungenerated is in itself necessary being. The consequent is
9 impossible; therefore that from which it follows [is impossible].[14]

The idea in [11.1–3] is that, if a nature can be exemplified more than once, then, provided there are no extrinsic blocks on its being exemplified by an indefinite number of things, it can in principle be exemplified by an indefinite number of things – a principle we encountered in [7] above. [11.3–4] is a consequence of divine necessity as understood by Scotus. [11.4–5] simply states that ingeneracy satisfies the antecedent in [11.1–2], and the reason for this is that *being determined to a certain number by something other than itself* is incompatible with *being ungenerated* [11.5–6] – presumably because determination is a kind of causation, and nothing can be causally prior to what is ungenerated. [11.7] makes the inference from [11.1–2] and [11.4–5], and [11.7–8] makes the required inference from [11.7] and [11.3]. There cannot be infinitely many actually existing *supposita*, so [11.7] is counterpossible, and thus the antecedent – namely that ingeneracy can be exemplified by more than one entity – is likewise impossible.

These last steps are simply the required logical moves, and are not controversial. But I suppose that the premisses are controversial. In particular, we could wonder whether the claim in [11.1–3] is true. On the face of it, there are some obvious counterinstances. *Duality* will not do, because duality can be exemplified as often as we like. But *being one of this set of triplets* is determined of itself to exactly three exemplifications. More damagingly, so (we might think) is the divine essence. Scotus would doubtless answer the triplet counterexample by pointing out that he is interested not in pseudo-properties of this kind, but with 'real' properties, ones corresponding to forms, or to whatever does duty in God for forms in creatures – that is, the divine essence and attributes. And on the specific issue of the divine essence, perhaps Scotus would hold that the essence is restricted to three exemplifications not in itself, but by something other than itself – perhaps the determined number of divine productions. But this would fall foul of Scotus's insistence – discussed in chapter 13 §4 below – that the divine essence is in some sense prior to the persons. There is nothing logically prior to it that could cause its restriction to just three exemplifications, and as we saw in discussing [7], Scotus does not believe that anything logically posterior to a nature can do the required job.

---

[14] Ibid., n. 370 (Vatican, II, 341).

Chapter 12

Divine Persons

Thus far, Scotus has taken great pains to show that there are exactly two necessary productions in God. This does not, on the face of it, entail that there are exactly two *persons* produced in God. Indeed, on the face of it, the things produced – acts of knowledge and love – seem pretty far removed from the status of persons. Oddly, Scotus devotes rather little space to showing that the divine products turn out to be persons, and it is hard to avoid the impression that he thinks the arguments in favour of this claim are just uncontroversial.

1 The Internal Products as Divine Persons

As we have seen, Scotus believes that the internal divine products whose existence he has established are both equal to the producer: infinite, necessary, and non-inherent. When first attempting to show, in distinction 2 of book 1 of the *Sentence* commentaries, that the products are persons, Scotus alludes to some but not all of these features:

[1]
1 Intellect ... is by some act of its productive of an end term equal to it (*adaequati*),
2 viz. infinite ([proved] from the preceding question). But nothing produces itself (*De*
3 *Trinitate* 1, c.1); therefore what is produced by an act of the intellect, is distinguished
4 in some way from the producer. But it is not distinguished essentially, because the
5 divine essence, and any essential perfection intrinsic to it, is indistinguishable
6 ([proved] from the question on the unity of God); therefore the product is
7 distinguished personally from the producer. There is therefore some person produced
8 by an act of intellect. The same is argued about the thing produced by an act of will.[1]

Equality and infinity are presupposed here **[1.1–2]**. And the notion of a production immediately entails a distinction of some kind, since nothing produces itself **[1.2]**. This yields two infinite *relata* **[1.3–4]**. How are they distinguished? Not as two individual divine essences, because there is only one divine essence – that is, one God **[1.4–5]**. Scotus infers immediately from this that the distinction between the two *relata* must be personal **[1.6–7]**. As it stands, this is puzzling, and Scotus does not spell out the notion of a person, even initially, until the next question of distinction 2. Roughly, what Scotus means is that the infinite producer and the infinite product are both *exemplifications* (as we would say) of the divine essence: the divine essence is *numerically* one and the same thing repeated in each divine

---

[1] Scotus, *Ord.* 1.2.2.1–4, nn. 355–6 (Vatican, II, 336); see *Lect.* 1.2.2.1–4, n. 165 (Vatican, XVI, 167–8). In **[1]** and **[2]** Scotus refers to Augustine, *De Trin.* 1.1.1 (CCSL, 50, p. 28).

person. And although Scotus does not make this clear at this point in his argument, neither one of these persons can be absolutely identical – formally identical, as Scotus would say – with the divine essence. (If the producer were, then he would be wholly contained by the product, since the product includes the divine essence and some further distinguishing feature. The same would hold, *mutatis mutandis*, for the product.) This yields (at least) two persons in God [1.7–8], and since parallel reasoning can be applied to the production from will, Scotus concludes to the existence of (at least) three persons [1.8]. And as we have already seen, Scotus holds that there can be no more than two productions in God: so what the argument thus far shows is that there are exactly two produced persons in God.

The argument is moving very fast, and various clarifications and additions are required. Scotus does not make them all here, but he does at other, later, points in his discussion. Perhaps the most pressing is this: why could the product not be somehow inherent in the producer – perhaps an infinite mental act belonging to the mind of the producer? Scotus in fact believes, as we have already seen, that the product cannot be thus inherent, since such inherence would require passive potency in the producer, and Scotus thinks he has sufficient warrant to reject the claim that God could include any passive potency. He makes the argument clearer in the context of a proof that the Holy Spirit is produced by means of will:

[2]
1 Nothing is infinite unless it is the divine essence itself. Therefore the [produced] love
2 is the divine essence. But the produced love is not by nature an inherent form, for
3 there is no such in God. Therefore it is *per se* subsistent. But it is not the same
4 subsistent as the producer, for nothing produces itself (*De Trinitate* 1, c. 1). Therefore
5 it is personally distinct, and this person I call the Holy Spirit (for the Son is not
6 produced in this way (as is clear from distinction 6), but rather through an act of
7 nature or intellect).[2]

[2] follows on directly from passage [7] of chapter 10 above. In this text Scotus argues in favour of an infinite product of will, and here he asserts that anything infinite must be (include, or be included by) the divine essence [2.1]. But an inherent form could presumably satisfy this description, in some sense belonging to (being included by) the divine essence. So Scotus immediately asserts that there could be no inherent form in God [2.2–3], and thus that the produced love is not an inherent form [2.2]. From the non-inherence claim, Scotus directly infers subsistence [2.3], and I will return to the nature of subsistence below. The argument then follows much the same pattern as [1.4–6], though the inference to personal distinction [2.4–5] is perhaps made more intelligible by the assertion that a non-inherent infinite thing must be a subsistent.

What is the sense of 'personally distinct' mentioned in [1.7] and [2.5]? The persons all include exactly the same essence. But they are not merely formally distinct: they are not distinct attributes of this essence, for example. Rather, they are fully real, subsistent entities, and as such really distinct from each other ('the Son is really distinguished from the Father'[3]). This is a specialized sense of 'really

---

[2] Scotus, *Ord.* 1.10.un., n. 9 (Vatican, IV, 342).

[3] Ibid. 1.2.2.1–4, n. 421 (Vatican, II, 366); I give other, more complex, evidence in my 'Scotus's Parisian Teaching on Divine Simplicity'.

distinct', at least in the context of Scotus's technical vocabulary. For separability is usually a necessary condition for real distinction, and the divine persons, while subsistent, are necessarily interdependent in various ways.[4] Indeed, Scotus claims that the divine persons are 'really identical' with the divine essence ('God or deity is not [really distinct from the Father]'[5]), and in this context he notoriously denies the transitivity of real identity.[6] So there is in this context a specialized sense of 'really identical' operative here; I discuss it more fully in chapter 13 below.

2 The Unproduced Producer as a Divine Person

Scotus provides, at various different places, arguments to show that the producer must be a subsistent – a person – too. One appears as part of a discussion to the effect that the divine essence itself cannot be essentially productive:

[3]
1 Every form sufficiently elicitive of some act, if it exists *per se*, acts *per se* by that
2 action (example: if heat is sufficiently a power for heating, separate heat will heat);
3 therefore if deity is a generative potency – and it is agreed that it is sufficient – it
4 follows that if deity exists *per se*, then it will generate *per se*. But deity exists first in
5 itself, in some way, before it is understood to exist in a person, for deity as deity is *per*
6 *se* existence (*esse*), such that the three persons are *per se* by the deity, and not vice
7 versa. ... Therefore in that first instant of nature in which [the deity] is understood,
8 before it is understood in a person, it will generate – and thus deity thus considered is
9 distinguished from what is generated.[7]

The gist of this *reductio* is to show that deity itself cannot be the relevant producer, since if it were then it would necessarily produce other divine essences, not persons. So coupling the claim that God is essentially productive with the claim that the production must be internal leads to the conclusion that something other than the divine essence must be what is internally productive: and this, of course, will be an (unproduced) divine person. Everyone agrees that, if the divine essence were the generator, then it would be sufficiently so [3.3]. And everyone agrees that the divine essence has some sort of *per se* existence – indeed, as I will make clear below, Scotus holds that it has some sort of *per se* subsistence [3.4–6]. The reason is that the divine essence explains the fact that the persons subsist, and to do this it must

---

[4] On separability for real distinction, see Part I, chapter 6 §3 above.

[5] See Scotus, *Ord.* 1.2.2.1–4, n. 421 (Vatican, II, 366); also passage [1] in chapter 14 below.

[6] I discuss this in detail in my 'Scotus's Parisian Teaching on Divine Simplicity'. The issue is of considerable complexity. Basically, Scotus claims that the Father is really identical with the divine essence, and the Son likewise, but that Father and Son are not really identical with each other. There are analogous cases amongst creatures: any individual substance is really identical with its nature, but two substances that share the same nature are not really identical. In this case, the nature, as we shall see in chapter 13 §1 below, lacks numerical unity; in such a case there is no reason to maintain that the two individuals are numerically the same as each other – indeed, this is the whole point of maintaining that creaturely natures lack numerical unity (see e.g. Scotus, *Ord.* 1.2.2.1–4, n. 412 (Vatican, II, 326)).

[7] Scotus, *Ord.* 1.7.1, n. 11 (Vatican, IV, 110).

itself subsist [**3.6**] – a complex argument to which I will return in chapter 13 below. Now, something that exists *per se* and is a sufficient cause of some action counts as the subject of the action [**3**.1–2]. So on the scenario described, the deity would be the subject of the action of generating: more perspicuously, the deity would generate [**3**.4]. But suppose deity does generate [**3**.7–8]. Anything which generates must produce something really distinct from itself [**3**.8–9]. But what could be really distinct from the divine essence? Creatures, to be sure, and other Gods. Generation is a univocal causal relation – something that generates produces things of the same kind as itself. So presumably the result of accepting that the divine essence – prior to its exemplification in even one person – could generate is that it would be necessary for God to produce another God. But there is necessarily only one God (see Part I, chapter 7). So the divine essence, prior to its exemplification in even one person, cannot generate. Since generation is necessary (as shown in chapter 10 §2 above), it follows that the divine essence must be exemplified by a divine person prior (logically speaking) to any internal generation.

Scotus's position, then, is that since something in God in essentially productive, and since this thing cannot be the divine essence, it must be something underlying this essence: namely, a divine person; *tertium non datur*. Elsewhere, Scotus tries to show that any essence must have an underlying *suppositum*:

[**4**]
1 It can be said that the [divine] essence determines for itself the first [personal]
2 property [viz. of the Father] as a formal principle: not however as an informing [form],
3 but as a quiddity is said to be a form of a *suppositum*, and [it can be said] that an
4 uncausable quiddity necessarily determines for itself some *suppositum* (as the pagans
5 would posit about an absolute *suppositum*, and we [posit] about the first relative
6 [*suppositum*]), and the reason is that such a quiddity of itself sustains itself (*sistit se*)
7 and is of itself the quiddity of something.[8]

The idea here is that every quiddity requires some *suppositum* for its existence – every exemplifiable or (in the technical medieval parlance) communicable entity, we might say, requires some incommunicable entity to exist in. Nothing *real* can be exemplifiable unless there are real exemplifications of it. (I return to the issues of communicability and incommunicability below.) Scotus, however, does not appeal to this general principle here, and simply focuses on the features proper to an uncausable quiddity. The first thing to note is that the proof for a first principle does not specify whether the entity whose existence is proved is communicable or incommunicable – roughly, shareable by many, or not so shareable. Scotus's claim is that any uncaused quiddity requires some sort of unshareable existence – 'determines for itself some *suppositum*' [**4**.3–4]. The relevant determination here is not causal: the quiddity does produce the first person. Indeed, Scotus in [**4**] is attempting to provide an alternative to the view that the divine essence somehow causes the Father: a view that he describes as a 'delusion (*phantasia*), very discordant with the sayings of the Saints'.[9] Scotus thus claims that, even if

8 Ibid. 1.28.3, n. 84 (Vatican, VI, 151).
9 Ibid., n. 82 (Vatican, VI, 149); the view is described at nn. 70–1, 75–81 (Vatican, VI, 146, 147–9).

(counterpossibly) Unitarianism were true, the divine essence would exist in some incommunicable thing – that is, in a *suppositum* [**4.4–5**]; *a fortiori*, then, the divine essence exists in at least one person – namely, that which is causally responsible for the others – as Trinitarians believe [**4.5**]. The claim that the quiddity of itself sustains itself means that it is altogether independent of anything external to it [**4.6**] – as we would expect for anything which is the quiddity of the first cause. But on the principle that any communicable entity is somehow related to something intrinsic and incommunicable, the quiddity must exist in (or as) a *suppositum* [**4.7**].[10]

Perhaps the way to give the argument some plausibility is to ask the following question: could everything be shareable, everything be universal? Perhaps so, unless we accept some theory of haecceity – as Scotus does – and apply it to the question of communicability too. But it is not clear that everything could *de facto* actually be shared. For even if nothing other than (overlapping) universals exist, still the precise overlaps of such universals would need to be unshared, on pain of there existing no discrete entities at all. So it seems to me that it is easy enough to give some sense to the fundamental insight that communicable entity must be somehow determined to incommunicable entity. And presumably the first entity – the first communicable quiddity – must determine itself to some incommunicable entity, since given that the existence of this entity is wholly uncaused, it hardly looks plausible to maintain that something external to it determines it to an incommunicable entity.

Another approach to the issue is to consider Scotus's claim that any pure perfection is communicable – such that it can be exemplified by (many) *supposita*.[11] In a nutshell, since the divine essence is perfect, it must be communicable.[12] But if it is communicable, it cannot be a *suppositum*, since no *suppositum* is communicable – a principle that I discuss in the next section. The first person must, therefore, be distinct from the divine essence – just as, on the same principle, the essence would have one underlying *suppositum* on the assumption that Unitarianism were true.[13]

---

[10] For the principle, see too Scotus, *Ord.* 1.2.2.1–4, n. 378 (Vatican, II, 344–5); *Ord.* 1.4.1.un., *text. int.* (Vatican, IV, 381, l. 20–p. 382, l. 4).

[11] I discuss this principle at length in chapter 18 below.

[12] Scotus, *Quod.* 5, n. 13 (Wadding, XII, 128; Alluntis and Wolter, 118–19 (¶ 5.30)); *Ord.* 1.2.2.1–4, nn. 382–3 (Vatican, II, 346–7).

[13] As we shall see, the distinction between communicable and incommunicable entity may be very slight – in creatures it is merely negation, in God something positive. Supposing Unitarianism were true, it is an interesting question whether divine subsistence would be constituted by some real entity distinct from the divine, or whether – as in creatures – subsistence could add to essence merely the negation of actual communication. Elsewhere, Scotus claims that limitation to just one thing is an imperfection for any communicable entity (*Ord.* 1.2.2.1–4, n. 382 (Vatican, II, 346); *Ord.* 1.28.1–2, n. 51 (Vatican, VI, 134–5)). This shows that, if the divine essence is communicable (and thus distinct in some way from any divine person, each one of which is incommunicable), then it must be communicated to more than one person. But this does not establish the prior claim that the essence is communicable.

3 Persons as Incommunicable Entities

Augustinian accounts that take seriously the analogy between the generation of the Word and the production of a mental entity – such as Scotus's – have to face an obvious problem. For a mental act – a concept – is a mental quality, with *intentional* or mental *contents*, and it is hard to see how such a thing could be a person – even in the admittedly mysterious context of the divine nature. Persons are surely things that do not themselves consist of mental contents in the way that concepts consist of (are) mental contents. But the whole point of the argument is to show that memory is productive of an entity that consists of mental contents. Scotus's very distinct account of the nature of intentional acts and objects, however, provides him with a solution. As we saw in Part I, chapter 4 §3 above, Scotus makes a strong distinction between the mental act and its contents. The act is a real quality, not an intentional entity at all; the intentional contents of the act somehow inhere in it, or somehow belong to it. While it seems very odd to think of a person as simply being intentional contents, it is not so hard to make the move from a real quality to a real person, particularly given Scotus's claims, mentioned in Part I, chapter 6 §3 above, that real qualities are individual things, in principle capable of independent existence.[14] Of course, Scotus does not believe that the divine persons are accidents. They are fully fledged substantial things. But Scotus's account of accidents means that there can be a strong family resemblance between substances and real accidents, and this, coupled with his view that mental acts are real qualities, makes his view about the generation of the divine Word not as susceptible as it would otherwise be to objections of the kind that I just outlined.

The argument that the internal divine producers and products are in fact persons, given in the first section of this chapter, relies on a somewhat unrefined account or series of accounts of what it is to be a person: thus, in **[1]** the notion is left wholly opaque, and in **[2]** non-inherence seems to be seen as a sufficient condition for some numerically singular thing to be a person. Needless to say, this condition far from exhausts Scotus's account of what it is to be a person, and no doubt he would have regarded the arguments in **[1]** and **[2]** as provisional, at least to the extent that they require adapting to take account of the full definition of 'person'. Still, as we shall see in the light of considerations introduced below, such an adaptation could be easily effected.

It may be thought that non-inherence is a sufficient condition for some numerically singular entity to be a person – let us say, a *suppositum*, for we, like the medievals, tend to reserve the use of the word 'person' for intellectual *supposita*. But the medievals, rightly, believe that more than this is required. For example, we would not say that my hand is a *suppositum*, and the reason for this is that, in so far as it is a singular entity at all, it is a *part* of me. So to non-inherence, we would immediately need to add the negation of parthood too. Still, neither parts nor (inherent) accidents are substances, and we might think that being an individual substance is sufficient for being a *suppositum*, and that if we add the further characteristic of rationality or intellectuality we will have a sufficient characterization of a person. This, of course, gives us Boethius's famous definition:

---

[14] For this last claim, see my *The Physics of Duns Scotus*, ch. 6, section 2.

'A person is an individual substance of rational nature.'[15] But this definition is not sufficient either. For we might well think that the divine essence fits this description. After all – as I make clear in a moment – the divine essence is not *divisible* into numerically many instances of itself, and is thus in some sense 'individual', and in some sense a substance. There are anthropological and Christological problems with the definition too.[16] Theologians have tried in various ways to overcome these difficulties. For our purposes, the most important and influential are the proposed revisions offered by Richard of St Victor. For, at least when applied to God, Richard sees that the definition must be amended in such a way as to exclude the possibility of the divine essence's being a person. Scotus agrees with Richard here, noting that the Ricardian definition of 'person' as 'incommunicable existence of an intellectual nature' is a marked improvement on Boethius's – among other reasons because it means that the divine essence does not count as a person.[17]

It is important here to understand what is not being said. Some modern theologians have seen the rejection of the applicability of the notion of *individuality* to the divine persons as an important corrective to views of the Trinity that neglect the notion of community and relationality in the Trinity. But this is a misunderstanding of medieval treatments, perhaps reflective of the painful tendency of certain theologians to argue simply by slogan, not taking any trouble to try to find out what is actually being asserted. Richard's clarification is entirely metaphysical, and has nothing to do with the quite independent questions of the *constitution* of the divine persons (by relations according to the common, Augustinian, medieval opinion), and of the kind of social existence enjoyed (or not) by the divine persons.

Scotus builds on foundations laid by Richard, and he does so in a very metaphysically sophisticated way, as we would expect. In doing so, it seems to me, he develops one of the most compelling and powerfully coherent accounts of the Trinity ever constructed. For Scotus, as for Richard, *incommunicability* is the key concept:

[5]
1 Something is said to be communicable either by identity, such that that to which it is
2 communicated is it, or by information, such that that to which it is communicated is
3 not it, but is by it (*ipso*).
4 In the first way, the universal is communicated to the singular, and in the
5 second way form [is communicated] to matter. For any nature, considered in itself
6 and under the description of nature, is communicable in either way – that is, to many
7 *supposita* of which each is it, and also as that 'by which' (*quo*), as a form, by which
8 the singular or *suppositum* is a being quidditatively (*ens quiditative*), or something

---

[15] Boethius, *Eut.* 3 (Moreschini, 214); for an excellent discussion of Boethius's definition and its subsequent history, see Corinna Schlapkohl, *Persona est naturae rationabilis individua substantia: Boethius und die Debatte über den Personbegriff*.

[16] For example, Scotus cites Boethius's definition, and notes that, on this definition, 'it would follow that the soul is a person – which is inappropriate – and the deity is a person': *Ord.* 1.23.un., n. 15 (Vatican, V, 356). I examine the claim that the divine essence is a subsistent entity in chapter 13 §5 below. For the Christological difficulty, see my *The Metaphysics of the Incarnation*, ch. 11.

[17] Scotus, *Ord.* 1.23.un., n. 15 (Vatican, V, 356); the definition Scotus gives is a composite of different claims from Richard: see *De Trin.* 4.22 and 4.23 (188).

9 that has a nature. And a *suppositum* is incommunicable with the opposed twofold
10 incommunicability.[18]

This is an extremely compressed passage. Part of the point is to show that the divine
nature is, in Scotus's account, a certain sort of universal; I discuss this issue in detail
in chapter 13 §1 below. The passage identifies two sorts of communicability – by
identity and by informing [5.1–3], and two corresponding sorts of
incommunicability, the negations of these two types of communicability [5.9].
Something is communicable by identity if it is really the same in various different
supposita [5.4], and this (as we discover elsewhere) can happen in one of two ways:
either by being an extramental universal (immanent in each *suppositum*), or by
existing as a concept that equally well represents various different *supposita*.[19] As
we shall see below, Scotus believes that only the divine essence can satisfy the first
of these descriptions. But since a common creaturely nature can be considered under
the accidental modification of being a concept that equally well represents various
different creaturely *supposita*,[20] it follows that every (common) nature is in one way
or another communicable by identity – communicable *ut quod*, as Scotus sometimes
puts it [5.5–7].[21] A *suppositum* is not communicable in this way. Thus, a *suppositum*
cannot be shared by many different entities such that it is identically the same in
each of them; neither can it exist as a concept representing many different *supposita*.
This gives us the first kind of incommunicability.

What this account shows, I believe, is that we have to be very careful in
supposing that the ascription of incommunicability to a person is anything other
than a highly technical way of denying that a person is a universal. Clearly, part of
the point of calling something 'individual' is to highlight its not being a common or
shared nature: it is not the sort of thing that can be *divided* into further instances. For
Scotus – as for all medieval thinkers – the divine nature is like this: it cannot be
divided into further Gods. But the divine nature – as I shall show in chapter 13 §1
below – is shareable in the sense of being fully exemplified in each person that
possesses it. By preferring 'incommunicable' to 'individual' as a description of a
divine person, Scotus is, basically, highlighting the metaphysical fact that no person
is exemplifiable in the way that the shared (universal) divine essence is.

The second kind of communicability – communicability *ut quo* – is if anything
rather more complex. The reason for this is that, it seems to me, Scotus makes
this second sort of communicability cover even more possible sorts of relation
than he makes the first cover. For he introduces the notion with the more basic
one of information, or informing: the relationship between a substantial form and
its matter, or an accidental form and its substance. And the point here is that the
relationship is between two really distinct items: hence the 'formal' component
is not the same as the item which it and the 'material' component compose

---

[18] Scotus, *Ord.* 1.2.2.1–4, nn. 380–1 (Vatican, II, 345–6); see too *Ord.* 1.23.un., n. 16 (Vatican, V, 357).

[19] I discuss this at length in my article, 'Divisibility, Communicability, and Predicability in Duns Scotus's Theories of the Common Nature'.

[20] On this, see Part I, chapter 4 §1 above, and the Appendix below.

[21] Scotus, *Ord.* 3.1.1, n. 10 (Wadding, VII, 16).

[5.2–3].[22] The notion of communicability *ut quo* is extended by Scotus beyond the standard types of information just mentioned, however, to include the communicability of a nature to its *supposita*. The purpose here is to highlight one of two possible relationships. Consider a creaturely nature. Such a nature, as I will show below, is not numerically the same in each *suppositum* that has it. So there is some sense in which it is not true that each *suppositum* is the nature; each one is a different (instance of) the nature. Thus, each one 'has' the nature, and the nature is that in virtue of which the *suppositum* belongs to a certain kind – is a being quidditatively **[5.8]**. Rather differently, the divine essence is numerically the same in each divine *suppositum*. But there is still a sense in which this nature is distinct from each *suppositum*, since each *suppositum* includes some entity not included by the nature – namely, the personal property. Hence, each divine *suppositum* has the divine nature **[5.7–9]**. Scotus goes on to make it clear that the relevant relationship here is not one of information.[23] Again, there is a corresponding negation, incommunicability, which is ascribed to a *suppositum*: a *suppositum* cannot inhere in anything, or be that in virtue of which something belongs to a certain kind.

How does Scotus know that the divine producer and products are incommunicable in these two ways? Let me begin with communicability *ut quod*. For something real to be communicated *ut quod*, it has to be identically the same in more than one complete thing (more than one *suppositum*). A necessary condition for being communicated in this way is being infinite, and indeed 'formally' infinite – infinite in such a way as to fail to include any finite elements. The divine producer and products are not formally infinite, since they include non-finite elements – the personal properties (on this, see chapter 18 below). Indeed, Scotus's view is that the only real entity communicable *ut quod* is the divine essence.[24]

Communicability *ut quo* is rather more complex, for – as I have just noted – Scotus uses it to cover at least two different cases, each one of which needs a separate treatment. The first is the relationship of divisibility (into parts of the same

---

[22] Of course, as I have presented Scotus's account of communication by identity, the same seems to be true in this case too. Some item is identically the same in various *supposita*, each one of which presumably includes some further item or items too. But Scotus presents this latter kind of communicability as a kind of identity, since the relevant further components are not in any way separable from each other: they are merely 'formally' distinct from the shared nature or essence. I will return to this below.

[23] Scotus, *Ord.* 1.2.2.1–4, n. 387 (Vatican, II, 348–9). I take it that part of the point of Scotus's repeated assertion that the essence is predicated of the persons 'by identity', rather than 'formally', is that the divine essence is not a form inherent in the persons: for the predication claims, see e.g. *Ord.* 1.5.1, n. 32 (Vatican, IV, 28); see chapter 17 §2 below.

[24] According to Scotus, being communicable *ut quod* entails being numerically one and infinite. Scotus at one point argues that it is not possible to infer simply from the nature of ingeneracy that ingeneracy cannot be divided (and thus that it is numerically one), and the reason is that ingeneracy is not formally infinite: Scotus, *Ord.* 1.2.2.1–4, n. 367 (Vatican, II, 339–40); see too Ibid., n. 385 (Vatican, II, 348); Ibid., 2.3.1.1, n. 39 (Vatican, VII, 408; Spade, 66); Ibid., 3.1.2, nn. 3–4 (Wadding, VII, 33–4). Since ingeneracy is not formally infinite, it is not the case that it is communicable *ut quod* to more than one *suppositum*. In this sense, it is incommunicable *ut quod*, and this is what Scotus wants to say about the divine persons too. For perfection rather than infinity as the relevant explanatorily basic feature, see Ibid., 2.3.1.2, n. 52 (Vatican, VII, 415; Spade, 70).

kind). I assume it to be obvious that no divine person is divisible into parts of the same kind. As we saw in chapter 11 §1 above, Scotus shows that there can be no more than one product of any given kind in God, and no more than one unproduced item. This entails that the natures of the products cannot be divided in the required way. What about the relationship of information? When talking about the relation between a form and its subject, Scotus highlights two different features of this relation: information and dependence.[25] No divine person could be a form of anything else, since being a form of something else would entail entering into composition with it in such a way as to compose a further thing. But no divine person can enter into composition with anything else in such a way, because components of substances are, as components, less perfect than the substances they compose – a state incompatible with being a divine person.[26] Neither could any divine person depend on anything else in the way in which (say) an accidental form depends on its substance, since every divine person is wholly unconditioned.[27]

This account of incommunicability helps us see just what Scotus thinks Richard of St Victor's definition of 'person' adds to Boethius's. Scotus, as I just mentioned, and shall show in more detail in chapter 13 §1, distinguishes two ways in which natures are shared by their *supposita*: by division (communicability *ut quo*), and by what we might call mere repetition – numerically one and the same nature in each exemplification (communicability *ut quod*). Scotus wants to draw attention primarily to the latter of these two sorts of relation, and deny it of a divine person. Scotus, as it happens, does not believe that the divine persons are individuals at all – presumably because he believes that anything individual is *eo ipso* communicable.[28]

One further important feature of the divine persons needs to be clarified. For Scotus believes that divine persons are not persons in just the same sense as created persons are persons. As he puts it, the notion of *person* is non-univocal between God and creatures.[29] This is, in fact, something that Scotus believes we find out from revelation: specifically from Christology. Clearly, no created extramental entity is communicable *ut quod*, since only the divine essence is communicable in this way.

---

[25] Scotus, *Ord.* 3.1.1, n. 3 (Wadding, VII, 6); *Quod.* 19, n. 13 (Wadding, XII, 502–3; Alluntis and Wolter, 428 (¶ 19.40)); I discuss all this in *The Metaphysics of the Incarnation*, 34–6.

[26] See Scotus, *Ord.* 3.1.1, n. 16 (Wadding, VII, 25); *Ord.* 3.6.3, n. 2 (Wadding, VII, 184); I discuss God's inability to enter into composition with anything else in Part I, chapter 6 §2 above.

[27] It might be thought that the divine persons depend on the divine essence in some way. But whatever way this is, it is neither causal, nor anything like the way in which a property depends on its subject. And this is sufficient to establish the *ut quo* incommunicability of a divine person. I discuss the relation between the divine substance and the divine persons in chapter 13 §1 below.

[28] See e.g. Scotus, *Quod.* 3, n. 17 (Wadding, XII, 82–3; Alluntis and Wolter, 74–5 (¶ 3.49)). This is a slightly odd terminology to adopt, though the doctrine itself does not seem strange – *pace* David Coffey, *Deus Trinitas: The Doctrine of the Triune God*, 168, n. 24. The point is that the domain of indivisible things is (generally) restricted to the domain of communicable things. Scotus obviously regards the point as unimportant: I mention at the end of the next chapter, for example, a text where Scotus claims that a divine person is indivisible, and that its indivisibility (unlike its incommunicability) formally derives from the divine essence.

[29] Scotus, *Ord.* 3.1.1, n. 10 (Wadding, VII, 16); *Quod.* 19, n. 20 (Wadding, XII, 509; Alluntis and Wolter, 435 (¶ 19.69)).

But Scotus holds that a created *suppositum* is communicable *ut quo* in at least one of the ways in which a created nature is communicable *ut quo*: it can depend on some extrinsic *suppositum* in a way analogous to that in which an accident or individual property depends on a substance.[30] Scotus has in mind the relation between Christ's human nature and the divine person. Scotus does not believe that something can be a created *suppositum* and actually dependent or communicated *ut quo* in the required sense. So every created *suppositum* has actual independence or non-communication *ut quo*. Indeed, independence is the natural status for a created *suppositum*, so every created *suppositum* has inclinational or aptitudinal independence too. But it is not impossible for something that is now a created *suppositum* to be caused by God to be a dependent particular. So no created *suppositum* has necessary independence or necessary incommunicability *ut quo*.[31] Scotus believes that, for a created *suppositum* to satisfy this condition, it cannot be the case that its independence (factual non-communication *ut quo*) is not the result of any additional entity over and above the individual substance that it is.[32] Contrariwise, the (broadly logical) impossibility of communication *ut quo* must be the result of some additional real property: as Scotus puts it, 'some positive entity' added to the nature or essence. The reason is that a block on communication requires some real explanation over and above the nature or essence of the relevant thing.[33] In the case of a divine person, this positive entity is the personal property of the divine person. The personal properties are thus the explanations for the persons' incommunicability.

---

[30] Scotus, *Ord.* 3.1.1, n. 10 (Wadding, VII, 16); *Quod.* 19, n. 11 (Wadding, XII, 502; Alluntis and Wolter 427–8 (¶¶ 19.33–19.35)).

[31] For these modal clarifications, see Scotus, *Ord.* 3.1.1, n. 9 (Wadding, VII, 15); *Quod.* 19, n. 19 (Wadding, XII, 508; Alluntis and Wolter, 434 (¶¶ 19.64–19.65)). See my *The Metaphysics of the Incarnation*, 301–7.

[32] So not all substances are *supposita*; only independent substances are *supposita*. I discuss this claim of Scotus's in *The Metaphysics of the Incarnation*, 297–301.

[33] Scotus, *Ord.* 3.1.1, n. 10 (Wadding, VII, 16); *Quod.* 19, n. 20 (Wadding, XII, 509; Alluntis and Wolter, 435 (¶ 19.69)); see my *The Metaphysics of the Incarnation*, 304–5.

Chapter 13

The Commonality of the Divine Essence

In the previous chapter, I introduced Scotus's claim that the divine persons are *exemplifications* (my word) of the divine essence: the divine essence is numerically one and the same thing in each divine person, shared by them. One obvious way of spelling this out would be to hold that the divine essence is a *universal*. On the whole, the Eastern tradition after Gregory of Nyssa is very happy to make just this claim. But the Western tradition, generally, does not. The reasons here are complex, to do with particular historical understandings of universals variously prevalent in the Eastern and Western traditions. In general, it seems to me, Western theologians after Augustine – following the philosophical (Aristotelian and Neoplatonic) tradition – tend to think of the relation between universal and particular in terms of *division*: a universal is somehow divided into the particulars that instantiate it. The relation of division can be understood in a variety of ways. For example, a nominalist might well hold that any extramental universal is just a collection of particulars, and that the division relation is just a matter of partitioning a collection into its various components. In this sense, there is no way in which a particular *is* the whole universal: the particular is simply a part of a collection, and the collection is the universal. Realists on the question of universals who want to persevere with the notion of division in this context tend to suppose that there is a sense of 'division' according to which the whole universal is somehow in the particulars, but in such a way as not to be numerically identical in each particular. Medieval writers refer to such particulars as 'subjective parts' of the nature. The view that universals are divisible in one or other of the ways I have begun to outline here predominated in the West. This makes it immediately clear why Western theologians on the whole reject the view that the divine essence could be a universal. The divine essence is supposed to be numerically one thing, really the same in each divine person. And neither sense of 'division' allows for numerical identity in more than one thing. The divine essence, then, is not divided into the persons considered as particulars.

The Eastern theologians, contrariwise, tend to dissociate the notion of division from that of universality. They thus have no difficulty in supposing that a universal is one and the same thing in each of its exemplifications.[1] Scotus follows the Eastern tradition here, which he has perhaps got from reading John of Damascus.[2] The situation is not wholly straightforward, but basically Scotus distinguishes two

---

[1] The thought seems to me to originate with Gregory of Nyssa: see my 'Gregory of Nyssa on Universals'.

[2] See e.g. Scotus's treatment of John of Damascus, *Exp. fid.* 8 (Kotter, 28, l. 238–p. 29, l. 246; Buytaert, 43, l. 268–p. 44, l. 277) at *Ord.* 2.3.1.1, nn. 39–40 (Vatican, VII, 408; Spade, 66–7). There is a sense in which this discovery by Scotus is somewhat accidental – the works that Scotus has access to do not make the Eastern point with unequivocal clarity.

different sorts of shared nature: created natures, which are divided into their instantiations, and the divine essence, which is a genuine universal, numerically identical in each divine person.

It seems to me that the question of whether or not the divine essence is a universal is, in part, a matter of terminology. It certainly is such in the medieval West, for Scotus assumes that the universality of the divine essence does not entail that it is an abstract entity (by 'abstract' I mean one incapable of causally interacting with other things) – or, if it does entail that the divine essence is an abstract entity, it does so only in a more specialized sense of 'abstract'. Indeed, the standard 'Augustinian' view of the divine essence – according to which the divine essence is not a universal – does not entail that the divine essence is not an abstract entity in just the same, very specialized sense that (I shall argue) Scotus holds it to be an abstract entity. Again, of this more below.[3]

The background to these issues is the famous debate between Joachim of Fiore and Peter Lombard, and the decision of Lateran IV, some 60 or more years after the event, in favour of Lombard's view that the divine essence is one thing that 'neither generates nor is generated, and does not proceed'.[4] As Scotus points out, this view is obviously true, and he cites Richard of Middleton's brief knock-down argument in its favour. The divine essence is identical in all three persons. So if it were generated when one person was generated, it would be generated in all. But if it were generated in all, it would be generated in the person generating too, and thus would be a self-generator. But (as Augustine points out), nothing generates itself. So the essence cannot be generated, and *pari passu* cannot generate.[5] Joachim's worry about Lombard's position is that it entails a quaternity of things in God: three persons, and a further thing too, the divine essence.[6] And this, indeed, is the standard objection to the kind of Trinitarian theology canonized at Lateran IV. The obvious reply is that the divine essence is not some fourth thing over and above the persons: it is simply their 'overlap'. And this is exactly what Scotus asserts. Immediately after quoting the Lateran decree, Scotus asserts, '[God] could not be a quaternity unless there were posited some fourth, really distinct from the three'.[7] The point here is that the divine essence is not something really distinct from any person: it is fully and inseparably included in each person, and in this sense quite unlike a person, which cannot be fully included in any other person or substance.

---

[3] I try to make some of these points about the interrelation between Eastern and Western traditions in Trinitarian theology in my 'Two Models of the Trinity?'.

[4] Lateran IV, const. 2 (*The Decrees of the Ecumenical Councils*, ed. Norman P. Tanner, I, 231), referring to Peter Lombard, *Sent.* 1.5, nn. 1, 6 (I, 80, 82).

[5] Scotus, *Ord.* 1.5.1.un., n. 13 (Vatican, IV, 16), citing Richard, *In Sent.* 1.5.1 c (I, 23vb); see Augustine, *De Trin.* 1.1.1 cited at n. 1 of chapter 12 above.

[6] On Joachim and the controversy in general, see Fiona Robb, 'Intellectual Tradition and Misunderstanding: The Development of Academic Theology on the Trinity in the Twelfth and Thirteenth Centuries'. Arguments against a quaternity have a small but interesting place in the history of Trinitarian thought: see, in addition to the famous example in Augustine (*Ep.* 120.2.7 (710)), the discussion in section 1 of my 'Perichoresis, Deification, and Christological Predication in John of Damascus'.

[7] Scotus, *Ord.* 1.5.1,un., n. 12 (Vatican, IV, 16). I have argued at length elsewhere that any coherent Trinitarian theology needs to be committed to the Lateran claim here: see my 'On Generic and Derivation Views of God's Trinitarian Substance'.

1 The Communicability of the Divine Essence

Scotus attempts to explain the way in which the divine essence is fully included in each divine person by distinguishing three *incommunicable* things (the persons) from one *communicable* thing (the essence). I introduced these notions in chapter 12 §3 above. Scotus argues that both created and uncreated natures are communicable, but that they are so in different ways:

[1]
1 Any nature is communicable to many by identity; therefore the divine nature is so
2 communicable. ... But it is not divisible, [as is clear] from the question on the unity
3 of God. Therefore it is communicable without division.[8]

The notion of communicability 'by identity', shared by all natures created and uncreated [1.1], is the notion of communicability '*ut quod*', outlined in chapter 12 §3 above. Created natures are communicable in this way by existing as concepts that identically represent all instances of the nature, but we need not pause on this clarification here.[9] The important point is that created natures are *divisible*: such a nature has a unity that is *less-than-numerical*, and as divided into its instances is numerically many:

[2]
1 What is common in creatures is not really one in the way in which what is common is
2 really one in the divine. For there the common is singular and indivisible because the
3 divine nature itself is of itself a 'this'. And it is plain that with creatures no universal
4 is really one in that way.[10]

No creaturely common nature is 'really one' in the way that the divine nature is [2.1–2, 3–4]. The divine nature, contrariwise, is *numerically one* ('singular and indivisible ... [and] of itself a "this"') [2.2–3], and its numerical unity prevents its divisibility [1.2–3]: 'The unity of God is proved from the fact that divine infinity is not divided into many essences.'[11] According to Scotus, the intrinsic infinity of the divine essence is what individuates this essence.[12] The divine nature is thus what modern philosophers would call an 'immanent' universal: numerically singular, indivisible, identical in each exemplification of it, and immanent in these exemplifications. In this it is contrasted with a created common nature, which is somehow divisible into many instances of itself.

Still, this does not mean that Scotus believes creaturely common natures to be just collections of particulars. The nature is an object that in itself has not numerical unity but some sort of 'less-than-numerical' unity.[13] It exists in each of the

---

[8] Scotus, *Ord.* 1.2.2.1–4, n. 381 (Vatican, II, 346).

[9] On this, see Part I, chapter 4 §3 above; see too my 'Divisibility, Communicability, and Predicability'.

[10] Scotus, *Ord.* 2.3.1.1, n. 39 (VII, 408; Spade, 66).

[11] Ibid. 1.2.2.1–4, n. 367 (Vatican, II, 339).

[12] Ibid. 1.8.1.3, n. 149 (Vatican, IV, 227).

[13] Ibid. 2.3.1.1, nn. 30 and 34 (Vatican, VII, 402, 404; Spade, 63–4).

particulars that possesses it, and has some extramental being of its own, prior to there being instances of it. I do not mean that Scotus's theory of common natures entails that common natures can exist separately from their instantiations; rather, the nature has a twofold being: its own intrinsic being, making it not nothing, and a further being as instantiated:

[3]
1 In the external thing where the nature is together with singularity, the nature is not *of*
2 *itself* determined to singularity, but is naturally prior to the aspect that contracts it to
3 that singularity. ... [Less-than-numerical unity] is a proper attribute of the nature
4 according to its primary entity.[14]

The nature has some sort of entity – and therefore unity – logically prior to its instantiation [**3**.1–2, 3–4]. Talk of 'contraction' here is a way of talking about the division of the nature into individuals – entities that cannot be divided in the same way that the nature is divided [**3**.2–3]. In creatures, it is the haecceity which is responsible for this contraction.[15]

Scotus's motivation in ascribing some being, some entity, to the common nature in itself is presumably that, if it had no such being, it would be nothing at all, and thus could not be the subject of a haecceity. Scotus holds that there can be a real object that in itself lacks numerical unity. This real object is divided into 'subjective parts': it is divided such that each instantiation of the common nature exhibits all the intensional features of that nature.[16] There is no feature of stone-nature that a stone lacks, for example. The unity of the common nature is supposed, on this account, to be much tighter than merely aggregative unity. There is no sense in which the parts of any aggregative whole really exhibit all the features of that whole defined extensionally. The common nature *in itself* (prior its instantiation) does not admit of an extensional description at all.

So Scotus makes a distinction between incommunicability and indivisibility: the divine essence is indivisible, but not incommunicable ('indivisibility does not entail incommunicability').[17] The essence can be really shared without being divisible. As suggested above, we might think of the divine essence as the 'overlap' of the persons, a notion that I will return to below.[18] Scotus claims that seeing the divine nature in this way can solve sophistical arguments of the form 'This God is the Father, the Son is this God, therefore the Son is the Father': the solution is to see that the divine essence, referred to as 'this God', is both individual and shared; the sophistical argument gains its force from the false understanding that 'the identity of the extremes in the conclusion is concluded as if the medium [viz. "God"] were a "this something"' – in this context something that cannot be shared.[19] This explains why Scotus is apparently so profligate about the transitivity of real identity in this context – something I mentioned in chapter 12 §1 above. Basically, relative to the persons,

---

[14] Ibid., n. 34 (Vatican, VII, 404; Spade, 64).
[15] Ibid. 2.3.1.5–6, n. 182 (Vatican, VII, 481; Spade, 195).
[16] See e.g. Ibid. 2.3.1.4, n. 106 (Vatican, VII, 443; Spade, 85).
[17] Ibid. 1.2.2.1–4, n. 367 (Vatican, II, 340).
[18] For an explanation of this way of thinking about the issue, see my 'Two Models of the Trinity?', 278, 284.
[19] Scotus, *Ord.* 1.2.2.1–4, nn. 414–15 (Vatican, II, 363–4).

Scotus persistently treats the divine essence as though it were a secondary substance (a 'such'), and thus the sense of 'real identity' that he has in mind when claiming that the Father is identical with the divine essence is a highly specialized one.

Real identity in this context has the formal characteristics of symmetry and intransitivity. This set of formal characteristics is exemplified by the modern notion of compresence, first introduced by Bertrand Russell to deal with a very similar problem to the one raised for Scotus by the divine essence: how universals – numerically singular universals such as Scotus considers the divine essence to be – could coincide to produce substances (persons in the Trinitarian context). Compresence is a basic unanalysed relation that is symmetrical and intransitive. Intransitivity allows two sets of compresent properties to overlap without thereby being identical with each other, or constituting some further whole.[20] Scotus's 'really distinct' is thus, in this context, something like the contradictory of 'compresent'. But the relations are not exactly the same, because Scotus holds, as I show in chapter 17, §§1 and 2 below, that the component properties of a person are really identical with the person, and *vice versa*, whereas compresence is a relation obtaining only between the constituent properties of a thing. But the definition of 'really identical' could easily be tightened up to take account of this.

As Scotus sees the issue, the notion that the divine essence is a universal in this way would entail that it is an abstract object only if we were to understand 'abstract' in a very specialized sense. For on the face of it Scotus seems to claim that the divine essence itself is capable of entering into causal relations with other things. We can best see this by considering some arguments that Scotus presents against the view that there are numerically singular immanent universals in the creaturely realm. The arguments all rely on the presupposition that, if there were such universals, they would not be abstract objects. For example, refuting an opinion that accepts the existence of *created* immanent universals of the kind that Scotus supposes the divine essence to be:

[4]

1 This opinion posits that that one substance [viz. the universal], under many accidents,
2 will be the whole substance of all individuals, and then it will be both singular and
3 this substance of this thing [*x*], and in another thing [*y*] than this thing [*x*]. It will also
4 follow that the same thing will simultaneously possess many quantitative dimensions
5 of the same kind; and it will do this naturally, since numerically one and the same
6 substance is under these [viz. *x*'s] dimensions and other [viz. *y*'s] dimensions.[21]

Here Scotus objects that immanent universals will be identically the same in all *supposita* [4.1–3], and are the subject of identically the same accidents – here, extension [4.4–6]. There are no creaturely universals identically the same in all exemplifications, then, because it is not the case that two things of the same kind have necessarily identically the same dimensions. Here, the 'substance' is the universal, and it is clearly presented as the subject of accidents.

[20] For an accessible account of Russell's view, see D. M. Armstrong, *Nominalism and Realism*, 89–91.

[21] Scotus, *Rep.* 2.12.5, n. 3 (Wadding, XI, 326ᵇ); see also *Ord.* 2.3.1.1, nn. 37, 41 (Vatican, VII, 406–7, 409–10; Spade, 65–7).

Elsewhere, Scotus makes a similar point about action:

[5]
1 If some *per se* existent form naturally had some proper action, [and] if it were to give
2 the same existence to many, [then] from the fact that *supposita* are denominated by the
3 action of the form only if they have existence through the form, they would be
4 denominated by the same action, just as [they are] if they have the same existence of
5 that active form. ... When therefore [the objection] states 'action belongs to a
6 *suppositum*, therefore there are many actions of many *supposita*', I deny the
7 consequence except in the case that the thing which is the *ratio agendi* [i.e. the form]
8 (through which, giving existence, these *supposita* are said denominatively to act) is
9 multiplied in [these *supposita*].[22]

The idea is that a *per se* existent form is a numerically singular item **[5.1]**, and an immanent universal, giving 'the same existence to many' **[5.2]**. This form is a concrete entity, in the sense that it has its own proper action **[5.1]**. This action is somehow communicated to all the *supposita* that exemplify the form **[5.3–5]**, and this means that the various *supposita* all share the same action (viz. the form's action) **[5.3–4]**. Forms that are *divided* into their *supposita*, contrariwise, are abstract entities in the sense that only the *supposita*, and not the forms, properly act **[5.5–9]**.

The presupposition is that an immanent universal would be in some sense an agent and, as I shall show below, Scotus tends to think of the divine essence in this sort of way too: at the very least, he thinks of the divine essence as something like a (reified) causal power shared by the persons. Still, the point that I want to bring out is that, in thinking of the divine essence as a universal, Scotus is not committed to thinking of it as an abstract entity in the sense of failing to be an agent, or at least a (reified) causal power shared by the persons. Thus, assuming that the Augustinian thinkers are less inclined to think of the essence as an abstract object in this sense, the distance between Scotus's view and that of thinkers who cling more closely to Augustine on the question is not as great as might at first sight appear.

2 The *Perichoresis* of the Divine Persons

One way in which the commonality of the divine essence is conveyed in the late Greek Patristic tradition is to talk about the 'perichoresis' of the divine persons. Henry of Ghent uses the notion of *perichoresis* (labelled 'circumincession') to talk about the 'overlap' of the divine persons, and I would judge his use to be in conformity with the Patristic tradition. On this view, each divine person is in each other person on the grounds that each includes the divine essence.[23] Scotus rejects

---

[22] Scotus, *Ord.* 1.12.1, n. 51 (Vatican, V, 54–5). At the passage marked with ellipses, Scotus talks of one and the same whiteness in two different surfaces 'doing' things: affecting the eye.

[23] See Ibid. 1.19.2, n. 42 (Vatican, V, 284), summarizing Henry, *SQ* 53.10 (II, fo. 74S–T). Supposing that the Greek Fathers use 'perichoresis' as a way of talking about the 'overlap' of the divine persons – as, in other words, a way simply of talking about the *homoousion* – is contentious (in the sense that modern commentators simply tend to assume that something more is meant), though I think it would be easy enough to demonstrate. Still, whatever the fact of the matter, it is clear that Scotus wants to say more than just this.

this view on the grounds that, since each divine person includes the essence, Henry's view would entail that each divine person is in himself, as much as in both other persons.[24] Circumincession is about the way in which one person can be another,[25] and Scotus distinguishes two relevant senses of 'in': first, something can be in another in the way that a form is in matter, or a (common) nature in a *suppositum*; or, secondly, something can be in another in the way that two subsistents might interpenetrate. Clearly, it is the second sense that is relevant in the case of the circumincession of the divine persons. Now, incommunicable subsistence pertains to a person not in virtue of its pertaining to any part of it, but pertains, rather, simply to the whole. The same, Scotus reasons, therefore obtains for any attribute that is a result of subsistence – such as 'interpenetration in the manner of a subsistent (*subsistenter inesse*)'. So it pertains to a person not in virtue of the divine essence, but to the whole person simply speaking.[26]

Of course, a great advantage of Henry's view is that it is easy to understand. In particular, supposing that persons' perichoresis is just their sharing the divine essence – and thus 'overlapping' – reduces the temptation to think of the interpenetration in spatial ways. Scotus's approach does not have this benefit, and it is hard to see in what way the elements which Scotus wants to add to the bare *homoousion* can be distinguished from more spatial models of perichoresis (for example, the Stoics' bodily interpenetration in a *krasis*).[27] Scotus is aware of this difficulty, and notes that there is no suitable direct analogue in the creaturely realm to the unique perichoresis of the divine persons. He suggests three more or less remote analogues, from each of which imperfect features must be excluded: God's presence (*illapsus*) in creation (excluding the notion of causal dependence);[28] the presence of the powers of the soul to the soul itself (excluding the notion of non-subsistence from the powers);[29] and the soul's relation to the body at the instant of death, or two glorious bodies interpenetrating (excluding the notion of numerical distinction of natures).[30] Of course, in the first two of these cases, Scotus has excluded the very way in which it is possible for the items to be present to each other, and in the third the notion seems irreducibly spatial, in the sense that at least one extreme is spatial, and that it is this spatiality that grounds the relation of indwelling. Scotus seems largely aware of the limitations of the analogies, but clearly prefers the last:

---

[24] Ibid., n. 45 (Vatican, V, 285–6).

[25] Ibid., n. 29 (Vatican, V, 280).

[26] Ibid., n. 54 (Vatican, V, 290); see too nn. 58–62 (Vatican, V, 294–5). Scotus cites Hilary of Poitiers, not Augustine, for this material, and there is no doubt that the origins of the notion in the Western tradition lie in the pre-Nicene era: the existence of the persons *in* each other is a way of talking about divine unity that predates the Nicene solution of the *homoousion*. For the references to Hilary, see Scotus, *Ord.* 1.19.2, nn. 54 and 63 (Vatican, V, 290 and 296), citing Hilary, *De Trin.* 7.41 (CCSL, 62, p. 310, ll. 27–9) and *De Trin.* 3.1 (CCSL, 62, p. 73, ll. 2–3, 11–12).

[27] On the relevance of this, see my 'Perichoresis, Deification, and Christological Predication', section 2.

[28] Scotus, *Ord.* 1.19.2, n. 64 (Vatican, 296–7).

[29] Ibid., n. 66 (Vatican, V, 297–8).

[30] Ibid., n. 65 (Vatican, V, 297).

[6]
1 For the sake of all of these examples ... it can be added that in this way of being 'in',
2 each extreme is in the other on the same basis (*rationem*), for here is denoted mutual
3 presence, not the containment of [one] extreme by [another] extreme – just as, if one
4 body is understood to be in a place, this is as what is contained [is in] a container; but
5 if two bodies are understood to be in the same place as each other, this is of the same
6 kind (*rationem*) [in each case], for they are simultaneous, and simultaneity implies a
7 common relation of one kind in both extremes. And if, *per impossibile*, the place is
8 excluded, and the simultaneous presence of bodies is posited, there will be a relation
9 of one kind in the extremes, and each in the other, without either being contained by
10 the other, or both being contained by a third.[31]

The relation of perichoresis is mutual [**6**.1–4], and an example is bodily interpenetration [**6**.5–7]. Still, bodily interpenetration by itself includes the notion that both bodies are contained by some further entity (the surrounding place) [**6**.3–4, 10].[32] But if, *per impossibile*, we think of bodily interpenetration without the notion of place – perhaps both bodies existing in a vacuum – we will have a relation that satisfies all the *formal* requirements for the perichoresis of the divine persons (viz. symmetry, transitivity, and non-reflexivity) [**6**.7–10].[33]

3 Against the View that the Divine Essence is a Substrate for the Persons

One Patristic route for explaining the commonality of the divine essence is to claim that the divine essence is some sort of substrate for the divine persons: that it is most like *matter* in the creaturely realm. Henry of Ghent takes this analogy very seriously, and uses it to explicate another obscure piece of Patristic heritage: the claim made at the Council of Nicaea – wisely dropped at the Council of Constantinople – that the Son proceeds 'from the substance of the Father'. Presumably, the Nicene claim is intended, at the very least, to ensure that the Son is not a creature: he is not produced from nothing, or from some substance other than God. The problem is that the Nicene claim is susceptible to a reading according to which the divine substance is identical with the Father in a way that it is not identical with Son or Spirit. Setting aside subordinationist worries here, the difficulty with this view is that it is simply incoherent. If the divine substance were properly identical only with the Father, then the Father would not be able to generate, for he would include no property other than the divine substance or essence.[34]

Henry takes the Nicene claim very seriously, and believes that, in order to block the claim that the Son is a creature, it should be understood as follows (I use Scotus's brief summary of Henry's characteristically prolix presentation):

[31] Scotus, *Ord.* 1.19.2, n. 67 (Vatican, V, 298).

[32] For this Aristotelian notion of place, see my *The Physics of Duns Scotus*, 193–202.

[33] As I indicated in Part I chapter 6 §1, Scotus seems to have a quite materialistic conception of divine immensity. I doubt that this conception is motivating his acceptance of the analogy here, however, since all he appears to be interested in are the formal aspects of the relation.

[34] On this, see my 'On Generic and Derivation Views', 465–71.

[7]
1 In this question it is said [by Henry of Ghent] that, just as in a generable created
2 substance something is potential, which is presupposed to generation (namely,
3 matter), and something [is] induced by generation (namely, form), and [something is]
4 produced by them (which is the generated thing): so there correspond proportionally
5 as it were (*quasi*) three similar things in God: for the person is a quasi-composite, and
6 the relation quasi-form, and essence quasi-matter. The Son is therefore generated
7 from the substance of the Father as from quasi-matter.[35]

This very nicely gives the general picture Henry has in mind. In the generation of a substance, on standard Aristotelian physics, there is a substrate for the change – namely matter, that somehow remains constant throughout the process – and there are the consecutive forms which structure the matter before and after the generation, respectively. Matter is seen as potential here, because it is what is structured by the form, and form actual, because it structures the matter. The result is a composite of matter and form – a material substance with a particular structure [7.1–4]. Henry argues that something analogous ('proportional') happens in the case of a divine generation [7.4–5]. The divine substance is like the substrate for the form, and the personal property is like the form. The Son is thus like a composite of essence and property [7.5–6]. And this gives us the correct interpretation of Nicaea: 'The Son is ... generated from the substance of the Father as from quasi-matter' [7.6–7]. And in line with this, Henry holds that the Son is generated from the divine substance 'not as it is in the three, but as it is the substance of the Father',[36] since 'only as it has existence in the Father does it have the *ratio* of a [passive] potency, so that something can be generated from it'.[37] The reason for this is the need to block the claim that the Son proceeds from himself (since he includes the divine substance), another obvious objection to the Nicene claim if understood as asserting that the divine substance is equally in all persons.

Clearly, the property of the Father is not lost in this process. Henry is not thinking of the generation of the Son as requiring the corruption of the Father, the inherence of the Son's form in that divine essence (the 'quasi-matter') after the inherence of the Father's form in the quasi-matter. We need to think rather of something like one chunk of matter with two different substantial forms (and, presumably, three once the Spirit is produced). Many medievals – including Henry – believe that there is nothing contradictory about this,[38] though it seems plausible only if the various forms are thought of as ordered in terms of potency and act – which presumably does not apply in the case at hand.[39] Why should Henry adopt this view about the divine substance? His reason is simple. The Son is not from nothing; therefore he is from something. According to Henry – very loosely citing Anselm – there are three ways of understanding the claim that something is 'from nothing'. On none of these

---

[35] Scotus, *Ord.* 1.5.2.un., n. 52 (Vatican, IV, 41), summarizing Henry, *SQ* 54.3 (II, fo. 84E–F).

[36] Ibid.., n. 58 (Vatican, IV, 45).

[37] Henry, *SQ* 54.3 (II, fo. 84F).

[38] See the discussion of Henry on the plurality of forms in my *The Physics of Duns Scotus*, 49–55.

[39] On this, see Scotus, *Ord.* 1.5.2.un., n. 90 (Vatican, IV, 59): 'Incompossible things cannot be simply speaking acts of the same thing, although the same thing [viz. a form] can be the act of incompossible things, as the soul [is the act of] organic parts.'

understandings is it true of the Son that he is from nothing. The relevant senses are the following: not produced at all; not produced from matter; produced after nothing.[40] The first sense is false both of the Son and of creatures. The third is, factually, true of the created universe, and false of the Son. But anyone who believes in the possible creation of a beginningless world would hold that the third sense could apply in this case too. Thus the third criterion would not be sufficient to distinguish the generation of the Son from the case of the production of creatures. As it happens, Henry rejects the possibility of a beginningless created world.[41] But if we allow the possibility, we can begin to see the shape of Henry's argument. For on this view, neither of the two obvious readings of 'from nothing' (the first and the third) is sufficient to distinguish the production of divine *supposita* from that of created *supposita*.

So what about the second sense of 'from nothing'? According to Henry, this sense is true of creatures and – in some sense – false of the Son. Scotus summarizes:

[8]
1 If we posit that the Son is from the Father [as from his originating or efficient
2 principle], there still remains the question, whether [he is] from something, as from
3 matter or quasi-matter, or from nothing. And since he is not from nothing (for in this
4 way a creature is from nothing), therefore he is from something, and the argument
5 stands.[42]

The point is that creatures are from nothing in the sense that creation does not require any sort of (material) substrate **[8.3–4]**. But the Son is from some sort of substrate: namely, the substance of the Father 'as quasi-matter' **[8.2–3, 4–5]**. And this is sufficient to distinguish the Son from every creature.

Henry's position is open to an obvious objection, one that Henry believes can be answered. If the divine substance is quasi-matter, and the property quasi-form, and the person quasi-composite, will it not follow that the divine substance is in potency to the quasi-form? And if it does, then the divine substance cannot be – as all medievals suppose – pure act (*actus purus*).[43] Henry believes that this objection can be met, and he does so in the usual scholastic way: by making a distinction. Henry's answer exploits the fact that the personal properties are relations, and the distinction that Henry makes is between two different sorts of potency: potency to receive an absolute form, and potency to receive a relation. Henry's general account of relations places them at a considerable ontological distance from non-relational items.[44] Relations are not things but modes, and something's potency for a relation is no more than rationally distinct from the thing itself: it is thus 'always naturally conjoined to act'. Contrariwise, a potency for an absolute thing involves going 'from potency to act by motion or transmutation', and receiving an

---

[40] Henry, *SQ* 54.3 (II, fo. 83D), citing Anselm, *Monol.* 8 (I, 23, ll. 3–21). Scotus cites the whole discussion in *Ord.* 1.5.2.un., n. 53 (Vatican, IV, 41–2).

[41] For this, see e.g. Henry, *Quod.* 1.7–8 (Macken, I, 35).

[42] Scotus, *Ord.* 1.5.2.un., n. 54 (Vatican, IV, 42), summarizing Henry, *SQ* 54.3 (II, fo. 84F).

[43] Ibid., n. 56 (Vatican, IV, 43–4).

[44] On Henry's account of relations, see Henninger, *Relations: Medieval Theories*, 52–8.

extramental form. This is incompatible with being pure act; but the potency for a relation is not.[45]

Richard of Conington develops Henry's position further, arguing that the divine essence can be said to be 'generated subjectively' – to be a 'subject of generation' – in the sense that the divine essence is a substrate that remains the same between the two terms of generation: 'the divine essence remains the same in Father and Son; therefore it is the subject [of generation]'.[46]

Against Henry's view, Scotus offers five arguments, of which I give the most interesting one, an argument that goes right to the heart of various derivation views of the divine Trinity – views according to which the Nicene 'from the substance of the Father' entails that the Father is somehow identical with the divine essence in a way in which the other persons are not. On Henry's view, the divine essence is the substrate of the production of the Son. Is this substrate to be identified as the essence considered as in all three persons, or simply in some one person? Clearly not the first of these, for then the Son would be generated from something in all three persons, and thus, *a fortiori*, from (in part?) himself. (If we reply that the generation of the Son simply makes the essence come to exist in the Son, then we will have Scotus's view, discussed in chapter 15 §1 below, that the essence is the formal end term of the generation, not the substrate at all.) If we opt for the second identification – as Henry does – then we will need to identify a person causally prior to the generation of the Son. If the Father, then since the essence in the Father would be that in which the Son's form is made to exist, the Son would be somehow 'in' the Father (and not *vice versa*); if some other person, then there would be two persons prior to the production of any divine person, which is false.[47]

This argument seems to me quite powerful, and what makes it so is that it forces Henry to think about the precise relation between Father and Son. For Henry's view is most naturally read as identifying the essence as, primarily, something in, or proper to, the Father. It is this priority which defines the one-way nature of the causal relation between Father and Son. If we hold that the essence as in all three persons is the substrate – presumably holding that the essence is somehow the substrate for the Father's relation to the Son and Spirit as much as it is the substrate for their relations to the Father – then it will be hard to see how the position Scotus opposes can secure the correct derivation relations between the persons: each will be 'from' the essence of every person. If, contrariwise, the essence is properly identified with the Father, then it will be hard to see how the Father could be distinct from the divine essence, and Henry's position will be open to all the objections that can be made to this extreme derivation view.[48]

Scotus replaces Henry's view with a different reading of 'from the substance of the Father', since, as he notes, 'from the time of Augustine until that [of Henry], no one dared to name the divine "matter" or "quasi-matter"'.[49] Scotus holds that the

---

[45] Scotus, *Ord.* 1.5.2.un., n. 56 (Vatican, IV, 43–4), summarizing Henry, *SQ* 54.3 (II, fo. 84G).

[46] Ibid., n. 60 (Vatican, IV, 46), summarizing Conington, *Quod.* 1.17: on this, see Dumont, 'William of Ware', 68–83.

[47] Scotus, *Ord.* 1.5.2.un., n. 73 (Vatican, IV, 51–2).

[48] On all this, see too Ibid. 1.28.3, nn. 68–9 and 82 (Vatican, VI, 145, 150).

[49] Ibid. 1.5.2.un., n. 93 (Vatican, IV, 60).

Father produces the Son without any passive substrate,[50] and proposes the following harmless reading of the rogue Nicene claim:

[9]
1 [In 'from the substance of the Father], the 'from' does not denote merely efficiency or
2 origination, for if merely efficiency, then creatures would be from the substance of
3 God; neither is there denoted by the 'from' merely consubstantiality, for then the
4 Father would be from the substance of the Son; rather, there is denoted both
5 origination and consubstantiality, such that by the case governed by the preposition
6 'from' [viz., 'substance' in the ablative] is denoted consubstantiality, such that the
7 Son has the same substance and quasi-form as the Father, from whom he exists by
8 origin; and by that which is construed in the genitive with this inflection [viz. 'of the
9 Father'] is denoted the originating principle, such that the complete sense of this
10 phrase 'the Son is from the substance of the Father' is this: the Son is originated by
11 the Father as consubstantial with him.[51]

'From the substance of the Father' denotes causal origin and consubstantiality [**9**.4–5, 9–11]. It cannot denote mere causal origin, for then creatures – which are causally originated by God – would be from the substance of God [**9**.1–2]. But it cannot denote mere consubstantiality, for then each divine person would be from the substance of every other divine person – since consubstantiality is a symmetrical and transitive relation [**9**.3–4]. More precisely, 'from the substance' denotes consubstantiality [**9**.5–8], and 'of the Father' denotes the causal origin: that the Son's substance derives from the Father [**9**.8–9]. The description of the essence as 'quasi-form' [**9**.7] – in marked contrast to Henry's description of the essence as 'quasi-matter' – draws attention to the fact that the divine essence is something like a universal, exemplified by the different persons – as discussed above. The persons are, as it were, the subjects of the essence; not *vice versa*.

4 The (Weak) Priority of the Divine Essence

All this might make us think that the essence, for Scotus, is straightforwardly posterior – from a logical point of view – to the persons. In the Aristotelian tradition, for example, universals depend on the individuals that exemplify them. But for Scotus things are rarely this simple. In this case, he holds that there is an important way in which the divine essence is in some weak sense prior to the persons. This looks to confirm all the worries of opponents of this kind of Trinitarian theology, so I should like to spend some time considering why Scotus adopts this view, and how precisely he understands it. As we shall see, the claim does not amount to anything very damaging, and serves various useful argumentative purposes.

When discussing the question of the Father's personal property – explained below in chapter 14 §2 – Scotus notes that the divine essence is prior to the personal properties for two reasons: it is infinite (and they are not), and because 'according

---

[50] Ibid., nn. 94–7 (Vatican, IV, 60–2).

[51] Ibid., n. 99 (Vatican, IV, 62–3).

to all' it is the foundation for the relations.[52] Elsewhere Scotus adds a further reason too:[53] *per se* existence formally belongs to the divine essence of itself, for the reason that, according to Augustine, the same (*per se* – non-relational) existence is common to the three persons.[54] Indeed, Scotus uses this insight to try to show that the divine essence is prior to the persons not merely in thought. The general principle Scotus states is this: 'What pertains [to something] primarily formally of itself, is in some way prior, outside the mind, to that which does not pertain to it of itself formally.' But being in a relational *suppositum* does not pertain to the divine essence of itself formally: 'therefore it exists *per se* prior to its being in this [*suppositum*].' The reason why being in a relational *suppositum* does not pertain to the divine essence of itself formally is that, if it did, then the essence would possess the relation in everything in which it exists. If, presumably, it pertains to the divine essence to exist *per se* 'prior' to its existing in a *suppositum*, then the essence is, in this sense, prior to any *suppositum*.

Still, this account raises as many questions as it answers. Among other things, if the essence is somehow the foundation for the various personal relations, then why is Henry of Ghent's theory about the quasi-materiality of the divine essence not true? After all, relations in some sense perfect – inhere in – their foundations, and this sort of relation is closely analogous to the one that Henry of Ghent proposes. Scotus's reply is of considerable complexity, and includes a further reason in favour of his view that the divine essence is somehow prior to the persons. He begins by considering an Aristotelian principle about a feature of the material world, namely, generation. The principle is that 'things that are posterior by generation are prior by species and substance', or, as Scotus has it, 'prior by perfection'.[55] The reason is that generation requires potency (the less perfect) prior to act (the more perfect). In case of God, however, 'it is necessary that the same is simply first, both by origin and perfection (even according to the Philosopher, in the same place[56]), for the whole order of generation is reduced to something first [in the order] of perfection'.[57] Given this, Scotus goes on to note that this insight would prioritize form or essence in the order of generation: if it obtained in creatures, then 'we would seek first the form which naturally gives act to matter, and secondly we would seek matter which naturally would receive existence by that form, or a *suppositum* that naturally subsists by that form.'[58] Scotus is not suggesting that we reject the Aristotelian

---

[52] Ibid. 1.28.3, n. 82 (Vatican, VI, 150), discussed above. The foundation of a relation is the form in virtue of which the relation obtains: and in the case of a simple form, it is that in which the relation 'inheres'. In the case of God, the relevant form is the divine essence: the divine essence is as it were the only available form, and indeed the only available entity prior to the constitution of the persons. But the relations must be founded in some entity prior to the existence of the persons, because the relations are supposed to constitute the persons, and to this extent be prior to the persons. (I discuss this issue in chapter 14 §1 below, when expounding Scotus's views on the personal properties of the persons.)

[53] For the whole discussion in the rest of this paragraph, see Scotus, *Ord.* 1.7.1, n. 85 (Vatican, IV, 144–5).

[54] See Augustine, *De Trin.* 7.3.6 (CCSL, 50, p. 254, ll. 107–8).

[55] Aristotle, *Metaph.* Θ.8 (1050ᵃ4–5); see Scotus, *Ord.* 1.5.2.un., n. 130 (Vatican, IV, 73).

[56] Ibid. (1050ᵃ7–9).

[57] Scotus, *Ord.* 1.5.2.un., n. 131 (Vatican, IV, 73–4).

[58] Ibid. (Vatican, IV, 74).

account of generation. What he is trying to show is that, if origin and perfection coincide, as they do in God, then we begin from the most perfect – the divine essence – not just as a way of looking at things, but because that is how things are. The divine essence is prior:

[10]
1 Beginning from the first instant of nature, the divine essence as it has *per se* existence
2 from itself occurs entirely first. This does not pertain to any created nature, for no
3 created nature has existence naturally prior to its [having existence] in a *suppositum*.
4 This essence – according to Augustine, *De Trinitate* 7 – is that by which the Father is,
5 and by which the Son is – though it is not that by which the Father is the Father and
6 the Son is the Son. *Per se* existence belongs to this essence, considered most
7 abstractly, as prior to every person, and in this first [instant the essence] occurs not as
8 something receptive of any perfection, but as infinite perfection, able indeed in the
9 second instant of nature to be communicated to another, not as a form informing
10 matter, but as a quiddity is communicated to a *suppositum* as to something formally
11 existing by it. And thus the relations spring forth (*pullulant*) from it (as some say),
12 and the persons spring forth into it (not as certain quasi-forms giving existence to [the
13 essence], or as certain quasi-*supposita*, in which it receives an existence that is simply
14 its), to which *supposita* it gives existence as that by which, formally, those *supposita*
15 exist, and by which they are God: and thus this relation of springing forth – if it is *per*
16 *se* subsistent – springs forth not as the form of the essence but as something naturally
17 God formally by that deity, though not as something informing it but as something
18 existent, the same as it by perfect identity. In no way, conversely, does the relation
19 belong to the essence as that by which the essence is formally determined or
20 contracted, or in some way actuated by it, for all of these are incompatible with the
21 infinity of the essence as it first occurs under the description of infinite act.[59]

This forbiddingly dense passage deals with the inference from priority to quasi-materiality. We need to think of the divine essence as most fully actual, with the relations and persons somehow springing forth from it. Scotus begins by drawing a contrast – one of many possible contrasts – with created natures. Created natures are posterior to their instantiations, in the sense that the existence of a nature depends on the existence of the *supposita*, but not *vice versa*: the nature is not a real singular thing in the extramental world; it exists in its own way only in so far as there are instances of it.[60] The divine nature, contrariwise, is prior to the persons [**10**.1–3]. According to Augustine, the essence is that by which each person exists, and is God: the divine essence, in Scotus's way of thinking of the issue, is exemplified by the divine persons [**10**.4–6]. And this essence has, in itself, *per se* existence [**10**.6–7]. So what is the relation between the essence, on the one hand, and the *supposita* and personal relations on the other? The divine essence does not *receive* either of these – it is not Henry's quasi-matter [**10**.7–8], nor is it somehow received in matter [**10**.9–10]. This much we already know. Scotus claims instead that the essence is communicable

---

[59] Ibid. (Vatican, IV, 74–5), referring to Augustine, *De Trin.* 7.6.11 (CCSL, 50, p. 262, ll. 20–2).

[60] The situation, again, is a little more complex. Common natures are independent in the sense that they are independent of the identity of their instantiations – provided there are humans, it makes no difference to human nature whether Socrates or his twin brother exists; instantiations are not independent of their natures in this way: on this, see my 'Medieval Theories of Haecceity', section 2.

to a person in a way analogous to that in which an (individual) nature is communicated to its *suppositum* [**10**.10–11]: the divine essence is more like the *act* of a person than it is like a passive potency for a form [**10**.14–15]. The rest of the passage elaborates on this thought, using Henry's language of the relations 'springing forth from' – somehow arising from – the essence, and the persons 'springing forth into' – somehow being actualized or perfected by – the essence [**10**.11–12].[61] Thus the essence is not perfected by the relations as quasi-forms [**10**.12–13]; neither does the essence receive its existence from the *supposita* [**10**.13–14]. The divine persons are subsistent relations [**10**.15–16], and the relations (again) are not forms of the essence: the essence is more like the form of the persons (i.e. of the subsistent relations) [**10**.16–17]; but not exactly a form of the persons, since that would imply composition: the essence and the persons are really (though not formally) identical – they are identical 'by perfect identity' [**10**.17–18]. All this is in full accord with Scotus's teaching on the exemplification of the divine essence by the divine persons; I deal with the precise issue of identity below. Even though the persons are exemplifications of the essence, we would not want to think of the relations as 'contracting' the essence, in the way that a haecceity contracts or actualizes a common nature [**10**.18–20] – and this is probably a consequence of the view that the essence is prior to the persons. The essence is infinite, and pure actuality, and thus not the sort of thing that can be contracted by a haecceity [**10**.20–21].

What is it for the relations to 'spring forth from' the essence, and for the persons to 'spring forth into' it? Scotus elsewhere makes it clear:

[**11**]
1 Not any sort of relations (even real) constitute the divine persons, or distinguish them.
2 Rather, relations of origin [constitute and distinguish the divine persons], for primarily
3 they spring into the divine essence, for the twofold fecundity is primarily in the
4 essence, in so far as it is infinite intellect and infinite will, and by these, as
5 intermediaries, the relations of origin pertaining to the communicability of the nature
6 spring forth – which nature or divine essence is communicated according to that
7 twofold fecundity just spoken of. When these relations are presupposed, the common
8 relations spring forth; for this reason these common relations, even if they are real,
9 neither constitute nor distinguish the persons.[62]

The purpose here is to show that, if the relation theory of the personal properties is true, then the relevant relations are relations of origin. Scotus holds that the 'common relations' – relations shared by the persons – presuppose the distinction of the persons, and so cannot have a role in distinguishing the persons [**11**.7–9] (the comments about the reality of these relations [**11**.1, 8] are directed against Henry's view that such relations are just rational; Scotus, for example, devotes a whole quodlibetal question to the issue of the reality of the relation of equality between the persons).[63] Scotus argues for his point in a way that makes it exactly clear what he understands by the notion of relations springing from the essence. The relations of

---

[61] On this, see Henry of Ghent, *SQ* 56.1 ad 2 (II, fo. 113D).
[62] Scotus, *Ord.* 1.26.un., n. 28 (Vatican, VI, 8–9).
[63] Scotus, *Quod.* 6 (Wadding, XII, 142–67; Alluntis and Wolter, 130–58); see too *Ord.* 1.42.un. (Vatican, VI, 341–9).

origin spring forth from the essence because they are produced by the activity of intellect and will in God, and these are features of the divine essence [11.2–5]. The relations of origin are prior to the common relations because intellect and will are the first productive powers in the divine essence [11.3–4]. (I discussed this at length above, in chapter 11 §1; see chapter 16 §1 on the common acts of intellect and will.) Intellect and will here are powers of the essence, and are thus the intermediaries in the essence's causality relative to Son and Spirit [11.4]. The essence is thereby communicated to Son and Spirit [11.5–7].

We should be careful not to suppose that Scotus's commitment to the priority of the divine essence means that he believes the exemplification of the essence to be a contingent matter, and thus God to be, essentially, something other than the Trinity of persons. Nothing could be further from the truth, of course. As we have already seen, Scotus's arguments in favour of the Trinity of persons require not only that God is necessarily a Trinity, but that we can come to have some reasonably secure understanding of this simply by reflecting deeply on the notion of God. But Scotus devotes considerable space to a consideration of the way in which the essence is, as a matter of logical necessity, exemplified by the three persons. The problem that Scotus sees in positing the priority of the divine essence lies in reconciling this with the (causal) priority of the Father. Specifically, how is the essence 'determined to the first person'?[64] Scotus's answer is that the essence is of necessity in all three persons, but that there is a certain order in its exemplification, corresponding to the causal ordering between the persons:

[12]
1 The divine essence does not have any one first subsistence, equal to it (for then it
2 could not be in another [subsistence]), but three subsistences are equal to that nature.
3 Nevertheless, there is an order in these three in having the nature, and for this reason
4 the essence is related by one primacy to the first of those ordered things, such that, just
5 as the essence would be of itself firstly in the three [persons] if it were in them without
6 order (and this as much by the primacy of equality as by the primacy of immediacy),
7 so now it is of itself in the three by the primacy of equality, but not [by the primacy] of
8 immediacy, but it is in the first of them [by the primacy of immediacy], and in virtue
9 of this is in the others, to which it is communicated by the first.[65]

The whole point here is that the essence is 'determined' to exactly these three persons,[66] and that (equivalently) they are 'equal' to it: there is, as it were, an exact and necessary 'fit' between essence and the three divine persons [12.1–2, 7]. But the essence is determined firstly to just one person – the Father – and through him to the others, in order [12.3–4]. If (counterpossibly) there were no order between the persons, it would still be necessary for there to be three divine persons. But the essence would then be immediately in all three persons [12.4–6]. As a matter of logical necessity there is an order between the persons; hence the essence is in the three by equality, but in the Father by immediacy [12.7–8]: the Father then communicates the essence to the other two persons [12.8–9].

---

64 See Scotus, *Ord.* 1.28.3, nn. 69 and 100 (Vatican, VI, 145 and 158).

65 Ibid., n. 104 (Vatican, VI, 159–60).

66 Ibid., n. 106 (Vatican, VI, 160–1).

5 The (Weak) Subsistence of the Divine Essence

The divine essence, as the causal power in virtue of which Son and Spirit are produced, is prior to the persons, and is somehow determined to its existence in exactly the three *supposita* that exist in God. Scotus believes, however, that this essence, although not a person or *suppositum*, is a subsistent in itself.[67] As we have seen, he believes it to be a substantial individual: substantiality is what the claim to *per se* existence amounts to, and individuality is entailed by numerical singularity. It may seem odd to think of the divine essence – as a universal substance – as a subsistent thing. It seems to me that there is a sense in which this issue is merely one of terminology. For on the face of it, 'being subsistent' and 'being a *suppositum*' are synonymous. Scotus disagrees. To be a *suppositum*, a subsistent thing needs to be: (i) not an inherent form; (ii) not a part; and (iii) incommunicable. Satisfying the first two criteria, however, is sufficient for being subsistent:[68]

[13]
1 'To subsist' is equivocal: in one way it is taken to mean existence *per se*, as this
2 excludes inherence and being in another as a part in a whole; and in this way there is
3 just one subsistence [in God], as there is one *per se* existence – and in this way the
4 authoritative passages of Augustine speak. In the other way, 'to subsist' is to exist *per*
5 *se* incommunicably, and in this way there are three subsistents, just as there are three
6 persons, because three things subsisting incommunicably (*tres subsistentes*
7 *incommunicabiliter*), even though there is only one *per se* being (*ens*). Therefore this
8 major premiss, 'that which constitutes the person gives subsistent being, or is the basis
9 for subsistence', should be understood in the second sense [of 'subsistence'], for it is
10 the basis for subsisting incommunicably.[69]

Scotus is here trying to show why the divine essence is not responsible for constituting the divine persons as persons, and [13] is a reply to a series of claims from Augustine to the effect that the divine substance is that by which the Father subsists.[70] Scotus agrees that the claims are true, provided that they are understood in a very specialized sense [13.3–4, 8–10]: specifically, the divine essence is that in virtue of which the divine persons are things that are neither forms nor parts [13.1–2] – 'inherence' in [13.2] is equivalent to the relation of *informing* in [5.2] of chapter 12 §3 above. The reference to one 'subsistence' makes it clear that Scotus here has in mind one item in virtue of which the divine persons are subsistents in the required sense [13.3]. Distinctive personal or hypostatic existence requires too incommunicability [13.4–6] – presumably in the senses outlined at the end of chapter 12 above. And this incommunicable existence is

---

[67] See e.g. Ibid.. 3.1.2, n. 6 (Wadding, VII, 37); see also *Ord.* 1.28.3, n. 81 (Vatican, VI, 149).

[68] Further complexities are added by other theological considerations. As I noted in chapter 12 §3 above, for example, Christological considerations require that not all substances subsist: Christ's human nature is, according to Scotus, a non-inherent particular substance that is nevertheless dependent on, and part of, some other whole.

[69] Scotus, *Quod.* 4, n. 20 (Wadding, XII, 104; Alluntis and Wolter, 98 (¶ 4.46)).

[70] Augustine, *De Trin.* 7.6.11 (CCSL, 50, p. 262); 7.4.9 (CCSL, 50, p. 260).

possessed by the persons in virtue of their possession of their personal properties.[71]

What about the claim here that there is only one *per se* subsistence in God? On the face of it, this is different from claiming that there are three *per se* subsistents, each of whose *per se* subsistence derives from the *per se* subsistent divine essence. But in fact Scotus seems to treat the two claims as equivalent (compare **[13.4–5]** with **[13.7]**, and with the equivalent claim elsewhere that the divine essence is a subsistent).[72] In any case, the difficulty could be covered under certain anomalous semantic rules that Scotus accepts in the context of the doctrine of the Trinity. Consider the claim that there is only one God, and that each of the divine persons is God. 'God' is in this context equivocal.[73] We could argue analogously about '*per se* subsistent'. This would make sense of the necessary independence of the divine persons. To be independent is to be a *per se* subsistent. There is only one independent item in God, namely, the divine essence. But each divine person is (in a different sense) *per se* subsistent – necessarily independent – just *derivatively* so, and derivatively from the divine essence not as an efficient cause, but as something like a 'formal' explanation for the person's subsistence.[74]

---

[71] See Scotus, *Quod.* 19, nn. 4 and 20 (Wadding, XII, 495, 509; Alluntis and Wolter, 422, 435 (¶¶ 19.14, 19.69)). Elsewhere, Scotus notes that divine persons have indivisibility and *per se* existence from the divine essence, since these are features of the divine essence that are communicated to the persons; incommunicability, however, is explained by the personal properties, not the divine essence: see Scotus, *Rep.* 1A.26.2 (MS M, fo. 115ᵛ), quoted at the end of chapter 14 below.

[72] Scotus, *Ord.* 3.1.2, n. 6 (Wadding, VII, 37).

[73] On this see my 'Duns Scotus on Divine Substance and the Trinity'.

[74] Recall Scotus's claim that the divine persons are not individuals, since there is only one individual thing in God – namely, the divine essence: see too the evidence I assemble in section 1 of my 'Duns Scotus on Divine Substance and the Trinity'. Here, Scotus assumes that individuality entails communicability.

Chapter 14

Personal Properties

In this chapter, I should like to consider Scotus's teaching on the precise identity of the personal properties. The standard Western medieval view has it that the properties are, respectively, paternity, filiation, and passive spiration, and that these properties are all relations. Thus what distinguishes the divine persons from each other are their relations to each other. Scotus accepts this account. But he does so only with a certain caution, and under some very precise understandings. For example, Scotus famously considered the view that the persons could be constituted of essence and absolute (non-relational) property, and, at least early in his life, regarded it as preferable to the standard view that the persons are constituted by relations. At the end of this chapter, I shall spend a little time discussing this issue, along with Scotus's changing views on the matter. In terms of the standard properties (paternity, filiation, and passive spiration), Scotus seems to think that the distinction between these properties is founded on something more basic, that is to say, on the different modes or manners in which the persons are produced. This view is associated in particular with certain Franciscans, and I shall briefly discuss the background below.

While there was general agreement that filiation and passive spiration are the personal properties of Son and Spirit respectively, there was some controversy about paternity as the property of the Father. For paternity is a relation, and seems to require the existence of an offspring – in the case of God, traditionally, the divine Son. But this seems to erode somewhat the monarchy and priority of the Father; at worst, it perhaps generates an inconsistency: how can the Father generate something that is itself responsible for the Father's identity. For this reason, some theologians preferred to argue for *ingenerate* as the property of the Father. As we shall see, Scotus rejects this rather controversial opinion in favour of the more common view that the Father's personal property should be identified as the relation of paternity. More debatable, however, is Scotus's rejection of the standard Western view that the distinction between Son and Spirit can be maintained only if the Son has a role in the origination of the Spirit. Scotus does not believe that *opposed* relations are required to distinguish the persons. He thus distinguishes filiation from active spiration, and claims that passive spiration is sufficient to distinguish the Spirit from the other two divine persons, irrespective of the subject of active spiration. This may sound highly abstruse, but as Scotus points out, the result is that the classic Western argument in favour of the *filioque* fails. (Scotus has his own, separate, argument for the *filioque*; I discuss it in chapter 15 §4 below.)

As I have just noted, Scotus is unclear as to whether the persons are distinguished by relations or by some non-relational features of them. But supposing them to be distinguished by relations, he makes it clear that he would accept the common view that the relevant relations are relations of origin.[1] That is

---

[1] Scotus, *Ord.* 1.26.un., n. 28 (Vatican, VI, 8).

to say, what distinguish the persons are the causal (originative) relations that exist between them: being a Father (paternity), being a Son (filiation), and being spirated (passive spiration).[2] Paternity, filiation, and passive spiration are three of the so called 'notions': intra-Trinitarian causal activities. The list of notions was usually taken to include two more: being ingenerated, and active spiration.[3] As we shall see, Scotus denies that these latter two properties could play any role in distinguishing the persons, and at least some of the discussion that follows will focus on the reasons why not.

1 Personal Properties as Relations of Origin

The fundamental reason why relations of origin are relevant is very simple. Scotus summarizes a series of passages from Henry of Ghent:

[1]
1 How a relation can constitute the persons and distinguish them, is declared by this,
2 that a producer is necessarily really distinguished from its opposite [viz. what is
3 produced], for the same thing cannot produce itself, according to Augustine, *De*
4 *Trinitate* 1, c.1; therefore there will be some real distinction of some things in the
5 divine essence. The [distinct things] cannot be there in any way by information, on
6 account of divine simplicity. Therefore there will be a *per se* subsistent in that nature;
7 therefore there will be really distinct persons.[4]

[1.5–7] provide a succinct summary of the inference from processions to persons, discussed in chapter 13 above, and we do not need to consider it further here. [1.2] simply notes that, when one thing produces another, there is a real distinction between them, for the simple reason that self-production is impossible [1.3]. I do not see why Scotus sees the need to cite Augustine, since the principle in [1.3] is more or less obvious, and certainly accepted by Scotus on rational grounds, not on the basis of faith. The distinction between producer and produced, as such, is a relation or pair of relations: 'producing ____' and 'being produced by ____' [1.1]. And this gives us the thesis that the personal properties are relations: relation of origin is sufficient to distinguish persons in God. Distinction and constitution [1.1] are not quite the same thing, and here Scotus is ascribing both to the relations. The argument in [1.2–5] focuses on distinction: the relations must be different in the different persons. Constitution, I take it, is more like an explanation for subsistence, or (more properly) for distinctively personal or hypostatic existence: an explanation, in other words, for incommunicability.

---

[2] Here and in what follows I use 'causal' for convenience; as indicated, 'originative' would perhaps be less tendentious, but it is more of a mouthful.

[3] See e.g. Scotus, 1.28.3, *text. int.* (Vatican, VI, 163, 1. 17). On the Patristic antecedents here, see e.g. J. N. D. Kelly, *Early Christian Doctrines*, 265. Scotus spends some time on 'inspirability' – the impossibility of being spirated – as a property of Father and Son: see *Ord.* 1.28.1–2, nn. 31–4 (Vatican, VI, 124–5), where he suggests that it could be added to the list.

[4] Scotus, *Ord.* 1.26.un., n. 29 (Vatican, VI, 9); see e.g. Henry, *Quod.* 6.1 (Macken, X, 9–14); for the Augustine reference, see chapter 12, passage [1].

I consider in Part I, chapter 6 §2, and in chapter 17 §3 below, the precise nature of the relations in Scotus's theory (i.e. not merely mind-imposed, but real extramental entities). For now, I want to focus on two further issues: first, how can a relation – paternity – be the personal property of the Father? and, secondly, in virtue of which of its features does a relation distinguish the persons? Both of these issues were the subject of some debate.

2 Paternity as the Personal Property of the Father

The problem with the first is this: how can a relation be the personal property of the Father? A relation such as 'producing ____' requires the existence of the product, and if a relation is the personal property of the Father, then the very constitution of the Father seems to depend on the existence of the Son: a conclusion that disturbs the 'causal' order between the persons required in Trinitarian theology.

The problem is so acute that some of Scotus's contemporaries – in line with certain trends in Patristic theology too – suggested that the relevant property of the Father was not a relation but something such as 'ingenerability' or 'innascibility'.[5] I take it that these two terms, if not synonymous, are nevertheless very close to each other in meaning. Scotus accepts that *ingenerate* is a property of the Father not shared by the other two persons. He understands 'ingenerate' to mean 'an unproduced subsistent (and it is understood in this way by the Saints)',[6] and holds that, in this sense, it is proper to the Father.[7] Still, Scotus does not hold that *ingenerate – unproduced subsistent –* is properly identified as the *constitutive* property of the Father – that which properly explains his hypostatic existence and distinction from every other divine *suppositum*. The reasons are made clear by Scotus's discussion of the near relation of 'ingenerate', namely 'innascible'.[8] Roger Marston, for example, holds that innascibility is the constitutive property of the Father.[9] The reason is that 'prior' to the production of the Son, the divine essence must be understood as actually non-communicated, and as such possessed by something that does not have the essence by communication: the essence is not somehow communicated to the Father, but is had by him without any causal activity. His possession of the essence is not the result of any causal activity. So the Father's personal property can be simply this: the negation of having the essence by any causal activity. And the correct term for this is 'ingenerate' (here treated as synonymous with 'innascible').[10]

---

[5] Note that this property – ingenerability – is distinct from its close relative, that of active generation, which Scotus takes to be really identical with paternity and only conceptually distinct from it: see *Quod.* 4, n. 26 (Wadding, XII, 110; Alluntis and Wolter, 102 (¶ 4.57)).

[6] Scotus, *Ord.* 1.28.1–2, n. 19 (Vatican, VI, 116–17).

[7] Ibid., n. 20 (Vatican, VI, 117).

[8] Scotus treats the two terms as simply synonymous at *Ord.* 1.28.1–2, nn. 36 and 40 (Vatican, VI, 127 and 128), and implies at n. 26 (Vatican, VI, 119–20) that 'ingenerate' signifies merely a negation (just as 'innascible' does).

[9] Marston, *De em.* 2 c, ad 23, ad 24 (pp. 28, 29, 31, 32–3); 3 c (pp. 55, 56).

[10] Scotus, *Ord.* 1.28.1–2, n. 36 (Vatican, VI, 126–7).

Scotus rejects this view for rather technical reasons. The reasons explain too why Scotus will not allow *ingenerate* to be the constitutive property of the Father. Scotus accepts that a negation can be incommunicable. But he does not believe that the negation can sufficiently *explain* its own incommunicability:

[2]
1 No negation is of itself incommunicable, for just as it is not of itself one, or indivisible
2 by some indivision, so it is not of itself *this* and incommunicable, but [is so] only by
3 an affirmation, with which being divided is primarily incompatible. Through this
4 [positive feature] it pertains to a negation not to be divided. It seems to be the same
5 for incommunicable existence, for being communicated is not incompatible with a
6 negation of itself, but [is so] only by some affirmation, to which incommunicability
7 primarily pertains. Therefore a negation will not be the primary explanation (*ratio*) of
8 incommunicability.[11]

Basically, the property of being ingenerated cannot be shared by any other person. But the reason for this, the explanation for it, must be something other than the mere property of ingeneracy: indeed, the explanation must be some positive feature of the person. Think of it like this: what feature of the property of ingeneracy could possibly be such as to render it unshareable (by various things of the same kind)? We might answer that the kind is of a sort that can only have one causal origin of the same kind. But in this case it is the features of the kind that explain the unshareability of ingeneracy, not ingeneracy itself. Whatever answer is given will always involve an appeal to some positive attribute. Scotus argues the case by considering the question of individuation. In his discussion of individuation in book 2 of the *Sentence* commentaries, Scotus considers the view of Henry of Ghent that the individuation of a substance could be explained simply by two negations: the negation of division *in se*, and of identity with others. Scotus's reply is that the explanation for individuation cannot be a twofold negation, because the twofold negation is precisely what needs explaining: *how* it can be that something is undivided *in se*, and divided from everything else, is what needs to be explained.[12]

Scotus uses something like this strategy against Marston's view on the personal property of the Father, though as we shall see the two answers are not entirely analogous. **[2.1–5]** sets up the parallel: the individuality of a negation cannot be explained by a negative feature; so neither can its incommunicability. **[2.5–6]** gives a reason for this: 'being communicated is not incompatible with a negation of itself'. Rather, the incommunicability of a negation requires some positive feature to explain it. It seems to me that here Scotus's argument is insufficient: we need some further reason to accept that the incommunicability of a negation requires extrinsic explanation. But, of course, the point could be argued inductively in the way that I tried to indicate above: simply try to think of examples in which a negation could be incommunicable, and then work out whether the explanation for this incommunicability could itself be a negation. **[2.7–8]** draws the required conclusion.

While it is true, then, that the Father is ingenerate and innascible, Scotus does

---

[11] Ibid., n. 44 (Vatican, 130).

[12] On all this, see too Part 1, chapter 4 §4 above.

not believe that these features could explain the distinction of the Father from Son and Spirit. Given this, Scotus concludes that the relevant feature must be something positive. But the only positive features obviously available are the divine essence and the relations of origin. Clearly, the divine essence cannot perform the required task, since it is shared by all three persons. So the Father's relation of origin must distinguish him from the other two persons. The personal property of the Father is thus *paternity*.[13] Still, this view raises the tremendous problem outlined above: surely this makes the existence of the Father somehow causally dependent on the existence of the other two persons? Scotus puts the objection as follows:

[3]
1 The first person is understood in personal existence before he generates, for acting
2 pertains to a *suppositum* (*agere enim est suppositi*); therefore he is understood
3 (*praeintelligitur*) to be a *suppositum* before he acts. If however he were constituted by a
4 relation to the second person, the second person would be understood to exist with
5 [the Father] existing, and for this reason the second person would be understood to
6 exist before the first generates, and thus the second person would not be the end term
7 of that generation.[14]

Scotus, in typical fashion, finds a rather complex way of making the point. He notes various relations of logical priority and posteriority involved in the generation of the Son. First is the Father existing as a person, logically prior to, secondly, his act of generating [3.1]. The reason for this ordering (Father – act of generating) is a marginal variant on the well-known scholastic tag '*actiones sunt suppositorum*' – it is only *supposita* that act [3.1–2].[15] So this means that the Father's being a *suppositum* is logically prior (*praeintelligitur*) to his act of generating [3.2–3]. Suppose, then, that what constitutes the Father as a *suppositum* is his relation to the Son [3.3–4]. In this case, the Father's existence as a *suppositum* requires the existence of the Son [3.4–5]. Now, since the Father's existence is logically prior to his act of generating, this means that the Son's existence too must be logically prior to the Father's act of generating [3.5–6]. But this in turn means that the Son cannot be the person generated by the Father [3.6–7], on pain of causal circularity. So the Father cannot be 'constituted in personal existence by some positive relation to the second person'.[16]

Scotus spends most of his discussion trying to work out how to circumvent this objection, given that it is true that the Father is constituted in personal existence by some positive relation to the second person. Scotus considers three views other than his own, and rejects them all. Oddly (since none of the three really provides anything like a plausible solution to the problem), all are harder to understand than

---

[13] Scotus, *Ord.* 1.28.3, n. 55 (Vatican, VI, 139–40).

[14] Ibid., n. 52 (Vatican, VI, 138–9).

[15] The origins are Aristotelian (*De an.* 1.4 (408^{b}13–15)), though the richness of the scholastic tradition here – a subject that could stand a monograph all of its own – far transcends the rather modest Aristotelian background.

[16] Scotus, *Ord.* 1.28.3, n. 52 (Vatican, VI, 138).

Scotus's own view: the first – that of Aquinas – particularly so. I consider here very briefly Aquinas's view, along with the third in Scotus – that of Henry of Ghent. The second view originates from Bonaventure, and is important for another aspect of Scotus's theory; I delay discussion of it until a little later in this chapter. According to Aquinas, we can distinguish two aspects of the Father's personal property: relation, and constitutive property. As constitutive property, it precedes the act of generation; as relation, it follows the act of generation.[17] Clearly, this does no more than restate the problem, and as Scotus points out, if the property is a relation, 'the difficulty [outlined in [3]] is not avoided'.[18] According to Henry of Ghent, we can think of the relation of origin as somehow potential prior to the act of generating, and hold that what constitutes the Father is the relation considered in this way: as potential.[19] Against this, Scotus objects that a merely potential relation is less perfect than an actual one (and thus that the Father is constituted by a property less perfect than the Son's property; this latter property consists in *actually* being generated);[20] and that, in any case, a merely potential relation added to a real common essence cannot constitute a real *suppositum* distinct from the essence in some way (I will return to this claim about the actuality of the personal properties in chapter 17 §3 below).[21]

Scotus's own view is that there is no need to distinguish different aspects of the relation of origin in the ways that his opponents want to: 'for whatever is varied [merely] according to [our] consideration is really the same, and in so far as it is real, it constitutes a real person'.[22] Scotus thus needs to show how the initial problem in [3] can be solved. His basic strategy is to distinguish causal from non-causal dependence:

[4]
1 The simultaneity of correlatives – by which they are said to be 'naturally simultaneous'
2 – is this simultaneity, namely, not be able to be without each other without
3 contradiction, if they are mutually relative: for one relation cannot be without its end
4 term, for if it could be without it, it would be a non-relational being (*ens ad se*); for the
5 same reason, neither can the relation that corresponds to it be without that end term.
6 Therefore these two relations, when they are mutual, cannot be without each other
7 without contradiction. ...
8   In this way, I concede that the first person and the second cannot be without
9 each other without contradiction (and there is no contradiction from anything
10 extrinsic, but from the formal *ratio* of these persons). Nevertheless, priority of origin
11 is consistent with this, for one is from another.[23]

What Scotus is trying to do here is distinguish causal dependence – 'posteriority of origin' – from non-causal dependence – the impossibility of one correlative being

---

[17] Aquinas, *ST* 1.40.4 c (I/1, 205[a–b]); see Scotus, *Ord.* 1.28.3, n. 57 (Vatican, VI, 140).

[18] Scotus, *Ord.* 1.28.3, n. 58 (Vatican, VI, 141).

[19] Henry, *SQ* 58.3 (II, fo. 134G); *SQ* 58.4 (II, fo. 134L–5L); see Scotus, *Ord.* 1.28.3, nn. 64–5 (Vatican, VI, 142–3).

[20] Scotus, *Ord.* 1.28.3, n. 66 (Vatican, VI, 143–4).

[21] Ibid., n. 67 (Vatican, VI, 144–5).

[22] Ibid., n. 93 (Vatican, VI, 155).

[23] Ibid., nn. 94–5 (Vatican, VI, 155–6).

without the other. Scotus, in common with standard medieval thinking on this matter, makes a distinction between two kinds of relation: real and rational. A mutual relation [4.3] is one which is real in both extremes. Scotus focuses on the relational properties themselves, and claims that the existence of a relational property requires the existence of whatever entity the property is directed towards, such that the following trivial *de dicto* claim is true: for any relation R, inherent in x and with y as its end term, it is logically impossible that R exist and y not exist [4.3–4]. Suppose there the relation between x and y is mutual. In this case, it is logically impossible that the relation R_1, inherent in y and with x as its end term, exists without R, and logically impossible that R exists without R_1 [4.2–3, 5]. R and R_1 are naturally simultaneous [4.1], and it is logically impossible that one exist without the other [4.6–7]. This mutual dependence is not, of course, causal: R does not *cause* R_1; neither does R_1 cause R. The mutual dependence is more like some logical relation that exists between R and R_1. This sort of relation exists between the divine persons: one cannot be without the other [4.8–9], and, furthermore, the explanation for this impossibility of independent existence is not something extrinsic to the persons; it simply follows from their identity (as, presumably, subsistent relations) [4.9–10].[24] But, as Scotus notes, none of this has any bearing on the causal relations that exist between the persons [4.10–11]; indeed, something like this is exactly what we would expect in a case in which one person is necessarily productive of another.

The upshot of this is, it seems to me, that Scotus basically supposes that his opponents are making the issue far more difficult than it really is. We do not need any complex analysis of different aspects of the causal relationship. All we need to understand is the *de dicto* claim that the state of affairs of x's causing y requires the existence of y. This does not mean that y in any sense causes x, or causes x to cause y. But Scotus clearly regards it as sufficiently robust to have a role in the 'individuation' of the persons. Perhaps his opponents could object that priority of origin is sufficient to generate the problem in [3]. Scotus's reply, I think, requires his particular view of relations as things that in some sense exist: the existence of the relation of causal origination is indeed logically simultaneous (in Scotus's sense) with the item originated. The individuation of this relation – this relational thing – could well be parasitic on the individuation of the thing produced, and it could be thus parasitic without this generating obvious problems of causal circularity. But it is harder to think of a substance in this way. Perhaps Scotus would simply rest content with the claim that, in the case of a substance that is a subsistent relation, this is precisely how we should think. In any case, I take it that, since Scotus's opponents agree that the persons are subsistent relations, his argument has at least an *ad hominem* success.[25]

---

[24] The persons do not have to be subsistent relations for this claim to be true. All that we need is the necessity of the relations of production in the Trinity. I will return to this below. (On subsistent relations, see, in addition to material cited above, Scotus, *Ord.* 1.26.un., n. 71 (Vatican, VI, 29); Scotus accepts that the persons include essence and relation as thing and thing (see below, chapter 17 §3) – so his view of subsistent relations is a little different from that of most other scholastic theologians.)

[25] On this, see too *Quod.* 4, n. 3 (Wadding, XII, 89; Alluntis and Wolter, 82 (¶ 4.6)).

3 Relations as Modes of Origin Distinguishing the Persons

On this 'relation theory' of the constitution of the divine persons, relations individuate the persons. How can a relation do this? In virtue of which of its features (very broadly construed) can the relation perform the differentiating function required of it? Scotus's own view, in a nutshell, is that the relations can do this by being different *kinds* of relation. But this was not the universal view, and tended to be accepted merely by Franciscan theologians, taking their lead from Bonaventure. According to Bonaventure, we can distinguish the causal actions of the persons from the relation between the persons. It is the causal action/passion that distinguishes the persons; the relations merely 'manifest' the distinctions.[26] Central to this theory is that the different *kinds* of causal action are sufficient to distinguish the persons: generation is irreducibly different in kind from spiration, for example, and these 'modes of origin' are what distinguish the persons.[27]

Aquinas thinks that Bonaventure's theory will not do the job required of it. Features that distinguish one *suppositum* from another must be *intrinsic* to that *suppositum*. But a mode of origin is not intrinsic to a *suppositum*; it is not, as Scotus puts it, a form.[28] It is rather a 'way' or causal 'route' between two things, and thus extrinsic to them: it is merely a dyadic property, and as such cannot individuate monadic *supposita*. (Medieval theories of relations posit that real relations include monadic properties: every real relation is (or involves) a monadic property in at least one of the two extremes. For Aquinas, it is these monadic properties that turn out to distinguish the persons, even though, puzzlingly, the properties are nevertheless identical with the divine essence.)

Scotus accepts Aquinas's response here.[29] But this is, in a way, misleading, for Scotus does not want to make such a strong distinction between relations and modes of origin as both Bonaventure's position and Aquinas's reply suppose. In common with Bonaventure, he holds that the modes of origin are fundamentally what distinguish the persons. But he does not see why these modes of origin should be somehow distinct from the relations. It is simply the *relations* that are different in kind. Actions and passions are, after all, relations; Scotus's position is just simpler and easier to understand than that of his Franciscan predecessors, who seem to want to make a distinction where none exists. We can see this if we consider Scotus's own response to Bonaventure's view (in the summary of this view Scotus takes from Roger Marston). Scotus cites with approval Aquinas's reply, as I have just noted. But he immediately makes a qualification:

---

[26] Bonaventure, *In Sent.* 1.26.un.3 c (I, 458ᵃ); see Aquinas, *ST* 1.40.2 c (I/1, 203ᵃ), and Scotus, *Ord.* 1.28.3, n. 61 (Vatican, VI, 141–2) for a presentation of Bonaventure's view.

[27] For a full discussion of the debate, see Russell Lance Friedman, '*In Principio erat Verbum*: The Incorporation of Philosophical Psychology into Trinitarian Theology, 1250–1325'.

[28] Scotus, *Ord.* 1.28.3, n. 62 (Vatican, VI, 142); see Aquinas, *ST* 1.40.2 c (I/1, 203ᵃ).

[29] Ibid.

[5]
1 If however this [i.e. Marston's view] is understood [to be] about quasi-principiative
2 distinction ... and not in the manner of a formal principle, then this position could
3 have truth, and this argument [viz. of Aquinas] would not be against it.[30]

The point is that there are causal relations between the persons, and that these relations are, as it were, the efficient cause of the distinction between the persons ('quasi-principiative distinction') **[5.2–3]**. The position opposed holds that, in addition to the relations, there are the origins of the person, and that these are the 'formal' causes of the distinction between the persons **[5.2–3]**. Scotus maintains, however, that there is no additional 'formal' cause of the distinction over and above the relation itself **[5.2]**. Indeed, the point of Scotus's argument in **[4]** is that the efficiently causal relations are also the required formal cause of the distinction between the persons, and that the relations can do this in virtue of the natural simultaneity of efficiently causal relations.

What Bonaventure's position makes clear is that it is possible to think of different *sorts* of causal origin here. Scotus makes a great deal of this insight, and in discussing the nature of the distinction between generation and spiration considers various different theories. He begins with Aquinas's account. As Scotus presents the issue, what distinguishes Aquinas's position from the others is that Aquinas simply refuses to think of different kinds of production. Generation and spiration are distinct *merely extensionally*, and the network of relations – of whatever kind – between the persons is somehow explanatorily sufficient and basic in the distinction between the persons. In Aquinas's presentation, this extensional understanding is manifested in the oft-repeated traditional assertion that what distinguish the persons are *opposed* relations: a divine person has relations with every other divine person. Scotus – and the Franciscans in general – tries to undermine this by arguing that persons can be distinct from each other by relation even if that relation is not directed at an opposed relation in the other person. It is not the mere *network* of relations that distinguishes the persons, but the *type* of relation.

The nature of the difference between Aquinas and Scotus can be seen if we consider Scotus's presentation of the standard (i.e. Thomist) argument in favour of the *filioque*. Thus, before I give a detailed account of the precise nature of the distinction between generation and spiration, it will be helpful to consider the standard arguments in favour of the *filioque* and Scotus's reaction to them. The question Scotus raises – a scholastic commonplace on this issue – is this: 'Whether, if the Holy Spirit were not to proceed from the Son, the real distinction of [the Spirit] from the Son could obtain'.[31] Of course, as we have seen, Scotus (in common with all who accept the existence of the Trinity) holds that the Trinity of persons is (broadly logically) necessary, and thus that the antecedent here is impossible, including incompatible or incompossible subject and predicate. This raises problems all of its own, because it is a standard logical rule that a counterpossible antecedent entails every proposition, even contradictory ones. Scotus begins his discussion, indeed, by considering the view of an anonymous theologian to the

---

[30] Ibid., n. 63 (Vatican, VI, 142); see too Ibid. 1.26.un., n. 58 (Vatican, VI, 23–4).
[31] Ibid. 1.11.2, n. 24 (Vatican, V, 9).

effect that 'the question is nothing', since if incompossible things are accepted then the logical rules that govern all disputation are inapplicable: these rules presuppose that incompossible things cannot be simultaneously affirmed.[32] Scotus's response – which I will not discuss in any detail here – involves distinguishing between different levels of incompossibility. Standard Aristotelian semantics distinguishes between essential and (merely) necessary properties of a thing: essential properties are the defining properties of the thing's kind; merely necessary properties are properties that the thing cannot be without, but which are not part of the definition of the thing's kind. The classic case is the definition of 'man' as 'rational animal'. 'Rational animal' is the essence; but there are other properties (classically, a capacity for laughter) that, while not definitional properties, are nevertheless necessary properties of any human being. Scotus's reply draws on this sort of distinction, claiming that it is one thing to assert something inconsistent with the essence of a thing, and another – much less damaging – to assert something inconsistent with a necessary property of something (compare: 'man is not an animal'; 'man does not have the capacity to laugh'). The second case is acceptable as the antecedent in a counterpossible implication, and in the case at hand generation is a defining property of the Son, but active spiration is not: it is a 'quasi-passion common to the Father and Son'.[33]

Opposing Scotus's view on the logical question became a commonplace amongst the followers of Ockham, and it is easy enough to see why.[34] Still, we do not need the counterpossible implication in order to deal with the question. As Scotus notes, 'the question is asked so that it may be enquired what the first real distinguishing feature between the Son and Holy Spirit is: whether filiation, or active spiration alone'.[35] It would be possible to deal with the issue entirely in this way, without appealing to the counterpossible implication at all. Scotus, as we shall see, holds that filiation (the Son's relation to the Father) is sufficient to distinguish Son from Spirit, and his (meaningful) answer to the counterpossible question is thus affirmative. The contrast is with Aquinas and his followers, who explicitly answer in the negative, holding that persons can be distinct from each other only if there are opposed relations between them.[36]

Scotus tackles Aquinas's *filioque* argument in two related ways. As I see it, the second way helps explain the first. According to the first argument, if a relation of origin – filiation – constitutes a person, then it sufficiently distinguishes that person from every other person irrespective of the presence or absence of opposed relations in every other person. Clearly, a relation of origin requires at least one opposed relation, and thus the distinction of a person requires at least one opposed person:

[32] Ibid., n. 27 (Vatican, V, 10). According to the Vatican editors (apparatus F *in loc.*), the Franciscan William of Nottingham ascribes the objection to his fellow friar John of Berwick, and to the Dominican William of Macclesfield.

[33] Ibid., n. 29 (Vatican, V, 11).

[34] On the whole topic, see Christopher Martin, 'Theories of Inference and Entailment in the Middle Ages', ch. 7.

[35] Scotus, *Ord.* 1.11.2, n. 28 (Vatican, V, 11).

[36] Ibid., n. 35 (Vatican, V, 14); see Aquinas, *ST* 1.36.2 c (I/1, 183^b–4^b); Giles of Rome, *In Sent.* 1.11.1.3 c (fo. 65rb); Thomas of Sutton, *Qu. ord.* 9 (p. 279, l. 304–p. 282, l. 382).

paternity–filiation, for example, distinguishing Father and Son. But, Scotus reasons, the distinction of the Son from every other divine person does not require opposed relations between the Son and every other divine person: an opposed relation between the Son and one other divine person will do.[37] The presupposition here must be that relations of origin are distinct of themselves, and one obvious way for this to be the case is if they are necessarily different in kind from each other. And this is just what Scotus holds. Thus his second argument against Aquinas is from the difference in kind between the relations – what he calls the different modes of emanation:

[6]
1 Generation is distinguished from spiration, and this even if we exclude, *per*
2 *impossibile*, everything else from the notion (*ratione*) of generation and spiration, or at
3 least if we exclude the fact that active spiration is from the Son, even while the
4 distinction of the principles of generating and spirating remains. Therefore with all of
5 this excluded, the distinction between Son and Holy Spirit would remain.[38]

The argument here derives from Henry of Ghent, who like Scotus takes a broadly Bonaventurean line on this question.[39] I discuss in a moment Scotus's lengthy treatment of the ways in which generation and spiration are distinct from each other. The presupposition here is that they are distinct [6.1], and irreducibly so, since they do not derive their distinction from the identity of the persons involved [6.1–4]. Scotus holds that this distinction is sufficient to account for the distinction of Son and Spirit even if there is no relation of origin between Son and Spirit (that is to say, even if the *filioque* does not obtain), and thus infers that Son and Spirit are distinct simply in virtue of the difference between the relations of generation and spiration [6.4–5]. The idea is that *being generated* is uniquely a property of the Son, and *being spirated* uniquely a property of the Spirit.

If generation and spiration are distinct from each other, what explains this? Scotus will argue that nothing does; generation and spiration are irreducibly distinct in every way just because they are the kinds of thing that they are. But he considers the positions of various opponents who try to find some explanation for the distinction. Scotus's representative of the paradigmatic extensionalist account is his almost exact contemporary, the Dominican Thomas Sutton. Scotus presents Sutton's view as reducing the distinction between generation and spiration to the distinction

---

[37] Ibid., n. 40 (Vatican, 16–17). Aquinas defends his view by noting that if non-originative relations (the so-called 'disparate relations') distinguish persons, then the Father's two disparate relations of active generation (paternity) and active spiration will result in two distinct Fathers (Aquinas, *ST* 1.36.2 c (I/1, 184ᵃ); see Scotus, *Ord.* 1.11.2, n. 37 (Vatican, V, 37)). Scotus responds that disparate relations are sufficient for distinction of persons only if those disparate relations are incompatible in one person. Active disparate relations – active generation and active spiration – are not incompatible, for there is no block on one person having two causal effects. But passive disparate relations – passive generation (filiation) and passive spiration – are incompatible in one person, in the sense that one person cannot receive existence from two complete and independent causes (Scotus, *Ord.* 1.11.2, n. 53 (Vatican, V, 24); see too n. 47 (Vatican, V, 20)).

[38] Scotus, *Ord.* 1.11.2, n. 46 (Vatican, V, 19–20).

[39] See Henry, *Quod.* 5.9 c (Paris, II, fo. 167P).

between the persons: it is just because the network of persons is as it is that generation and spiration are distinct. The account is extensionalist because the distinction can be fully captured simply by highlighting the fact that generation (active and passive) is the relation between Father and Son, and spiration (active and passive) the relation between (Father + Son) and Spirit. This extensionalist view of the distinction between generation and spiration does not require any difference in kind between generation and spiration; as a result of this the *filioque* is a necessary part of Sutton's Trinitarian thinking. Aquinas accepts a very close analogue to Sutton's position: the relations are distinct because one relation is to one origin, and the other relation to two origins.[40] This is, of course, a likewise extensionalist account of the distinction between the relations.

Here, first, is Scotus's presentation of Sutton's position, and his brief response:

[7]
1 In one way it is posited that these productions are distinguished by the formal terms,
2 which are the persons produced. ...
3 Against this: [the productions] do not have existence through the end terms,
4 therefore neither [do they have] distinction. The antecedent is clear, because the end
5 terms have existence formally from [the productions]; I prove the consequence, for
6 existence and distinction are had from the same thing.[41]

[7.1–2] describes the basic extentionalist position. According to Scotus, this account is open to an objection in terms of the relevant explanatory order. Production is a causal relationship, and the end terms (Son and Spirit) are causally posterior to the causal relationship itself: they are what is produced in virtue of this relationship [7.4–5]. But a productive relationship cannot be individuated by its end term, because effects are individuated by their causes – through the things that give them existence [7.5–6]. The relations are not effects of the persons produced [7.3]; so they cannot be individuated by the persons produced [7.4]. There is on the face of it a problem here: the effect may be individuated by its cause, but the identity of the causal relation between effect and cause is surely dependent on the identity of the effect? I think Scotus could respond that the identity of an effect is relevantly determined by two things: the identity of the cause, and the identity of the productive action (relation) in virtue of which the effect is brought about. Think about the identity of some effect of mine: it is mine because of my identity, and it is this effect rather than that (of the same kind) because of the identity of the action in virtue of which I bring it about. So the relations cannot be individuated by their end terms, and Sutton's extensionalist account is insufficient to account for the difference between generation and spiration.

Scotus's view is that the explanation for the distinction between generation and spiration should not be located in anything extrinsic to the two relations: neither in anything prior (the causal principles) nor in anything posterior (the persons produced). Thus, generation and spiration are distinct relations of emanation, and, as Scotus points out, it is these relations of emanation that

---

[40] See Aquinas, *ST* 1.36.2 ad 7 (I/1, 185ᵃ), mentioned at Scotus, *Ord.* 1.13.un., n. 12 (Vatican, V, 69).
[41] Scotus, *Ord.* 1.13.un., nn. 8 and 10 (Vatican, V, 68 and 69); see Sutton, *Quod.* 4.2 ad 1 (p. 508, ll. 235–44).

distinguish the persons.⁴² Generation and spiration are irreducibly distinct relations of emanation:

[8]
1 Each production is distinguished formally by itself. For generation is formally
2 generation by itself, and spiration is formally spiration by itself, and from their formal
3 definitions (*rationes*) it is impossible for generation to be spiration (if *per impossibile*
4 everything else is excluded), such that it is not necessary to ask by what they are
5 distinguished, for the whole formal definition of one is not the same as the formal
6 definition of the other.⁴³

The kind of thing one production is – its formal *ratio* – is just different from the other **[8.1–3, 5–6]**: and this is true even if we exclude from consideration the relation between these productions and any other thing whatsoever **[8.3–4]**. There is nothing else other than the productions that is responsible for their being different in kind from each other **[8.4–5]**. Although Scotus does not provide any explicit definition of either type of production, he seems to hold that these different kinds of production amount to production by an act of intellect, and production by an act of will:

[9]
1 A person is truly produced by an act of intellect as a productive principle, and another
2 person by an act of will as a productive principle – and not merely metaphorically, on
3 account of some extrinsic likeness [between the production of a person and the act of
4 intellect or will].⁴⁴

So Scotus holds that the notion of generation is just that of being produced by intellect, and the notion of spiration just that of being produced by will **[9.1–2]**, and he is perfectly serious that the persons are produced in this way. Talk of production from intellect and will is *literal*, not merely metaphorical, as some suppose **[9.2–4]**. On the face of it, this is a surprising claim. But it is in fact wholly consistent with Scotus's arguments for the existence of productions in God, which begin from the notion that perfect memory and perfect will are necessarily productive. Scotus, then, thinks that his refutation of the theories of Aquinas and others on the question of the distinction between generation and spiration is as secure as his attempt to find probable arguments in favour of the Trinity.

4 Personal Properties as Relational or Non-relational

One of the more important aspects of Scotus's Trinitarian theology is his defence – in his earlier writings – of the view that the persons might be constituted not by relations but by some sort of absolute (non-relational or monadic) property.⁴⁵ The

---

⁴² At *Ord.* 1.13.un., n. 78 (Vatican, V, 106) Scotus ascribes this view to Augustine, *De Trin.* 5.27.50 (CCSL, 50, pp. 532–3, ll. 94–109).

⁴³ Scotus, *Ord.* 1.13.un., n. 77 (Vatican, V, 105–6).

⁴⁴ Ibid., n. 23 (Vatican, V, 75).

⁴⁵ For a detailed summary of Scotus's changing position on this question, see Friedrich Wetter, *Die Trinitätslehre des Johannes Duns Scotus.*

debate has ramifications well beyond the question merely of the constitution of the persons, however, for – as we shall see – the main arguments in favour of the view that the persons are constituted by relations entail that the only distinctive properties that the persons could possess are relations. And this would likely be thought false by anyone who – for example – tended towards some kind of social Trinitarianism. So Scotus's arguments against the relation theory will be of direct relevance to such a theologian. Of course, the truth or otherwise of social Trinitarianism is not something that is of concern here, though I will return to the issue briefly in chapter 15 §5 and chapter 16 §1 below.

In the *Lectura* and book 1 of the *Ordinatio*, Scotus presents arguments for and against both relation and absolute-property (non-relation) theories of the constitution of a divine person, and is clearly more enthusiastic about the non-relation theory than he is about the more usual relation theory. Thus, he offers no replies to the arguments in favour of the non-relation theory, and is – indeed – unable to find replies to at least one argument against the relation theory. And he offers an extensive discussion to show that the relation theory is not required by either scriptural or ecclesiastical authority.[46] There are two central arguments – commonplaces in the scholastic tradition – in favour of the traditional, relation theory. Both arguments go right back to the motivations for the relation theory in the first place. Relations are not things, and thus the relation theory secures both the simplicity of a divine person, and the fact that the essence is numerically identical in all three persons.[47] Thus, Scotus's first argument is that if a divine person is constituted by a non-relational property, a divine person will include two non-relational features: essence and non-relational personal property. But 'an absolute added to an absolute necessarily makes composition';[48] hence any person thus constituted will be composed. And the second argument is that if the divine persons are distinguished by non-relational properties, then the divine essence 'is distinguished and numbered in' the persons.[49] Distinction by relational property is necessary for the numerical singularity of the essence.

Against the first of these arguments, Scotus reasons as follows:

[10]
1 It can be said that if some absolute reality constitutes the persons, it nevertheless does
2 not make composition with the divine essence, just as a relation constituting the
3 persons does not make [composition]; which is confirmed by an argument *a fortiori*,
4 for the proper reality of subsistence in a creature does not make composition with an
5 essence, whereas a relation in creatures does make composition with a foundation. ...
6 Therefore if a relation here [i.e. in God] can make non-composition with the essence,
7 much more does the reality of a *suppositum* not make composition with the reality of
8 the nature.[50]

---

[46] Scotus, *Ord.* 1.26.un., nn. 67–72 (Vatican, VI, 27–9); *Lect.* 1.26.un., nn. 55–7 (Vatican, XVII, 332–3).

[47] On these, see my 'Two Models of the Trinity?'.

[48] Scotus, *Ord.* 1.26.un., n. 24 (Vatican, VI, 6); see e.g. Henry of Ghent, *Quod.* 3.1 c (Paris, I, fo. 52R–T).

[49] Ibid., n. 26 (Vatican, VI, 6); see e.g. Henry of Ghent, *Quod.* 6.1 c (Macken, X, 8–9); *Quod.* 6.7 c (Macken, X, 75–6).

[50] Ibid., n. 80 (Vatican, VI, 36–7).

The basic point is that it is simply not clear that constitution by a non-relational property entails composition [**10**.1–3]. Scotus considers the case of a haecceity (the 'proper reality of subsistence') [**10**.4]. A haecceity is a non-relational property. But it is only formally distinct from the nature or essence of an individual, and thus 'does not make composition' with this essence [**10**.4–5]. Indeed, Scotus holds that categorial relations – the temporary and accidental relations that creatures have with other creatures – are *things*,[51] and thus to this extent enter into composition with their 'foundations', the feature of the creature in virtue of which it has such-and-such a relation [**10**.5]. So at least some non-relational features of creatures are less 'real' than relational ones, and so make less of a composition with their substances. Furthermore, if a relation in God need not result in composition with the divine essence, *a fortiori* a non-relational feature need not [**10**.6–8].

The reply to the second argument is simply that the explanation for the numerical indivisibility of the divine essence is not that the persons are constituted by relations, but rather that the essence is *infinite* (and thus unrepeatable):

[**11**]
1 If we posit relational persons, it is necessary to posit that they truly subsist, and that
2 the same undivided nature is in them. But it is not in virtue of some imperfection of
3 the persons in subsisting that this can be posited, for they are posited to be as truly
4 subsistent as [they would be] if they were absolute. Therefore it is necessary that it is
5 posited on account of the infinity of the essence that is in the subsistents. But the
6 infinity of the essence would be the same if the persons were absolutes. Therefore it
7 would not be necessary in that case for the nature to be divided, just as now the
8 [relational] property [does not divide it].[52]

As Scotus understands the argument of his opponents, it relies on the assumption that relational subsistence is somehow less perfect than non-relational subsistence. It is this that explains how relational subsistence is not sufficiently 'robust' to divide the divine essence into particular instantiations [**11**.2–3]. But Scotus disputes this assumption: relational persons are as robustly subsistent as non-relational persons [**11**.3–4]. So there must be some other explanation for the indivisibility of the divine essence, and Scotus proposes that this explanation is the essence's own infinity [**11**.4–5]. (On this, see chapter 13 §1 above.) The key thing for the argument in [**11**] is that the infinity of the essence is wholly independent of any claim about the personal properties of the divine *supposita*: 'the infinity of the essence would be the same if the persons were absolutes' [**11**.5–6]. So the question of the constitution of the persons is simply irrelevant to the question of the indivisibility of the divine essence [**11**.6–8].

In both the *Lectura* and book 1 of the *Ordinatio*, Scotus offers a series of three arguments against the relation theory too, and at this stage in his career does not know of an answer to the most damaging – the third of them. The first is that the Father (at least) cannot be constituted by a relation, since the Father's constitution is logically prior to the existence of the entity to which he is related, namely the

---

[51] On this, see Part I, chapter 6 §2.
[52] Scotus, *Ord.* 1.26.un., n. 82 (Vatican, VI, 37).

Son.[53] We have already seen how Scotus deals with this sort of objection.[54] A second argument is likewise easily dealt with: a relational property cannot be produced unless the non-relational *suppositum* in which it inheres is first produced.[55] Scotus's response is simply to deny the inference: a relational property cannot be produced unless the *suppositum* in which it inheres is first produced; but the relevant *suppositum* can be a relational *suppositum*: the requirement for logical priority is irrelevant provided that the *suppositum* does not pre-exist the relation.[56]

The third argument against the relation theory is far more damaging, and at this stage in his career Scotus is stumped for an answer: as he notes in the *Ordinatio*, 'these arguments seem more difficult, though soluble if the second opinion [viz. the relation theory] is true: let him who knows how solve them.'[57] The *Lectura* is even more terse: 'I say that I do not know well how to solve [them]'.[58] The argument that causes all of this difficulty runs as follows:

[12]
1 Whatever constitutes in some existence, and in the unity corresponding to that
2 existence, is wholly and primarily incompatible with the distinction opposed to that
3 unity. ... And this proposition is proved, for if such a distinction is incompatible with
4 the whole constituted, therefore it is incompatible with it through something. Let that
5 thing be '*a*'. If it is wholly incompatible with *a*, what is proposed is proved; if not, but
6 if it is incompatible with it through *b*, there will be a regress to infinity, or, wherever
7 we stop [the regress], that will be the ultimate constituent in such a unity, and the
8 distinction opposed to such a unity will be wholly incompatible with it. Therefore if
9 paternity constitutes the first *suppositum* in personal existence under the description
10 of 'incommunicable', it is necessary that communicability is primarily incompatible
11 with paternity in its definition. But this seems false in many ways.[59]

Basically, if paternity is in any way communicable – shareable – then paternity cannot be the constituent of a person that explains the person's incommunicability [12.8–11]. The reason is that an explanation for any sort of unity exhibited by something must itself have sufficient unity to do the relevant explanatory task [12.1–3]. For example, an explanation for numerical unity must itself have numerical unity, and indeed must have it in such a way that its own numerical unity has no further explanation outside itself. The point of the regress argument in [12.3–8] is that if there be no such entity – no constituent of me, for example, that has explanatorily basic numerical unity, then there will be no explanation for my numerical unity. Scotus is anxious to find an explanation that would render something absolutely unique, and nothing that consists wholly of shareable features could be absolutely unique: anything so composed could be exactly replicated.

Scotus claims that paternity is indeed shareable [12.11], and goes on to give a total of five arguments to show this. First, as his opponent Henry affirms, every

---

[53] Ibid., nn. 33–7 (Vatican, VI, 10–12).

[54] See here Ibid., nn. 84–8 (Vatican, VI, 39–47).

[55] Ibid., nn. 38–44 (Vatican, VI, 13–15).

[56] Ibid., nn. 89–92 (Vatican, VI, 48–9).

[57] Ibid., n. 94 (Vatican, VI, 49).

[58] Scotus, *Lect.* 1.26.un., n. 75 (Vatican, XVII, 339–40).

[59] Scotus, *Ord.* 1.26.un., nn. 45–6 (Vatican, VI, 15–16).

quiddity – every definable property – is communicable. But paternity is such a property, and is thus communicable.[60] Secondly, infinity is necessary for a quiddity to be individual of itself; paternity is not of itself infinite, and therefore not individual of itself. And if it is not individual of itself, it is *a fortiori* not incommunicable of itself, for 'incommunicability presupposes singularity [i.e. individuality]'.[61] Thirdly, at least some intra-divine relations are communicable: active spiration is shared by Father and Son, for example. And if some are, there is no reason why all – including paternity – cannot be.[62] Fourthly, if active spiration is communicable, there is no reason why passive spiration cannot be; but then passive spiration could not constitute the Holy Spirit, and on the assumption that relations constitute persons the Holy Spirit could not be constituted as a person.[63] Fifthly, if active spiration is communicable, then there is no reason in principle why active generation could not be. But active generation and paternity are the same property.[64]

What gives Scotus trouble is working out how paternity in God could – despite appearances – actually be incommunicable in the required way. His instinct in all of these objections is something like the following: there are good *prima facie* grounds for supposing that paternity is a shareable property (after all, it is something had by – for example – my father and seemingly by God the Father too). By the time he revised book 3 of the *Ordinatio*, he found an argument to show how paternity in God could be primarily incommunicable – the explanatorily basic ground of the Father's incommunicability. The text appears in a marginal addition to the discussion in book 1, and is clearly derived from the later book 3 discussion.

The basic reply to the objection is that paternity in God is incommunicable of itself, even though paternity as such is not. Paternity had by God the Father is logically unshareable; paternity had by my father, and other creaturely fathers, is just an instance of a shareable essence. Scotus deems the question of shared univocal concepts irrelevant;[65] it is the real extramental properties that he is interested in: 'that reality which is in God, that is not formally the divine essence'.[66] **[13]** is the (not wholly straightforward) argument in favour of the incommunicability of paternity in God:

[13]
1 The reason for its incommunicability is this, that just as the [divine] essence is
2 ultimate act, and for this reason cannot be determined by anything with respect to
3 which it is quasi-potential, so whatever is in it [i.e. the divine essence] is ultimate, in
4 the ultimate actuality compatible with it [i.e. whatever is in the divine essence], so that
5 in that instant of nature in which wisdom springs forth (*pullulat*) in the essence, it
6 springs forth according to the ultimate determination which it can have, such that the
7 reality which is formally wisdom, is not determinable. Likewise, whatever can be
8 incommunicable in the first instant of nature in which it springs forth in the nature,

---

[60] Ibid., n. 46 (Vatican, VI, 16), referring to Henry, *SQ* 53.6 ad 5 (II, fo. 69R).
[61] Ibid., n. 47 (Vatican, VI, 16).
[62] Ibid., n. 48 (Vatican, VI, 16).
[63] Ibid., n. 49 (Vatican, VI, 16–17).
[64] Ibid., n. 50 (Vatican, VI, 17).
[65] On this, see the Appendix below.
[66] Scotus, *Ord.* 1.26.un., *text. int.*, n. [45] (Vatican, VI, 49, ll. 20–1) = *Ord.* 3.1.5 (MS A, fo. 142[vb]).

9 springs forth as incommunicable, and not primarily as communicable, for then it
10 would be determinable by something, by which it would be made incommunicable.[67]

The divine essence is fully actual, incapable of any further determination [13.1–3].
Therefore anything that is somehow intrinsic to God, and whose existence is
ultimately explained by the divine essence, is fully actual, incapable of further
determination [13.3–4] – be it attribute [13.4–7] or personal property [13.7–10].
(Talk of 'springing forth in the essence' ('in' + ablative) is, I take it, a way of
claiming that the entity that springs forth is somehow explained by the essence, and
yet not really distinct from it.) In the case of personal property, one such
determination would be determination to incommunicability. If the personal
property is incommunicable, then it cannot be so other than intrinsically [13.9–10].
So if paternity in God can be incommunicable, then it is, without further explanation
[13.7–9]. Wisdom in God is different: it is intrinsically shareable, and its ultimate
determination is as a communicable thing.
     This is not an argument from reason, for it makes an assumption that paternity
in God is incommunicable;[68] the argument in [13] is simply designed to show how
paternity can be incommunicable given that it somehow 'springs forth' from a
communicable essence. Basically, Scotus holds that the incommunicability of
divine paternity is just basic, not admitting of any further explanation, and *a
fortiori* not explained in any sense by its springing forth from the communicable
divine essence. If the assumption is correct, Scotus needs replies to the five
arguments summarized above (after [12]) to the effect that paternity cannot be
incommunicable. Against the first, Scotus reasons that quiddities that are
communicable in the required way are either pure perfections or divisible (into
subjective parts). But nothing in God is divisible, and the personal properties (as
we shall see in chapter 18 below) fail to be pure perfections (perfections that are
better for anything that possesses them). So divine paternity, despite being a
quiddity (i.e. not a bare particular), is not communicable to many.[69] Against the
second, Scotus reasons, in line with [13], that infinity is not necessary for a
quiddity's being intrinsically singular. The numerical singularity of something
intrinsic to God can derive from the infinite and numerically singular divine
essence. And, as [13] makes clear, something incommunicable can in some sense
derive from this essence, even though the essence is not the 'formal' explanation
for its incommunicability.[70]
     The replies to the remaining three arguments simply deny that the
communicability of one term of a relation entails that the other term is
communicable too: there is no reason, for example, to suppose that the
communicability of active spiration entails the communicability of passive
spiration,[71] and the reasons for the incommunicability of some of these intra-divine
relations, and the communicability of others, may just be intrinsic to the relations

---

[67]   See Ibid. (Vatican, VI, 49, l. 22– p. 50, l. 8) = *Ord.* 3.1.5 (MS A, fo. 142[vb]).

[68]   Ibid. (Vatican, VI, 49, ll. 18–19) = *Ord.* 3.1.5 (MS A, fo. 142[vb]).

[69]   Ibid., n. [46] (Vatican, VI, 51, ll. 16–20) = *Ord.* 3.1.5 (MS A, fo. 142[vb]).

[70]   Ibid. (Vatican, VI, 51, ll. 6–15) = *Ord.* 3.1.5 (MS A, fo. 142[vb]).

[71]   Ibid. (Vatican, VI, 51, ll. 21–5) = *Ord.* 3.1.5 (MS A, fo. 142[vb]).

themselves.[72] It is easy to think of analogous examples: *being the cause of this effect* may be communicable (perhaps the effect is caused jointly by more than one agent), and yet *being this effect* incommunicable (indeed, and roughly, *being this effect* seems by definition incommunicable).

So by the time he revises book 3 of the *Ordinatio*, Scotus knows of replies to all the arguments he can think of against the relation theory. He still leaves the truth of the relation theory an open question, though – unlike his earlier account – he now claims that the relation theory is more likely than the absolute-property theory, on the grounds of the force of Patristic authority in favour of the relation theory.[73] This represents a shift in position, since in the earlier discussion Scotus goes to great lengths to show how a careful reading of the relevant authorities can avoid the relation theory. The date or dates of the revisions of book 3 of the *Ordinatio* are unknown, but it seems to me that the revisions must predate the examination of book 1 of the *Reportatio*, since in this text Scotus knows an answer to arguments in favour of the absolute-property theory, arguments that he earlier left unanswered – presumably because he regarded the absolute-property theory with some sympathy. So by book 1 of the *Reportatio* Scotus finds not only authority but also reason in favour of the traditional view that the persons are subsistent relations.[74]

The arguments in favour of the non-relation theory found in Scotus's earlier works derive from a particular interpretation Scotus offers of Bonaventure's Trinitarian theology. According to Bonaventure, a person is fundamentally an Aristotelian primary substance, something that is in some sense prior to any relational property it may possess, and something that is distinct from any shared secondary substance.[75] Scotus reasons in favour of this view that subsistence – being a primary substance – is fundamentally a non-relational matter, and thus cannot be explained by a relation.[76] In the *Reportatio*, Scotus offers a similar argument in objection to the relation theory. Among creatures, it is a perfection for an essence to have a *suppositum* of the same kind as itself. For accidents depend on substances, and thus have a *suppositum* different in kind from themselves – that is, a substance. Substances are more perfect than accidents, and thus having a *suppositum* of the same kind as the nature is a perfection. If divine *supposita* were constituted by relations, then they would be constituted by something different in genus from the divine essence. They would thus – falsely – be less perfect as subsistents than created *supposita* are.[77]

---

[72] Scotus argues that supposing the opposite can easily be made to generate contradictions: Ibid., n. [47] (Vatican, VI, 51, ll. 26–35) = *Ord.* 3.1.5 (MS A, fo. 142ᵛᵇ).

[73] Scotus, *Ord.* 3.1.5 (MS A, fo. 142ᵛᵃ).

[74] For the possibility that Scotus's earlier, non-relation theory may have got him into trouble, see Vatican, VI, 23*; some of the debates are outlined in Michael Schmaus, *Die Liber Propugnatorius des Thomas Anglicus und die Lehrunterschiede zwischen Thomas von Aquinas und Duns Scotus: II. Teil: Die Trinitarischen Lehrdifferenzen: Erste Band: Systematische Darstellung und historische Würdigung*, 482–550.

[75] Bonaventure, *In Sent.* 1.25.1.1 c (I, 437ᵃ), quoted in Scotus, *Ord.* 1.26.un., n. 57 (Vatican, VI, 23).

[76] Scotus, *Ord.* 1.26.un., nn. 60 and 66 (Vatican, VI, 24, 26–7).

[77] Scotus, *Rep.* 1A.26.2 (MS M, fo. 115ᵛ):

Et si quaeratur quare non potest essentia divina quantum ad omnes conditiones habere suppositum sui generis sicut suppositum creatum, cum hoc sit perfectionis in substantia creata,

In reply, Scotus notes that incommunicability – since it is possessed by accidents as much as by substances – is not a perfection, and thus need not be explained by the divine essence or something of the same genus as the divine essence. Indeed – and this is the argument in favour of the relation theory – it cannot be, because anything possessed simply in virtue of possession of the divine essence is communicable, and the personal property is by definition incommunicable, as we have seen.[78] What Scotus has in mind is that the personal property cannot be anything of the same genus as the divine essence – that is, the genus of substance. But the property cannot be a non-relational accident of the divine person, for there are no such in God (see Part 1, chapter 6 §2 above). So the personal property must be a relation, *tertium non datur*. And this is the argument against the absolute-property theory.

---

quia convenit sibi ut distinguatur ab accidentibus, et ita sicut suppositum creatum constituitur incommunicabiliter per aliquid de genere substantiae, ita constitueretur incommunicabiliter suppositum increatum per aliquid generis absoluti, et non per relationem ...

(Note that the text in Wadding, XI, 139[b] (n. 13) is defective.)

[78] Ibid.:

Respondeo: in supposito [in]creato perfectionis est quod habet per se esse et indivisibiliter esse. Sed quod habet esse incommunicabiliter, hoc est sibi et accidentibus commune, et ideo hoc non est perfectionis in eo. A simili, quod suppositum increatum habet esse per se et indivisibiliter, hoc convenit sibi ratione essentiae et ita per aliquid generis substantiae convenit sibi quod est perfectionis. Sed quia quicquid est perfectionis in divinis communicabile est, ideo non potest suppositum substantiae per aliquid illius generis habere incommunicabilitatem et esse incommunicabile, et ideo ad hoc quod haberet tale esse oportuit ipsum contrahi et determinari per aliquid quod non est perfectionis simpliciter, cum illud esse sit perfectum simpliciter

(Note again that the text in Wadding, XI, 139[b] (n. 13) is defective; the text here follows directly from that in the previous footnote.)

Chapter 15

Persons and Essence in the Production of Son and Spirit

In this chapter, I should like to discuss the following two issues: first, in virtue of which of his properties – namely, essence or personal property – is it true of a divine person that he is produced? Secondly, what is the causal interrelation of a divine person's properties – namely, essence and personal property – in the production of other divine persons? Which – in other words – should be identified as the relevant causal power, and what if anything is the causal role of the other? Both of these questions are complex, and both raise further issues too. Perhaps the most important, which I discuss in this chapter, arises from the second, and it is the question of the *filioque*. As we shall see, Scotus uses his account in a novel and powerful defence of the *filioque*.

The background again is Lateran IV's adjudication in favour of Peter Lombard's view that the divine essence does not generate, and is not generated, mentioned in chapter 13 above. While Scotus forcefully accepts the teaching of Lateran IV, he does not think it has told the whole story. For he holds that, while the divine essence does not generate, it is that in virtue of which a person (viz. the Father) can generate: it is the formal basis for production. Likewise, Scotus holds that, just as the divine essence is the formal basis for production, so too it is the formal basis for being produced (it is that in virtue of which a person can be produced).

1 The Divine Essence as the Basis for a Divine Person's Being Produced

It seems odd to think of a person having a property 'in virtue of which it can be produced', and indeed the notion needs a little sorting out before we can continue. 'In virtue of which' translates 'is the formal basis (*ratio*) for'. Talk of a formal *ratio* for some property requires us to be able to arrange the properties of a thing in a certain explanatory order: x's possessing φ explains x's possessing ψ, and so on, and in each case the explanatory property is the formal *ratio* for the *explanandum*. In my example, x's being φ is the formal *ratio* for x's being ψ. But the property of *being produced* is a relational one, and the formal *ratio* is a way of picking out an *intrinsic* explanatory condition. So in this case, the formal *ratio* is not a sufficient condition; it is, however, the relevant *intrinsic* necessary condition: if x has a formal *ratio* for a relation, x has every intrinsic property necessary for the relation. (So perhaps 'in virtue of' is a bad translation: I do not mean to suggest that the relevant feature is a sufficient condition for being produced.) Equally, we should not think of the property as existing prior to the production. The question is rather about the explanation for something's (continued) relation to a cause on which it depends for as long as it exists. Doubtless, there are such features of things. I am sustained in existence by the air I breathe, and the formal basis in me for this relation is my capacity to process oxygen – my respiratory system, blood, and so on. Equally, there is no reason for this explanation to be different in the first instant of a thing's existence from the way the explanation obtains during the period of a thing's existence. And in the case of the divine Son there is no first instant of existence: as we saw above, Scotus (unsurprisingly) holds that the existence of the Son, and likewise his dependence on the Father as generator, is eternal.

The presupposition here seems to be that that in virtue of which a person can be produced is one or other of the features of that person: in the case of a divine person, essence or property. Again, this need not be too odd a thought. It is certainly clear that some of (e.g.) my relations to sustaining causes of me are based on specific features of mine: particular aspects of my physical structure, for example, explain the fact that various different natural objects have a role in sustaining me in existence (lungs for air, digestive system for nourishment, and so on). Could all of my dependence relations be like this? I am not sure. But it seems to me that there is an important principle that can be made plausible, and the principle is that in any case of dependence, the formal basis in the dependent thing for dependence must be a feature that can be shared with other things of the same type. It cannot, for example, be an individuating feature. Consider my biological dependence relation on my parents (admittedly not a relation that persists after my birth, but let that pass). I should say that what specifically grounds this is my being the *kind* of thing that I am. It cannot be my being the *individual* that I am, because my parents would have conceived a quite different child in even marginally different circumstances. The case of my dependence on (e.g.) liquid is similar. My kidneys are one of many parts of my body that have a role in processing liquids, and it is not my having just the kidneys that I now have, but my having kidneys as such that is relevant to my dependence relation. Kidneys, after all can be transplanted. Obviously, the two cases are not quite similar, for although I could exist without the kidneys I now have, I cannot exist without being the individual I am. But the principle is the same: given a cause and an end term, the *identity* of the end term is a matter of (causal) indifference to the cause: the causal relation obtains irrespective of the identity of the end term. In terms of the relevant explanation for the dependence of the end term, the identity of the end term cannot be the explanation. If it were, then nothing else of the same kind would have the relevant basis. But on the principle of causal indifference, this cannot be true.

Scotus appeals to precisely this general claim in defending his view that the formal basis for being produced is the divine essence:

[1]
1 In creatures, nature, and not individual or hypostatic property, is the formal end term
2 of production – as is clear in *Physics* 2, where it is stated that generation is natural, or
3 is said to be nature, because it is 'a way into a nature'.[1]

The argument is intended as a proof of the claim that 'the essence is the formal end term of the production and generation of the Son'. The general claim is that natures

---

[1] Scotus, *Ord.* 1.5.2.un., n. 68 (Vatican, IV, 49), referring to Aristotle, *Ph.* 2.1 (193^{b}12–18).

or essences are the formal end terms of production **[1.1–2]**. Nature is contrasted with 'individual or hypostatic property' **[1.1]**, and Scotus just means to pick out whatever feature of a *suppositum* is responsible for distinguishing it from all others of the same kind. (Using 'hypostatic' helps ease the transition from creatures to God, for 'hypostatic' just means 'personal', and thus is an instance of the kind of property that distinguishes divine persons from each other.) The reason is Aristotelian: generation is a 'way into a nature': nature is what is replicated in generation **[1.2–3]**. Obviously, the parallels to the case of divine production are not exact, not least because the divine nature is not 'replicated' in the production of a person: it is numerically identical in each person. Still, it seems to me that the general principle has some plausibility, for the reason outlined.

Scotus's other argument seems to take it for granted that, of essence and property, exactly one must be the formal end term of production. This is not obviously the case, but if we suppose that it is true, then the argument looks successful:

[2]
1 No formally univocal entity, simply speaking more perfect than a formal end term, is
2 had through production. But the essence is formally infinite, and relation not.
3 Therefore if relation were the formal end term of production, the person would not
4 have the essence through production.[2]

It is not possible for something to be communicated by generation that is more perfect than the formal end term of the generation **[2.1–2]**.[3] But the divine essence is more perfect than the personal property, because the essence is infinite, and the property not **[2.2]**. Since the essence is communicated in generation, generation cannot have property as its formal end term **[2.3–4]**.

Scotus's position on the first question asked above, then, is that the essence is the 'formal' end term in the production of a person. This, incidentally, is understood by Scotus to give him a further argument against Henry's view that the Son is generated from the divine essence as quasi-matter, discussed in chapter 13 §3 above. Scotus makes a fundamental distinction between the subject of generation and the end term or result of generation: one and the same thing cannot be both subject and result of one act of generation.[4] Nevertheless, Scotus is, apparently, perfectly happy with the thought that one and the same thing could be both the causal power responsible for the production and the end term of the production, and this is the second issue that I want to look at in this chapter.

---

[2] Ibid., n. 67 (Vatican, IV, 48–9); see too n. 140 (Vatican, IV, 79).

[3] I am not sure what the force of 'univocal' in **[2.1]** is: perhaps Scotus is supposing that in cases of equivocal causation, something can be communicated that is more perfect than the end term (though, presumably, no more perfect than the cause). In any case, the generation of a divine person is an instance of univocal causation, since all agree that the three divine persons are the same in kind.

[4] Scotus, *Ord.* 1.5.2.un., n. 64 (Vatican, IV, 47); see too n. 97 (Vatican, IV, 62); 1.5.1.un., nn. 27–9 (Vatican, IV, 25–7).

2 The Divine Essence as the Productive Power

In answer to the second question, Scotus basically holds that the divine essence is that power in virtue of which a divine person can produce other divine persons. For example, whereas, in the production of a mental word, Scotus holds that soul and object are joint causes, in the case of the generation of the Son, Scotus holds that the Father's perfect memory is the sole cause of the product. And memory is possessed by the Father in virtue of his possession of the divine essence – as indeed it is by Son and Spirit too. As we have seen, Scotus – in line with standard Trinitarian theology – holds that each divine person includes essence and a personal property uniquely his own. As so often, Scotus sets up the discussion by presenting two opposing views, in this case those of Aquinas and Henry. All agree that the personal property alone cannot be the causal principle of the production. Aquinas, for example, argues from the empirical data about created causal relations that the divine essence alone is the relevant causal principle. He reasons that it is universally the case that causal powers belong to things in virtue of other shared properties – natures, in Aquinas's account, but presumably he could include accidents too. Analogously, the causal power involved in the production of a divine person must belong to the productive person in virtue of the divine essence, not of the (unshareable) personal property.[5] Henry does not accept Aquinas's general principle here, but argues on the basis of a different, explicitly Aristotelian one. According to standard Trinitarian orthodoxy, the divine personal properties are *relations*. But Aristotle teaches that relations cannot be causes or causal powers. So the divine essence must be the relevant causal power in the production of a divine person.[6]

This makes it look as though Aquinas and Henry basically agree. But they do not, for Henry holds that Aquinas's theory – or one like it – will not allow for any differentiation between the various productions in God. So he holds that divine relations, while not having any causal role, nevertheless are necessary conditions for differentiation in God, and thus for the exercise of any internal causal power. As Scotus summarizes Henry's position, the essence is 'of itself undetermined to many persons and to the actions of many persons; therefore, for it to be a principle of determined action, it is necessary that it is determined' – determined, that is to say, by a personal property.[7]

Scotus sides with Aquinas here, and I shall return to the rejection of Henry's view below. As far as I can tell, however, Scotus has no objection to the arguments proposed by both Aquinas and Henry in favour of the basic claim that the divine essence is the causal power relevant in the production of a divine person. Scotus adds some arguments of his own too. He divides his reasons into two sorts: reasons that show that the causal principle cannot be the relation, and reasons to show that the causal principle must be the essence. Most telling against the relation view is this argument:

---

[5] Ibid., 1.7.1, n. 10 (Vatican, IV, 109–10); see Aquinas, *ST* 1.41.5 c (I/1, 210a).

[6] Ibid., n. 18 (Vatican, IV, 112–13); see Henry, *SQ* 39.4 arg. 1 in opp. and c (I, fo. 247A, BC), referring to Aristotle, *Ph.* 5.2 (225b11–13).

[7] Ibid. (Vatican, IV, 113).

[3]
1 If paternity is the principle of the generation of the Son, the same relation will be the
2 principle of itself, for paternity exists only if the Son does, to whom [paternity] is
3 formally directed. ... If therefore paternity is the principle of the generation of the
4 Son, it will be the principle of itself.[8]

Suppose that the causal power responsible for (e.g.) the Father's generation of the Son is the Father's personal property. As discussed at length in chapter 14 §2 above, this personal property is paternity, and 'exists only if the Son does' [3.1–2]. For paternity is that in virtue of which the Father is related to the Son: and such a relation can exist only if the Son does [3.2–3]. According to Scotus, then, the existence of the Son is a necessary condition for the existence of paternity. But if the existence of the Son is a necessary condition for the existence of paternity, then it seems that paternity is a self-cause (i.e. causes its own *existence*) [3.3–4]. For paternity exists only if the Son does, and if paternity causes the Son, it causes a necessary condition of its own existence: and this clearly entails being a self-cause – much as if I were to cause one of my parents to exist.

Having shown that the productive principle cannot be the personal property, Scotus tries to show too that this principle must be identified as the divine essence. Scotus's major argument has the kind of *a priori* feel that many of his Trinitarian arguments have:

[4]
1 No perfection in a productive principle removes from anything the notion of
2 *productive principle*. But to communicate oneself in numerical identity by a
3 communication equal to oneself is a perfection in a productive principle. Therefore
4 this does not remove from anything the notion of *productive principle*. But if *per*
5 *incompossibile* God were to generate another God, and that other [God] a third, deity,
6 not relation, would be posited as the productive principle of the other [God]. And in
7 this case deity would not communicate itself in numerical identity; neither would it
8 communicate itself by a communication equal to itself under the description of
9 *productive principle*, for deity could be a principle of another communication, for
10 example, one made – *per incompossibile* – by the second God. Therefore since deity is
11 not communicated in numerical identity and by a communication equal to itself (such
12 that there cannot be numerically another communication by deity of the same kind as
13 this [communication]), it follows that an absolute is posited now to be the productive
14 principle more than would be posited then.[9]

The argument is not straightforward – though anyone who has followed my discussion of the Subtle Doctor up to this point will perhaps not be surprised by this. Scotus is imagining that the production of a divine person is a kind of univocal causation: a divine person produces another of the same kind. As we saw in Part I, chapter 1 §1 above, in standard Aristotelian accounts of causation, univocal causation involves the communication of a form from the agent to the patient, and in such a case the causal principle is the form. (Scotus immediately gives an

---

[8] Scotus, *Lect.* 1.7.un., n. 47 (Vatican, XVI, 489); see *Ord.* 1.7.1, n. 37 (Vatican, IV, 122).
[9] Scotus, *Ord.* 1.7.1, n. 39 (Vatican, IV, 123).

example of fire generating fire:[10] it would be odd to say that the causal principle here was not fire but, for example, the haecceity of a fire.) The argument tries to imagine a more conventional type of causation than that of the intra-Trinitarian production of a divine person, and the example of this more conventional causation is counterpossible: the production of another God [4.4–5]. This would be a case of univocal production, and thus the divine essence would be the relevant causal principle [4.5–6]. In the case of the Trinitarian productions, there are two differences from the production of another God: (1) the things produced are not merely the same in kind, but include numerically the same essence, and (2) the productive acts are such that there can be only one of any given kind (each productive act is 'equal' to its cause in the sense employed in chapter 11 §1 above) [4.6–9, 10–13]. (The second of these features is not exhibited by external production of another God since, Scotus reasons, the second God could itself produce further objects of the same kind – perhaps a third God – and do so in the same way as the first God [4.9–10].) These two features are perfections of a productive cause [4.2–3], and no perfection of a productive cause can be such as to prevent some such cause from being productive [4.1–2]. So the distinctive features of Trinitarian production are not such as to prevent the divine essence from being the relevant productive principle – indeed, the divine essence is the relevant productive principle *a fortiori*, given that essence is productive even in the envisaged counterpossible scenario [4.13–14].

Scotus later formulates a similar argument without use of counterpossible entailments. If what is communicated is form (here the divine essence), then *ceteris paribus* we would expect form to be the relevant productive principle. The notion of a Trinitarian production differs from standard types of production in the two respects just outlined. But neither of these respects seems incompatible with the notion of production – indeed, they are both perfections of production. Since *ceteris paribus* essence is the relevant productive principle, and since neither of the two features of divine production blocks the divine essence's being the productive principle, it follows that essence is the productive principle.[11]

This might make it seem as though Scotus has overlooked something obvious: namely, that essence and relation might *jointly* be the relevant causal power. After all, it is not obvious that essence alone or relation alone are exhaustive disjuncts. But Scotus's arguments against the possibility of relation being the relevant causal power are effective too against the view that essence and relation might jointly be the relevant causal power. In any case, Henry, as we have seen, proposes a somewhat more nuanced view, one that Scotus devotes considerable time to refuting. On Henry's view, the role of the personal property is not causal; rather, the property has a role in determining the essence to its different actions – the personal property allows the essence to act in different ways. Scotus objects to Henry's view that the divine essence is 'of itself undetermined to many persons and to the actions of many persons'. According to Scotus, it is true that the divine essence is 'of itself undetermined' in the sense that it can produce (say) two different effects – that is, Son and Spirit. But it is nevertheless of itself determined such that the Son is

---

[10] Ibid., n. 41 (Vatican, IV, 124).

[11] Ibid., n. 40 (Vatican, IV, 123–4).

produced first, and, given the production of the Son, the Spirit second, since it is such that, necessarily, it is related to the act of generation before the act of spiration.[12]

As we saw in chapter 13 §4 above, Scotus is convinced that there is a certain sense in which the divine essence is prior to the divine persons. This reply to Henry's position makes clear that this priority claim should be understood very carefully. For Scotus's claim is that it is necessary that the divine essence is exemplified in just the way that it is: and not only that it is necessary, but that it is, as it were, *intrinsic* to the divine essence that it is exemplified in this way: it is determined 'of itself' to be exemplified in this way.

3 The Possession of Internal Productive Powers by All Three Divine Persons

It might be thought that maintaining that the divine essence is the relevant causal power would result in the breakdown of all relations between the persons. For if possession of the divine essence is sufficient for possession of the relevant causal powers, then, since every person possesses the divine essence, every person possesses the relevant causal powers, and every person thus produces every other person. Scotus agrees that all three persons possess the divine essence, and thus that all three persons possess all the causal powers necessary for the internal productions. But he claims that the possession of the divine essence is sufficient for producing a divine person only if the essence is possessed prior to the relevant production. 'Prior' here does not, of course, mean, temporally prior, but in some sense 'causally' prior. The most important discussion of the general principle occurs in a lengthy interpolated note on the discussion of the production of the Holy Spirit:

[5]
1 In whatever there is a perfect productive principle – not impedable from outside, or
2 dependent – that thing can produce an end term by that [principle] unless it is
3 incompatible with the end term to be produced by [the principle]. Likewise, it cannot
4 produce the end term by that [principle] if it is incompatible with the end term to be
5 produced by it. Each of these seems to be an immediate major premiss.
6   Or thus: in whatever there is a perfect principle before the end term is
7 produced, it is not incompatible with the end term to be produced by it. And likewise,
8 [the end term] cannot be produced by the cause if [the principle] is not in [the cause]
9 before the end term is produced. Each of these seems to be an immediate minor.
10   First conclusion: in whatever there is a perfect productive principle before the
11 end term is produced, that thing can produce the end term by that principle. Second
12 conclusion: in whatever there is no principle before the end term is produced, that
13 thing cannot produce the end term (whether [the end term is] simultaneous [with the
14 cause] (for which reason the Word does not speak himself), or posterior (for which
15 reason the Holy Spirit does not generate)).[13]

---

12 Ibid., n. 22 (Vatican, IV, 115).
13 Ibid. 1.10.un., *text. int.* (Vatican, IV, 369, l. 19–p. 370, l. 9, p. 370, ll. 16–17).

Scotus here states two related but logically independent 'syllogisms'[14] (as he rather profligately describes them) of considerable formal complexity. The major premisses are [5.1–5], the minors [5.6–9], and the conclusions [5.10–13]. The material in [5.13–15] is an addition to the interpolation that briefly applies the conclusions to the theological questions of the productions of the divine persons. The argument is not straightforward, and the reader more interested in the theological issues could easily skip to [6] without too much doctrinal loss.

The first syllogism runs as follows:

(Major) If a cause x has an independent and unimpedable causal power for the production of an effect y, and if all causal conditions intrinsic to y, necessary for the production of y, are satisfied, then x can produce y [5.1–3].
(Minor) If x has, prior to the production of y, an independent and unimpedable causal power for the production of y, then all causal conditions intrinsic to y, necessary for the production of y, are satisfied [5.6–7].
(Conclusion) If x has, prior to the production of y, an independent and unimpedable causal power for the production of y, then x can produce y [5.10–11].

(I take 'independent and unimpedable' to be glosses on 'perfect'.) First, the structure of the argument. As it stands, it is not quite sound. Let 'P' = 'x has an independent and unimpedable power for producing y'; 'Q' = 'all causal conditions intrinsic to y, necessary for the production of y, are satisfied'; 'R' = 'x can produce y'; and 'S' = 'x has, prior to the production of y, an independent and unimpedable perfect causal power for the production of y'. The argument runs as follows:

(Major) $(P\&Q)\rightarrow R$
(Minor) $S\rightarrow Q$
(Conclusion) $S\rightarrow R$

Scotus has missed out a key premiss:

$S\rightarrow P$

For $((S\rightarrow P)\&(S\rightarrow Q))\rightarrow(S\rightarrow(P\&Q))$, and coupled with the major premiss of Scotus's argument, this entails $S\rightarrow R$, the required conclusion. But '$S\rightarrow P$' is just 'If x has, prior to the production of y, an independent and unimpedable causal power for the production of y, then x has an independent and unimpedable causal power for the production of y', a premiss that Scotus presumably thought too obvious to need spelling out.

Supposing, then, the argument to be valid, we still have the formidable problem of understanding the premisses. 'P' ascribes a real causal power to some item. 'Q' is a way of asserting that there is nothing about y that prevents it being produced by an agent with a causal power to produce y. 'S' specifies that the causal power for the production of y is possessed *prior* to the production of y. 'R' asserts that the causal

---

[14] See Ibid. (Vatican, IV, 371, l. 7).

constitution of the actual world is such as to allow an agent with a power to produce *y* actually to do so. The point of the argument is to spell out one way in which this causal constitution can be satisfied, namely in the following case: the agent possesses an independent and unimpedable power prior to the production of the effect. The powers that Scotus is talking about are powers for effect *tokens*, not effect types, and the case that Scotus is aiming to exclude is that in which something possesses the relevant power, but exists only after the relevant effect is produced. In this case, something would possess a power that the causal constitution of the actual world made it impossible to exercise.[15]

This argument is directly relevant for Scotus's discussion of the *filioque*, and I shall return to it in discussing **[6]** below. The second argument in **[5]**, however, is relevant to the question at hand, namely, how to prevent every divine person being a cause of every other divine person:

(Major) If a cause *x* has an independent and unimpedable causal power for the production of *y*, and if some causal condition intrinsic to *y*, necessary for the production of *y*, is not satisfied, *x* cannot produce *y* **[5.3–5]**.
(Minor) If it is not the case that *x* has, prior to the production of *y*, an independent and unimpedable causal power for the production of *y*, then some causal condition intrinsic to *y*, necessary for the production of *y*, is not satisfied **[5.7–9]**.
(Conclusion) If it is not the case that *x* has, prior to the production of *y*, an independent and unimpedable causal power for the production of *y*, then *x* cannot produce *y* **[5.11–13]**.

The structure of the argument is exactly the same as the first argument, and indeed the argument is invalid in just the same manner and needs correcting in the way proposed for the first argument. The conclusion is that the causal constitution of the world is such that something which possesses the relevant power, but exists only after the relevant effect is produced, does not – and cannot – produce the effect.[16]

The second argument shows how it is that, even given that the divine essence is the relevant causal power in the production of divine persons, it is not the case that every divine person causes every other divine person. In effect, Scotus holds that Son and Spirit possess causal powers (for generation, and in the case of the Spirit, for spiration). Since the existence of the Father is *logically* necessarily prior to the production of the Son, and the production of the Son likewise necessarily prior to the production of the Spirit, it follows that Son and Spirit possess a power that it is *logically* impossible for

---

[15] Presumably, Scotus's point is that the relevant block on the exercise of a naturally unimpedable power is that the power is possessed somehow too late to produce the effect. 'Independent and unimpedable', excludes, for example, the necessity of spatial proximity, and perhaps every natural block excepting the required 'temporal' relation between cause and effect. When commenting on the argument, Scotus certainly talks as though the nature of the priority relations makes all the difference to the plausibility of the argument. See e.g. Scotus, *Ord.* 1.10.un., *text. int.* (Vatican, IV, 370, 10–11; p. 371, l. 19–p. 372, l. 4, ll. 15–19, p. 373, ll. 16–17).

[16] These modalities are not logical. They would be read so, however, in the case that it is logically necessary for the effect to be produced prior to the possession of the relevant causal power. In the case of the Trinity, this reading becomes relevant, as we shall see.

them to exercise.[17] And the reason for this is that they do not exist 'prior' (in some sense) to the exercise of the causal power. [5.13–15] draw the conclusion explicitly. The Word does not generate himself because he fails to possess the divine essence prior to his own production. The Son is 'simultaneous' (in the relevant sense) with the relation of generation, and thus not prior to it [5.13–14]. The Spirit does not generate the Son, for the production of the Spirit is posterior to the production of the Son, and thus not prior to it [5.14–15]. The lesson, I take it, is that logical possibility in this context requires both power and the opportunity to exercise the power.[18]

4 In Favour of the Filioque

As we saw in chapter 14 §3 above, Scotus rejects the standard argument against the *filioque*, as found for example in Aquinas. But Scotus nevertheless believes that a good argument can be found in favour of the *filioque*. The basic assumption is that the divine essence is the causal power in virtue of which persons produce other persons, and, as we learn from [5], the cogency of this view requires the cogency of the principle that a divine person can possess a causal power that it is logically impossible for him to exercise.

[6]
1 Anything that has a perfect productive principle before it is understood to have a
2 product, can produce by that principle, when, that is to say, the principle is so perfect
3 that it neither depends on a patient, nor can be impeded by anything. The Son has the
4 [divine] will, which is the productive principle of equal love, and it is [the will] as it is
5 presupposed to the thing produced by the act of will. Therefore he can produce it.
6 Therefore he does produce it.
7   Proof of the minor: generation and spiration have a certain order, such that
8 generation is in some way prior to spiration, and in that prior [instant] every divine
9 perfection is communicated to the generated thing that is not incompatible with it, and
10 thus will [is communicated]. Therefore he has the will as prior to the thing produced
11 by the act of will, for here [viz. in generation] there is not understood to be any
12 production made by the mode or manner of will.[19]

As we saw above, Scotus holds that '*x* can produce *y*' is true if *x* has a power that is not impedable, not dependent on anything external, and prior to *y*, and he asserts this without argument in [6.1–3]. The divine will certainly fits the first two descriptions,

---

[17] See too e.g. Scotus, *Ord.* 1.26.un., n. 28 (Vatican, VI, 8): 'There is *in the divine essence* a twofold fecundity, in so far as it is infinite intellect and infinite will' (my italics). It is not clear to me that it is absurd to think of there being a power that it is logically impossible to exercise. Consider, perhaps, God's power to perform an action in circumstances that would make it sinful. For example, it seems odd to suppose that God does not have the power to make any noise that he wishes, and hence a power to utter the words 'hate me': but it is logically impossible for him to utter these words in circumstances in which he believes that they will be understood. I doubt that we should consider the possession of a power to be dependent on the circumstances in which it is exercised; hence God's inability to utter 'hate me' in the circumstances outlined does indeed amount to his possession of a power that he could not exercise.

[18] On this, see the explicit statement in Scotus, *Ord.* 1.7.1, n. 27 (Vatican, IV, 118).

[19] Ibid. 1.11.1, nn. 11–12 (Vatican, V, 4).

and Scotus argues that the Son has the will prior to the production of the Spirit [**6**.3–5]. The spiration of the Spirit is, moreover, an act of will [**6**.4–5]. So the Son satisfies all the criteria sufficient for being able to produce the Holy Spirit [**6**.5]. And, Scotus infers, therefore the Son does produce the Spirit [**6**.6]. This last claim looks somewhat controversial, and I will return to it below, for Scotus elsewhere provides a defence that does not rely on arguments of a crudely modal nature.

The minor premiss in this argument is that the Son has the divine will prior to the production of the Spirit [**6**.3–5], and Scotus defends this by appealing to the order in the production of the persons. Generation is prior to spiration [**6**.7–8]. Now, as we saw above, in the production of a divine person, the divine essence – along with all the divine attributes – is made to belong to a divine person. So the generation of the Son entails the Son's possession of the divine essence and all the divine attributes [**6**.8–9]. One of these attributes is the divine will [**6**.9–10], so the Son possesses the divine will. But given that generation is prior to spiration, all of this is prior to the spiration of the Spirit [**6**.10–11], and thus the minor premiss in [**6**.3–5] is true. By way of strengthening his conclusion, Scotus notes that there is no act of will involved in the generation of the Son [**6**.11–12]; the point here is that there is no act of divine will that cannot be elicited by the Son.[20]

Why suppose that generation is prior to spiration? Scotus, needless to say, has an argument:

[7]
1 When first acts have an order in something, [it follows] if each is perfectly active that
2 they have the same order in eliciting their acts. ... In the Father, intellect and will are
3 perfectly active, and have a certain order, for the fecundity of intellect constitutes the
4 Father, not the fecundity of will. Therefore that fecundity of intellect in some way has
5 its act before the fecundity of will has its act.[21]

Being perfectly active here means being unimpedable and independent, and it seems uncontroversial to hold that where two causes (two 'active first acts') have some sort of order, their acts will exhibit the same sort of order [**7**.1–2]. Intellect and will in the Father are perfectly active, and have a certain order [**7**.2–3]. Thus their acts will have the same order [**7**.4–5]. The order that Scotus suggests involves the priority of intellect over will, for the reason that 'the fecundity of intellect constitutes the Father, not the fecundity of will' [**7**.3–4]. It seems clear enough that a constitutive property is somehow prior to a non-constitutive one. But why suppose that the fecundity of intellect is constitutive of the Father? It is easy enough to think of arguments here, but hard to find one that is not circular. For example, if we grant the *filioque*, it is easy to see that production by mode of intellect, but not production by mode of will, constitutes the Father. After all, production by mode of will, on the sort of theology that Scotus is attempting to develop, is shared by Father and Son, and so cannot be a constitutive property of the Father.[22] There is a clear argument

---

[20] There is no positive act of the Father's will in the generation of the Son: this will is simply complacent, not willing against the generation: I discuss this in chapter 16 §1 below.

[21] Scotus, *Ord.* 1.11.1, n. 13 (Vatican, V, 4–5).

[22] Scotus uses precisely this argument in *Ord.* 1.28.3, n. 55 (Vatican, VI, 139–40). Note that defending this claim against all possible objections would take considerable time, and I do not want to pause on it here.

from revelation here. For we learn from revelation that 'Father' is the proper name of the first divine person, and this suggests that the Father is constituted precisely by his relation to the Son, not to the Spirit. This leaves undefended the identification of the Son as the person produced by intellect, and so does not establish the priority of natural over free production. But it would establish the priority of generation over spiration, provided that the precise nature of these two distinct relations is left unspecified. So it would show that the Son has whatever is required to produce the Spirit, which is all Scotus needs.

Scotus does not at this point in his argument make clear something required for a full defence of the *filioque*, namely, that the production of the Son must be (logically) prior to the production of the Spirit. But material considered above in Part I, chapter 4 §1 adds a step that Scotus is obviously presupposing, namely that every act of love requires the presence of something known as the object of that love. Even given this, **[6]** is not a complete defence of the *filioque*, for it in any case leaves undefended the crucial inference from possibility to actuality. Later, Scotus shows how he would go about defending this inference. As we shall see in chapter 16 §2 below, Scotus uses much the same sort of argument to defend the undivided external causal activity of the Trinity of persons. I have quoted the relevant passage as **[5]** in chapter 13 §1 above. Basically, Scotus argues that the numerical identity of one causal power in more than one *suppositum* entails that, if one *suppositum* acts by that causal power, any other *suppositum* that has both the power and the opportunity to act by the power does so. Thus,

[8]
1 Since the fruitful will is one principle of spirating, whatever is denominated by this
2 action, since it has existence by this form, is denominated by the same action.[23]

Elsewhere, when discussing a Trinitarian problem raised by the doctrine of the Incarnation, Scotus draws precisely this conclusion:

[9]
1 In anything in which there is a formal basis for acting (*ratio formalis agendi*), [this
2 thing] acts in accordance with this basis, or at least can act in accordance with this
3 basis, and that [basis] is the basis and principle of its acting, prior to its act being
4 actually elicited, or [its] end term being [actually] produced. As was often stated in
5 book 1, the Father and Son spirate the Holy Spirit because they have the spirative
6 power, and both [have this] prior by origin to the Holy Spirit's being spirated, and for
7 this reason too the three persons create, such that the power for creating is for each
8 person the basis for creating, and for this reason each can create, for each has [the
9 power for creating] prior by nature to a creature's being produced.[24]

---

[23] Scotus, *Ord.* 1.12.1, n. 51 (Vatican, V, 54–5).

[24]   In quocumque est ratio formalis agendi, agit secundum istam rationem vel saltem potest agere secundum istam rationem, et prius natura quam actio eius sit elicita actu vel terminus productus, et illud est ei ratio et principium agendi. Sicut frequenter declaratum est in primo libro, quod propter hoc Pater et Filius spirent Spiritum Santum, quia habent vim spirativam, et uterque prius origine quam Spiritus Santus spiretur, et propter hoc etiam tres personae creant, ita quod potentia creandi est etiam cuilibet personae ratio creandi, et quare potest creare, quia

This does not add substantively to **[8]** in the sense that **[8]** entails the *filioque*; it does, however, make the point about the *filioque* explicit, where in **[8]** Scotus is content to argue about any form without attention to the peculiarities of the *filioque*. Consider a causal power that is (identically) the same in many *supposita* **[9**.1**]**. Any *suppositum* in which the power exists 'acts', or 'can act in accordance with this' power **[9**.2–3**]**, provided that the *suppositum* has the power prior to the existence of the effect **[9**.3–4**]**. Notice that there are two distinct claims in **[9**.2–3**]**: first, that the *suppositum* 'acts' on the basis of its power, and secondly that it 'can act' on the basis of this power. The rest of the passage makes it clear that it is the first, stronger claim that Scotus is interested in making: that is to say, that the presence of the power is *sufficient* for the action, provided, presumably, that the three criteria for the possibility of action outlined in **[5]** above are satisfied (indeed, Scotus makes the priority criterion clear here **[9**.3–4**]**). Thus, in **[9**.4–6**]** Scotus makes it clear that the possession of the spirative power is sufficient for the spiration of the Spirit, provided that the power is possessed by the agents *prior* to the production of the Spirit. It is of course for this last reason that the Holy Spirit is not a self-spirator. The spirative power is identified as the divine essence, but the divine essence is not possessed by the Spirit prior to his own passive spiration. The Spirit, then, possesses a power that it is logically impossible for him to exercise, since the relevant priority criterion is not satisfied. In **[9**.6–8**]** Scotus applies the same consideration to the question of the external activity of the three divine persons – I return to this in chapter 16 §2 below. In **[9**.8–9**]** Scotus makes it clear that the possession of the power to create is not just sufficient for creation but necessary: thus the power is that in virtue of which the persons 'can' create. (I suggest that we read **[9**.2–3**]** in this way too: the causal power possessed in the way outlined is both sufficient and necessary for the production of the effect.)

In summary:

[10]
1 In that instant of origin in which the Father produces by an act of will, the productive
2 principle is the same in Father and in Son, and for this reason the Son produces the
3 Spirit by the same production as the Father.[25]

The instant of origin here is simply a position on a logical sequence: specifically, the Father's production of the Holy Spirit by his will **[10**.1**]**. At this instant, the Son has numerically the same will as the Father **[10**.1–2**]**, and this is sufficient for the Son's producing the Spirit by the same production as the Father **[10**.2–3**]**. The *filioque* is thus true. My guess is that the argument is, for all its complexity, actually successful, provided that it is agreed that the divine essence is that in virtue of which divine persons produce.

---

quilibet habet eam prius naturaliter quam creatura producatur. (Scotus, *Ord.* 3.1.5, n. 6 (MS A, fo. 142ᵛᵃ).)
The text in Wadding, VII, 55–6, is garbled and evidently defective.
[25] Ibid. 1.11.1, n. 18 (Vatican, V, 6–7); see *Ord.* 1.12.1, n. 7 (Vatican, V, 27).

5 Father and Son as One Principle in the Production of the Spirit

Given that the *filioque* is true, Scotus tries to provide various clarifications to deal with obvious problems and questions that arise. Perhaps the most interesting has to do with the way in which Father and Son act together. In particular, Scotus spends considerable time defending the view that the Father and Son spirate 'as one agent', and not, for example, as two things acting in concert. Scotus takes this view against, among others, Augustine. According to Augustine, the Holy Spirit is the mutual love of Father and Son, and, as Scotus suggests in an objection to his own view, this might seem to imply that they spirate the Holy Spirit as two distinct things.[26] The thought is not that Father and Son are not one principle of the Holy Spirit, for two things acting in concert can count as one principle:[27] consider two causes of the same kind acting cooperatively to produce an effect (two horses pulling a cart are one principle in this sense). The two persons are on this view one principle consisting precisely of the two persons acting in concert. And this is the view that Scotus wants to reject. Father and Son are one principle, but they are not so by acting in concert.

Henry of Ghent develops the 'Augustinian' view – that Father and Son are one principle by acting in concert – with considerable sophistication. According to Henry, it is true that Father and Son share the 'spirative power', but true too that no one person has this spirative power, and thus that 'the proximate and immediate principle of spirating ... is not will considered as will, but as it is the joint (*concors*) will of Father and Son'.[28] Henry cites Richard of St Victor's refined presentation of the Augustinian position to the effect that perfect love (*amor iucundissimus*: the 'most agreeable' love) has to be mutual, such that it is only mutual love that can be the principle of the Holy Spirit.[29] On the basis of this, Henry distinguishes two senses relevant to the identity and/or distinction between Father and Son in the spiration of the Holy Spirit. Scotus summarizes his view:

[11]
1 [Father and Son are distinct] in one way, as they are described as eliciting the act; and
2 in another way, [they are distinct] as they are understood to be concordant (*concordes*)
3 in mutual love and will in relation to the act to be elicited. From their distinction
4 considered in the first way, they are in no way to be said to spirate as many, for
5 although those who spirate are many, they do not spirate on account of the plurality
6 which is principally in them, but rather only as a result of their distinction in the
7 second way: and thus Father and Son do not spirate the Holy Spirit in so far as they
8 are many in the action elicited – although they agree in the one *ratio* according to
9 which the act is elicited – but [they spirate the Holy Spirit] as they are in one will,
10 which is the basis for eliciting the act, by concord in their love, in that mutuality.[30]

---

[26] Ibid. 1.12.1, n. 1 (Vatican, V, 25). This, of course, is Augustine's argument for the *filioque*. It is not open to Scotus for, as I show in a moment, Scotus holds that love that the Father and Son share is not mutual: it is their shared love of the divine essence. Having one and the same object of love minimizes the motivation to think of the Son and Spirit as two things acting in concert.

[27] See Ibid, nn. 7–8 (Vatican, V, 27–8).

[28] Henry, *SQ* 54.6 ad 8 (II, fo. 95E); see Scotus, *Ord.* 1.12.1, n. 9–10 (Vatican, V, 28–30).

[29] Henry cites Richard *De Trin.* 3.3 (p. 138) and 3.16 (pp. 151–2).

[30] Scotus, *Ord.* 1.12.1, n. 13 (Vatican, V, 32); see Henry, *SQ* 54.6 ad 8 (II, fo. 95E).

Henry makes a distinction between two ways in which the unity and/or distinction of Father and Son can be considered, relative to the act of spiration. The first way is the unity or distinction of the cause of the act; the second is the unity or distinction of the ways in which the agents relate to the act (the love is 'not of the same *ratio* as it is given (*impensus*) from the Father to the Son, and, on the contrary, as it is returned (*repensus*) from the Son to the Father').[31] In the first way, Henry reasons, the two persons are identically the same cause of the love (they are one cause of the act); in the second way, however, they are distinct, since their love is mutual and thus differently directed in each.

Scotus subjects this admittedly appealing Trinitarian theology to rigorous intellectual scrutiny, and finds it philosophically wanting. One argument relies on the claim that the divine essence is the first object of the divine will: if this is so, then the divine will is directed to the divine essence prior to its being directed to any divine person. Since the first product of the divine will is the Spirit, it follows that the Spirit is sufficiently produced by the love of Father and Son for the divine essence.[32] A second argument seems more compelling:

> **[12]**
> 1 A principle that is equally as perfect in one *suppositum* as in two is equally the
> 2 principle of acting in one as in two, for there is not required for action anything other
> 3 than a perfect principle by which [the action is caused] and a perfect agent
> 4 *suppositum*. But will is equally as perfect in one *suppositum* as in two, and one
> 5 *suppositum* is equally as perfect as two (by the perfection required for an agent
> 6 *suppositum*). Therefore will can be equally as much a principle of producing in one as
> 7 in two; so the mutuality [proposed in Henry's theory] is not, on the part of the
> 8 productive principle, any basis for producing.
> 9   The major is proved, for the principle 'by which' does not receive perfection
> 10 belonging to it from the *suppositum*, but rather gives [perfection belonging to it] to the
> 11 *suppositum*, for the *suppositum* is perfected by [the principle]. Therefore such a
> 12 principle is not more perfect in more than in one, when the principle is the same in
> 13 many as in one.[33]

The last clause here, in **[12.12–13]**, makes clear the important presupposition of this argument, which is that the divine will is numerically one and the same in Father and Son. (Divine) action requires merely a perfect principle and a perfect *suppositum* **[12.2–4]**. Suppose, therefore, that (numerically) one and the same perfect principle exists in two perfect *supposita*. Such a principle, if it is a principle for acting in the one *suppositum*, is a principle in the other *suppositum* too **[12.1–2]** (nothing about either the principle or the *suppositum* blocks this, for each is perfect **[12.4–6]**). The divine will fits this description of 'principle', and is in perfect *supposita* **[12.4–5]**. So will satisfies the requirements of the middle term of the syllogism (it is a principle equally as perfect in one *suppositum* as in two), and is thus equally the principle of acting in one as in two **[12.5–7]**. In this case, the ascription of some causal function to the mutuality of the persons is superfluous – it cannot be 'any basis for producing'

---

[31] Ibid., n. 12 (Vatican, V, 31); see Henry, *SQ* 54.6 ad 8 (II, fo. 95E).

[32] Ibid., n. 19 (Vatican, V, 35).

[33] Ibid., n. 24 (Vatican, V, 38).

[**12**.6–8]. In defence of the major premiss ('A principle that is equally as perfect in one *suppositum* as in two is equally the principle of acting in one as in two'), Scotus proposes that numerically identical formal principles [**12**.12–13] – such as the divine will – are not different in perfection in different things [**12**.11–12]. The reason for this is that a *suppositum* cannot increase the perfection of the formal principle (and presumably cannot decrease it either), because the only communication of perfection is from the form to the *suppositum*, and not *vice versa* [**12**.9–11] – a standard feature of developed Aristotelian talk about forms.

The argument gains its force from the fact that Henry apparently accepts that Father and Son spirate the Holy Spirit as one principle, and that the relevant causal principle is the will. In other words, Scotus is trying to show that Henry's distinction between, on the one hand, Father and Son as eliciting the act, by divine will, 'as one', and on the other Father and Son as two distinct things 'concordant in mutual love' cannot be sustained. If eliciting a single act by shared will is sufficient for spiration, mutuality cannot be necessary. Perhaps the objection shows at least this much, that someone wanting to defend Augustine's mutuality claim needs to be a social Trinitarian, accepting two distinct wills in Father and Son respectively.

Scotus's concerns are not merely philosophical, however. At one point, he argues against Richard of St Victor on the grounds that the view Richard defends, if understood at face value, is simply heretical.[34] He later tries to save Richard from this very undesirable conclusion by glossing Richard's account in such a way that the account no longer involves a commitment to the supposedly heretical view.[35] The alleged heresy consists in this: that if mutual love is the most agreeable sort of love, then, since that love by which a divine person is beatified is the most agreeable love, 'the Father is not formally beatified in himself as object, but only in the Son, which is heretical'.[36]

I am not sure why Scotus thinks this view is heretical. But Scotus in any case tries to find an argument to show that mutual love is not, for God, the most agreeable kind of love:

[13]

1 In us, mutual love is more agreeable [than non-mutual love], because by such
2 mutuality a greater reason for lovability is found in the thing loved. For any loved
3 thing that is able to love makes itself more lovable, because the reason for lovability is
4 not only whatever goodness is in it, but also the returned love (*redamatio*) is another
5 reason for lovability, and for this reason someone having the goodness which is the
6 first basis for lovability, and [having] too the returned love, is more lovable.
7 Therefore the opposite will be [the case] in God, where this reason for lovability
8 cannot in any way be found or posited: for the Son is not more lovable than the Father
9 for the reason that he returns love to the Father than [he is lovable] on account of the
10 divine essence [in him] (on account of which he is primarily loved); neither is this
11 returned love any other basis for lovability in the Son.[37]

---

[34] Ibid., n. 32 (Vatican, V, 42).

[35] Ibid., nn. 38–41 (Vatican, V, 45–8).

[36] Ibid., n. 32 (Vatican, V, 42).

[37] Ibid., n. 33 (Vatican, V, 42–3). The Vatican text of my ll. 8–10 (= Vatican, V, 43, ll. 8–10) makes no sense, and the reason is that the text in MS A, prioritized by the Vatican editors over all other

Central here is Scotus's view that the first object of love for each divine person is the divine essence. Scotus is not denying that the love of Father and Son is mutual. All he wants to deny is that this mutuality adds any love to the love that they share for the divine essence. If there is any mutuality in Scotus's account, it is to be located in the fact that the divine persons equally *share* their love for the divine essence. (I am not referring here to the spiration of the Spirit, a 'notional' act of Father and Son, but simply to the 'essential' love that all three persons share. I discuss the distinction between notional and essential acts below.) Scotus's claim is that we creatures love to a greater extent things that love us back than things that do not, because the returned love provides, in the object that we love, a further reason for loving that object, over and above its essential goodness [13.1–6]. Scotus does not see that this could apply in God. The first object of divine love is the divine essence, and – putting it bluntly – what could be more lovable than the divine essence? If each divine person is, in himself, infinitely lovable, then what difference can the return of love make? In accordance with this, Scotus wants to assert that what makes the Son lovable is simply the presence of the divine essence in him – it is (paraphrasing) 'on account of the divine essence that the Son is primarily loved' [13.9–10]. The love that Father and Son have for each other does not add to this in any way [13.8–9, 10–11]. I take it that what Scotus is trying to say is that the three persons share their love for the divine essence, which is the object of their love. But the divine essence is fully in each person; by loving the divine essence, they are *eo ipso* loving (something in) each other, and (something in) themselves; Scotus does not see what could be added to this. If nothing can make a divine person more lovable than the presence of the divine essence in him does, then *eo ipso* the reciprocity of mutual love does not make the person more lovable. It is worth noting too that Scotus clearly intends the act of love in Father and Son to be numerically the same in each one of them: again showing his distance from any form of social Trinitarianism.

I will discuss in the next chapter the relation between notional and essential acts in God. But one part of that discussion is relevant here. In his *Sentences*, Peter Lombard states of the question 'whether the Father and Son love by the Holy Spirit' that it is 'insoluble, overcoming human sense'.[38] Scotus does not agree, and after lengthy discussion of a closely related question, 'whether the Father and Son love each other by the Holy Spirit', concludes that the statement is false, unless understood in the following highly restrictive sense: 'The Father and Son produce Love'.[39] In no sense is the Holy Spirit the mutual love of Father and Son for each other. (I will give in chapter 16 §1 Scotus's reasons for holding this, since understanding his arguments requires a firm grasp of his views on the distinction between notional and essential acts, which I discuss in that chapter.)

As we have seen, Scotus holds that the object of the divine will in the active spiration of the Holy Spirit is the divine essence. His view on the question of the

---

witnesses, makes no sense, either grammatical or conceptual. Here, then, the editors are content to print gibberish – a wonderful example of the triumph of ideology over common sense. I have followed the variant reading in the apparatus.

[38] Lombard, *Sent.* 1.33.1, nn. 1 and 2 (I, 232, 233).

[39] Scotus, *Ord.* 1.32.1–2, n. 33 (Vatican, VI, 238).

principle of this active spiration is that Father and Son spirate the Holy Spirit 'by will, in so far as [will] is entirely one (*inquantum omnio una*)':

[14]
1 For the notion of a principle, precisely as a principle, requires only its perfection in
2 itself and that it is had in a person before it is understood to have an equal end term.
3 But will is entirely one in Father and Son, and is in them earlier by origin than it is
4 understood to have an equal term (because both are spirative); and for this reason will,
5 as in them [viz. Father and Son], is the same productive principle with respect to the
6 Holy Spirit.[40]

The notion of a causal principle requires the perfection of the principle, and its existence in a *suppositum* prior to the production of the end term [**14**.1–2]. The divine will is the causal principle of the Holy Spirit. But this will is perfect and has existence in a *suppositum* prior to the production of the end term (the Holy Spirit) [**14**.3–4]. So will satisfies the requirements for being the productive principle of the Holy Spirit. But this will is numerically one in Father and Spirit: it has existence in two *supposita* [**14**.3]. So the two *supposita* spirate by this numerically one will [**14**.5–6]. Since the will is numerically one in the two persons, the active spiration is numerically the same in both of them: the one power is actualized in both of them.

Given that the Father and Son are one principle of the Holy Spirit in the way described, what, if anything, could Scotus say to the objection of certain post-Photian Eastern theologians that this compromises the so-called 'monarchy' of the Father – the view that the Father is the sole causal origin of the other two divine persons? Scotus's view is that there is a certain priority to be given to the Father, namely that the Father is the sole *ultimate* causal origin of the other persons. To this extent, the act of spiration is not 'uniform' in Father and Son:

[15]
1 An act can be considered in three ways: in itself, or in so far as it pertains to the end
2 term, or in so far as it is compared to the agent *supposita*. In the first two ways, there
3 is entire uniformity [in active spiration], or better, unity, for [there is] most truly one
4 act and one produced end term. Speaking in the third way, just as the power of
5 spiration is communicated to the Son by the Father, so too the Son has from the Father
6 that he spirates. And thus the Father spirates from himself, and the Son not from
7 himself.[41]

The question is the uniformity of the act, and to deal with it Scotus reasons that there are three aspects to an act: the act itself, the relation between the act and its end term, and the relation between the act and the agent [**15**.1–2]. In the first two of these ways, the act of spiration is uniform, because it is numerically one act with numerically one end term [**15**.2–4]. In relation to the agent, however, there is not complete uniformity, because one productive *suppositum* (the Son) receives the relevant power from the other (the Father) [**15**.4–7]. As Scotus makes clear, this does not entail that the Father has an act of spiration prior to that of the Son. They

[40] Ibid. 1.12.1, n. 36 (Vatican, V, 44).
[41] Ibid. 1.12.2, n. 60 (Vatican, V, 59).

have one and the same act. The point is simply that the Son possesses the relevant causal power 'after' the Father does, and spiration is (in terms of origin) posterior to the Son's possession of the power of spiration.[42] There is nothing much original in this view: it is found, for example, in Aquinas,[43] and, following Henry of Ghent, Scotus uses it to construe claims to the effect that the Father spirates the Holy Spirit 'through' the Son. According to Henry, 'through' in this context, following a transitive verb (as in, e.g. 'the Father creates through the Son'), indicates 'sub-authority' ('*subauctoritas*') – a derived power – and this is precisely what the medievals understand in the case of the Son's power to spirate.[44] Although the power in the Son is numerically the same as the power in the Father, the Son derives this power – just as he derives the divine essence – from the Father.

As **[15]** makes clear, even though there is one power, one act, and one end term, there are nevertheless two agent *supposita*. Would we want, therefore, to say that there is one *spirator* (something that spirates the Holy Spirit) or two? Scotus holds that there is one spirator, because there is only one agency involved, but two spirating persons, Father and Son. Scotus notes that this question is 'quasi-grammatical', and he notes, 'since the force [of the question] concerns the significate of a word, I will not delay much [on it]';[45] but the discussion is a little more serious than this might suggest, for it reinforces Scotus's view that Father and Son, although they are one principle – one spirator – of the Holy Spirit, do not include any real principle shared by themselves but not by the Spirit.

I will not spend a great deal of time discussing the grammatical aspects of the question, because I have discussed these at length elsewhere.[46] Basically, Scotus holds that, while it is true that there are two spirating persons, there is only one spirator. The reason is that substantive terms ascribing agency – such as 'spirator' – signify 'the principle of the act ... as [the act] denominates an active *suppositum*.' Such substantives taken in the plural therefore signify numerically many principles – numerically many causal powers. Since there is only one causal power in the spiration of the Son, 'it does not seem to be conceded, from the force of the words, that there are two spirators'.[47]

Having said this, Scotus wants nevertheless to claim that Father and Son, in spirating, do not constitute some one *person*, or *who*, or *something*, and he uses this insight to interpret any Patristic statement to the effect that Son and Spirit are not one spirator.[48] Richard of Middleton proposed that the one spirator was some sort of *per se* existent common to Father and Son – though not a person (because not incommunicable).[49] The proposed communicable entity would be a 'sub-essence',

[42] Ibid., nn. 61–2 (Vatican, V, 59–61).

[43] Aquinas, *ST* 1.36.3 ad 2 (I/1, 186ª).

[44] Scotus, *Ord.* 1.12.2, n. 66 (Vatican, V, 62–3), following Henry, *SQ* 54.7 ad 2 and ad 3 (II, fo. 98N–99N, 99P).

[45] Ibid. 1.12.1, n. 42 (Vatican, V, 48).

[46] See my *The Metaphysics of the Incarnation*, 231–2.

[47] Scotus, *Ord.* 1.12.1, n. 42 (Vatican, V, 48).

[48] Ibid., n. 46 (Vatican, V, 51–2); the Patristic statements to which Scotus refers are found in Lombard, *Sent.* 1.12.2, nn. 109–11 (I, 82–3).

[49] Richard of Middleton, *In Sent.* 1.11.5 c (I, 41ʳᵇ⁻ᵛᵃ).

common only to Father and Son. Scotus rejects this view, focusing precisely on the relation between this sub-essence and the Spirit:

[16]
1 There does not seem to be here any *per se* existent, common to the Father and Son and
2 not to the Holy Spirit, because [if there were] that singular *per se* (but not
3 incommunicable) existent would be really related to the Holy Spirit, and there would
4 be something really related internally, in some way earlier than the first person is
5 understood to be, and thus not every real internal relation would be a person, which
6 does not seem probable.[50]

Richard is presumably troubled by the thought that one action can be the action of two *supposita*. Scotus, as I showed above, believes that this is exactly the situation in the case of the spiration of the Spirit (just as one action is the action of three *supposita* in the case of divine external activity: I discuss this in chapter 16 §2 below). According to Scotus, Richard's view has the undesirable consequence that, since the proposed singular existent would have a real relation (viz. active spiration) to the Holy Spirit [16.2–3], there is a real relation in God that is not a person [16.4–5] (since the relevant singular existent, the 'sub-essence' shared by Father and Son, is not a person). The priority claim [16.4] is entailed by Scotus's view that possession of the divine will, prior to spiration, is sufficient for spiration – precisely analogous to the sort of consideration that makes the divine essence weakly prior to the persons (see chapter 13 §4 above). Since the proposed singular existent spirates, and the Father does not, it follows that the proposed singular existent is somehow prior to the Father. Still, we do not need the priority claim to establish the conclusion that there would be a real relation in God that is not a person.

The one spirator, then, is simply the Father and the Son causing one product by means of one causal power. This causal power is shared by the product, but is such that it is logically impossible for the product to cause by means of it. The causal power, in short, is the divine essence, and the spirator is the Father and Son 'using' (or able to 'use') this numerically single, shared causal power – perhaps we should more accurately say not 'using', but 'causing in virtue of this numerically single, shared causal power'.

---

50 Scotus, *Ord.* 1.12.1, n. 50 (Vatican, V, 53–4).

Chapter 16

Notional and Essential Acts

Taking Augustine's Trinitarian analogy of memory, understanding, and will literally in every respect could have some odd consequences. The Father, for example, would be memory with no actual act (operation) of understanding; the Son would be an act of understanding inherent in no intelligence; and the Spirit would be an act of love inherent in no will. I have already shown the various ways in which these analogies should not be taken thus literally (even though Scotus holds that the relevant *productions* are literally productive acts of the Father's memory and will). In this chapter, I will consider the way in which the Trinity of persons can all understand and will – where understanding and willing are *essential* (common) actions that are in fact quite distinct from the *notional* actions of generation (act of memory) and spiration (act of will). As is clear from material discussed in Part I, chapter 4 §1, and Part II, chapter 15 §3 above, these notional acts result from powers common to all three persons (because possessed in virtue of the divine essence). Memory and will are the relevant causal powers, and it may be thought that the notional acts that are elicited from these powers are somehow related to the essential acts of these powers. Henry of Ghent adopts this view for the Trinitarian processions, and extends it too to the question of God's external creative activity, holding that the Father somehow creates through the knowledge and love that are (respectively) Son and Spirit. Scotus rejects all of this account – fundamentally for the reason that he does not believe that Son and Spirit are actually the Father's acts of knowledge and love respectively: they are persons that are produced by memory and will, but do not in any way inhere in (the Father's) intelligence and will. The Father produces them, but they are not his acts. In this chapter, I should like to look at these two debates, focusing first on Henry's claim that the notional acts productive of the persons are causally dependent on the essential acts of knowledge and love, and secondly on Henry's claim that the Father creates through the Son and Spirit.

1 The Priority of Essential Acts

As we saw above, Scotus holds that intellect and will are pure perfections, and as such, had by all three divine persons in virtue of their possession of the divine essence: 'The intellect of the three is the same, and the will [of the three is the same], and consequently entirely the same act of understanding is there, and of willing, and the same object.'[1] This follows straightforwardly, I think, from the

---

[1] Scotus, *Quod.* 8, n. 6 (Wadding, XII, 205–6; Alluntis and Wolter, 201 (¶ 8.10)); see Scotus, *Ord.* 2.1.1, nn. 18, 32 (Vatican, VII, 10–11, 18–19)); for the relation between perfection and the divine essence, see chapter 18 below; Scotus makes the point specifically about intellect at e.g. *Quod.* 1, n. 11

proofs of divine perfection and unicity discussed in Part 1 above, though I will consider in a moment the detailed alternative view proposed by Henry of Ghent, and Scotus's attempts to refute it. It is worth noting that this makes it look as though Scotus – perhaps unsurprisingly – would reject social Trinitarianism, at least as it is understood as implying three divine consciousnesses, or at least three distinct sets of mental acts or contents.[2]

Scotus accepts the view of Henry, described in a moment, that there is a sense in which the essential acts are somehow prior to the notional acts of generation and spiration, and that to this extent the notional acts presuppose essential acts. As Scotus puts it, the essential acts are 'closer' to the divine essence than the notional acts are. But Scotus does not agree that there is any direct *causal* link between the essential acts, on the one hand, and the notional acts on the other. For example, perfect memory – memory with its intelligible object present – is prior to the generation of the Son. But perfect memory is essential, not notional, for memory is possessed by all three persons; the same can be argued about will relative to spiration.[3] This might make it seem as though, for example, the Son possesses memory somehow prior to his own production. But Scotus is clear that this is not the case. As we saw above, Scotus holds that the Father possesses the divine essence prior to the generation of the Son. According to Scotus, this does not mean that the Son cannot possess the divine essence, for there is nothing contradictory about the Son's possessing the divine essence. The same point could be made about the divine memory. As we saw above, the Son cannot possess the productive act of generation, for then he would generate himself, and this would indeed be self-contradictory. But this does not prevent the Son from possessing the divine memory.

The notional productions are, then, correlated to – and posterior to – the relevant essential causal powers of memory and will. Henry develops an insight like this to show that there are only two productions in God. Almost all of Scotus's account of the generation of the Son from divine memory in the Father (described in chapter 10 above) forms part of an extended refutation of vast areas of Henry's Trinitarian thinking. According to Henry, as Scotus summarizes his view,

[1]
1 Notional acts are grounded on essential acts, but there are only two essential acts
2 remaining internal [to God], and these are understanding and willing. Therefore there
3 are only two notional acts which are internally productive, grounded on the same
4 essential acts.[4]

(Wadding, XII, 11–12; Alluntis and Wolter, 15-16 (¶ 1.34)). Augustine is explicit that all three persons know and understand: see e.g. *De Trin.* 15.14.23 (CCSL, 50A, pp. 496–7), cited by Scotus at *Ord.* 2.1.1, n. 11 (Vatican, VII, 6).

[2] One puzzling feature: Scotus believes that divine persons are capable of making self-reference (using the word 'I'): see e.g. *Ord.* 3.16.1–2, n. 15 (Wadding, VII, 374). I do not know how he would integrate this claim (evidently correct, given Scotus's interpretation of the text under discussion in the passage just cited (i.e. John 10.18)) with his claims about the persons' shared mental contents, though there clearly are strategies that could be used.

[3] Scotus, *Quod.* 1, n. 17 (Wadding, XII, 21; Alluntis and Wolter, 22 (¶ 1.54)).

[4] Scotus, *Ord.* 1.2.2.1–4, n. 271 (Vatican, II, 287); see e.g. Henry, *SQ* 54.8 (II, fo. 101D).

Scotus agrees that notional acts in God – acts proper to particular persons – are all *productive* acts [**1**.3]. But he does not believe that these productive acts are grounded on the essential acts of understanding and willing [**1**.1–2, 3–4]. Part of Henry's reason for accepting his view is that he believes that the production of a mental word in creaturely cognition is a *consequence* of an act of understanding: the production of a perfect act of understanding from confused knowledge.[5] Scotus, however, rejects the Henrician claim that the essential acts of knowing and loving are themselves causal principles for the production of knowledge and love. For Scotus, the correlation between essential and notional extends only as far as essential *powers* (or memory and will; not *acts* of knowledge and love) grounding the notional acts (of generation and spiration – productions of knowledge and love). As he puts it:

[**2**]
1 This opinion [viz. Henry's] posits four articles that I do not believe to be true. The
2 first is that the divine Word is generated by impression; the second is that [it is
3 generated] by impression on the intellect as converted on itself; the third is that
4 essential knowledge is the formal basis for generating declarative knowledge; the
5 fourth is that [the Word] is generated by impression on the intellect considered as
6 bare.[6]

The claims about generation 'by impression' [**2**.1–2] and by impression on the intellect 'considered as bare' [**2**.5–6] relate in this context to Henry's views about the divine essence as quasi-matter, discussed in chapter 13 §3 above.[7] The claims about the intellect's conversion 'on itself' [**2**.2-3] and about essential knowledge as the causal principle of generated knowledge [**2**.4] all tie in with Henry's account of the generation of the mental word. The gist of Henry's view, as applied to the Trinity, is that the Father generates not by his memory considered as including habitual knowledge but by his intellect considered as actually knowing something (claim three [**2**.3–4]), and that the Word is somehow impressed on the Father's same intellect (claims one, two, and four [**2**.1–3, 5]). Henry's position allows him to assert that the Word is the knowledge of the Father (and indeed of the other divine persons): the Word is, in short, God's essential act of understanding.[8]

One very important general Scotist consideration against Henry's view is that any sort of passive impression – impression in a substrate or 'quasi-matter' – would be an imperfection.[9] No produced object can somehow 'belong' to a divine person. Such an internal product will simply be a divine person. So there is no way in which the Son can be an act of knowledge belonging properly to any divine person. How then do essential and notional acts correlate for Scotus? The question of the relation between essential powers and notional acts is easy: the powers cause the acts (I have discussed

---

[5] Henry, *SQ* 54.9 (II, fo. 104C); see Scotus, *Ord.* 1.27.1–3, nn. 11–12 (Vatican, VI, 67–8); *Ord.* 1.2.2.1–4, nn. 276–9 (Vatican, II, 289–92). For a clear summary of Henry's view, see Friedman, '*In Principio erat Verbum*', 257–8; for more detail, see pp. 135–53.

[6] Scotus, *Ord.* 1.2.2.1–4, n. 282 (Vatican, II, 294–5).

[7] See e.g. Henry, *SQ* 54.10 (II, fo. 105L).

[8] Ibid. 59.6 (II, fo. 151B).

[9] See Scotus, *Ord.* 1.2.2.1–4, nn. 233–5, 262, 266 (Vatican, II, 266–9, 282–3, 285).

this at great length above, in chapter 10 §§2–3 and chapter 15 §§2–3 above). But the question of the relation between essential and notional acts themselves is more obscure. The basic principle is that essential acts are, *ceteris paribus*, prior to notional acts – though not in such a way as to be causally responsible for the notional acts. This is clearest in the Father, who exists 'prior' to any notional act: the Father's act of understanding is prior to his notional act of generating the Word. I will return to Son and Spirit once I have discussed the easier case of the Father.

Why should essential acts be prior to notional acts?

[3]
1 Whatever perfection the Father can possess, he possesses it as prior in origin to the
2 Son, because he possesses it in himself, for he can have no perfection other than from
3 himself – and therefore not from the Son. Therefore if the Father can distinctly know
4 every intelligible thing actually, he knows as he is prior in origin to the Son.
5 Therefore he does not distinctly know any intelligible things precisely in the Son.[10]

The Father is – as all agree – the 'causal' source of the other two divine persons – here the Son **[3.1–2]**. As such, there is a sense in which he is prior to them: his existence does not causally presuppose theirs. (The priority is not, of course, temporal.) Since all his perfections are necessary features of his, there is a sense in which he possesses them prior to the existence of the other persons **[3.1–3]**. The rest of the passage applies this insight to Henry's claim that the Father knows (merely) in the Son, or through the Son **[3.5]** – that the Son is, in short, the Father's act of knowledge just as he is that of the other persons too. The Father's knowledge is a perfection, and thus possessed by him causally prior to the production of the Son **[3.3–4]**. The Son cannot therefore be that in whom or through whom the Father knows. Elsewhere, Scotus notes that 'nothing can be formally in the Father other than the ungenerated'.[11] The generated Word cannot belong to the Father in the way that a generated mental word belongs to (e.g.) a human intelligence. The generated Word is a divine person, and as such is not related to another person as attribute to subject.

Given that the Father's essential internal acts precede any notional act, what is the relation between the two acts? Scotus raises the issue in the form of a *dubium*:

[4]
1 There is a doubt about these productive acts [viz. the notional acts], how they belong
2 to the productive principles to which the essential acts belong; for since acts
3 distinguish powers (*On the Soul*, 2), it seems that notional acts should not belong to
4 the powers to which essential acts belong.[12]

There are powers for the essential acts **[4.2]**. But one power cannot bring about different sorts of act **[4.2–3]**. So the powers to which the essential acts belong cannot be the powers to which the notional acts belong **[4.3–4]**. Scotus's reply brings out nicely his view of the complex interrelation of notional and essential:

---

[10] Scotus, *Quod.* 1, n. 20 (Wadding, XII, 28; Alluntis and Wolter, 26 (¶ 1.68)). Scotus ascribes this view to Augustine, *De Trin.* 15.7.12 (CCSL, 50, pp. 475–7).

[11] Scotus, *Ord.* 1.2.2.1–4, n. 321 (Vatican, II, 318).

[12] Ibid., n. 305 (Vatican, 310), referring to Aristotle, *De an.* 2.3 (415ª16–20).

[5]
1 The memory in the Father is the Father's operative principle, by which, as first act, the
2 Father formally understands in second act. The same memory in the Father is a
3 productive principle, by which the Father, existing in first act, produces generated
4 knowledge in second act. The productive act is not grounded on the essential act,
5 which consists in second act, that is, which is a quasi-operation on the formal basis
6 (*ratio*) of eliciting that second productive act, but in a certain way presupposes that
7 second act, for a first act that is operative and productive is the basis for perfecting a
8 *suppositum* in second act, in which [the first act] exists before (in a certain order) that
9 which is produced is understood to be produced or perfected. For what operates and
10 produces, by that principle, operates before it produces. ...
11 Understanding (which is the operation of the Father) and 'saying' (which is the
12 productive act of the Father with respect to generated knowledge) are understood to
13 have a certain order to the same first act, which is the memory of the Father: not such
14 an order that the understanding of the Father is the cause or elicitive principle of the
15 'saying' of the Word, but that understanding is more immediately 'produced' (as it
16 were) by the memory of the Father than the 'saying' or Word is produced by the same
17 [memory].[13]

Basically, the Father has two acts: an operation, which is his own act of understanding, and a production, which is the generation of the Word – generated knowledge. The Father's own act of understanding, then, is not generated. Memory is the principle of both of these acts **[5.1–4]**. The Father's own act of knowledge is not produced, for 'nothing can be formally in the Father other than what is ungenerated',[14] but can be thought of as 'quasi-produced': somehow belonging to the Father's intellect, reflective of the contents of the Father's memory **[5.15–16]**. Scotus seems to suggest that the operation – the Father's own act of understanding – somehow perfects his memory (the 'formal basis of eliciting that second act'), not his intelligence, and for this reason should count as merely a 'quasi-operation' **[5.5–6]**. (Recall that, in the case of creaturely cognition, the operation produced by the memory is indeed a perfection of the intelligence.) Elsewhere, Scotus appears to suggest that the Father's act of knowledge perfects his intelligence.[15] But I do not see that anything significant turns on this. At any rate, Scotus wants to deny Henry's claim that there is a causal connection between the operation of the Father's intelligence and the production of the Word **[5.4]**. Scotus holds instead that, if one thing can both operate and produce in virtue of the same causal principle, then operation is prior to production **[5.6–10]**, and the reason seems to be that operation – and not production – is properly perfective of a *suppositum* **[5.7–9]**. **[5.11–17]** simply reiterates the claim that operation is prior to production: and of course, the operation here is the essential act, and the production the notional act; so the Father's essential act is prior to his notional act **[5.13–17]**.[16]

---

[13] Ibid., nn. 311–12 (Vatican, II, 314–15); see too n. 237 (Vatican, II, 269–70).

[14] Ibid., n. 321 (Vatican, II, 318).

[15] Ibid., n. 320 (Vatican, II, 318).

[16] Henry denies that intellect includes memory and intelligence as separate faculties; for Henry, the simple intellect both understands (operates) and produces mental acts (see e.g. Henry, *SQ* 58.5 c (II, fo. 135P)). Since on this account the productive faculty is identical with the operative one, Scotus simply glosses 'intellect' as 'intelligence', since intelligence for him is the relevant operative faculty. I discuss the distinction between memory and intelligence in Scotus in Part I, chapter 4 §3 above.

Presumably much the same holds too for the spiration of the Spirit: Father and Son are 'lovers' – they have their intrinsic operation – prior to the production of the Spirit. As Scotus makes clear, all three persons share the same memory, intelligence, and will.[17] Scotus makes the point only in the case of the Father, when discussing how the Father's will is involved in the generation of the Son. The problem is that, on the one hand, the generation of the Son cannot be without the Father's will – it cannot fail to be something that the Father wants – but, on the other hand, the generation cannot be caused by will, for then the Son would be spirated. Godfrey of Fontaines solves this problem by simply accepting that (as summarized by Scotus) the Father 'does not generate the Son willingly, but merely by natural necessity, as fire heats, though if the act of generation is, as it were, granted, then the will of the Father takes pleasure [in it], as it were'.[18] Godfrey's reason, as summarized by Scotus, is that 'the intellection of the Father in some way precedes the will; but the intellection of the Father seems to be the generation of the Son; therefore the generation of the Son as Son precedes any volition of the Father'.[19]

Scotus rejects this view, holding that, in general, the will can take pleasure in an intellectual act without eliciting any act of will: the will can operate without *producing* any act of will.[20] In the case of the generation of the Son, he argues as follows:

[6]
1 In the first instant of origin, the Father formally understands, and then he can have
2 formally an act of willing; in the second instant of origin he generates the Son – and
3 neither does he will that generation by a volition that follows the generation, but [he
4 wills it] by a volition that is had in the first instant of origin, by which the Father
5 formally wills, presupposing now some intellection by which the Father understands,
6 but not the generation of the Son.[21]

[6.1–2] relates to the Father's essential acts, prior to the notional acts of generating and spirating. As we saw, Scotus holds that the production of an act of understanding is posterior to these essential acts **[6.2]**. Thus, the Father can will the generation of the Son by his essential act of love, not his notional act of love **[6.3–5]** – which latter, of course, is the Holy Spirit, posterior to the generation of the Son. So the act of will presupposes the essential act of understanding, 'but not the generation of the Son' **[6.5–6]**. Presumably the same is true of the spiration of the Spirit: the essential operation of Father and Son loving precedes the production of an act of love – the Holy Spirit.

What should we make of certain passages in Augustine in which it is suggested that the Word is somehow the 'art' or 'reason' of the Father?[22] Henry of Ghent uses these passages to defend his claim, summarized by Scotus, that the Word, as

---

[17] Scotus, *Ord.* 1.2.2.1–4, n. 320 (Vatican, II, 317–18).

[18] Ibid. 1.6.un., n. 8 (Vatican, IV, 89); see Godfrey, *Quod.* 8.4 (PhB, 3, p. 298).

[19] Ibid., n. 9 (Vatican, IV, 90); see Godfrey, *Quod.* 6.1 (PhB, 3, p. 97).

[20] Ibid., n. 13 (Vatican, IV, 93).

[21] Scotus, *Ord.* 1.6.un., n. 15 (Vatican, IV, 95).

[22] Scotus, *Quod.* 1, n. 18 (Wadding, XII, 26; Alluntis and Wolter, 23 (¶ 1.59)); see e.g. Augustine, *De Trin.* 6.10.11 (CCSL, 50, p. 241).

'expressive of all those things which are somehow contained or involved (*quasi involute continentur*) in the divine essence', is somehow that in which 'God understands whatever he understands distinctly', such that 'in the divine intellect, no actual distinction can be accepted between essence and memory, somehow preceding the production of the Word'.[23] Scotus agrees that the Word is expressive of everything in the divine essence. But he holds that every divine person is expressive of everything in the divine essence: that is to say, the contents of every person's understandings include equally fully the divine essence.[24] This 'expressiveness' is appropriated to the Son – it is ascribed to him by convention, even though expressiveness is no more fully an attribute of the Son than it is of any other person – and the reason is that he is produced by an act of the memory, and such an act 'expresses knowledge' – expresses the contents of the memory.[25]

In the *Ordinatio*, Scotus adds more detail to his very attenuated account of the Word's role as an intellectual act. The account turns on an ambiguity in the notion of *expression*. In English, we can talk of *expression* both as something done by a speaker, and as something done by the words spoken. The Latin '*declaratio*' is open to a similar treatment, and Scotus exploits it in talking about the expressive (declarative) role of the Son. The Son includes, in his knowledge, knowledge of the divine essence, and he does this by having the contents of his knowledge given to him by the Father (just as he has the divine essence given to him by the Father). The Son is thus the 'formal' expression of the divine essence: that by means of which the essence is expressed, to the extent that any generated knowledge expresses its object. The Father 'efficiently' causes the Word – the expression of the divine essence. The Father is thus the efficient or effective expression of the divine essence: the Father produces the expression.[26] Still, Father and Son share memory and intelligence, and the contents of this memory and intelligence are the same. The essential act of each likewise includes the expression of the divine essence.[27]

Precisely the same sort of situation holds in the case of the spiration of the Holy Spirit. The Holy Spirit is an act of love, and such act has the divine essence as its object. In virtue of the production of the act, there is a certain loose sense in which the producer can be 'denominated by the relation' between act and object: hence there is a certain loose sense in which the Holy Spirit can be the love of Father and Son for the divine essence.[28]

2 The Unity of External Activity

None of this is, I think, remotely surprising, given Scotus's claim that essential acts of knowledge are prior to notional productions. All three persons equally know and love the divine essence and each other. Much the same is true of the role of the Son

---

[23] Ibid.; for hints of the argument ascribed to him by Scotus, see e.g. Henry, *SQ* 59.6 (II, fo. 151A–C).

[24] Ibid., n. 20 (Wadding, XII, 28; Alluntis and Wolter, 27 (¶ 1.70)).

[25] Ibid. (Wadding, XII, 28; Alluntis and Wolter, 27 (¶ 1.71)).

[26] Scotus, *Ord.* 1.32.1–2, nn. 24–5 (Vatican, VI, 231–3).

[27] Ibid., n. 28 (Vatican, VI, 234–5).

[28] Ibid., nn. 32–3 (Vatican, VI, 237–8).

in creation. Henry of Ghent develops a complex theory according to which the Son has, in general, a role in the relation between God and creatures, and as a consequence a more specific role too in creation. The general idea is that the Son is God's knowledge both of himself and of all possible creatures. The Son is thus the 'pattern' of creation: he has some sort of formal causality in relation to creation,[29] or, more properly, is the causal power (form) in virtue of which creation can be brought about.[30]

Scotus rejects this, for both general and specific reasons. Generally,

[7]
1 Something notional is more immediate to the essence than anything essential
2 including a relation to something extrinsic. ... This is proved, for such an essential
3 thing pertains to God only through the operation of an intellect comparing [him] to
4 something external. But the notional really pertains to the essence, without any
5 comparison by the intellect to something external. Therefore there is required a
6 medium between the essence and the notional less than between the essence and an
7 essential thing, where an act of the intellect necessarily mediates.[31]

[1.1–2] is the point to be proved: at least one notional act is prior to anything requiring a relation to something other than the divine essence. Any essential act of (e.g.) knowledge the object of which is something other than the divine essence requires a relation to some secondary object – that is, something extrinsic to the divine essence as such. Such a secondary object is related to the divine essence only by an act of intellect [7.2–4] (on this, see Part I, chapter 4 §3 above). The notional, on the other hand, is really related to the divine essence, prior to any act of the intellect comparing the divine essence to anything external [7.4–5]. And this makes the notional 'more immediate' to the divine essence than the essential act is [7.5–7]. The idea is that a rational relation is not as straightforwardly 'automatic' as a real relation: in a rational relation, someone – a mind – has to do something additional; that is, think of the relation.

More specifically:

[8]
1 The formal and proximate basis for causation in God is the intellect or the will, or
2 some act of intellect or will. But the intellect of the three persons is the same and the
3 will [of the three persons] is the same, and consequently entirely the same act of
4 understanding and willing is theirs, and the same object, whether primary or
5 secondary. Therefore too the same formal basis of causing – even the proximate
6 [formal basis] – is common to the three persons.[32]

A proximate basis for a causal action [8.1, 5–6] is the final member of a set of necessary conditions intrinsic to the causal agent. The idea is that a mere change in

---

[29] Scotus, *Quod.* 8, n. 8 (Wadding, XII, 208; Alluntis and Wolter, 203 (¶ 8.15)); see too n. 21 (Wadding, XII, 216; Alluntis and Wolter, 213 (¶ 8.45)).

[30] Ibid., n. 5 (Wadding, XII, 205; Alluntis and Wolter, 201 (¶ 8.9)); see too *Ord.* 1.27.1–3, nn. 91–4 (Vatican, VI, 100–2); see Henry, *SQ* 59.5 (Paris, II, fo. 149F–H).

[31] Ibid. 1, n. 16 (Wadding, XII, 20; Alluntis and Wolter, 21 (¶ 1.51)).

[32] Ibid. 8, n. 6 (Wadding, XII, 205; Alluntis and Wolter, 201–2 (¶ 8.10)).

extrinsic circumstances is sufficient for the agent to be active. A formal basis [**8.1, 5**] is simply one that has an appropriately explanatory role in causal activity. All divine external activity results from intellect, will, or some act of theirs [**8.1–2**]. But all of these are identical in all three persons [**8.2–5**]. And this means that the proximate formal basis for external activity is common to all three persons [**8.5–6**]. It cannot, then, be proper to the Son.

In the *Ordinatio*, Scotus develops this line of thought in some detail. The key insight is that all external divine activity is contingent, whereas all internal divine activity is necessary. Connecting the two activities in some way seems to break this distinction down.[33] Since necessary productions – the communication of the divine essence – are prior to contingent ones in God, it follows that all causal powers are communicated to the divine persons prior to the contingent productions.[34] Secondly, the divine essence is an object of divine cognition logically prior to the production of any secondary objects of cognition. The divine essence is a sufficient object of the memory, and memory in the presence of a sufficient object is naturally productive. So the Father's memory is productive (of the Word) prior to the presence of any secondary object to that memory.[35] Equally, Scotus is clear that the understanding and love of the divine essence that he identifies as the productions of Son and Spirit are prior to any divine understanding of external objects.[36]

What Scotus is prepared to concede is that, just as the Son and Spirit have the divine essence from the Father, so too they have all attributes consequent upon the divine essence from the Father. Just as in the case of the spiration of the Spirit Scotus talks about the 'sub-authoritative' action of the Son (see chapter 15 §5 above), so here Scotus talks about the Son and Spirit both being a 'sub-authoritative' (*subauthenticum*) principle of creation. He means by this simply that their possession of creative power, just like their possession of the divine essence, is derivative in the way described – they create under the authority of the Father in the sense that their creative power derives from him.[37]

One obvious way in which it may seem that the external activity of the Trinity must be divided is in the divine *missions*: the sending of the Son by the Father, and the sending of the Spirit by Father and Son. As Scotus understands the missions, they are instances of sub-authoritative action:

[9]
1 The Father is said to create through the Word, and thus it can be conceded that the
2 Son creates through the Holy Spirit, and not *vice versa*, for 'creating through the Son'
3 does not imply absolutely an external action, but action with authority, and in this it
4 connotes the active production in the operator with respect to that person through

---

[33] See e.g. Scotus, *Ord.* 2.1.1, n. 24 (Vatican, VII, 14), considering the view that the Holy Spirit could be spirated as the love not only of the divine essence but also of everything that can be loved: 'Thus in virtue of his production he would be the love of a creature as of the divine essence; therefore either God would necessarily love creatures, or the Holy Spirit is not necessarily produced: both of which are false.'

[34] Ibid., n. 17 (Vatican, VII, 9).

[35] Ibid., n. 18 (Vatican, VII, 10).

[36] Ibid., nn. 30–2 (Vatican, VII, 16–19).

[37] Scotus, *Quod.* 8, n. 19 (Wadding, XII, 215; Alluntis and Wolter, 211 (¶ 8.32)); *Ord.* 1.32.1–2, *text. int.* (Vatican, VI, 235, ll. 15–17).

5 whom he operates, by, as it were, sub-authority. So it can be said that sending a person
6 is to operate through him and thus to bring about an effect with that person through
7 the mode of authority, giving to that person an action that pertains to the producing
8 person only with respect to the produced person – and to be sent means the same as to
9 operate with sub-authority, in the power of the sending person, which happens only
10 when the operating person receives from another the power to act.[38]

In the case of creating, 'creating through the Son', for example, means: the external activity of creation, brought about by Father and Son [**9**.2–3], such that the Son derives his creative power from the Father producing the Son [**9**.3–5]. The Father has authority, and the Son sub-authority (authority produced by the Father) [**9**.5]. Mission is like this. All three persons act externally without division. For the Son, for example, to be sent, means: Father and Son bringing about an effect [**9**.5–6], such that the Son derives the one causal activity from the Father just as he derives the divine essence from the Father [**9**.7–8]. The Son has sub-authority, acting in the power of the sending person [**9**.8–9], and this happen when the Son receives from the Father the power to act (just as he receives the divine essence from the Father) [**9**.9–10].[39] The missions of the persons do not imply any sort of distinct activity for the different persons.[40]

Note too that, given that Father and Son send the Spirit, this understanding of the divine missions entails the *filioque*. The more usual Western defence of the *filioque* from the notion of mission is an argument from fittingness: the external missions somehow reflect the internal processions. On Scotus's account, the external missions cannot fail to reflect the internal processions, for 'mission' just means procession coupled with unified external activity.

---

[38] Scotus, *Ord.* 1.14–16.un., n. 12 (Vatican, V, 131).

[39] It is not clear to me what is meant in [**9**.7–8]: an action 'that pertains to the producing person only with respect to the produced person': there is no parallel to this in *Lect.* 1.14–16.un., n. 12 (Vatican, XVII, 181–2).

[40] It might be thought that the Incarnation is an obvious counterinstance to this. But Scotus – in line with the other scholastics – holds that all divine causal activity relevant to the Incarnation is common to all three persons; the Son is merely the subject of human predicates. I discuss this at length in my *The Metaphysics of the Incarnation*, chs 6 and 10.

Chapter 17

The Constitution of a Divine Person

What metaphysical 'components' or 'constituents' does a divine person have? As we saw above, the divine persons are exemplifications of the divine essence, and each divine person includes a personal property – be it relational or non-relational – all his own. As we have already seen, Scotus does not think of the divine essence as wholly simple. The divine attributes are 'circumstances' of the essence: the essence is somehow constituted by the divine attributes. I dealt with the question of the essence–attribute distinction in Part I, chapter 6 §4, above. Here I focus on the essence–personal property distinction. Various questions arise. First, what is the nature of the distinction between essence and property? Secondly, what is the ontological status of essence and property? Thirdly, given that essence and property have some sort of distinction, and some sort of reality, what explanation can be given of their unity? It is easiest to start with the last of these questions, and then go on to consider the first two in order.

1 The Unity of a Divine Person

Scotus's opponent on the question of the explanation for the unity of essence and property is Henry of Ghent. As we saw above, Henry holds that the divine essence is the quasi-matter of the divine person, and the personal property is quasi-form. According to Henry, the union of quasi-matter and quasi-form results in a quasi-composite – the divine person. As we also saw above, Scotus vehemently rejects this view. One advantage of Henry's account is the relative ease with which he can explain the unity of a divine person, simply by appealing to a more or less close analogy with standard material substances. In such substances, unity is the result of the nature of the physical components: matter (as potential) and form (as actual).[1] When discussing Henry's view, Scotus is fully aware of this appealing feature, and tries to work out ways in which the unity of a divine person can be explained given the falsity of Henry's account. Scotus considers the problem by discussing one of four related 'difficulties' that arise from the rejection of Henry's position.

The first is the crucial difficulty: 'how is a divine person one, unless this [i.e. relation] is act, and that [i.e. essence] potency?'[2] Scotus argues against this that the divine essence is the actuality of a divine person, much like a form or quiddity is the actuality of any primary substance. Scotus pinpoints three features in the relation between a created quiddity and its substance. First, the quiddity is the explanation

---

[1] On this, see my *The Physics of Duns Scotus*, chs 4 and 5.

[2] Scotus, *Ord.* 1.5.2.un., n. 107 (Vatican, IV, 66).

for a substance's being of such-and-such a kind.[3] Secondly, the quiddity is divided into subjective parts by a 'contracting' entity: what Scotus elsewhere calls a haecceity.[4] Thirdly, both quiddity and haecceity – the metaphysical 'constituents' of a substance – are act, though the quiddity is more perfectly actual than the haecceity.[5] The first of these relations does not imply any sort of imperfection,[6] and so is directly applicable to the relation between the divine essence and a divine person.[7] The second however – divisibility and contraction – requires potency in the quiddity (for division and contraction). The divine essence, as we have seen, is indivisible, of itself 'this', and not contractible. So the second feature is entirely lacking in the case of the relation between the divine essence and a divine person.[8] The third feature of the relation between a quiddity and a primary substance, however, has some correlate in God: essence is infinite *act*, and the relation too is the proper *act* of a person.[9] In some sense, then, a person is a subject of two actualities: essence and property.

Still, this does not yet answer the question about composition,[10] so Scotus proposes the following:

[1]

1 Necessarily, the unity of a composite is from the natures of act and potency. ... But a
2 divine person is not composed, or quasi-composed, but is simple, and as truly simple
3 as the essence itself is, considered in itself, having no real composition or quasi-
4 composition, even though the formal definition of the divine essence is not the formal
5 definition of the relation, or *vice versa*.[11]

Scotus's solution, then, is simply to deny that essence and relation are really distinct **[1.2–4]**. Essence and relation are formally distinct **[1.4–5]**. An explanation for unity is required only if the components are really distinct **[1.1]**. Since essence and relation are not really distinct, there is no need for an explanation of unity.

In this discussion, Scotus claims that essence is more perfectly actual than relation. Later, he claims that essence somehow 'has the mode of form with respect to relation, just as nature [has the mode of form] with respect to *suppositum*, in so far as it is that by which a subsistent relation is God'.[12] Since the person includes merely relation and essence, we can think of the person as actualized – made to be the kind of thing he is – by the essence; and since the only other 'component' of the person is the relation, we can think of the relation as actualized by the essence too: analogous to the way in which both matter and material composite are actualized by form. Scotus in effect, then, reverses Henry's claims about the quasi-materiality of

---

[3] Ibid., n. 108 (Vatican, IV, 66).
[4] Ibid., n. 109 (Vatican, IV, 66). On subjective parts, see chapter 13 § 1 above.
[5] Ibid., n. 110 (Vatican, IV, 66–7).
[6] Ibid., n. 108 (Vatican, IV, 66).
[7] Ibid., n. 112 (Vatican, IV, 67).
[8] Ibid., n. 113 (Vatican, IV, 67–8).
[9] Ibid., n. 114 (Vatican, IV, 68).
[10] Ibid., n. 115 (Vatican, IV, 68).
[11] Ibid., n. 116 (Vatican, IV, 68).
[12] Ibid., n. 137 (Vatican, IV, 77).

the divine essence. If the essence resembles anything in the constitution of a material substance, it is form, not matter.

2 The Distinction Between Essence and Property

[1] makes it clear that essence and property are *formally distinct*. Elsewhere, Scotus develops the point more fully:

> [2]
> 1 Here there remains a further difficulty. Unless some distinction is posited between the
> 2 notion of essence and the notion of *suppositum*, it does not seem intelligible that the
> 3 essence is numerically one while the *supposita* are many. ... I say without asserting it,
> 4 and without prejudice to some better opinion that the notion by which a *suppositum* is
> 5 incommunicable (let it be 'a') and the notion of essence as essence (let it be 'b') have
> 6 some distinction prior to every act of intellect, whether created or uncreated. I prove it
> 7 thus: The first *suppositum* [viz. the Father] formally possesses communicable entity
> 8 [viz. the divine essence], otherwise he could not communicate it; and he really
> 9 possesses incommunicable entity too, otherwise he could not positively be a
> 10 *suppositum* in real entity.[13]

The passage contains two distinct arguments for the distinction of essence and *suppositum*. First, essence and *suppositum* must be (at least) formally distinct [2.1–2], since each admits of different and contradictory attributes: unity and plurality respectively [2.2–3]. Secondly, the Father has two distinct attributes: communicable entity (essence), which he actively shares with the other persons [2.7–8], and incommunicable entity (property), which constitutes him as an (incommunicable) entity – a *suppositum* [2.8–10]. Scotus here posits the view somewhat tentatively ('without asserting it, and without prejudice to some better opinion') [2.3–4].[14] Since the *suppositum* includes something (incommunicable entity: i.e. the personal property) not included by the essence [2.4–5], it follows that essence and *suppositum* are distinct 'prior to every act of intellect, whether created or uncreated' [2.5–6].

There is a problem with this account. As I shall note below, Scotus's early account of the formal distinction entails that a formal – *diminished* – distinction obtain only between formalities – *diminished* beings. And this raises a problem of consistency, since Scotus is quite clear that the divine essence is fully real, as is

---

[13] Ibid. 1.2.2.1–4, nn. 388–90 (Vatican, II, 349–50); see too Ibid. 1.11.2, n. 52 (Vatican, V, 23–4); Ibid. 1.26.un., n. 31 (Vatican, VI, 9–10).

[14] Some have suggested that Scotus's application of this formal distinction to the doctrine of the Trinity provoked some controversy in the early fourteenth century – compare for example his somewhat reserved exposition in [2.3–4] with the rather drier and more distinctive version from the earlier *Lectura* (usually dated to the last two or three years of the thirteenth century): 'Let him who can grasp this grasp it, because that it is so my intellect does not doubt': Scotus, *Lect.* 1.2.2.1–4, n. 375 (Vatican, XVI, 217). I have dealt with the claim that Scotus later moderates his view – which seems to me mistaken – in 'Scotus's Parisian Teaching on Divine Simplicity'. As we shall see below, Scotus develops the teaching in the later *Rep.* and if anything strengthens his application of the formal distinction in this context.

made clear by my discussions in chapter 13 §5 above. Be this as it may, Scotus comes in any case to modify his view. His reason is that a constituent must be as real as the thing it constitutes. I shall try, in the rest of this chapter, to show briefly how and why Scotus comes to change his view on the matter.

Scotus, as we have just seen, claims that essence and relation are formally distinct. And this is the first of my questions above. This material is closely related to the second, since Scotus vacillates on the question of the ontological status of formally distinct items. As just indicated, Scotus modifies his view on the nature of the formal distinction. The way I introduced the formal distinction in Part I, chapter 6 §3 above, I presented it as 'the kind of distinction that obtains between (inseparable) properties on the assumption that nominalism about properties is false'. Furthermore, as I noted there, in the context of the formal distinction between the various divine attributes, the distinction is somehow less 'real' than real distinction: it is in some sense a *diminished* distinction, and the mark of such a distinction is that it obtains between not things but *formalities* – little or diminished things. In the *Reportatio*, Scotus provides a great deal of further reflection on this sort of diminished distinction. In particular, he clarifies his account in two ways. The first is that he introduces a further variety of distinction midway between real and rational, namely *adequate* non-identity (more properly, non-adequate identity). And the second – more important in many ways – is that he drops his earlier claim that items that are formally distinct cannot themselves count as things. I shall suggest that Scotus comes to believe that a formal distinction between *things* obtains in the case that the items so distinguished have a role in the *constitution* of some further thing. This does not entail that all formally distinct items are things; indeed, it seems clear to me, as I noted in Part I, chapter 6 §3 above, that Scotus does not modify his account of the simplicity of the divine essence and attributes in any significant way during his life. Since Scotus's most mature treatment of the issue – that in the Parisian *Reportatio* – is by far the most fully developed, I focus on this treatment in what follows. I have dealt with the shifts in his position fully elsewhere.[15] In the *Reportatio*, Scotus talks about a 'qualified' distinction to cover both formal and adequate non-identity; qualified identity, likewise, is either formal or adequate identity. Scotus thus treats unqualified distinction as inconsistent with qualified identity and qualified non-identity. But in the *Reportatio* – the main locus for discussion of qualified and unqualified identity and non-identity – he does not always treat *real* distinction in this technical way, and sometimes talks as though any extramental distinction is real. I note below a relevant case of this. For the sake of consistency with Scotus's other discussions, I treat 'real' here as synonymous with 'unqualified'; nothing of substance turns on this merely terminological issue.[16]

When explicating the sense in which essence and property are distinct, Scotus lists the criteria for real or unqualified distinction. The first is that real distinction is 'of actual things, not merely potential [things], as those things that are in matter are not distinguished *simpliciter*, because they are not actual'.[17] Secondly, real

---

[15] See my 'Scotus's Parisian Teaching on Divine Simplicity'.

[16] On this, see Martin M. Tweedale, *Scotus vs. Ockham – A Medieval Dispute over Universals*, II, 453.

[17] On the relevant senses of the excluded 'potential', see my *The Physics of Duns Scotus*, 17–23.

distinction requires 'formal, and not just virtual existence, as effects are in their cause virtually, not formally'.[18] Thirdly, real distinction is of things that have unconfused existence, not like 'the extremes in a medium, or mixable things in a mixture', but of things that have 'existence distinct by proper actualities'.[19] Fourthly, real distinction requires 'non-identity, which alone completes a perfect distinction'.[20]

Qualified distinction of really identical things is satisfied when the first three conditions are met, but not the last.[21] Essence and property satisfy the first three criteria, but not the last, and for this reason fail to be really distinct. Essence is (1) actual, (2) formal, and (3) unconfused, 'as if nothing else were there'; property likewise, 'as if nothing were there other than it'. But non-identity does not hold, because the essence is infinite, and thus on Scotist teaching really the same as anything in it: if the essence could be part of a composite, it would not itself be infinite; and the relation is not part of a composite because it can (and does) exist in the infinite essence, 'springing from its fruitfulness'. So the two have perfect (i.e. unqualified) identity, 'as if [relation] were not distinguished from [essence]'; their non-identity can be only *secundum quid*, that is, qualified.[22]

---

[18] On virtual existence in a cause, see Part I, chapters 4 §3 and 5 §2 above.

[19] On the existence of elements in a mixture, see my *The Physics of Duns Scotus*, 71–6.

[20] Ad hoc quod aliqua simpliciter distinguuntur quatuor requiruntur conditiones. Prima est quod sit aliquorum in actu et non in potentia tantum, quomodo distinguuntur ea quae sunt in potentia in materia, et non simpliciter, quia non sunt in actu. Secunda est quod est eorum quae habent esse formale et non tantum virtuale, ut effectus sunt in sua causa virtualiter et non formaliter. Tertia conditio est quod est eorum quae non habent esse confusum ut extrema in medio et miscibilia in mixto sed eorum quae habent esse distinctum propriis actualitatibus. Quarta conditio [est] quae sola completiva est distinctionis perfectae est non identitas, ut patet per Philosophum 4 Metaphysicae ubi dicit diversum et distinctum esse et idem esse non. Illa ergo distinguuntur perfecte quae secundum esse eorum actuale proprium et determinatum sunt non eadem simpliciter, et illa secundum quid distinguuntur quae non habent non identitatem simpliciter sed non identitatem secundum quid. (Scotus, *Rep.* 1A.33.2 (MS M, fo. 151ᵛ; Wadding, XI, 186ᵃ (n. 9)).)
Tweedale reads 'quae sola completiva est distinctionis perfectae' to mean that the fourth condition is alone sufficient for real distinction (Tweedale, *Scotus vs. Ockham*, II, 450). As he points out, this – if the correct reading – entails that Scotus understands the fourth condition to entail the first three (Ibid., 449).

[21] 'Diversitas autem in omnibus tribus primis conditionibus salvata identitate est distinctio secundum quid quia non est non identitas nisi secundum quid': Scotus, *Rep.* 1A.33.2 (MS M, fo. 151ᵛ; Wadding, XI, 186ᵃ (n. 9)).

[22] Essentia vero et relatio habent tres primas conditiones, quia non habent esse possibile nec virtuale nec confusum, sed actuale formale et proprium et deteminatum, quia essentia est ita perfecte secundum omnes tres primas conditiones in persona ac si nihil aliud esset ibi; similiter paternitas est ita perfecte ibi sicut si nihil aliud esset ibi praeter eam. Eis tamen non competit quarta conditio, quae est completiva distinctionis, scilicet non identitas simpliciter, quia non habent sed tantum secundum quid, scilicet secundum tres primas conditiones; sunt enim idem simpliciter quia alterum, scilicet essentia, est infinita formaliter. Infinitum autem est cuilibet sibi compossibili idem, cui repugnat etiam aliquo alio perfici vel actuari, quia sic esset compossibilis cum illo addito et per consequens non esset simpliciter infinitum. Relatio autem originis est sibi compossibilis, cum oriatur ex fecunditate eius, ut visum est supra, et ideo relatio est eadem perfectissima identitate ac si nullo modo distingueretur ab ea, et ideo non identitas eorum est tantum secundum quid, et per consequens distinctio eorum tantum est

What precisely is the fourth criterion for real distinction? Scotus distinguishes two sorts of *secundum quid* distinction: formal non-identity and adequate non-identity. In the *Reportatio*, Scotus gives his definitive account of formal non-identity:

[3]
1 Things are said to have formal non-identity when one does not belong to the *per se*
2 and primary concept of the other, as a definition or the parts of a definition belong to
3 the concept of what is defined, or when neither is included in the formal *ratio* of the
4 other even though they are really the same.[23]

Formal non-identity here allows both for complete definitional disjunction [3.3–4], and for definitional overlap in such a way that one concept is fully included in the other but not (presumably) *vice versa* [3.1–3]. Scotus goes on to draw the obvious conclusion, namely that relations of formal identity and formal distinction are asymmetrical. Specifically, Scotus here holds that the Father is formally identical with paternity on the grounds that the person is a 'certain whole [that] includes the property in its formal *ratio*', and that paternity is formally distinct from the Father.[24] It has been argued that this approach is in conflict with Scotus's standard treatment of the issue. Crucially, Scotus seems to regard formulations of the form '*x* and *y* are formally distinct' as equivalent to those of the form '*x* is formally distinct from *y*', and this seems to entail symmetry, since we would expect the first formulation to entail too '*y* is formally distinct from *x*'.[25] But I think this is a mistaken reading, and that Scotus is serious in supposing that these two claims do not jointly entail symmetry:

[4]
1 Property and person are really distinguished *secundum quid* ... for their non-identity
2 is *secundum quid*. ... Person and property are formally the same ... but, on the other
3 hand ... property is not formally the same as the person.[26]

Here Scotus treats '*x* and *y* are formally distinct' [4.1] as entailing '*x* is formally distinct from *y*' [4.3], but *not* '*y* is formally distinct from *x*' [4.2]. So nothing in his treatment forces us to take the relation of formal distinction as symmetrical.[27]

---

secundum quid. Potest enim essentiae et relationis distinctio vocari secundum quid ex natura rei quia est eorum non identitas secundum quid ac si utrumque ex natura rei actualiter et proprie determinate existeret sine alio. (Scotus, *Rep.* 1A.33.2 (MS M, fo. 151ᵛ–2ʳ; Wadding, XI, 186ᵃ (n. 10)).)

[23] 'Dicuntur autem aliqua habere non-identitatem formalem quando unum non est de per se et primo intellectu [eius] alterius, ut definitio vel partes definitionis sunt de intellectu definiti, sed quando neutrum includitur in formali ratione alterius licet tamen sunt eadem realiter': Scotus, *Rep.* 1A.33.2 (MS M, fo. 152ʳ; Wadding, XI, 186ᵇ (n. 11)).

[24] Scotus, *Rep.* 1A.33.3 (MS M, fo. 153ʳ; Wadding, XI, 188ᵇ (n. 6)). See too Ibid. 1A.34.1 (MS M, fo. 54ʳ; Wadding, XI, 190ᵃ (n. 2)).

[25] See for example Tweedale's comments to this effect on *Qu. misc.* 1, n. 3 (Wadding, III, 442ᵃ) in *Scotus vs. Ockham*, II, 476–7.

[26] Scotus, *Rep.* 1A.33.3 (MS M, fo. 153ʳ; Wadding, XI, 188ᵇ (n. 6)).

[27] I discuss this problem in greater detail in my 'Scotus's Parisian Teaching on Divine Simplicity'.

So much for the relations between person and property. Scotus holds too that essence and property are formally distinct from each other, for if they could be defined, neither would be included in the *per se* definition of the other, even though the infinity of the divine essence guarantees that they are really identical.[28]

The second sort of *secundum quid* non-identity is adequate non-identity:

[5]
1 Essence and property are not the same by adequate identity, of which kind are those of
2 which neither exceeds the other but is precisely that thing, neither more nor less, as
3 definition and what is defined. Those things are said to be non-adequate in identity of
4 which one exceeds the other, or the unity of one exceeds the unity of the other, as
5 animal is related to man. ... But excess or non-adequation of one to another can be
6 understood in two ways: either according to predication and non-convertibility, as
7 animal and man are non-adequate according to predication, for animal is said of more
8 than man; or according to power and perfection, as man is a more perfect thing than
9 animal, or form than matter.[29]

Adequate identity is stronger than mere formal identity: it entails definitional coincidence; two items lack adequate identity if their definitions do not coincide [5.1–5]. Adequate identity entails formal identity, though not *vice versa*. Equivalently, formal non-identity entails adequate non-identity, though not *vice versa*.[30] The cases of 'excess' are presumably supposed to provide suitable tests for adequate non-identity even in cases where the contents of the various things (or of the concepts representing the relevant things) overlap: the concepts can differ in extension (predication/non-convertibility) [5.5–8] or in perfection [5.8–9], and presumably satisfying one of these is sufficient for adequate non-identity.

Essence and property satisfy both 'excess' criteria; they are thus things with adequate non-identity. The perfection excess is obvious enough: essence exceeds personal property in perfection for essence is formally infinite in a way that personal property is not. We might think that essence exceeds property in predicability too, for it is predicated of more things than any one personal property is. But Scotus

---

[28]   Nunc autem si essentia et relatio in divinis definerentur neutrum caderet in per se definitione alterius nisi ut additum, ergo essentia non est de formali intellectu paternitatis nec e converso. Sed differunt formaliter et habent non identitatem formalem et quidditativam, quia formalis ratio essentiae est esse ad se, formalis ratio relationis esse ad alterum, quae differunt quidditative, et tamen propter non identitatem formalem non sequitur quin unum simpliciter sit idem alteri. Patet de ente et passionibus eius, et hoc in proposito propter infinitatem alterius extremi. (Scotus, *Rep.* 1A.33.2 (MS M, fo. 152ʳ; Wadding, XI, 186ᵇ (n. 11)).)

[29]   Essentia et proprietas non sunt eadem identitate adaequatae, cuius illa quorum neutrum excedit alterum, sed est praecise illud neque magis neque minus, ut definitio et definitum, sed non-adaequata in identitate dicuntur illa quorum unum excedit aliud, vel unitas unius excedit unitatem alterius, sicut se habet animal ad hominem. Essentia autem et proprietas non sunt eadem adaequate. Excessus autem vel non-adaequatio unius ad alterum potest intelligi dupliciter, vel secundum praedicationem vel non-convertibilitatem, ut se habent animal et homo secundum praedicationem inadaequate, quia animal dicitur de pluribus quam homo. Alio modo secundum virtutem et perfectionem, ut homo est perfectius quid quam animal vel forma quam materia. (Scotus, *Rep.* 1A.33.2 (MS M, fo. 152ʳ; Wadding, XI, 186ᵇ–7ᵃ (n. 12)).)

[30]   For this point, see Tweedale, *Scotus vs. Ockham*, II, 457.

disagrees. He focuses on 'personal property' as a second-intention concept – a concept of a concept, or a merely logical concept – and holds that this second-intention concept is predicated of the persons 'formally and substantially'. Contrariwise, the first-intention concept of essence is not thus formally predicated of the persons.[31] Of course, all of this is consistent with the view outlined that property is *formally* distinct from essence, and *vice versa*: neither is included in the definition of the other.

Overall, then, Scotus posits that each person is formally identical with the divine essence and with its personal property, since each person includes these in an account of what that person is. Contrariwise, both essence and property are formally distinct from each person, and from each other. All of these various things – person, essence, and property – are non-adequately identical: none of them is adequately identical.

3 The Reality of Essence and Property

The *Reportatio* makes clear another very important feature of Scotus's mature account of qualified non-identity, namely that – in distinction from his earlier works – a formal distinction no longer requires the diminished status of the entities so distinguished. That is to say, Scotus comes to see that a formal distinction can hold between *undiminished things*. In his earlier works, Scotus assumes that every distinction between fully fledged things is real, such that the mark of a qualified (i.e. formal) distinction is that the things so distinguished are *formalities* – inseparable properties of a thing somehow less real than either the substance itself or the accidental features from which it is separable.[32] In the *Reportatio*, Scotus claims that both the divine essence and a divine personal property count as undiminished things. He rejects two views according to which essence and property could be qualifiedly entities, such that there is an unqualified distinction between two qualified entities.[33] The first opinion is that essence is an absolute thing, and

---

[31]   Primo modo proprietas transcendit essentiam quia de pluribus formaliter praedicatur quam essentia, quia secundum Damascenum c. 8, essentia tantum est communis tribus personis communitate reali; proprietas autem, ut prius ostensum est, prout abstrahitur ab hac et ab illa et tertia (paternitate, filiatione et spiratione), est communis eis communitate rationis et praedicatur de eis formaliter et in quid, et sic proprietas non est eadem essentiae adaequate secundum praedicationem. E converso autem essentia excedit proprietatem secundum virtutem et perfectionem, quia ipsa est formaliter infinita, non sic aliqua proprietas personalis, ergo non sunt eadem adaequate secundum perfectionem et virtutem. Patet ergo quod essentia et proprietas non sunt eadem identitate adaequata. (Scotus, *Rep.* 1A.33.2 (MS M, fo. 152ʳ; Wadding, XI, 187ᵃ (nn. 12–13)).)
The reason for the fact that essence cannot be predicated of the persons is that, according to Scotus, '(divine) essence' in standard syntactic contexts is to be understood as signifying precisely the divine essence, in abstraction from any divine person. Thus it is not the sort of thing that can be predicated formally of anything – as in (e.g.) 'the Father is (a) divine essence'. On this, see *Ord.* 1.5.1, n. 24 (Vatican, IV, 22–3).
[32]   See e.g. Scotus, *Ord.* 1.2.2.1–4, n. 407 (Vatican, II, 358); *Lect.* 1.2.2.1–4, n. 271 (Vatican, XVI, 215).
[33]   Scotus, *Rep.* 1A.33.2 (MS M, fo. 151ʳ; Wadding, XI, 185ᵃ (n. 3)).

property a relative thing. The second opinion – ascribed by Scotus to Bonaventure – is that the property is no more than a mode of the essence.[34] According to Scotus, essence and property are not distinct in either of these ways – that is to say, Scotus wants to reject the view according to which essence and/or property are just *qualified things*.[35] Thus, as far as I can see, he rejects the first opinion on the grounds that it uses the fact that the property is a relative thing to show that there can be some sort of distinction between essence and property without this compromising divine simplicity; he rejects the second opinion for holding that the property is not a thing but a mode. Rather, the relevant distinction is not a distinction of 'realities *secundum quid*' (qualified things), for the reason that the divine essence is a thing *simpliciter* (an unqualified thing) – and Scotus, as I shall show in a moment, is elsewhere clear in his late work that the property is a thing in much the same way.

Thus Scotus holds that there is a qualified distinction between two *things*, essence and property:

[6]
1 In another way this qualification '*secundum quid*' can be referred to the distinction, so
2 that the sense is that essence and property are really but qualifiedly (*secundum quid*)
3 distinguished, and thus it is true that the distinction of essence and property is of
4 unqualified thing and thing, but the distinction is qualified.[36]

Here, Scotus claims that '*secundum quid*' qualifies the distinction **[6.1]**. 'Real' is not being used here in a technical sense; thus, claiming that the distinction is 'real' is a way of asserting that it is not merely mind-imposed **[6.2–3]**: the contrast here among extramental distinctions is between *unqualified* distinctions and *qualified* distinctions. Unlike the earlier accounts, however, qualified distinction does not require that the entities so distinguished are likewise qualified or diminished in some way. Thus Scotus asserts that each of essence and property is unqualifiedly a thing **[6.3–4]**, and the point of the passage is that it is not the things that are qualified, but the distinction between them. Talking about two things makes it clear

---

[34] Ibid. 1A.33.1 (MS M, fo. 150ʳ; Wadding, XI, 183ᵇ (n. 14)); see Bonaventure, *In Sent.* 1.33.un.2 (I, 575ᵇ); *In Sent.* 1.22.un.4 (I, 398ᵃ⁻ᵇ).

[35]   Dico quod essentia et relatio sic distinguuntur quod ante omnem actum intellectus haec proprietas distinguitur ab essentiam secundum quid. Sed distinctio aliquorum realis secundum quid potest intelligi dupliciter. Uno modo ut haec determinatio 'secundum quid' referatur ad realitatem et sic opiniones priores dixerunt essentiam et relationem distingui secundum quid, quia realitas relativa non dicit realitatem simpliciter, sed cum determinatione realitatis relativae, ut dicit prima opinio. Secunda etiam opinio ponit quod relatio dicit aliquem modum super essentiam, qui modus non est res simpliciter sed modus talis rei. Sed non sic pono ego essentiam et relationem distingui secundum quid realiter, quia tunc esset sensus quod distinctio essentiae et relationis est distinctio realitatum secundum quid, quod est inconveniens, quia essentia est res simpliciter cum sit formaliter infinita. (Scotus, *Rep.* 1A.33.2 (MS M, fo. 151ᵛ; Wadding, XI, 186ᵃ (nn. 8–9)).)

[36] 'Alio modo potest haec determinatio "secundum quid" referri ad distinctionem, ut sit sensus quia essentia et relatio ex natura rei distinguuntur secundum quid, et sic est verum quia distinctio essentiae et relationis est rei et rei simpliciter, sed distinctio est secundum quid': Scotus, *Rep.* 1A.33.2 (MS M, fo. 151ᵛ; Wadding, XI, 186ᵃ (n. 9; note that the Wadding text is defective, omitting the required 'et rei' ('and thing') in **[6.4]**)).

that both essence and property count as (undiminished) things. The claim that property could be such an undiminished thing is clearly new, without precedent in either *Lectura* or *Ordinatio*.

This teaching is accepted and developed in detail in the very late *Quodlibet*.[37] The discussion in *Quodlibet* 3 builds on the *Reportatio* account by providing arguments for the new claim that property, as much as essence, must count as a thing. The account begins with a simple analysis of the different senses of 'thing', which is, as Scotus notes, 'an equivocal term'. From broadest to most specific, Scotus discerns four possible senses: anything non-contradictory; anything extramental; anything non-relational; anything substantial.[38] Scotus holds that the personal property of a divine person is a relation, and that it is a thing in the first two senses.[39] The basic reason is that the relevant sort of relation is not just mind-dependent: it is a property responsible for relating one thing to another, and in order to do this it must have some entity of its own, distinct from the entity of the thing it relates.[40] But what sort of entity is this? Not as fully real as non-relational entities, for 'they lack the sort of being found in the things of which they are the circumstances, and to the extent that something departs from perfect reality it approaches the rational'.[41] So a relation has some sort of diminished being. But this diminution cannot be great, because Scotus goes on to note that a categorial relation and the thing it relates are *really distinct* (i.e. unqualifiedly distinct, in the *Reportatio* language), such that the thing related is separable from the relation and can exist without it.[42] Thus Scotus holds that a categorial relation in creatures 'has its own accidentality, for it is a thing in itself and yet it is not the thing on which the relation is based nor is it a thing that is a *per se* being, as substance is'.[43] There is no thought that a relation in God is *less real* than a relation in creatures – all it lacks is accidentality, and, as Scotus notes a little later, the issue of the *identity* of a relation in God with the divine essence is a different question from that of its degree of reality: 'the question about the reality of a relation is not a question about its otherness'.[44] Categorial relations in creatures are really distinct from their foundations, because their foundations can exist without the relations. Relations in God are no less beings than relations in creatures are: indeed, the relevant parts of the argument in *Quodlibet* 3 rely on the presupposition that, in terms of entity, divine and categorial relations are equal in their degree of being (though, of course, different in terms of their distinction from their subjects). Scotus at one point talks about the inseparability of essence and relation in God by using the traditional language of the relation 'merging' with the essence:

---

[37] I take it that this is strong evidence in favour of ascribing a date to the *Reportatio* later than either the *Lectura* or book 1 of the *Ordinatio*.

[38] Scotus, *Quod.* 3, nn. 2–3 (Wadding, XII, 67–8; Alluntis and Wolter, 61–3 (¶¶ 3.6–3.14)).

[39] Ibid., nn. 3, 5 (Wadding, XII, 68, 71; Alluntis and Wolter, 63–4, 65 (¶¶ 3.16–3.17, 3.21)).

[40] Ibid., nn. 8, 9–10 (Wadding, XII, 75, 76; Alluntis and Wolter, 67–9 (¶¶ 3.29–3.30, 3.32–3.33)).

[41] Ibid., n. 9 (Wadding, XII, 76; Alluntis and Wolter, 68 (¶ 3.31)).

[42] Ibid., n. 15 (Wadding, XII, 81–2; Alluntis and Wolter, 73–4 (¶ 3.46)).

[43] Ibid. (Wadding, XII, 81; Alluntis and Wolter, 73 (¶ 3.44)). On the reality of categorial relations, see too Part I, chapter 6 §2.

[44] Ibid., n. 22 (Wadding, XII, 84; Alluntis and Wolter, 78–9 (¶ 3.57)).

[7]
1 In this way [i.e. merging in such a way as not to remain really distinct but nevertheless
2 to retain relational entity of its own], it does not remain really distinct, and
3 nevertheless [is] a thing outside the soul with proper reality which is relational. And
4 thus 'it remains', to the extent that 'remaining' excludes merging destructive of its
5 proper reality.[45]

Property 'merges' with essence, such that it is really (unqualifiedly) identical with the divine essence **[7.1–2]**. But relations and non-relational items cannot be qualifiedly (formally or adequately) identical, since their definitions are wholly disjoint – relational versus non-relational **[7.3]**. No amount of real identity can destroy the relation's 'proper [relational] reality' **[7.4–5]**.

We have seen why Scotus in the *Reportatio* holds that the divine essence is a thing. Why does he hold too that the relation is a thing in the sense just outlined? In the *Quodlibet*, Scotus gives two arguments, the first of which I discuss here. The argument casts light not only on his position in the *Reportatio*, but also on his metaphysics in general. The argument relies on the view that essence and property are somehow constituents of a divine person. The qualification here is important, for, as we have seen, composition is a relation that obtains between really (unqualifiedly) distinct things. Anything composed includes at least one potential and at least one actual thing, and Scotus of course does not believe that there could be potency in God:

[8]
1 When things distinct in some way constitute a third, they constitute it only as they are
2 related to each other in some way, or are united in some way. And this is clear in
3 extrinsic causes, which only ever cause if they concur in some way for the purpose of
4 causing, and more [clear] for intrinsic causes, which constitute a *suppositum* only as
5 they are united in some way: for essence and relation, whatever sort of principles they
6 are, constitute a person according to all. Therefore this is in so far as they concur,
7 which can be only as the relation is in the essence. From this I infer that essence and
8 relation constitute a person only if the relation is in the essence. But for the relation to
9 be in the essence is for the relation to have a most real reference (*comparationem*) to
10 the essence beyond that which it can have through the consideration of the intellect.
11 Therefore, the relation constitutes the person only as compared to the essence. But it
12 does not constitute a person other than as a thing, otherwise the person, as formally
13 constituted, would not be a thing; therefore the relation, as compared to the essence, is
14 a thing.[46]

This is a later, more complex, version of the material in **[1]** above. Constitution, in any manner at all, requires union **[8.1–2, 4–5]**. And union requires components that are in some sense distinct **[8.8–10]**. (Usually it requires too a relation between the components; here the relation is real identity, not any sort of categorial relation at all: hence, Scotus talks about the real *comparatio* between the two constituents, not their real relation to each other **[8.9–10]**.) Essence and property are in some sense the constituents of a divine person **[8.5–6]**: specifically, the relation is in some sense

---

45 Ibid., n. 21 (Wadding, XII, 84; Alluntis and Wolter, 78 (¶ 3.55)).
46 Ibid., n. 4 (Wadding, XII, 70; Alluntis and Wolter, 64 (¶ 3.19)).

'in' the essence [**8.**7–8]. (As I suggested in chapter 14 §4 above, the relevant sense is that, while the relation is not really distinct from the essence, it is 'in' the essence; nevertheless the essence explains the relation, and not *vice versa*: hence, presumably, the essence is not 'in' the relation.) But why should the distinct components count as things? Scotus presupposes that the essence counts as a thing, and that a divine person must be in some sense distinct from the essence. Suppose that what distinguishes the person from the essence that is a constituent of it is not itself a thing. This entails, Scotus reasons, that a person, 'as formally constituted', is 'not a thing'. A person, on the scenario envisaged, would not be a thing distinct from the essence; but the person 'as formally constituted' must be distinct from the essence; hence, as distinct from the essence, the person would not be a thing [**8.**11–14].

This looks about right. If we are supposing that there are two correlative constituents in a thing, we would want those constituents to be of equal ontological 'density'. This does not mean that we would want either of them to be things. But on the supposition that one of them is, we would want the other one to be too. As Scotus presents his position, what is important about it is that the components of a person have some *explanatory* work to do – specifically, the components are to explain (among other things) how the item they compose should count as a thing. What distinguishes something that is as real as the essence from the essence must itself be as real as the essence.

It seems to me that there are some important ontological consequences of Scotus's late view. For on the late view, at least some formally (qualifiedly) distinct constituents are as real as really (unqualifiedly) distinct constituents. What ties really distinct constituents together are categorial relations between them, and these relations are really identical with their own relations of inherence (thus allowing them to be the bedrock explanation of unity).[47] But it would be odd to think of there being such categorial relations between formally distinct items. In the case of something constituted of merely formally distinct things, I take it that the non-categorial relation of real identity between the constituents is the basic, bedrock, explanation of the substantial unity of such a thing.[48]

---

[47] Ibid., nn. 15–16 (Wadding, XII, 81–2; Alluntis and Wolter, 73–4 (¶¶ 3.44–3.48)).

[48] Recall the relationship between our notion of compresence and Scotus's notion of the real identity of constituents to which I drew attention in chapter 13 §1 above.

Chapter 18

Anti-subordinationist Strategies

Clearly, Scotus emphasizes – perhaps to a greater extent than his immediate predecessors – the genuinely causal nature of the origination relations between the divine persons. This seems to me quite right. Origination relations seem, by their very nature, to be causal in some way or another. Nevertheless, some theologians have objected to this sort of account on the grounds that it appears to be subordinationist. For example, when the doctrine of the divine processions was first being properly developed, Gregory of Nazianzus replied to such worries by noting that, even though the persons are not equal in terms of causal relationships (since two are dependent on the third), the divinity of each person is equal, and that this is sufficient to rebut any serious subordinationism charge.[1] The subordinationism objection seems to me particularly weak: Gregory's reply is surely, and obviously right, and sufficient to deal with the difficulty; though if it is felt that more should be said, then surely Gregory's reply coupled with the *necessity* of the production – its being *internal* to the divine essence, as outlined in chapter 10, and in chapter 14 §2 – should be sufficient to dispose of the objection. In the course of his discussion, Scotus proposes various arguments against subordinationism, and I discuss these in case the reader thinks that Scotus's robustly causal account of the origination relations makes him particularly susceptible to the objection.

A standard form of the worry would be to infer imperfection from causal or originative dependence. Scotus, for example, raises a complex series of objections to the effect that, if the Son has his existence from the Father, then his existence is contingent, dependent, and mutable, and any of these would in effect make him a creature.[2] Scotus's response is to deny that the notion of being produced entails any of these further properties. The Son is formally necessary in himself in the sense that he is a necessary exemplification of a necessary essence. But the Father is the 'efficient' cause of this state of affairs. The two claims are not incompatible since, as we have seen, Scotus holds that it is necessarily the case that the Father generates the Son.[3] Anyone who thinks that it is necessary for God to create just those things that are *de facto* created – the 'Philosophers', as Scotus puts it – will hold that creatures are necessary in the sense that it is necessarily the case that all and only those things that now exist exist. Still, even in such a case creatures would not be necessary in the way that the Son is.[4] The Son is formally necessary in the sense that he shares with the

---

[1] See Gregory of Nazianzus, *Or.* 29.15, ll. 1–2, 15–17 (*Discours 27–31*, 208).
[2] See Scotus, *Ord.* 1.2.2.1–4, nn. 201–8 (Vatican, II, 251–5).
[3] Ibid., n. 259 (Vatican, II, 280).
[4] Ibid., n. 261 (Vatican, II, 281–2).

Father the same causally independent essence.[5] Neither does production entail mutation: as noted in chapters 10 §2 and 13 §3 above, the relevant notion of production abstracts from all notions of passive substrate and mutation.[6]

Scotus's strategy is to claim that the personal properties are neither pure perfections nor in any way imperfect. They cannot be pure perfections, since pure perfections are essential divine perfections (on this, see Part I, chapter 3 above). Such perfections in God are perfections of the infinite divine essence, had by every divine person; no personal property is a perfection of every person. But nothing about the personal properties entails any kind of imperfection either. So *lacking* such and such a personal property (e.g. the Father's lacking filiation) is not an imperfection.[7]

Scotus devotes the whole of his fifth quodlibetal question to this topic, and proposes a total of three very lengthy arguments to show that no personal property can be formally infinite (and hence that no personal property can be a pure perfection). I briefly examine two of these.[8] Infinity here is *intensive*, not extensive: infinity in perfection, not in quantitative extent or magnitude.[9]

The first argument is based on the unity of an infinite being:

[1]
1 There cannot be many really distinct and formally infinite things. But there are many
2 really distinct relations of origin. Therefore they are not formally infinite intensively;
3 neither, consequently, is any of them, because for any reason [that] one [is infinite],
4 every other [is] too.[10]

It may be thought that the claim that the relation of origin itself could be infinite misses the point about the infinity of a divine person: it is the persons that are infinite. But Scotus's point is that the one divine essence is infinite, and that it is in virtue of this that a person is infinite. There is only one properly – formally – infinite entity, and that is the essence. Infinity 'piggy-backs' from the essence to the persons: the persons overlap at this formally infinite entity. The personal property is not, itself, infinite, for then there would be at least three (and probably four) infinite entities: the three properties, and (probably) the divine essence too. Scotus goes on to note that every pure perfection is infinite or limitless,[11] and

---

[5] Ibid., n. 267 (Vatican, II, 286).

[6] Ibid., nn. 266 and 269 (Vatican, II, 285 and 286–7).

[7] For the claim that the personal properties are not imperfect, see Scotus, *Quod.* 19, n. [10] (Wadding, XII, 498; Alluntis and Wolter, 426 (¶ 19.31)); for a denial that the personal properties are pure perfections, see Ibid., n. 10 (Wadding, XII, 498; Alluntis and Wolter, 427 (¶ 19.32)). Presumably Scotus means that possessing one or other disjunctively is a perfection, but not possessing any given property; or perhaps (less likely) that the personal properties are qualitatively neutral. For the precise meaning of the question, see Ibid. 5, n. 5 (Wadding, XII, 120; Alluntis and Wolter, 112 (¶ 5.12)).

[8] The teaching exists too in the various *Sentence* commentaries: see e.g. Scotus, *Lect.* 1.8.1.4, n. 189 (Vatican, XVII, 69); *Ord.* 1.8.1.4, n. 221 (Vatican, IV, 276).

[9] Scotus, *Quod.* 5, nn. 3–4 (Wadding, XII, 118–19; Alluntis and Wolter, 109–11 (¶¶ 5.7–5.9)).

[10] Ibid., n. 7 (Wadding, XII, 125; Alluntis and Wolter, 114 (¶ 5.17)).

[11] Ibid., n. 7 (Wadding, XII, 125; Alluntis and Wolter, 114 (¶ 5.19)); see too *Ord.* 1.19.1, n. 25 (Vatican, V, 277).

contained in the divine essence in a way in which the personal properties are not (the persons overlap at all the essential attributes, which somehow compose the one essence). If every pure perfection is infinite, then no personal property is a pure perfection.

Scotus's second argument makes use of the notion of communicability:

[2]
1 Every pure perfection (*perfectio simpliciter*) is communicable; every intensively
2 infinite thing is a pure perfection. Therefore [every intensively infinite thing is
3 communicable]. No personal property, however, is communicable, since it is the
4 formal ground for existing incommunicably. Therefore, no personal property is
5 intensively infinite.[12]

The argument is clearly valid, and can be used easily to infer too that no personal property is a pure perfection (every pure perfection is communicable [2.1]; no personal property is communicable [2.2–3]; therefore no personal property is a pure perfection). I explained in chapter 12 §3 above the way in which Scotus holds that personal properties explain incommunicability [2.2–3]. But why accept the claim that every pure perfection is communicable? Pure perfections are the sort of thing that it is in general better to be than not to be. Now, what is incommunicable is unshareable. But it cannot be *in general* better to be this incommunicable thing than not to be it, for by definition only one thing can be this incommunicable thing.[13] Of course, *incommunicability* is shareable; but a personal property, like an individuating feature, is not.[14]

In the light of this, Scotus simply maintains that the divine persons are equal in all respects. This equality is explained by the divine essence, which is equally perfect in all divine persons. Again, the fullest discussion of this issue is in the *Quodlibet*. Basically, Scotus holds that the three divine persons are equal, and (more controversially) that this equality is a real relation between them. Scotus holds that there are various sorts of relevant equality: perfection (called by him 'magnitude' in this context[15]), eternity, and power.[16] The divine essence is infinite

---

[12] Ibid., n. 13 (Wadding, XII, 128; Alluntis and Wolter, 118–19 (¶ 5.30)).

[13] Ibid, n. 14 (Wadding, XII, 128–9; Alluntis and Wolter, 119–20 (¶¶ 5.31–2); note in particular the following:

> What is incompatible with something is not simply better for it than what is not such, for as it is incompatible with it, it would destroy the other as such. But what is of itself incommunicable is incompatible with everything [else], even *qua suppositum*, and hence is not better for it *qua suppositum* than what is not it. We have therefore this major: No pure perfection is formally incommunicable.

[14] The problem of the shareability of the attribute of incommunicability caused the medievals some difficulty, closely related to the analogous difficulty, originating from Augustine, of the communicability of *being a person* (see Augustine, *De Trin.* 7.4.7–9 (CCSL, 50, pp. 255–60). I discuss the whole issue at length in *The Metaphysics of the Incarnation*, 176–8.

[15] Scotus, *Quod.* 6, n. [5] (Wadding, XII, 143; Alluntis and Wolter, 134 (¶ 6.13)).

[16] On these, see Scotus, *Quod.* 6, nn. 4 and 17 (Wadding, XII, 144 and 152; Alluntis and Wolter, 132–3 (¶¶ 6.8–6.9) and 144 (¶ 6.40)); *Ord.* 1.19.1, nn. 12–13 (Vatican, V, 270–1); Ibid. 1.20.un., nn. 24–7 (Vatican, V, 313–15).

in all these required ways.[17] Equality is not a reflexive relation, so for a relation of equality in any respect, the *relata* must be really distinct.[18] The divine persons are really distinct.[19] And they include identically the same essence. So they are equal.[20]

---

[17] For magnitude, see Scotus, *Quod.* 6, n. [6] (Wadding, XII, 144; Alluntis and Wolter, 135 (¶ 6.16)); for eternity, see Ibid., n. 13 (Wadding, XII, 149–50; Alluntis and Wolter, 141 (¶ 6.33)); for power, see Ibid., n. 17 (Wadding, XII, 152; Alluntis and Wolter, 144 (¶ 6.40)).

[18] Ibid., nn. 19–20 (Wadding, XII, 157; Alluntis and Wolter, 145–6 (¶¶ 6.45–6.46)).

[19] Ibid., n. 19 (Wadding, XII, 157; Alluntis and Wolter, 145 (¶ 6.44)); I discussed this in chapter 13 above.

[20] Ibid., n. 33 (Wadding, XII, 166; Alluntis and Wolter, 156-6 (¶ 6.82)); see too *Quod.* 6, nn. 32–3 (Wadding, XII, 166; Alluntis and Wolter, 156 (¶¶ 6.79–6.81)).

Appendix: Religious Language and Divine Ineffability

Scotus is clear that there is some sense in which the divine essence cannot be known: specifically, it cannot be known by creatures by natural knowledge: 'God is not known naturally by the wayfarer in a particular and proper way, that is, as this essence, as this and in itself.'[1] The sort of knowledge of the divine essence that Scotus has in mind would be like knowledge of the definition of 'God': knowledge sufficient to allow us to infer all other features of God too. Scotus describes this knowledge as '*per se*, proper, and immediate knowledge': essential ('*per se*'), specific to one kind ('proper'), and definitional ('immediate'): complete knowledge, in other words, of the features of an essence.[2] The divine essence, in such a case, is an object of cognition 'according to the whole *ratio* of its knowability'.[3] Knowledge of the defining features of divinity would be a very full sort of knowledge; in denying this sort of knowledge to the wayfarer, Scotus is not making any strongly apophatic sort of claim. God is supremely knowable, both by himself[4] and by creatures.[5] In two ways, indeed, Scotus's theory of our knowledge of God is not at all apophatic. For he holds that it is possible for the divine essence to be known in this full sort of way if God wills to make it known. And he holds that, even without revelation, we can have some more limited knowledge of God's essence.

First, then, according to Scotus, we can have knowledge of the divine essence 'according to the whole *ratio* of its knowability'. But, whether in the wayfaring or the beatific state, such knowledge is had only by divine will:

[1]
1 Any such intellection – that is, *per se*, proper, and immediate – requires the object
2 present under the proper *ratio* of an object, and this either in its own existence (if the
3 [intellection] is intuitive), or in something perfectly representing it under the proper
4 and *per se ratio* of its knowability (if it is abstractive). But God, under the proper *ratio*
5 of divinity, is not present to any created intellect other than voluntarily.[6]

Full intellectual understanding of an object requires its full presence – either immediately (as in intuitive cognition), or via a mental representation (as in abstractive cognition) [1.1–4]. And God is present in this way only by his will [1.4–5].

---

[1] Scotus, *Ord.* 1.3.1.1–2, n. 56 (Vatican, III, 38; *PW*, 25–6; Frank and Wolter, 114).

[2] Scotus, *Quod.* 14, n. 10 (Wadding, XII, 369; Alluntis and Wolter, 324–5 (¶ 14.36)).

[3] Ibid., n. 21 (Wadding, XII, 400; Alluntis and Wolter, 336 (¶ 14.74)).

[4] Scotus, *DPP* 4, n. 17 (Wolter, 109 (¶ 4.51)).

[5] Ibid., n. 24 (Wolter, 123 (¶ 4.65)).

[6] Scotus, *Quod.* 14, n. 10 (Wadding, XII, 369; Alluntis and Wolter, 324–5 (¶ 14.36)).

Why accept that God is present to creatures only by his will? Scotus maintains that, for an object to be known, the object must be a (partial) cause of the knowledge. And, as we have seen, Scotus holds that all external divine causal activity is contingent, subject to the divine will. This entails, then, that God cannot be a natural cause of a creature's knowledge of him, and Scotus makes just this point:

[2]
1 To move to a beatific act is not proper to the divine essence, and neither is this prior to
2 the act of the will. Rather, it is properly the act of that will. ... If the essence were not
3 formally a voluntary agent, then it could cause absolutely nothing *ad extra*, for it could
4 not cause other than naturally, and whatever is extrinsic [to it], since it is formally
5 possible, could not [be made to] exist by what is necessary, other than contingently.[7]

If God were not to cause things external to himself contingently and voluntarily, then he could not cause them at all [**2.2–4**]. So God cannot be other than voluntarily an object that causes beatific knowledge in a creature [**2.1–2**]. 'Possible' means something like 'causable and logically contingent'; a necessary being such as God can thus only bring about voluntarily and freely what is in this sense possible [**2.4–5**]. The relevant effect, of course, is the beatific act of a creature. This beatific act, then, can be brought about in a creature only by divine will.

Scotus clearly believes that this restriction holds not just for intuitive knowledge of the divine essence – knowledge by immediate encounter – but for abstractive knowledge too – knowledge by means of mental representations:

[3]
1 Nothing created can be the cause of this presence in the intellect, even abstractively,
2 because [nothing created] can cause something that is a proper and *per se*
3 representation of the divinity under the proper *ratio* of its knowability, for such a
4 representation can be caused only [in one of the two following ways]: by the knowable
5 thing itself, or by something that perfectly contains it under the *ratio* of its
6 knowability. Therefore even if God could be known by some representation, that
7 would nevertheless not be caused other than immediately by God voluntarily causing
8 it.[8]

In the case of intuitive cognition, the (external) object is a partial cause of the act of knowledge. In the case of abstractive cognition, the (external) object is a partial cause of the intelligible species representing the object [**3.3–5**],[9] or, at the very least, the intelligible species needs to be caused by something that fully contains the relevant object [**3.5–6**]. The sort of thing that Scotus has in mind would be the intelligible representations of creatures caused in the divine memory as objects of divine thought. Nothing, presumably, can contain the divine essence in this way. So the argument in [**2**] applies in the case of abstractive knowledge too.

Still, God can cause in the creature both intuitive and abstractive knowledge of his essence.[10] And while it is clear that the human mind is finite, and that there is

---

[7] Ibid., n. 17 (Wadding, XII, 382; Alluntis and Wolter, 333 (¶ 14.67)).

[8] Ibid., n. 11 (Wadding, XII, 369; Alluntis and Wolter, 325 (¶ 14.37)).

[9] See e.g. Scotus, *Ord.* 1.3.1.1–2, n. 35 (Vatican, III, 21–4; *PW*, 22-3; Frank and Wolter, 112).

[10] On this, see Dumont, 'Theology as a Practical Science'.

some sense in which God remains incomprehensible,[11] Scotus never makes clear just in what way this is, given that God can give creatures the kind of knowledge of his essence that I have been describing. As we saw in Part II, chapter 10 §2 above, Scotus talks about God's knowledge of his own essence being – uniquely – infinite and unlimited. Whatever creatures' knowledge of the divine essence is like, it is not like this.

The fact that we cannot know this essence without revelation does not, according to Scotus, mean that without revelation we can know nothing about God's essence. We can know of the divine essence that it necessarily includes in its content or intension certain attributes, the contents or intensions of which are in turn known to us ('a concept can be had in which God is conceived *per se* and quidditatively').[12] What account does Scotus give of this knowledge about the divine essence available to us without revelation? Basically, as is well known, Scotus believes that there must be some concepts that are *univocal* between God and creatures. There must be some concepts under whose extensions both God and creatures fall, such that the concepts are identically the same in both cases. Scotus proposes the following two conditions, necessary and (presumably) jointly sufficient for univocity:

[4]
1 I call that concept 'univocal' that is one in such a way that its unity is sufficient for a
2 contradiction when it is affirmed and denied of the same thing, and is sufficient too
3 for a syllogistic middle term, so that when the extremes are united in a middle term
4 that is one in this way, they may be concluded to be united between themselves
5 without the fallacy of equivocation.[13]

Necessary and jointly sufficient for the univocity of concepts is (1) that it is contradictory to affirm and deny one and the same concept of one thing [**4**.1–2]; and (2) that the concept can serve as the middle term in a syllogism [**4**.2–5]. Scotus is thinking that arguments, for example, are fundamentally a matter of the relation of concepts to each other. The fallacy of equivocation, in this context, amounts to drawing an inference on the basis of one concept to a wholly different concept. It is not hard to think of examples when we mistakenly suppose two concepts to be the same when they are not, and in such cases it is a lack of *information* that causes the problem. I can suppose, for example, that when two people are talking about the same idea, they in fact are not. And on the basis of this supposition, I can draw inferences that can be shown to be false. This would be an example of the fallacy of equivocation about concepts, not words.

One final note. As just observed, Scotus's claim is about *concepts*, not *words* or terms. So there is no reason for the two criteria to be thought of as sufficient for the univocity of terms.[14] How we know that we are using one word in the same sense (signifying the same concept) in two different contexts is a further, semantic, question, and Scotus offers no help.

---

[11] Scotus, *DPP* 4, n. 14 (Wolter, 103 (¶ 4.46)).

[12] Scotus, *Ord.* 1.3.1.1–2, n. 25 (Vatican, III, 16–17; *PW*, 19; Frank and Wolter, 108).

[13] Ibid., n. 26 (Vatican, III, 18; *PW*, 20; Frank and Wolter, 108).

[14] *Pace* Janice Thomas, 'Univocity and Understanding God's Nature', 90–3.

Scotus offers a number of arguments for his position. The most basic one is simply that discussion about God could not get started unless the univocity theory were true. In the *Ordinatio*, Scotus puts it as follows:

[5]
1 Every intellect certain about one concept and dubious about others has a concept
2 about which it is certain, distinct from those about which it is dubious (the subject
3 includes the predicate). But the intellect of someone in this life can be certain that
4 God is a being but doubtful about finite or infinite [being], or created or uncreated
5 [being]. Therefore the concept of being, [affirmed] of God is different from the other
6 concepts, and thus [is] neither of itself, and is included in both of them, and is
7 therefore univocal.[15]

Suppose we accept that God is wise (Scotus's example is *(a) being*, but I choose a less contentious case so that we are not misled into irrelevant complaints about God's not being an object in the universe). We thus accept that God falls under the extension of the concept of wisdom **[5.5]**. But this concept must be distinct from the further concepts *finite wisdom* and *infinite wisdom*, or from *created wisdom* and *uncreated wisdom* **[5.5–6]**. For we can accept that God falls under the extension of the concept of wisdom, but yet not know whether God falls under the extension of *finite wisdom* or the extension of *infinite wisdom* **[5.3–5]**. Furthermore, it seems that the concept of wisdom is included in both the concept of finite wisdom and the concept of infinite wisdom **[5.6]**.

The apophatic objection to this – if I may so put it – is that knowing that God is wise does not require knowing the contents of the concept of wisdom as ascribed to God. In some ways, it looks as though Scotus does not take this objection seriously. For his second argument in favour of his theory is that, if there are concepts applicable only to God and not to creatures, we could not know what these concepts are since we have no cognitive mechanism for constructing them.[16] This, of course, would not be of concern to the apophatic theologian, for such a theologian would want to deny that we can know the contents of concepts under whose extension God falls. Aquinas, for example, makes it clear enough that we can affirm certain perfections of God on the basis of the resemblance that necessarily obtains between an effect (creatures) and its cause (God). But he is adamant that we do not know the contents of these perfections.[17]

Scotus's worry about this sort of approach is, I think, fundamentally *formal* – not as such connected with the material content of a theological claim. As **[5]** hints, if we do not know at least something of the contents of the concepts that we ascribe to God, then no theological discussion can even get off the ground. In the *Lectura*, Scotus makes the point explicitly:

[6]
1 Unless 'being' implies one univocal intention, theology would simply perish. For
2 theologians prove that the divine Word proceeds and is generated by way of intellect,

---

[15] Scotus, *Ord.* 1.3.1.1–2, n. 27 (Vatican, III, 18; *PW*, 20; Frank and Wolter, 110).

[16] Ibid., n. 35 (Vatican, III, 21–4; *PW*, 22; Frank and Wolter, 112).

[17] Compare Aquinas, *ST* 1.13.6 c (I/1, 69ᵃ) with 1.3 praef. (I/1, 13ᵃ): 'Because we cannot know of God what he is, but what he is not, we cannot consider about God how he is, but rather how he is not.'

3 and the Holy Spirit proceeds by way of will. But if intellect and will were found in us
4 and in God equivocally, there would be no evidence at all that, since a word is
5 generated in us in such and such a fashion, it is so in God – and likewise with regard to
6 love in us – because then intellect and will in these two cases would be of a wholly
7 different kind (*ratio*).[18]

Note that Scotus is here talking about the Trinity. He is thus concerned with theology, not metaphysics **[6.1]**, and therefore ultimately with revealed theology (since he does not believe that there are *demonstrative* arguments in favour of the Trinity, as we saw in Part II, chapter 9 above). The argument is that authoritative theologians have in the past drawn inferences about the Trinity on the basis of human will and intellect **[6.3–7]**. If *intellect* and *will* were not univocal concepts **[6.3–4, 6–7]**, then, 'theology would simply perish' **[6.1]**.

It could be objected that Scotus has neglected the apophaticism of – say – the Church Fathers in this sort of context. Scotus could reply, however, that any instance of a deductive theological argument is sufficient to establish his point on the basis of authority. And whatever the status of arguments about intellect and will in the Trinity, it is clear that there are plenty of rigidly deductive arguments to be found in the Church Fathers. Analogy will not do here; for a valid syllogism, the concepts must be identically the same in the two premises. The argument about univocity is thus fundamentally one from authority – the authority of the Fathers' own practice of theology – and it is that anyone whose theological praxis includes deductive arguments implicitly or explicitly accepts that there are univocal concepts. I will return to this in just a moment.

As Scotus sees it, then, there are concepts under whose extensions God and creatures fall. He holds too that there are concepts proper to God, and concepts proper to creatures. But at least some of these will be complex, made up of more than one component concept. Thus, in the example I used to explicate **[5]** above, there is a (complex) concept proper to God, *infinite wisdom*, and a (complex) concept proper to creatures, *finite wisdom*; each concept includes the simple concept of wisdom, along with a further qualifier – infinite and finite, respectively:

[7]
1 I say that we can arrive at many concepts proper to God that do not pertain to
2 creatures. Of this kind are the concepts of all perfections simply in the highest
3 [degree], and the most perfect concept, in which – in a certain description, as it were –
4 we most perfectly know God, is by conceiving all the perfections simply and in the
5 highest [degree]. But a more perfect and at the same time simpler concept, possible
6 for us, is the concept of infinite being. For this is simpler than the concept of good
7 being, true being, or of others like this, for the infinite is not a quasi-attribute or
8 passion of being, or of that of which it is said, but it implies an intrinsic mode of that
9 entity, such that when I say 'infinite being', I do not have a concept [composed]
10 accidentally, as it were, of subject and passion, but a *per se* concept of a subject in a
11 certain degree of perfection, namely, infinity.[19]

---

[18] Scotus, *Lect.* 1.3.1.1–2, n. 113 (Vatican, XVI, 266–7).
[19] Scotus, *Ord.* 1.3.1.1–2, n. 58 (Vatican, III, 40; *PW*, 26–7; Frank and Wolter, 116).

The highest degree of any perfection [7.2–3, 4–5] is infinity [7.11],[20] and the basic point is that any concept of an infinite degree of a pure perfection is proper to God, and is descriptive of the divine essence [7.3]. Scotus holds that 'infinite *being*' is the most perfect concept we can have of God [7.5–6]. The reason has to do with the theory of the transcendentals. As I mentioned in Part I, chapter 3 above, Scotus holds that 'being' is predicable of any substance or accident, and he holds that there are certain 'passions' of being – 'one', 'good', and 'true' [7.6–7] – that are entailed by *being*, and likewise predicable of every substance and accident. Scotus holds that *being* is the explanatory attribute that somehow 'contains' all the others ('virtually includes' them, as Scotus puts it).[21] Anything which is a being is *eo ipso* one, good, and true.[22] But there is some intensional content to these concepts or predicates; hence *true being*, for example, is a concept of more complex contents than merely *being*. For this reason, in addition to being the most perfect concept we can have of God without revelation, *infinite being* is also the simplest [7.5–6]. The reason is that infinity is merely a degree of perfection of an attribute; it does not add any further *intensional* content. Infinity is, as we saw in Part I, chapter 6 §5, an *intrinsic mode* of a substance, and such modes do not add further intensional content.

Scotus's presupposition in all of this is that there is a complex network of concepts arranged hierarchically as genus and species, ultimately traceable to certain irreducibly simple, non-overlapping 'genera', and irreducible, non-overlapping 'specific differences'. The origins of this theory lie in Porphyry's famous 'tree', his attempt to analyse each one of Aristotle's categories as a descending series of ever more specific genera, with (taking the category of substance as an example) *substance* at top, and the most specific species of substances at the bottom (*man, cat, dog, tree* and so on).[23] The medieval theory of the transcendentals modifies this scheme, continuing the hierarchy above the categories, such that (for example) *being* is the supreme 'genus' of all the categories. On Scotus's understanding, the disjunctive transcendentals (on these, see Part I, chapter 6 §5 above) are the relevant 'differences'. Each of these transcendentals will be wholly simple, not inter-definable. The same follows of the various 'specific differences' that appear all the way down the modified scheme (classically, 'rational' as the specific difference of 'man').[24]

The univocity theory is fundamentally a cognitive theory. It makes important semantic assumptions, but – contrary to the rather simple-minded way it is sometimes presented in modern theological literature – it does not make any metaphysical assumptions.[25] The semantic assumptions are about the theory of

[20] Ibid., n. 60 (Vatican, III, 41; *PW*, 28; Frank and Wolter, 116–18).

[21] Ibid., n. 59 (Vatican, III, 40–1; *PW*, 27; Frank and Wolter, 116).

[22] Ibid. 1.8.1.3, nn. 114–15 (Vatican, IV, 206–7; *PW*, 3).

[23] See Porphyry, *Isag.*, 4, l. 15–p. 5, l. 1; Spade, 4 (¶¶ 21–3).

[24] A consequence of Scotus's position, in fact, is that ultimate specific differences, the 'transcendental differences' (*infinite, finite, necessary, contingent*, and so on), and the passions of being (*one, good, true*) all fail to fall under the extension of the concept *being*: see Scotus, *Ord.* 1.3.1.3, n. 137 (Vatican, III, 85; Frank and Wolter, 120).

[25] I explore this issue at length in my '"Where Angels Fear to Tread": Duns Scotus and Radical Orthodoxy'.

concepts that Scotus accepts.[26] For Scotus supposes that concepts are, basically, either definitions or the components of definitions, such that there are simple, undefinable, primitive concepts that are used in complex definitions. Concepts are thus in principle fixed, and satisfying a concept requires the concept to be identically the same in its various cases. In line with this, sound argumentation requires identically the same concept to link the relevant premises. Aquinas forms a contrast. For Aquinas, satisfying a concept does not require the concept to be identically the same in its various cases. All that is required is that the things that satisfy the concept are related to each other by some definable similarity relation. In line with this, sound argumentation does not require satisfying such stringent conditions as it does on Scotus's account. Aquinas's theory will amount to a set of claims about knowing how to *use* certain words, irrespective of any capacity to *define* the relevant terms. It is doubtless for this reason that Aquinas provides an account not of the analogy of concepts, but of the analogy of terms (words).

Scotus's objection is that, on Aquinas's theory, there are no relevant similarity relations that can be defined in a philosophically principled way. The semantic link for Aquinas is sustained by a metaphysical theory – that while we do not know the meanings of words in case of God, we know that the relevant words are predicable of God on the basis of resemblance between effect and cause. Scotus's objection, I suppose, is that if the semantic theory is correct, then in fact any 'scientific' – deductive – system is rendered impossible.[27] For deductive syllogisms whose

---

[26] The whole of Aquinas, *ST* 1.13 is about *naming* God; Scotus's discussion of univocity occurs entirely in the context of *knowing* God. In fact, like Aquinas, Scotus holds that we can speak of God more clearly than we can know him. The claim is connected with some technical medieval semantic theories about the imposition of words, theories that we do not need to concern ourselves with here. The gist of Scotus's position is that we can use words about God whose sense is fixed merely extensionally – the Tetragrammaton is Scotus's example – such that the sense of the word is indeed 'the divine essence as this' (the divine essence in itself), but that this sense is secured merely extensionally: see Scotus, *Ord.* 1.22.un., nn. 10–11 (Vatican, V, 345–6). The reason, however, is different from Aquinas's: not that we cannot know the contents of the concepts we ascribe to God. Rather, Scotus ascribes to Aquinas and others the view that 'as something is understood, so it is named' (Scotus, *Ord.* 1.22.un., n. 4 (Vatican, V, 343)) – that something cannot be spoken of more clearly than it can be understood – and maintains that, since we have biblical warrant that we can speak of God in a way that expresses the divine essence (the Tetragrammaton), Aquinas's view would entail that we can in this life have an understanding of the divine essence in itself. The relationship with Aquinas is complex. Aquinas maintains that 'Something can be named by us in the manner that it can be known by us', and goes on to argue that, since we know God through our knowledge of creatures, we name him in this way too (Aquinas, *ST* 1.13.1 c (I/1, 63ᵇ)). This, of course, is one of the motivators for Aquinas's relative apophaticism. Still, Aquinas maintains that the sense of the Tetragrammaton is 'being itself', and holds too that only God is identified as his being. For this reason, the Tetragrammaton 'most properly names God' (*ST* 1.13.11 c (I/1, 74ᵃ)). I suppose that Aquinas agrees that the sense of the Tetragrammaton is fixed extensionally; but Aquinas takes it that a concept whose contents are fixed extensionally is no more obscure than a word whose sense is fixed extensionally. Scotus's criticism to this extent seems to miss its mark.

[27] Objecting to the semantic theory does not, of course, constitute an objection to the metaphysical theory that it entails. Scotus is perfectly clear that creatures derive from God, and on this basis resemble him. Thus he holds that creatures imitate their exemplar cause, and that this relation is real only in the creature: they are 'measured' by their exemplar cause, and dependent on it, without any correlative relation in this cause: see Scotus, *Ord.* 1.3.2.un., n. 297 (Vatican, III, 180): on this, see my '"Where

validity is to be evident require unambiguous middle terms – and Scotus's thought is that such unambiguity cannot be secured other than through univocity. Aquinas is on the face of it vulnerable, to the extent that he is serious about holding theology to be a science.[28] As Scotus puts it, 'Masters who write of God and of those things that are known of God, observe the univocity of being in the way in which they speak, even though they deny it with their words'.[29]

Why suppose that Scotus's theory makes no metaphysical assumptions? In order to understand and support this claim, we need to consider again Scotus's theory of the transcendentals. When I discussed the theory above, I used inverted commas around the word 'genus', and this was to warn that the transcendentals are not really genera in Scotus's usual specialized sense of 'genus'. For a genus, according to Scotus, is a real feature of a thing, formally distinct from the species that includes it and the specific difference that modifies it.[30] The transcendentals are not like this: the bare transcendental (*being*, or whatnot) is not a real feature of a thing at all, but merely a vicious abstraction.[31] Scotus is a nominalist about these properties (nominalist in the sense of denying that the properties are in any sense really universal or common). One consequence of this view is that the relevant concepts apply properly – that is, without qualification – to neither God nor creatures.[32] *Being* is just a vicious abstraction, proper to nothing; proper to God is the (marginally) more complex property *infinite being*, and to creatures *finite being*. As Scotus puts it, the univocity theory is a 'logical' theory, not a metaphysical one, by which he means that it deals *not* with things but merely with concepts.[33]

More importantly, Scotus uses this nominalist insight about the transcendentals to show how his theory of our knowledge of God is consistent with the traditional claim that God is not in a genus. In strict propriety, the transcendentals are not in fact genera, and the modifications of the transcendentals (Scotus's examples here are *infinite/finite* and *necessary/contingent*[34]) not specific differences. The reasons are that (1) a genus cannot be indifferent to finite and infinite (since a genus is potential to specific differences, and nothing that can be infinite can be potential to

---

Angels"', 18–20; it is, indeed, impossible to imagine that Scotus could have thought otherwise. His rejection of the semantic theory of his opponents leaves this metaphysical claim – about which both he and they agree – untouched.

[28] See Aquinas, *ST* 1.1.2 c (I/1, 3ᵇ).

[29] *Rep.* 1.3.1, n. 7 (Wadding, XI, 43ᵇ), noted in Richard Swinburne, *The Coherence of Theism*, 76.

[30] Scotus, *Ord.* 1.8.1.3, n. 137 (Vatican, IV, 221–2).

[31] Scotus discusses this at length in *Ord.* 1.8.1.3, n. 137–50 (Vatican, IV, 221–7), where he tries to show how it can be the case that 'a concept can be common without any community (*convenientia*) in the thing or in reality': *Ord.* 1.8.1.3, n. 82 (Vatican, IV, 190).

[32] See Scotus, *Ord.* 1.3.1.1–2, nn. 38–40 (Vatican, III, 25–7 = *PW*, 24–5; Frank and Wolter, 114) and the discussion in my *Duns Scotus*, 38.

[33] Scotus, *Super El.*, 15, n. 7 (Wadding, I, 237a); see the helpful discussion in Giorgio Pini, *Categories and Logic in Duns Scotus: An Interpretation of Aristotle's* Categories *in the Late Thirteenth Century*, 178–9. The relevant concepts, of course, are not merely logical, in the sense that real objects, not just concepts, fall under their extension: in the technical medieval vocabulary, the relevant concepts are first intentions, not second intentions.

[34] See Scotus, *Ord.* 1.8.1.3, nn. 101–9 (Vatican, IV, 199–203) and Ibid., nn. 110–111 (Vatican, IV, 203–4), respectively.

anything);[35] (2) that infinity cannot be a specific difference, because unlike a specific difference it has no intensional contents;[36] and (3) that necessary being cannot be a genus (for reasons outlined in Part I, chapter 2 §4).[37]

The metaphysical claim that there are no real features or attributes shared in any way by God and creatures may seem to have a consequence for Scotus's theory of knowledge. For Scotus holds that material creatures come to know by abstraction, and what is abstracted are the common natures and essences of things. Common natures, for Scotus, have a degree of reality of their own; a property that admits merely of nominalist analysis seems not the sort of property suitable for being known abstractively. Nevertheless, Scotus holds that the transcendental attributes are known by abstraction, by means of a process that is (presumably) analogous to the process whereby common natures are abstracted from particulars.[38] Scotus's cognitive theory allows for this degree of flexibility about abstraction since – as we saw in Part I, chapter 4 §3 – he believes that real forms are not necessary conditions for concepts: the concept is caused *efficiently* by the external object and the mind, and is fundamentally a representation of external reality, and only in a qualified sense a mentally existent common nature.

Thus far, I have presented Scotus's claim that there are univocal concepts under whose extension both God and creatures fall. This claim does not mean that he has no theory of analogy; quite the reverse, in fact. In a late addition to the *Ordinatio* Scotus explicitly accepts such a theory in this context. He presents a version of the argument in **[4]** that presents the unity between two complex concepts that share one simpler univocal concept as analogy.[39] The idea is, presumably, that the complex concepts of (say) infinite wisdom and finite wisdom are analogous to each other. Now, the context is a refutation of the opinion of Henry of Ghent that there is no 'real likeness' between God and creatures, and hence that forms predicated of God and creatures are merely analogous to each other.[40] So I take it that Scotus is in this context merely using the words of his opponent. But the position seems wholly compatible with the sort of theory that Scotus develops in his theological writings, and whatever label is given to the relation between the concepts of (say) infinite wisdom and finite wisdom, that relation is clearly closer than the relation that obtains between two concepts that have nothing in common.[41]

In Part I, chapter 6 §3, I argued that Scotus's account of divine simplicity is ultimately entailed by his univocity theory of religious language. The reason is that, supposing some creaturely properties to be in some sense distinct from each other and from their subjects, univocity entails that the same is the case for corresponding divine properties. There is nothing about univocity as such that requires Scotus's

---

[35] Ibid., nn. 101–7 (Vatican, IV, 199–202).

[36] Ibid., nn. 108–9 (Vatican, IV, 202–3).

[37] Ibid., nn. 110–11 (Vatican, IV, 203–4).

[38] Ibid. 1.3.1.1–2, n. 35 (Vatican, III, 21–2; *PW*, 22; Frank and Wolter, 112).

[39] Ibid. 1.8.1.3, n. 67 (Vatican, IV, 183).

[40] Henry, *SQ* 19.2 c (I, 124F–I).

[41] In his early philosophical writings, Scotus presents analogy as a metaphysical theory relevant in the case of the dependence of one essence on another (on this, see Pini, *Categories and Logic*, 178–9). But if there is a shift, it seems to me to be terminological, not substantive.

doctrine of divine simplicity. The simplicity doctrine is required only if coupled with Scotus's realist claims about creaturely properties ('realist' not about universals, but simply about properties as such, be they universals or particulars, whether or not realism about common natures is true). Scotus would assert, I believe, that if his doctrine of divine simplicity were false, this would be because *creatures* too are simpler than his metaphysics supposes.

Is Scotus's theory of our natural knowledge of God 'onto-theology', as is often asserted?[42] A lot depends on what this term means, and I have explored this at length elsewhere.[43] Let me suppose, in line with what I take to be the general recent consensus, that its meaning is something like this, that God is somehow subordinated to, and dependent on, some higher entity or concept, *being*. Heidegger sometimes objects to the whole tradition of Western metaphysics from Aristotle onwards for making God dependent on being, where being is identified as the ground of all that is, whether created or uncreated. And the ground of something is in turn something presupposed to its existence. On this view, there is something prior even to God.[44]

There is some ambiguity in this account as to whether being here is to be understood as a thing, Being, or merely some concept, *being*, in some way prior to God. If Being, then of course Scotus's theory of religious language does not amount to onto-theology, since it is his contention merely that if we are to have abstractive knowledge of God then we need the concept *being* (or, more properly, at least some concept under whose extension both God and creatures fall), and this concept is itself merely a vicious abstraction, not picking out a real property of anything. If, contrariwise, onto-theology is the claim that there is a concept, *being*, prior to God, then Scotus's position amounts, with qualification, to some form of onto-theology. But if Scotus's argument about religious language is plausible, then all theologians are, to a greater or lesser extent, practitioners of onto-theology. For the claim is merely about the conceptual requirements for some limited knowledge of God. There is no thought – in Scotus at least – that the concept *being* has any real existence, or is any sort of requirement in the order of reality. The concept *being* is a mental abstraction that is required for abstractive knowledge of aspects of God. It is in no sense 'more absolute' than God; it *is* in no sense at all.

Whatever we make of the issue of onto-theology, one question perhaps remains. As we have seen, despite his official hesitancy about perfect-being theology, Scotus is generally happy to argue in ways that transfer perfections in the creaturely realm to the divine. And it might be thought that this is ultimately too anthropomorphic, and should be replaced by what has become known as the 'eliminative' method, merely eliminating imperfections from God. But the issue is not quite this simple. As Scotus sees it, the eliminative method itself presupposes a solidly cataphatic theology:

[8]
1 We should not make a distinction between God's being known negatively and [his
2 being known] affirmatively, for a negation is known only through an affirmation. ...

[42] On this, see for example my '"Where Angels"', 11–14.
[43] See Ibid., 25–7.
[44] See Ibid., 26 for the references to Heidegger.

3 And it is clear that we know negations about God only through affirmations through
4 which we remove other things incompossible with those affirmations.[45]

Scotus goes on to explain what he means: if *all* we know are negations, then we will
not be able to distinguish God from non-being. If, contrariwise, we know negations
that are proper to God, this can be the case only on the basis of some positive and
specific understanding that we have of God.[46] The eliminative method can proceed
only on the basis of positive knowledge. To be unlimited is to be perfect, and the
exclusion of any given limitation amounts to the ascription of a corresponding
perfection. Consider Scotus's argument about the necessity of an internal divine
production. Scotus holds that lacking internally productive powers is a limitation,
and that lacking the necessary activity of these powers is likewise a limitation.
Eliminating these limitations or imperfections entails the conclusion that God
possesses necessarily active internally productive powers. It may be that the
premises are false; but that has nothing to do with the legitimacy of the method. If
we are to be so robustly apophatic as to exclude even this sort of eliminative method,
then it will be hard to see how any speculative or systematic theological project
could get off the ground. And we would certainly be more apophatic than is
warranted by the Christian theological tradition. To pursue cataphatic theology is
not to be naively anthropomorphic.

[45] Scotus, *Ord.* 1.3.1.1–2, n. 10 (Vatican, III, 4; *PW*, 15).
[46] Ibid., n. 11 (Vatican, III, 5; *PW* 15–16).

Bibliography

Manuscripts

Assisi, Biblioteca Communale, MS 137 (= MS A; Duns Scotus, *Ordinatio*).
Merton College, Oxford, MS 53 (= MS M; Duns Scotus, *Reportatio*).
Vatican Library, MS Lat. 13687 (Henry Harclay, *Quaestiones in libros Sententiarum*).

Printed Primary Sources

Anselm, *Opera Omnia*, ed. Franciscus Salesius Schmitt, 6 vols (Edinburgh: Thomas Nelson and Sons, 1946–61).
Aquinas, Thomas, *De ente et essentia*, ed. M.-D. Roland-Gosselin, Bibliothèque Thomiste, 8 (Kain, Belgium: Revue des Sciences Philosophiques et Théologiques, 1926).
——, *Summa theologiae*, ed. Petrus Caramello, 3 vols (Turin and Rome: Marietti, 1952–6).
Aristotle, *Opera*, ed. Immanuel Bekker, 5 vols (Berlin: Georgius Reimer, 1831).
Augustine, *Epistulae (I–CXXIII)*, ed. A. Goldbacher, CSEL, 34/2 (Prague and Vienna: Tempsky; Leipzig: Freytag, 1885).
——, *De trinitate*, ed. W. J. Mountain, 2 vols, CCSL, 50 (Turnhout: Brepols, 1968).
Avicenna, *Liber de philosophia prima sive scientia divina [Metaphysics]*, ed. S. van Riet, 3 vols, Avicenna Latinus (Louvain, Peeters; Leiden: Brill, 1977–83).
Boethius, *De consolatione philosophiae; opuscula sacra*, ed. C. Moreshini, Bibliotheca Scriptorum Graecorum et Romanorum Teubneriana (Munich and Leipzig: K. G. Saur, 2000).
Bonaventure, *Opera Omnia*, 10 vols (Quaracchi: Collegium Sancti Bonaventurae, 1882–1902).
Denifle, H., and E. Chatelain (eds), *Cartularium universitatis Parisiensis*, 4 vols (Paris, Delalain, 1889–97).
Duns Scotus, John, *Opera Omnia*, ed. Luke Wadding, 12 vols (Lyons, 1639).
——, *Opera Omnia*, ed. C. Balić and others (Rome: Typis Polyglottis Vaticanis, 1950–).
——, *God and Creatures: The Quodlibetal Questions*, ed. and trans. Felix Alluntis and Allan B. Wolter (Princeton, NJ and London: Princeton University Press, 1975).
——, *A Treatise on God as First Principle*, ed. Allan B. Wolter, 2nd edn (Chicago, IL: Franciscan Herald Press, 1982).
——, *Philosophical Writings: A Selection*, ed. and trans. Allan B. Wolter (Indianapolis, IN and Cambridge, UK: Hackett, 1987).

——, *Contingency and Freedom: Lectura I 39*, ed. A. Vos and others, The New Synthese Historical Library, 42 (Dordrecht, Boston, and London: Kluwer, 1994).

——, *Opera Philosophica*, ed. Girard. J. Etzkorn and others (St Bonaventure, NY: The Franciscan Institute, 1997).

Frank, William A. and Allan B. Wolter (eds and trans.), *Duns Scotus, Metaphysician*, Purdue University Press Studies in the History of Philosophy (West Lafayette, IN: Purdue University Press, 1995).

Giles of Rome, *In primum librum Sententiarum* (Venice, 1521).

Godfrey of Fontaines, *Les Quodlibets cinq, six et sept de Godefroid de Fontaines*, eds M. de Wulf and J. Hoffmans, Les Philosophes Belges, Textes et études, 3 (Louvain: Institut Supérieur de Philosophie, 1914).

Gregory of Nazianzus, *Discours 27–31 (Discours théologiques)*, ed. Paul Gallay, Sources Chrétiennes, 250 (Paris: Editions du Cerf, 1978).

Henry of Ghent, *Quodlibeta*, 2 vols (Paris, 1518).

——, *Summa quaestionum ordinariarum*, 2 vols (Paris, 1520).

——, *Opera Omnia*, ed. R. Macken and others, Ancient and Medieval Philosophy, De Wulf-Mansion Centre, Series 2 (Leuven: Leuven University Press; Leiden: Brill, 1979–).

Hilary of Poitiers, *De trinitate (I–VII)*, ed. P. Smulders, CCSL 62 (Brepols: Turnhout, 1979).

John of Damascus, *Die Schriften des Johannes von Damaskos*. vol. 2: *Expositio fidei*, ed. Bonifatius Kotter, Patristische Texte und Studien, 12 (Berlin and New York: Walter de Gruyter, 1973).

——, *De fide orthodoxa: The Versions of Burgundio and Cerbanus*, ed. Eligius M. Buytaert, Franciscan Institute Publications: Text Series, 8 (St Bonaventure, NY: The Franciscan Institute; Louvain: E. Nauwelaerts; Paderborn: F. Schöningh, 1955).

Lombard, Peter, *Sententiae in quatuor libris distinctae* 3rd edn, 2 vols, Spicilegium Bonaventurianum (Grottaferrata: Collegium Sancti Bonaventurae ad Claras Aquas, 1971–81).

Marston, Roger, *Quaestiones disputatae*, Biblioteca Franciscana Scholastica Medii Aevi, 7 (Ad Claras Aquas: Collegium Sancti Bonaventurae, 1932).

Noone, Timothy B., 'Scotus on Divine Ideas: *Rep. Paris. I–A*, d. 36', *Medioevo*, 24 (1998), 359–453.

Olivi, Peter John, *Quaestiones in secundum librum Sententiarum*, ed. Bernardus Jansen, 3 vols, Bibliotheca Franciscana Scholastica Medii Aevi, 4–6 (Quaracchi: Collegium S. Bonaventurae, 1922–6).

Porphyry, *Isagoge et in Aristotelis Categorias commentaria*, ed. Adolfus Busse, Commentaria in Aristotelem Graeca, IV/1 (Berlin: G. Reimer, 1887).

Richard of Middleton, *Super quatuor libros Sententiarum ... quaestiones*, 4 vols. (Brescia, 1591).

Richard of St Victor, *De trinitate*, ed. Jean Ribaillier, Textes Philosophiques du Moyen Age, 6 (Paris: J. Vrin, 1958).

Spade, Paul Vincent (ed. and trans.), *Five Texts on the Mediaeval Problem of Universals: Porphyry, Boethius, Abelard, Duns Scotus, Ockham* (Indianapolis, IN and Cambridge, UK: Hackett, 1994).

Summa fratris Alexandri, 4 vols (Quaracchi: Collegium Sancti Bonaventurae, 1924–48).

Tanner, Norman, P. (ed.), *The Decrees of the Ecumenical Councils*, 2 vols (London: Sheed and Ward; Washington, DC: Georgetown University Press, 1990).

Thomas of Sutton, *Quaestiones ordinariae*, ed. Johannes Schneider, Veröffentlichungen der Kommission für die Herausgabe ungedruckter Texte aus der mittelalterlichen Geisteswelt, 3 (Munich: Bayerischen Akademie der Wissenschaften, 1977).

——, *Quodlibeta*, ed. Michael Schmaus with assistance from Maria González-Haba, Veröffentlichungen der Kommission für die Herausgabe ungedruckter Texte aus der mittelalterlichen Geisteswelt, 2 (Munich: Bayerischen Akademie der Wissenschaften, 1969).

Vos, A., and others, *Duns Scotus on Divine Love: Texts and Commentary on Goodness and Freedom, God and Humans* (Aldershot, UK and Burlington, VT: Ashgate, 2003).

Wolter, Allan B., *Duns Scotus on the Will and Morality*, 1st edn (Washington DC: Catholic University of America Press, 1986).

——, and Marilyn McCord Adams (eds and trans.), 'Duns Scotus' Parisian Proof for the Existence of God', *Franciscan Studies*, 42 (1982), 248–321.

Secondary Sources

Armstrong, D. M., *Nominalism and Realism* (Cambridge, UK: Cambridge University Press, 1978).

Bąk, F., 'Scoti schola numerosior est omnibus aliis simul sumptis', *Franciscan Studies*, 16 (1956), 144–56.

Boland, Vivian, *Ideas in God according to Saint Thomas Aquinas: Sources and Synthesis*, Studies in the History of Christian Thought, 69 (Cologne, Leiden, New York: Brill, 1996).

Brown, Stephen F., 'Henry of Ghent (b. ca. 1217; d. 1293)', in Gracia (ed.), *Individuation in Scholasticism*, 195–219.

Catania, Francis J., 'John Duns Scotus on *Ens Infinitum*', *American Catholic Philosophical Quarterly*, 67 (1993), 37–54.

Coffey, David, *Deus Trinitas: The Doctrine of the Triune God* (New York and Oxford: Oxford University Press, 1999).

Courtenay, William J., *Schools and Scholars in Fourteenth Century England* (Princeton, NJ: Princeton University Press, 1987).

Craig, William Lane, *The Cosmological Argument from Plato to Leibniz*, Library of Philosophy and Religion (London and Basingstoke: Macmillan, 1980).

——, *The Problem of Divine Foreknowledge of Future Contingents from Aristotle to Suarez*, Brill's Studies in Intellectual History, 7 (Leiden: Brill, 1988).

Cross, Richard, 'Duns Scotus on Eternity and Timelessness', *Faith and Philosophy*, 14 (1997), 3–25.

——, *The Physics of Duns Scotus: The Scientific Context of a Theological Vision* (Oxford: Clarendon Press, 1998).

——, *Duns Scotus*, Great Medieval Thinkers (New York and Oxford: Oxford University Press, 1999).

——, 'Identity, Origin, and Persistence in Duns Scotus's Physics', *History of Philosophy Quarterly*, 16 (1999), 1–18.

——, 'Perichoresis, Deification, and Christological Predication in John of Damascus', *Mediaeval Studies*, 62 (2000), 69–124.

——, '"Where Angels Fear to Tread": Duns Scotus and Radical Orthodoxy', *Antonianum*, 76 (2001), 7–41.

——, *The Metaphysics of the Incarnation: Thomas Aquinas to Duns Scotus* (Oxford: Oxford University Press, 2002).

——, 'Gregory of Nyssa on Universals', *Vigiliae Christianae*, 56 (2002), 372–410.

——, 'Philosophy of Mind', in Williams (ed.), *The Cambridge Companion to Duns Scotus*, 263–84.

——, 'Two Models of the Trinity?', *Heythrop Journal*, 43 (2002), 275–94.

——, 'Divisibility, Communicability, and Predicability in Duns Scotus's Theories of the Common Nature', *Medieval Philosophy and Theology*, 11 (2003), 43–63.

——, 'Duns Scotus on Divine Substance and the Trinity', *Medieval Philosophy and Theology*, 11 (2003).

——, 'Medieval Theories of Haecceity', in Edward N. Zalta (ed.), *The Stanford Encyclopedia of Philosophy*, <http://plato.stanford.edu/archives/fall2003/entries/medieval-haecceity>.

——, 'On Generic and Derivation Views of God's Trinitarian Substance', *Scottish Journal of Theology*, 56 (2003), 464–80.

——, 'Scotus's Parisian Teaching on Divine Simplicity', in *Duns Scot à Paris: Actes du colloque de Paris, 2–4 septembre 2002*, ed. Olivier Boulnois and others, Textes et Etudes du Moyen Age, 26 (Turnhout: Brepols, 2004), 519–62.

Davidson, H. A., *Alfarabi, Avicenna, and Averroes on Intellect: Their Cosmologies, Theories of the Active Intellect and Theories of Human Intellect* (New York and Oxford: Oxford University Press, 1992).

Davies, Brian, *The Thought of Thomas Aquinas* (Oxford: Clarendon Press, 1992).

Dumont, Stephen D., 'The quaestio si est and the Metaphysical Proof for the Existence of God according to Henry of Ghent and John Duns Scotus', *Franziskanische Studien*, 66 (1984), 335–67.

——, 'Theology as a Practical Science and Duns Scotus's Distinction between Intuitive and Abstractive Cognition', *Speculum*, 64 (1989), 579–99.

——, 'William of Ware, Richard of Conington and the *Collationes Oxonienses of John Duns Scotus*', in Honnefelder, Wood, and Dreyer (eds), *John Duns Scotus*, 59–85.

Evans, Gillian R., *Old Arts and New Theology: The Beginnings of Theology as an Academic Discipline* (Oxford: Clarendon Press, 1980).

Friedman, Russell Lance, '*In Principio erat Verbum*: The Incorporation of Philosophical Psychology into Trinitarian Theology, 1250–1325', unpublished doctoral dissertation, University of Iowa, 1997.

Geach, Peter, 'Causality and Creation', in Geach, *God and the Soul*, Studies in Ethics and the Philosophy of Religion (London and Henley: Routledge and Kegan Paul, 1969), 75–85.

Gracia, Jorge J. E. (ed.), *Individuation in Scholasticism: The Later Middle Ages and the Counter-Reformation*, SUNY Series in Philosophy (Albany: State University of New York Press, 1994).

—— and Timothy B. Noone, *A Companion to Philosophy in the Middle Ages*, Blackwell Companions to Philosophy, 24 (Malden, MA and Oxford: Blackwell, 2003).

Henninger, Mark G., *Relations: Medieval Theories 1250–1325* (Oxford: Clarendon Press, 1989).

Hissette, R. *Enquête sur les 219 articles condamnés à Paris le 7 Mars 1277*, Philosophes Médiévaux, 22 (Louvain: Publications Universitaires de Louvain; Paris; Vander Oyez, 1977).

Hoffmann, Tobias, 'The Distinction Between Nature and Will in Duns Scotus', *Archives d'histoire doctrinale et littéraire du moyen age*, 66 (1999), 189–224.

——, *Creatura Intellecta: Die Ideen und Possibilien bei Duns Scotus mit Ausblick auf Franz von Mayronis, Poncius und Mastrius*, BGPTM, N. F., 60 (Münster: Aschendorff, 2002).

Honnefelder, Ludger, *Scientia transcendens: Die Formale Bestimmung der Seiendheit und Realität in der Metaphysik des Mittelalters und der Neuzeit (Duns Scotus, Suárez, Wolff, Kant, Pierce)*, Paradeigmata, 9 (Hamburg: Felix Meiner, 1990).

——, Rega Wood, and Mechthild Dreyer (eds), *John Duns Scotus: Metaphysics and Ethics*, STGM, 53 (Leiden, New York, and Cologne: Brill, 1996).

Kelly, J. N. D., *Early Christian Doctrines*, 5th edn (London: A. and C. Black, 1977).

Kenny, Anthony, *The Five Ways: St Thomas Aquinas' Proofs of God's Existence* (London: Routledge and Kegan Paul, 1969).

King, Peter, 'Duns Scotus on the Common Nature and Individual Differentia', *Philosophical Topics*, 20 (1992), 51–76.

——, 'Duns Scotus on the Reality of Self-Change', in Mary Louise Gill and James G. Lennox (eds), *Self-Motion from Aristotle to Newton* (Princeton, NJ: Princeton University Press, 1994), 229–90.

——, 'Duns Scotus on Mental Content', in *Duns Scot à Paris: Actes du colloque de Paris, 2–4 septembre 2002*, ed. Olivier Boulnois and others, Textes et Etudes du Moyen Age, 26 (Turnhout: Brepols, 2004), 65–88.

Knuuttila, Simo, 'Modal Logic', in Norman Kretzmann, Anthony Kenny, and Jan Pinborg (eds), *The Cambridge History of Later Medieval Philosophy* (Cambridge, UK: Cambridge University Press, 1982), 342–57.

——, *Modalities in Medieval Philosophy*, Topics in Medieval Philosophy (London and New York: Routledge, 1993).

——, 'Duns Scotus and the Foundations of Logical Modalities', in Honnefelder, Wood, and Dreyer (eds), *John Duns Scotus*, 127–43.

Lerner, Ralph and Mahdi, Muhsin (eds), *Medieval Political Philosophy: A Sourcebook* (New York: The Free Press of Glencoe, 1963).

Lewis, Neil, 'Space and Time', in Williams (ed.), *The Cambridge Companion to Duns Scotus*, 69–99.

Loux, Michael, 'A Scotistic Argument for the Existence of a First Cause', *American Philosophical Quarterly*, 21 (1984), 157–65.

Mann, William E., 'Divine Simplicity', *Religious Studies*, 18 (1982), 451–71.

Martin, Christopher, 'Theories of Inference and Entailment in the Middle Ages', unpublished doctoral dissertation, Princeton University, 1999.

Menn, Stephen, 'Metaphysics: God and Being', in A. S. McGrade (ed.), *The Cambridge Companion to Medieval Philosophy* (Cambridge, UK: Cambridge University Press, 2003), 147–70.

Noone, Timothy B., 'Universals and Individuation', in Williams (ed.), *The Cambridge Companion to Duns Scotus*, 100–28.

Normore, Calvin, 'Scotus, Modality, Instants of Nature and the Contingency of the Present', in Honnefelder, Wood, and Dreyer (eds), *John Duns Scotus*, 161–74.

——, 'Duns Scotus's Modal Theory', in Williams (ed.), *The Cambridge Companion to Duns Scotus*, 129–60.

O'Connor, Timothy, 'Scotus's Argument for a First Efficient Cause', *International Journal for Philosophy of Religion*, 33 (1993), 17–32.

Owens, Joseph, 'The Special Characteristics of the Scotistic Proof that God Exists', *Analecta Gregoriana*, 67 (1954), 311–27.

Pasnau, Robert, 'Cognition', in Williams (ed.), *The Cambridge Companion to Duns Scotus*, 285–311.

Paulus, Jean, *Henri de Gand: Essai sur les tendances de sa métaphysique*, Etudes de philosophie médiévale, 25 (Paris: Vrin, 1938).

Pegis, A. C., 'Toward a New Way to God: Henry of Ghent', *Mediaeval Studies*, 30 (1968), 226–47.

——, 'Toward a New Way to God: Henry of Ghent II', *Mediaeval Studies*, 31 (1969), 93–116.

——, 'Henry of Ghent and the New Way to God III', *Mediaeval Studies*, 33 (1971), 158–79.

Pini, Giorgio, *Categories and Logic in Duns Scotus: An Interpretation of Aristotle's Categories in the Late Thirteenth Century*, STGM, 77 (Leiden, Boston, and Cologne: Brill, 2002).

Prentice, Robert P., 'Some Aspects of the Significance of the First Chapter of the *De primo principio* of John Duns Scotus', *Antonianum*, 36 (1961), 225–37.

——, 'The *De primo principio* of John Duns Scotus as a Thirteenth Century Proslogion', *Antonianum*, 39 (1964), 77–109.

——, *The Basic Quidditative Metaphysics of Duns Scotus as Seen in his De Primo Principio*, Spicilegium Pontificii Athenaei Antoniani, 16 (Rome: Antonianum, 1970).

Robb, Fiona, 'Intellectual Tradition and Misunderstanding: The Development of Academic Theology on the Trinity in the Twelfth and Thirteenth Centuries', unpublished doctoral dissertation, University College, London, 1993.

Roest, Bert, *A History of Franciscan Education (c. 1210–1517)*, Education and Society in the Middle Ages, 11 (Leiden and Boston: Brill, 2000).

Ross, James F. and Todd Bates, 'Duns Scotus on Natural Theology', in Williams (ed.), *The Cambridge Companion to Duns Scotus*, 193–237.

Schlapkohl, Corinna, *Persona est naturae rationabilis individua substantia: Boethius und die Debatte über den Personbegriff*, Marburger Theologische Studien, 56 (Marburg: N. G. Elwert, 1999).

Schmaus, Michael, *Die Liber Propugnatorius des Thomas Anglicus und die Lehrunterschiede zwischen Thomas von Aquinas und Duns Scotus: II. Teil: Die Trinitarischen Lehrdifferenzen: Erste Band: Systematische Darstellung und historische Würdigung*, BGPTM, 29/1 (Münster: Aschendorff, 1930).

Söder, Joachim Roland, *Kontingenz und Wissen: Die Lehre von den futura contingentia bei Johannes Duns Scotus*, BGPTM, N. F., 49 (Münster: Aschendorff, 1999).

Swinburne, Richard, *The Coherence of Theism*, revised edn (Oxford: Clarendon Press, 1993).

Thomas, Janice, 'Univocity and Understanding God's Nature', in Gerard J. Hughes (ed.), *The Philosophical Assessment of Theology: Essays in Honor of Frederick C. Copleston* (Tunbridge Wells: Search Press; Washington, DC: Georgetown University Press, 1987), 85–100.

Tweedale, Martin M., *Scotus vs. Ockham – A Medieval Dispute over Universals*, 2 vols, Studies in the History of Philosophy, 50 (Lewiston, Queenstown, and Lampeter: The Edwin Mellen Press, 1999).

Valkenberg, Wilhelmus G. B. M., *Words of the Living God: The Place and Function of Holy Scripture in the Theology of St Thomas Aquinas*, Publications of the Thomas Instituut te Utrecht, N. S., 6 (Leuven: Peeters, 2000).

Vos, Antonie, 'The Scotian Notion of Natural Law', *Vivarium*, 38 (2000), 197–221.

Wetter, Friedrich, *Die Trinitätslehre des Johannes Duns Scotus*, BGPTM, 41/5 (Münster: Aschendorff, 1967).

Williams, Thomas (ed.), *The Cambridge Companion to Duns Scotus* (Cambridge, UK: Cambridge University Press, 2002).

Wippel, John F., *The Metaphysical Thought of Godfrey of Fontaines* (Washington, DC: Catholic University of America Press, 1981).

Wolter, Allan B., *The Transcendentals and their Function in the Metaphysics of Duns Scotus*, Franciscan Institute Publications, Philosophy Series, 3 (St Bonaventure, NY: The Franciscan Institute, 1946.

——, 'Duns Scotus on the Existence and Nature of God', *Proceedings of the American Catholic Philosophical Association*, 28 (1954), 94–121. (Reprinted in Wolter, *The Philosophical Theology of John Duns Scotus*, 254–77.)

——, *The Philosophical Theology of John Duns Scotus*, ed. Marilyn McCord Adams (Ithaca, NY: Cornell University Press, 1990).

——, 'Duns Scotus on Intuition, Memory, and Our Knowledge of Individuals', in Wolter, *The Philosophical Theology of John Duns Scotus*, 98–122.

Wood, Rega, 'Scotus's Argument for the Existence of God', *Franciscan Studies*, 47 (1987), 257–77.

Index Locorum

General Index

abstraction, ultimate 113; *see also*
  cognition, abstractive
act, categorial, *see* production
act, second, *see* operation
action, ascribed to *suppositum* 187; *see*
  also causation, efficient; operation;
  production
actiones sunt suppositorum, see action
analogy
  in Aquinas 255
  in Duns Scotus 157
  in Henry of Ghent 257
  see also apophatic theology; religious
    language; univocity
Anselm
  'from nothing' ac. to A. 172–3
  ontological proof for God's existence in
    A. 36–7
  perfect-being theology in A. 49–50
apophatic theology 252–3, 258–9; *see also*
  analogy
Aquinas, Thomas
  on analogy 255
  use of Bible 9 n. 23
  on concepts and meaning 255
  and the condemnations of 1277 4
  and Duns Scotus 4
  on *filioque* 191–2
  on God's essence as productive power
    in Trinity 200
  on God's knowability 252, 255 n. 26
  on God's knowledge of creaturely
    essences 60–61
  on God's knowledge of extramental
    reality 81
  on God's knowledge of individuals 78
  on God's knowledge of tensed facts 83,
    85 n. 109, 121
  on God's lack of idea of matter 78 n. 87
  on God's lack of passive capacities 10
  on God's omnipresence 101
  on God's simplicity 103
  on indemonstrability of the Trinity 13

on infinite regress of causes 24
on the infinite 25
on infinity as negation 96–7
on intelligible species 66–7
on matter 78
on non-reality of creaturely
  essences/natures 62 n. 32
on origination of foetus 22–3
personal properties distinct from
  relations in God ac. to A. 188
personal properties not modes of origin
  ac. to A. 190
personal properties in God distinct
  merely extensionally ac. to A. 191–2
on religious language 104, 255
on theology as science 256
Aristotle
  acts distinguish powers ac. to A. 226 n.
    12
  charitable readings of 7 n. 22
  on demonstration 13–14, 38–9
  on four causes 26–7
  on free vs natural 135
  on freedom 58 n. 13
  on generation 177, 178, 205
  on God's lack of body 100
  on goodness and perfection 49 n. 3
  on identity of knower and known 67
  on infinity 24, 96
  influence of in West 3–4
  as origin of *actiones sunt suppositorum*
    187
  on origination of foetus 22–3
  on perfection 49 n. 3
  on potential infinite 92–3
  priority defined in 25
  relations not causal powers ac. to A. 206
  on science 13–14, 38–9
  unmoved mover in 119
Armstrong, D. M. 169 n. 20
Augustine
  on causation 7
  on commonality of divine essence 177

279

foetus, origination of 22–3
form
  and actuality 19
  and causation 19–20
  immaterial 20
forms, plurality of in Henry of Ghent 173
Frank, William A. 91 n. 1
freedom
  argument for in Aristotle 58 n. 13
  compatible with necessity 138–42
  and contingency 56–8
  contracausal account of 56–7, 141 n. 25
  defined 56
  in God 120–21
  and impeccability 140
  vs nature 132, 147
  vs nature in Aristotle 135
  see also contingency
Friedman, Russell Lance 190

Geach, Peter 19
generation of divine Son, *see* filiation;
    God, internal productions in; God,
    memory in; Son, divine
Giles of Rome, extensional account of
    divine personal properties in 192 n.
    39
God, attributes of
  distinct from each other 104–11
  formal distinction between 107–11
  and intrinsic modes 114
  reality of 105–10
  real identity with each other 111–13
  Trinitarian argument for distinction of
    106–7
God, *esse* of 114 n. 56
God, essence of
  abstractive knowledge of 129, 250–51
  as act of person 234–5
  as act of relation 234–5
  as agent 170
  basis for divine persons' being produced
    203–5
  as collection of really identical
    attributes 111–13
  common to persons ac. to Augustine
    177, 178
  communicability of 159–62, 167–70
  distinct from attributes ac. to John of
    Damascus 111 n. 47
  as end term of production 205
  explains subsistence of persons 181–2

  formally distinct from personal
    properties 234, 235–40
  formally distinct from persons 238–40
  as foundation for internal divine
    relations 176–7
  individuality of 159
  indivisibility of 159–60
  intuitive knowledge of 129, 250–51
  known only by divine will 249–50
  known *per se* and quidditatively 251
  in Nicaea 172–3, 176
  non-relational 177
  not known naturally 129
  numerically one 153–4, 167–9
  object of divine knowledge 133
  object of divine will 141, 216–18
  personal properties spring from e.
    178–80
  persons spring into e. 179
  prior to persons 176–80, 244
  productive power in God 206–9
  quasi-act of persons 179
  subsistence of 155–6, 181–2
  as subject for divine persons ac. to
    Richard of Conington 175
  as substrate for divine persons ac. to
    Henry of Ghent 106, 172–5, 233,
    234–5
  substrate view rejected 175–6
  as thing 166, 240–44
  as universal 165–6
God, essential acts in
  ac. to Augustine 226 n. 10
  prior to notional acts 223–9
  see also God, external activity of; God,
    memory in
God, as exemplar 110–11
God, external activity of
  contingent 56–9, 87, 119–20, 231, 250
  Son's role in ac. to Henry of Ghent 230
  undivided 231
  unity of 229–32
God, freedom of 56–9, 87, 119–20
  and immutability 120–21
  see also God, external activity of; God,
    will of
God, image of 130 n. 17
God, imitability of 65, 110–11
God, immateriality of 50, 99–100
God, immutability of
  argument for from simplicity 119–20
  and divine freedom 120–21

Gracia, Jorge J. E. 6 n. 13
Gregory of Nazianzus against
subordinationism 245
Gregory of Nyssa on divine essence as
universal 165

haecceity
defined 60
and individuation 78, 157, 234
Harclay, Henry, on reality of divine
attributes 107
Heidegger and onto-theology 258
Henninger, Mark G. 62 n. 32, 103 n. 22,
174 n. 44
Henry of Ghent
on analogy 257
on causal powers 106 n. 30
and Duns Scotus 6
on divine essence as substrate for
persons 106, 172–5, 233
on divine essence as productive power
206, 208
on *esse essentiae* 62, 71
on God as pure act 174
on God's knowledge of creaturely
essences 61–2, 64
on God's knowledge of extramental
reality 80–81
on God's knowledge of possible
individuals 78–80
on God's knowledge as scientific 14
on identity of divine memory and
intelligence 227 n. 16
on individuation 78–9
on internal divine production 147–8
on monarchy of Father 221
notional acts founded on essential ac. to
H. 224–5
on perichoresis of divine persons
170–71
on personal properties 150
on personal properties and relations of
origin 184, 188
personal properties spring from essence
ac. to H. 179
and proofs for God's existence 29
on science 39 n. 22
on Son's causal role in creation 230
on Son as Father's reason 228–9
Hilary of Poitiers on perichoresis of divine
persons 171 n. 26
Hoffmann, Tobias 76 n. 88, 75 n. 74, n. 75

Holy Spirit, *see* Spirit, Holy
Honnefelder, Ludger 2 n. 6

ideas, divine 60–69
term rejected 66 n. 43
see also God, knowledge in
identity, adequate 237–40
identity, formal 237–44
identity, non-adequate 237–44
identity, real 109, 237–40
and compresence 169
defined 112–13
intransitivity of 155, 168–9
immateriality, divine, *see* God,
immateriality of
immutability, divine, *see* God, immutability
of
impossibility
divine origination of 72–7
and unintelligibility 71–2
see also counterpossible arguments;
modality; possibility
incommunicability
defined 156–7, 159–63, 167–70
of negation 186–7
not a perfection 202
ut quo 160–62
ut quod 159–60
individuality
distinct from incommunicability 168–9
and indivisibility 159–60
see also common nature; divisibility
into subjective parts
individuation
by haecceity 60, 78, 157
ac. to Henry of Ghent 78–9
Henry of Ghent's view rejected 79
of qualitatively indiscernible individuals
78
infinite
actually i. multitude impossible 24–5
argument from potential i. to actual
93–4
exemplifiability 148–9, 151–2
as intrinsic mode 97–8
as negation in Aquinas 96–7
see also God, infinity of
infinity, divine, *see* God, infinity of
ingeneracy
as 'notion' of Father 183–4, 185–7
property of Father ac. to Roger Marston
185

DATE DUE

			Printed in USA